PRAISE FOR

Beyond the Influence

"SCIENTIFICALLY BASED, USEFUL, AND
AUTHORITATIVE FOR EVERY FAMILY AND EVERY
PERSON TOUCHED BY THIS DISEASE."
—G. Douglas Talbott, M.D., FASAM, FACP, medical director,
Talbott Recovery Campus, past president of the American
Society of Addiction Medicine

"DESTINED TO BE ONE OF THE MOST WIDELY READ AND DIS-
CUSSED BOOKS ON ALCOHOLISM."
—William White, author of *Slaying the Dragon: The History of Addiction,
Treatment, and Recovery in America*

"PROVIDES HOPE TO THOSE SUFFERING ALCOHOLICS, THEIR
FAMILIES, AND FRIENDS."
—Terence T. Gorski, author, trainer, and president of the CENAPS
Cooperation, and clinical director of the Relapse Prevention Certification
School

Beyond the Influence

UNDERSTANDING AND DEFEATING ALCOHOLISM

Katherine Ketcham
and William F. Asbury

**with Mel Schulstad and
Arthur P. Ciaramicoli, Ed.D., Ph.D.**

BANTAM BOOKS

New York Toronto London Sydney Auckland

Library of Congress Cataloging-in-Publication Data

Ketcham, Katherine, 1949–
Beyond the influence : understanding and defeating alcoholism /
by Katherine Ketcham and William F. Asbury with
Mel Schulstad and Arthur P. Ciaramicoli.
p.   cm.
Includes bibliographical references and index.
ISBN 0-553-38014-1
1. Alcoholism.   2. Alcoholism—Treatment.   3. Alcoholics—Rehabilitation.
I. Asbury, William F.   II. Title.
HV5035 .K53 2000
362.292'8 —dc21   99-058107

CONTENTS

———

FOREWORD

———

Five years have passed since my daughter Terry left a Christmas-festooned Wisconsin bar, stumbled into a snowbank, and froze to death. Coming from a family of four daughters and a son, Terry had struggled—and her family had struggled with her—to overcome her alcohol addiction for most of her adult life. One of the paradoxes of Terry's life is that despite the dreadful affliction of alcoholism, which was complicated by depression, she was a lovable, compassionate, witty, intelligent human being. She was a devoted mother who left two daughters, now twelve and fourteen, who are living with their father in Florida. They are both doing straight A work in school, except for frequent A-pluses. All indications are that they are happy, well-adjusted, talented girls.

After Terry's death at Christmastime 1994, I began a search to discover why this daughter with whom I was especially close became so seriously addicted to alcohol that it dominated her life. Was it my fault?

Why wasn't I more aware that alcoholism is a fatal disease if not brought under control? Had I neglected my children because of my preoccupation with politics, foreign policy, and travel? In view of the frequent incidence of alcoholism in the McGovern clan going back generations, should I have been more alert to the genetic danger of alcoholism? Or is this a myth—the notion that alcoholism is a disease that might be transmitted genetically? Is it possible that Terry became an alcoholic simply because she didn't have the self-discipline to regulate her alcohol intake sensibly? And if that is true, did I contribute to my daughter's death by not teaching her how to live a disciplined life? After all, over the years my wife, Eleanor, and I have dropped by countless Washington cocktail parties, had a drink, and gone home or out to dinner without any problems. Why couldn't we have taught precious Terry to do the same?

In trying to come to terms with these questions, I came across a book that I wish with all my heart I had read when Terry was alive—*Under the Influence: A Guide to the Myths and Realities of Alcoholism*, co-authored by Dr. James R. Milam and Katherine Ketcham. This book made more sense to me than any other I had read on the subject of alcoholism. It was a pioneering book when it was published in 1981 and now it is a classic. If I could have only one book in my personal library on the subject of alcoholism, this is the one I would take.

Colonel Mel Schulstad captured the essence of the Milam-Ketcham book in his foreword:

> *Under the Influence* closely points out that the accumulated evidence from all the life sciences positively indicates that physiology, not psychology, determines whether a drinker will become addicted to alcohol or not. The alcoholic's genes, enzymes, hormones, brain and other body chemistries work together to create his or her abnormal and unfortunate reaction to alcohol.

As Colonel Schulstad pointed out at the time, that point of view was not shared by a majority of alcohol treatment professionals, who tend to see alcoholism as an outgrowth of psychological factors. Anecdotal evidence is not conclusive, but I cite the case of my daughter, who went through five years of psychotherapy while a student at the University of Virginia and extensive follow-up counseling in Madison, Wisconsin. Meanwhile, her alcoholism worsened. Not until she became active in Alcoholics Anonymous did she achieve eight years of sobriety.

But now comes the needed companion volume to *Under the Influence—Beyond the Influence: Understanding and Defeating Alcoholism*. This book is perfectly named because it builds upon but carries well beyond the first volume. It contains nearly twenty years of scientific findings that have become available since 1981. It makes a powerful and nearly irrefutable case for the view that alcoholism is a disease which attacks some people because of their genetic heritage.

No one who wants to be conversant with a scientific approach to alcoholism can fail to own this book. This invaluable work will contribute much to the battle against our number one disease.

George McGovern
Fall 1999

INTRODUCTION

---

*The philosophers have interpreted the world in
different ways — the task is to transform it.*

—KARL MARX

Alcoholism is a disease characterized by abnormalities in brain chemistry. Susceptibility to this disease can spring from many factors, but one of the most significant is that of genetic transmission. If you inherit certain genetic mutations, you will be at risk for developing alcoholism if you drink. These are the simple facts.

We have written this book in an attempt to present the known facts about alcoholism. We hope to dispel the prevailing myths and misconceptions and create some calm in what has for many decades been a tempestuous storm of controversy about the nature of this disease and its victims. We believe it is possible to get beyond the influence of the drug alcohol and the pain and suffering it causes for so many millions of people all over the world.

Our qualifications for writing this book are diverse:

Katherine Ketcham is a nonfiction writer, who has coauthored eleven books including *Under the Influence: A Guide to the Myths and Realities of Alcoholism* (Bantam, 1983) with James R. Milam, Ph.D., and *The Spirituality of Imperfection: Storytelling and the Journey to Wholeness* (Bantam, 1992) with Ernest Kurtz, Ph.D. Both books are considered classics in the alcoholism literature.

William F. Asbury is a journalist and former editor in chief of the *Seattle Post-Intelligencer.* After retiring from the newspaper business, Bill served as director of the Washington State Office of International Relations and chief of protocol for Washington Governors John Spellman and Booth Gardner. He was appointed by Governor Mike Lowry to help write new ethics and campaign finance laws for the state. He was then appointed to the state's Legislative Ethics Board and elected chairman of that board. Bill has lectured and written frequently about the need for changes in alcohol policies at all levels of government.

Bill is a recovered* alcoholic with twenty-five years of sobriety.

Mel Schulstad is the cofounder and former president of the National Association of Alcoholism and Drug Abuse Counselors. In 1978 the editor/publisher of *The Alcoholism Report* established the Mel Schulstad Award to recognize outstanding contributors to the then-new profession of addiction counseling. This annual award is given to the nation's most outstanding alcoholism counselor. In 1994 Mel received the National Association of State Alcoholism and Drug Addiction Directors Lifetime Achievement Award for outstanding work in the field of alcoholism and drug addiction.

A retired colonel in the U.S. Air Force, he was twice awarded the Distinguished Flying Cross for valor in air combat operations over Europe during World War II.

Mel is a recovered alcoholic with thirty-four years of sobriety.

Arthur P. Ciaramicoli, Ed.D., Ph.D., is a licensed clinical psychologist and director and chief psychologist at the Alternative Therapy Center, MetroWest Wellness Center in Natick, Massachusetts. Dr. Ciaramicoli is also an instructor of psychology in the department of psychiatry at Harvard Medical School, where he supervises the Harvard Couples Project for alcoholics and their spouses. He has worked with alcoholics in inpatient, outpatient, and day treatment alcohol programs for more than twenty-five years; in the last decade he has developed an expertise in advising alcoholics in alternative medicine modalities. Dr. Ciaramicoli's unique approach to group psychotherapy programs for alcoholics is featured in his book *Treatment of Abuse and Addiction: A Holistic Approach* (Northvale, New Jersey: Jason Aronson, 1997).

In *Beyond the Influence* our purpose is to present a clearheaded approach to the facts about the drug alcohol and the disease of alcoholism. Our common denominator is a deep understanding of the suffering of alcoholics and their families and a commitment to presenting the truth not as we would like to perceive it but as the scientific facts present it.

We offer this book with great optimism, believing that it is possible to reduce the suffering caused by the drug alcohol and the disease we call alcoholism. The facts about alcoholism are known; the solutions are within our reach.

---

* *In this book we use the word* recovered *to describe alcoholics with more than six years sobriety. After six years of continual sobriety, relapse is relatively rare (see References section).*

PART I

The
Problem

1

Still Under the Influence

All truth passes through three stages. First, it is ridiculed. Second, it is violently opposed. Third, it is accepted as being self-evident.

— SCHOPENHAUER

Don't remember where I was flying to, but was taken off the plane in Twin Cities, ambulanced to Hennepin County Detox—nightmare—went to Hazelden from there—started stealing, then drinking—then to detox center in Hastings, Minnesota. Scotty picked me up, got drunk at his home nearby, had to leave on bus to Madison, got drunk couldn't stay at Sharon's. My wallet stolen that night. Tried to sleep outside at Ray's old apt. Neighbors called. Woke up in detox. Began series of staying with AA people.

Ran out of places to go, no insurance, no halfway house, no money. Went to D.C.—stayed sober one month.

Terry McGovern wrote these words in her journal when she was forty-three years old. Two years later she was dead. Around 8:30 P.M. on December 14, 1994, Terry left the Crystal Corner Bar in Madison, Wisconsin, and wandered into an unlit parking lot, where she either fell or lay down in the snow and froze to death. Her body was discovered around noon the next day. The coroner's report stated that death was due to "hypothermia while in a state of extreme intoxication."

Many of us will hear Terry McGovern's story and shake our heads in dismay—perhaps even in disgust. Why, we wonder, did this gentle, intelligent, much-loved daughter of former senator and presidential candidate George McGovern choose to kill herself with booze? How did she get caught up in such a self-destructive way of life when she was so talented and privileged, surrounded by people who loved her and wanted to help her? What, exactly, was wrong with her? What demons possessed her?

The answers to these questions are hotly debated by those who insist that alcoholism is a primary, progressive, physiological disease and those who argue that alcoholism is not a true medical disease at all but a symptom of underlying psychological and emotional problems to which the individual responds by engaging in increasingly self-destructive behavior. The disease theorists engage in vociferous exchanges with those who do not see alcoholism as a disease, and each side carefully amasses research studies and dramatic anecdotes to fortify its position.

After the smoke clears, little if anything seems to have been resolved. Witnessing the bitter disagreements among experts, most of us end up bewildered by the conflicting theories. If alcoholism is a behavior, what quirk of personality or circumstance would lead good, decent, intelligent people such as Terry McGovern to destroy everything in their lives for alcohol? Are alcoholics inherently weak, selfish, emotionally immature individuals?

If, on the other hand, alcoholism is a disease, why do its victims suffer from such intense guilt, shame, and self-loathing? Why can some diagnosed alcoholics return to "moderate" or "controlled" drinking for weeks or even months? Why do some alcoholics stop drinking and recover with no treatment at all? And why are psychological counseling and spirituality considered such important elements of recovery?

These questions and the contentious debates they engender lead many people to throw up their hands, concluding as the Supreme Court did in April 1988, that alcoholism is a consequence of "willful misconduct."

Alcoholism is not a mysterious illness, nor is it "willful misconduct." Alcoholism is a true medical disease rooted in abnormalities in brain chemistry—biochemical aberrations that are inherited by the great majority of alcoholics and, in some cases, acquired through intense and sustained exposure to alcohol and other drugs. *When the alcoholic drinks, something different happens.* This difference between alcoholics and nonalcoholics is not created by personality disorders, emotional instability, character defects, or traumatic circumstances; it is a difference in the way the alcoholic's body responds to the drug alcohol.

Physiology, not psychology, determines whether one drinker will become addicted to alcohol and another will not. This is not theory but fact, based on thousands of research studies detailing the nature, causes, and progression of this ancient yet perpetually misunderstood disease. More than fifty years of experimentation and investigation by distinguished scientists in such diverse fields as neurology, biochemistry, pharmacology, and psychology have provided the basic facts needed to understand the drug alcohol and the disease it creates in biologically susceptible individuals. We know what this disease is, we know how to treat it, and we know how to prevent it. The knowledge is in our hands.

Yet the myths and misconceptions that distort our thinking about alcoholism, complicating both treatment and recovery, remain firmly in place. Two decades ago the myths and realities about alcoholism were presented in *Under the Influence: A Guide to the Myths and Realities of Alcoholism*, coauthored by James R. Milam and Katherine Ketcham. Despite stunning scientific advances in alcoholism research in the last twenty years, these myths continue to influence the way we treat alcoholics.

Myth:	Alcohol has the same chemical and psychological effects on everyone who drinks.
Reality:	Alcohol, like every other substance we take into our bodies, affects different people in different ways.
Myth:	Addiction to alcohol is often psychological.
Reality:	Addiction to alcohol is physiological and involves profound chemical disruptions in the brain.
Myth:	Alcohol is an addictive drug, and anyone who drinks regularly for a long enough period of time will become physically addicted to it.
Reality:	Alcohol is a *selectively* addictive drug; only a minority of drinkers will experience the need or desire to consume alcohol in sufficient quantities and over a long enough period of time to become physically addicted to it.
Myth:	People become alcoholics because they have psychological or emotional problems that they try to relieve by drinking.
Reality:	Alcoholics have basically the same psychological problems as nonalcoholics before they start drinking, but these problems are aggravated (and new disturbances are created) by addiction to alcohol.
Myth:	If people would drink responsibly, they would not become alcoholics.

Reality: Many responsible drinkers become alcoholics. Because of the nature of the *disease*—not the person—they begin to drink irresponsibly.

Myth: Some alcoholics can learn to drink normally as long as they limit the amount.

Reality: Alcoholics, who by definition suffer from a permanent brain addiction, can never safely return to drinking.

A little history may help here. Originally published in 1981, *Under the Influence* detailed the biochemical and neurophysiological factors—metabolic abnormalities, alterations in brain chemistry, heredity, ethnic susceptibility, and prenatal influences—that determine why some people become addicted to alcohol while others do not. The book helped fuel the "recovery boom" of the 1980s, a time of remarkable advances in alcoholism treatment and prevention efforts and a period marked by a growing commitment to the scientifically proven understanding that alcoholism is a primary, progressive, physiological disease requiring lifelong abstinence for recovery.

As the recovery boom gained momentum, growing numbers of behaviorists, social critics, and popular writers raised their voices to criticize the "disease concept," arguing that it failed to account for psychological and emotional factors. Many critics contended that focusing attention on the physical addiction released problem drinkers from moral responsibility for their behavior. What about willpower and simple human decency? If we call alcoholism a disease, the critics continued, we might as well call fingernail biting, obsessive TV viewing, and chronic boredom "diseases." One psychiatrist used a sunburn analogy: Redheads tend to burn more easily than brunettes or blondes, so shouldn't they protect themselves by staying out of the sun? And shouldn't those redheads who continually get sunburned take responsibility for and accept the consequences of their misbehavior?

Alcohol problems should be redefined as "maladaptive lifestyle habits," argued behavioral psychologist Alan Marlatt of the University of Washington. An outspoken critic of the "disease concept," Marlatt insisted that excessive drinking is a behavior that people *do*, not a symptom of what they *are*, and that alcoholics and problem drinkers can be taught how to modify their maladaptive habits through stress management, lifestyle changes, and basic learning principles. For those who want to reduce their drinking and avoid the health problems associated with excessive use of alcohol, Marlatt and other behavioral psychologists argued that moderation is the key.

In *Heavy Drinking: The Myth of Alcoholism as a Disease* Herbert Fingarette, a professor at the University of California and a consultant on alcoholism and addiction to the World Health Organization, dismissed fifty years of research on the neurological and biochemical nature of alcoholism with this statement: "No leading research authorities accept the classic disease concept." In *The Diseasing of America: Addiction Treatment Out of Control* psychologist Stanton Peele argued that disease definitions actually "undermine the individual's obligations to control behavior and to answer for misconduct."

Popular writers quickly latched on to the behaviorist trend. Audrey Kishline, a moderate drinker who believes she was mistakenly diagnosed as an alcoholic, observed in *Moderate Drinking,* "The act of lifting a drink to your lips too often is not a 'disease.' Drinking too much is a behavior, something that a problem drinker *does,* not something that he or she *has.*"

As concepts such as "moderation," "responsible drinking," and "maladaptive habits" caught the public's imagination, society as a whole became less tolerant of alcoholics and their "misbehaviors." Changing attitudes toward alcoholics were reflected clearly in the increasingly popular use of the word *abuse.** Beginning in the 1980s, government agencies charged with overseeing alcohol education and treatment programs abandoned the word *alcoholism* in favor of the term *alcohol abuse* and, more recently, *substance abuse.* In recent years the word *alcoholism* seems to have disappeared from official language while the term *substance abuse* has become as familiar as Budweiser's trio of frogs.

As alcoholism gradually became linked in the public mind with alcohol "abuse," efforts to teach "irresponsible" and "abusive" drinkers how to moderate their drinking grew in popularity. Critics of the disease concept argued vehemently that controlled-drinking therapy—tellingly translated as "behavioral self-control"—should be considered a valid alternative to lifelong abstinence. In the 1990s "harm reduction" programs such as DrinkWise, S.M.A.R.T., and Moderation Management expanded to the point where a 1997 *U.S. News and World Report* article predicted that controlled-drinking programs would someday "be as commonplace as Weight Watchers and Smokenders."

Insurance companies were quick to pick up on the argument that

---

* *Whenever we use the word* abuse *in this book, we will put quotation marks around it. As we explain in more detail in Chapter 16, we consider this word a powerful tool of the liquor industry, which hopes to portray alcohol as wholly benign for all drinkers, except for those who "choose" to "abuse" it.*

alcoholism is not a true medical disease but a behavior of "self-abuse." Uncontrollable growth in the addiction treatment field, one of the fastest-growing health care markets in the early 1980s, led to a severe backlash when insurance companies turned to the concept of managed care in an effort to control health care costs. By the early 1990s, many insurance carriers began to refuse the more expensive inpatient treatment programs in favor of less expensive outpatient treatment, arguing that it doesn't matter what treatment you offer alcoholics, because they are all equally ineffective (an argument we will counter in Chapter 10).

Alcoholics, who for decades received inappropriate and sometimes lethal treatments for their "psychological" problems, were once again crowded under the massive umbrella of the mental health bureaucracy. As insurance coverage for alcoholism was drastically reduced, health care providers struggled to reduce costs by consolidating mental health and chemical dependency units. In the always fiercely fought battle over who should oversee alcoholism treatment, psychiatrists (many of whom still subscribe to outdated psychological theories about alcoholism) gained control of administering treatment and overseeing patient care.

Meanwhile, society's problems with alcohol continue to escalate:

• An estimated fourteen million Americans are addicted to the drug alcohol or suffer from serious problems related to alcohol use.*

• Alcohol and alcohol-related problems drain more than $166 billion yearly from our economy.

• Every year more than a hundred thousand Americans die from alcohol-related causes.

• In 1998, 15,935 people died in alcohol-related traffic accidents in the U.S., an average of 44 every day (nearly two deaths per hour) and 308 every week—the equivalent of two jetliners crashing every week. These deaths represent 38.4 percent of the total 41,471 traffic fatalities.

• Alcoholics are five times more likely than others to die in motor vehicle crashes.

• One out of every 280 babies born today will die in a crash with an intoxicated driver.

This conservative figure does not include many early- and middle-stage alcoholics who are mislabeled problem drinkers or alcohol "abusers." Many experts in the alcoholism field believe the number may be as high as twenty to twenty-five million.

• Alcohol is associated with 47 to 65 percent of adult drownings and half of all boating accidents; alcoholics are sixteen times more likely than others to die in falls and ten times more likely to become fire or burn victims.

• Up to 40 percent of industrial fatalities and 47 percent of industrial injuries can be linked to alcohol consumption and alcoholism.

• In 40 percent of all fatal pedestrian accidents, the driver, pedestrian, or both were intoxicated.

• Thirty-seven percent of rapes and sexual assaults, 15 percent of robberies, and 27 percent of aggravated assaults involve alcohol use by the offender.

• More than half of all incidents of domestic violence involve alcohol, with women most likely to be battered when both partners have been drinking.

• At the end of 1996, more than 1.7 million American adults were behind bars and 80 percent—1.4 million men and women—were considered "seriously involved" with alcohol and other drugs. Among these 1.4 million inmates are the parents of 2.4 million children, many of them minors.

• An estimated 6.6 million children under the age of eighteen live in households with at least one alcoholic parent.

• More than half of our country's middle and high school students drink alcoholic beverages.

• Two of every five college students (43 percent) are binge drinkers (drinking five or more drinks at a time in the previous two weeks) while four out of five (81 percent) of those living in fraternity or sorority houses are binge drinkers. Among students who drink, 52 percent say a major motivation was "to get drunk."

• Almost half of all college students who are victims of campus crimes said they were drinking or using other drugs when they were victimized.

• Forty-seven percent of people admitted to hospital emergency rooms have positive blood alcohol levels; in the great majority of cases, the patient is treated and discharged with no effort to diagnose or treat the underlying alcohol problem.

• Alcoholism among certain minorities—Latinos, Asians, and African-Americans, for example—is increasing, due in large part to aggressive "target marketing" by the liquor industry. Among Latinos, for example, chronic liver disease and cirrhosis are the sixth and seventh leading causes of death (compared to the ninth leading cause of death in the general U.S. population); 12 percent of Latino homicide victims are killed in bars.

Most disheartening of all, people such as Terry McGovern—talented, intelligent, loving human beings in the prime of their lives—continue to progress in their disease as family members agonize over their inability to find effective help for their loved ones. In *Terry: My Daughter's Life-and-Death Struggle with Alcoholism*, George McGovern asks the questions that haunt so many people who love alcoholics: "How could this have happened? Why did she drink so much and die so young? Why do some people recover from alcoholism while my daughter died despite all her struggles to overcome her addiction? Why did my daughter become addicted at all?"

We will attempt to answer these questions, bringing into clear focus the problems we face as individuals and as a society as we attempt to understand the disease of alcoholism and find appropriate help for its victims. In Part I we explore the uniquely complex nature of alcohol, a drug that is addictive for only a minority of users. We look at the central role played by dopamine, serotonin, norepinephrine, GABA, and other neurotransmitters in paving the way for addiction. We follow alcoholism through its early, middle, and late stages, detailing the differences between social drinkers, problem drinkers, and alcoholics.

In Part II we focus on practical approaches to diagnosis, intervention, treatment, and recovery. What treatments work, and which should you avoid? Why does a physical disease require psychological and spiritual approaches in treatment and recovery? How safe and effective are the various drug treatments for alcoholism, including the opiate antagonist naltrexone, Prozac-type drugs, and Campral (acomprosate)? Do nontraditional healing methods such as exercise, nutritional therapy, acupuncture, herbal remedies, and amino acids help prevent relapses and solidify recovery? Which methods are most effective and why?

In Part III we investigate the central role played by the beer, wine, and distilled-spirits industries in promoting the prevailing view of alcoholism as a psychological disorder rather than a true physiological disease. We detail innovative education, prevention, and treatment programs that can be instituted in our medical, legal, educational, and political systems to help dispel the prevailing myths and misconceptions about alcoholism.

In these pages we hope to establish a foundation—both philosophical and practical—upon which alcoholics, their families, and those who seek to help them can build a broader understanding of both the disease and the recovery process. While there are certainly gaps in our knowledge about alcoholism—as there are numerous voids in our understanding of all diseases—we have the basic facts in hand, and we have sufficient knowledge and expertise to create effective education, prevention, and treatment programs. What stands in our way is not a lack of scientific evidence but a wealth of misinformation and misconceptions about the drug alcohol and its varied, diverse effects on human beings.

2

Alcohol:
A "Simple" Chemical

Why did I drink? What need was there for it? I was
happy. Was it because I was too happy? I was
strong. Was it because I was too strong? Did
I possess too much vitality? I don't know why I
drank.

—JACK LONDON

Jack London, the prolific turn-of-the-century writer and intrepid adventurer, was five years old when he got drunk for the first time. Carrying a pail of beer to his father, who was plowing a distant field, he stopped for a rest and took a drink, figuring that since the grown-ups always seemed to take so much pleasure in their beer, maybe a few sips would be good for him, too. It was a hot day, and he gulped the bitter brew like medicine, considerably lightening his load. After sleeping the afternoon away, he awoke to a spinning head, a heaving stomach, and the firm conclusion that he had been poisoned.

Two years later London got drunk again, this time on red wine. Sick for days afterward, the seven-year-old vowed never again to touch the stuff. "No mad dog was ever more afraid of water than was I of alcohol," he recalled later. Yet as time went by, London began to look back at that nausea-inducing episode with a more affectionate eye. "It had been something ticklishly, devilishly fine," he concluded, "a bright and gorgeous episode in the monotony of life and labor."

Early on in life Jack London—who died at age forty of kidney failure—came to understand the strange twin nature of the simple chemical ethanol, commonly known as alcohol: a foul-tasting, stomach-heaving, head-spinning liquid that possesses the nearly miraculous power of transforming everyday experience into something extraordinary and memorable. Within moments of ingestion, alcohol loosens the tongue, frees inhibitions, induces laughter, and dispels the gray monotony of day-today life. Only hours later is the overimbiber forced to confront the longer-term penalties bestowed by this convivial chemical: nausea, headaches, memory lapses, and, often enough, shame and guilt that last for hours, even days.

Yet, oddly enough, the memory of alcohol's fleeting salutary effects often overpowers more unpleasant remembrances. Looking back on yet another drinking occasion, London describes what he "got" from alcohol that kept him coming back for more. (Most alcoholics will know exactly what he's talking about.)

> *I had got into the cogs and springs of men's actions. . . . I had caught a myriad enticing and inflammatory hints of a world beyond my world. . . . I had got behind men's souls. I had got behind my own soul and found unguessed potencies and greatnesses. . . . Yes, that day stood out above all my other days. To this day it so stands out. The memory of it is branded in my brain.*

How can a simple chemical have such complex, even contradictory effects on our thoughts, feelings, and behaviors? What is it about alcohol that allows it to gain such a hold on the human mind and imagination that even with all the lingering physical pain and psychological torture it bestows on its regular users, they look forward with great anticipation to its fleeting pleasures? Why are some people vulnerable to alcohol's charms, while others can take it or leave it and still others have no desire to touch the stuff?

We cannot hope to understand the reasons why people drink or why they become addicted to alcohol until we grasp the inherent paradox of a substance that can be praised and damned in one breath. Alcohol, some say, is an inherently benign, euphoria-inducing substance capable of reducing tension and adding significantly to the pleasure of life. Alcohol, others caution, is a potent drug, as dangerous as heroin or cocaine; in fact, alcohol causes more death and destruction and kills more innocent bystanders than all illegal drugs combined. Alcohol, intones another voice, is dangerous only for those who drink too much and too often; the problem lies not in alcohol itself but in the person who "abuses" it.

Whom are we to believe? While there is a measure of truth in each of these statements, the whole truth can be assembled only when we look at alcohol's actions in the body and its varying effects on different individuals. This chapter describes what happens in your body when you drink alcohol. We follow alcohol's journey from the stomach and small intestine into the bloodstream, explaining how different factors including weight, gender, hormones, and body fat influence blood alcohol levels. Finally, we accompany alcohol into the liver, describing the enzymes involved in metabolism and the various enzyme combinations that create highly individual reactions to alcohol.

Alcohol is a simple chemical, but its effects on the body are extraordinarily complex and highly individual.

THE ACTIONS OF ALCOHOL

What is alcohol? Yeast poop. When yeast, a microorganism that evolved around two hundred million years ago, encounters the water and plant sugars in fruits, berries, and grains, something very interesting happens. In the process known as fermentation, yeast releases an enzyme that converts the sugars into carbon dioxide (CO_2) and ethanol (CH_3CH_2OH, more commonly called alcohol). A simple one-celled organism, yeast doesn't know when to call it quits and continues to produce alcohol until it expires, the very first victim of acute alcohol poisoning.

Because most strains of yeast cannot survive an alcohol concentration much above 14 percent, naturally fermented wines generally contain between 10 and 14 percent alcohol. In beer, which is made from barley, corn, rice, wheat, or other cereal grains, brewers artificially halt the fermentation process somewhere between 3 and 6 percent alcohol. Malt liquors are allowed to ferment longer, thereby increasing their alcohol concentration; some brands of malt liquor contain 10 percent alcohol or more.

Human beings have been drinking beer for almost seven thousand years and wine for approximately five thousand years. Around A.D. 800, Arabian chemists figured out how to overcome yeast's natural limitations by boiling alcohol away from its sugar bath and condensing it into "pure" alcohol. Because pure alcohol isn't very appetizing (chemists use it in the laboratory as a solvent, an extracting agent, fuel, and the starting material for the production of acetic acid, lacquers, varnishes, and dyes), distillers dilute the "spirits" with water.

To impart a distinctive taste and aroma to their beverages, brewers, vintners, and distillers mix their products with various additives such as glucose, fructose, acetic and lactic acids, vitamins, salts, acids, ketones, and esters as well as metals such as aluminum, lead, manganese, silicon, and zinc. They may also add other alcohols (called congeners), including propyl, butyl, amyl, hexyl, hyptyl, octyl, nonyl, decyl, and methyl, or fusel oil, all of which bestow a unique flavor on the beverage. Wood alcohol (also called methyl alcohol or methanol), for example, gives vodka its unique taste; Russian vodkas, favored by many vodka connoisseurs, contain relatively high amounts of wood alcohol.

While various additives and congeners are generally used in such minuscule amounts that they are considered harmless, some experts believe that severe hangovers, headaches, aggressive or violent behavior, and various medical complications may be caused by an individual's unique (possibly allergic) reaction to one or more of these substances.

ALCOHOL'S JOURNEY THROUGH THE BODY

When you drink a beer, glass of wine, or mixed drink, alcohol travels down your esophagus directly into your stomach. Because alcohol is a very small molecule (just two and a half times the weight of water), it requires little or no preliminary enzyme activity and passes directly through cell membranes. In contrast, a starch molecule weighs 250,000 times as much as alcohol and requires three to four hours in a rich stew of stomach acids and pancreatic enzymes before it can be broken down into smaller molecules that then can be absorbed into the bloodstream.

ABSORPTION

Five to 10 percent of the alcohol you drink is absorbed into the bloodstream through the lining of the mouth and esophagus. Approximately 20 percent is absorbed into the bloodstream through the stomach, although the rate varies according to gender. The remaining 70 to 75 percent is absorbed through the walls of the small intestine.

When alcohol mixes in with your bloodstream, your blood alcohol concentration (BAC), also known as blood alcohol level (BAL), rises. BAC is the amount of alcohol in the bloodstream, measured in percentages. A BAC of 0.10 percent, for instance, means that a person has 1 part alcohol per 1,000 parts blood in the body. How quickly and how high your BAC rises depends not only on how much you drink and the percentage of alcohol in the drink, but on weight, body fat, gender, age, nutritional status, physical health, and emotional state.

Weight

The more you weigh, the greater your blood volume; the greater your blood volume, the more liquid there is to dilute alcohol. A 200-pound man has more pints of blood circulating in his body than a 150-pound man; the more blood there is to dilute the alcohol, the slower the rise in BAC.

Body Fat

Alcohol does not dissolve as readily in fat as it does in water, muscle, or bone. Alcohol is a polar molecule (one end is positively charged and the other end is negatively charged) and easily dissolves in other polar substances such as water. Fat, on the other hand, is nonpolar, and alcohol has a difficult time getting into fatty tissues; more of it will remain in your bloodstream instead. As a result, the greater the amount of body fat you have, the higher your BAC will be.

Gender

Even if a man and a woman weigh the same and drink the same amount, the woman will have a higher BAC for two basic reasons.

First, women have a smaller amount of body water to dilute the alcohol (somewhat like mixing the same amount of alcohol into a smaller pail of water). Women also tend to have a higher percentage of body fat; as we explained in the section above, alcohol does not dissolve readily in fat, so the concentration of alcohol in the bloodstream will be greater. Perhaps most significant, however, is the fact that women have lower activity of the alcohol metabolizing enzyme alcohol dehydrogenase (ADH) in their stomachs. The deficiency in ADH levels causes a larger proportion of the alcohol to reach the bloodstream, creating a higher BAC, which in turn leads to more rapid intoxication. Because of these factors, women are more vulnerable than men to alcohol-induced liver and heart damage.

A woman's BAC will also vary according to the phases of her menstrual cycle. The highest BACs occur during the premenstrual phase. Because hormone levels can vary day to day and month to month (and BACS vary with them), women are less able to predict accurately the effect of a given amount of alcohol. Alcohol metabolism may contribute to increased production of a form of estrogen called estradiol (which contributes to increased bone density and reduced risk of coronary artery disease) and to decreased metabolism of this hormone. Thus in some women, alcohol consumption significantly elevates estradiol levels over the short term.

Age

Body fat typically increases with age while enzyme actions tend to slow down as you get older. As a result, a few drinks will hit you harder at age sixty than they will at age thirty, forty, or fifty.

Although teens and preteens are not fully grown, their livers can process alcohol just as well as adult drinkers'. The problem with teen-agers is that they tend to drink large quantities of alcohol in very short periods of time, leading to rapid intoxication, vomiting, loss of consciousness, and even death. (See section on binge drinking, pages 101–102.)

Nutritional Status

If you eat when you drink, alcohol mixes in with the more complex food molecules, which slows down the rate at which the stomach's contents empty into the small intestine. Since 70 to 75 percent of alcohol is absorbed through the small intestine, this delay results in a slower rise in blood alcohol concentration. If, on the other hand, you drink on an empty stomach (the 5 P.M. happy hour is a perfect example), the process of absorption is faster because there are fewer competing food molecules and circulating enzymes in the stomach to slow down the absorption process. As a result, alcohol is released immediately into the small intestine, where it is rapidly absorbed into the bloodstream.

In one study, subjects who drank alcohol after a meal that included fat, protein, and carbohydrates absorbed the alcohol about three times more slowly than when they consumed alcohol on an empty stomach.

Health of the Stomach, Intestines, and Bowel

Ulcers and bowel disorders such as colitis, Crohn's disease, and irritable bowel syndrome create raw, irritated surfaces in the bowels, which make these surfaces more permeable or "leaky." This leads, in many cases, to a higher BAC.

Emotional State

Anxiety, fear, anger, stress, and fatigue signal the body to release the hormone epinephrine (adrenaline). Adrenaline mobilizes fats and glycogen (the body's primary source of sugar) for energy use, diverting blood away from the stomach and intestines into the skeletal muscles; this reduced blood flow will slow down the process of alcohol absorption. However, chronic and intense emotional states may have the *opposite* effect, damaging the stomach and intestines, and thereby speeding up absorption.

Drink Strength

The stronger a drink is—that is, the more alcohol it contains—the greater the amount of alcohol that will get into your bloodstream. In distilled spirits (scotch, whiskey, gin, vodka, etc.) the alcohol molecules make up a much larger percentage of the total volume; in addition, most distilled liquors do not contain significant amounts of complex sugars or carbohydrates, which are present in wine and beer and help slow down absorption through the stomach and intestine. This explains why a 2-ounce martini, which consists of approximately 35 to 40 percent pure alcohol, is absorbed more rapidly than a 4-ounce glass of Chablis, which contains approximately 12 percent alcohol.

Mixers and Food

When you mix alcohol with nonalcoholic substances such as orange juice, tomato juice, or milk, the fats and sugars in the mixers will slow down absorption. And as we've seen, if you accompany your drinks with food, absorption will be slower as well. Neither mixers nor food, however, will keep you from getting drunk if you drink enough alcohol.

Carbonation

Carbonated alcoholic beverages such as champagne, wine spritzers, scotch and sodas, or gin and tonics can accelerate absorption. The carbonated bubbles irritate the pylorus, the ring of muscle that serves as a gate between the stomach and small intestine. The pylorus opens up prematurely to empty the stomach contents into the small intestine, from which alcohol is absorbed quickly into the bloodstream.

BAC levels depend on a number of factors, some of which you can control—food intake, weight, how much, how fast, and what kind of beverage you drink—and others that are beyond your control—age, gender, hormonal fluctuations. The following table offers a rough idea of how alcohol affects behavior at different doses:

TABLE 2-1 Impact of alcohol on BAC

Number of Drinks and BAC in One Hour of Drinking			Number of Drinks and BAC in Two Hours of Drinking		
Male 170 lbs.	BAC	Female 137 lbs.	Male 170 lbs.	BAC	Female 137 lbs.
5 drinks (.09–.10)	.10			.10	4 drinks (.09–.10)
	.09		5 drinks (.07–.08)	.09	
	.08	3 drinks (.07–.08)		.08	
4 drinks (.06–.07)	.07			.07	3 drinks (.06–.07)
	.06		4 drinks (.05–.06)	.06	
3 drinks (.04–.05)	.05			.05	
	.04	2 drinks (.04–.05)		.04	
2 drinks (.02–.03)	.03		3 drinks (.02–.03)	.03	2 drinks (.02–.03)
	.02			.02	
	.01		2 drinks (.01)	.01	
	BAC			BAC	

Source. National Highway Traffic Safety Administration

ALCOHOL METABOLISM:
HOW THE BODY ELIMINATES ALCOHOL

Think of the bloodstream as a fast-flowing river crammed with barges of nutrients and chemicals that require unloading and processing at the liver, an incredibly efficient factory. When alcohol is present in the bloodstream, it zips in and out of the steady flow of traffic like a speedboat with a thrill-seeking teenager at the wheel. The heavily loaded barges move out of the way, allowing alcohol to pass quickly through the congestion and gain easy entry to the liver.

If only one or two speedboats enter the bloodstream, the liver has no difficulty stripping them down into scrap metal. If the speedboats keep coming, however, the liver has a traffic jam on its hands. A normal, healthy liver can process alcohol at the approximate rate of 0.5 ounce of pure alcohol per hour, the equivalent of one 12-ounce beer, 5 ounces of table wine, or 1.5 ounces of 80-proof distilled spirits. Thus, if you drink one and a half cans of beer, 6 ounces of wine, or 2 ounces of 80-proof gin in one hour or less, that's more alcohol than your liver can process. The remainder will circulate in your bloodstream until your liver is ready to deal with it. If you continue to drink, your BAC will continue to rise.

Here's an example: It's Sunday evening in Denver, the Broncos have just won the Super Bowl, and Joe is in a party mood. Around 8 P.M. he joins some friends at a local tavern, and in the next four hours he downs twelve beers and four shots of 80-proof tequila. In all the excitement, Joe, who weighs 165 pounds, forgets to eat dinner, munching on pretzels and potato chips instead.

By midnight, when Joe falls into bed, his liver has burned up 2 ounces of pure alcohol (about four beers). By 6:00 A.M., when he wakes up, his liver has eliminated an additional 3 ounces (six more beers). On his way to work at 7:00 A.M., Joe still has approximately 2 ounces of pure alcohol circulating around in his bloodstream (the remaining beers and 4 ounces of tequila).

Seven hours after Joe stopped drinking, he is still legally drunk.

Unfortunately for Joe, there's nothing he can do to nudge his liver along and accelerate the metabolic process. Coffee, cold showers, fruit juice, and exercise are all basically useless, for the fact remains that if you drink more than your liver can process at one time, your BAC will rise. If you keep drinking, you'll get drunk. And the more you drink, the drunker you'll get. This is true no matter what you drink—the liver treats all alcohol the same way, and it takes just as long to metabolize the alcohol in a can of Coors as it does to burn up a straight shot of tequila. You would have to drink a larger volume of the lower-alcohol-content beverage to attain the same BAC, but alcohol is alcohol, and the liver doesn't care what package it comes in.

The liver metabolizes (breaks down) alcohol through three different enzyme systems or pathways: (1) the alcohol dehydrogenase (ADH) pathway; (2) the microsomal enzyme oxidizing system (MEOS); and (3) the catalase oxidation system. Because the catalase oxidation system contributes relatively little to alcohol metabolism in the liver, we will discuss only the ADH and MEOS pathways.

THE ADH PATHWAY

The ADH pathway, which processes most of the alcohol you drink, involves two basic steps. In the first stage, alcohol is converted into acetaldehyde through the actions of the enzyme alcohol dehydrogenase

(ADH) and the cofactor NAD+ (nocotinamide adenine dinucleotide, derived from the vitamin niacin). In the second step, acetaldehyde is changed into acetate, with the help of the enzyme aldehyde dehydrogenase (ALDH) and NAD+. Both steps involve additional enzymes, isoenzymes, and cofactors, but ADH, ALDH, and NAD+ are the major players.

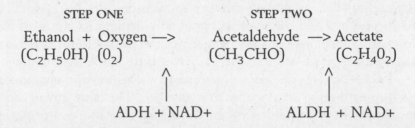

STEP ONE

STEP TWO

Ethanol + Oxygen —>   Acetaldehyde —> Acetate
(C_2H_5OH) (O_2)   (CH_3CHO)   ($C_2H_4O_2$)

ADH + NAD+   ALDH + NAD+

Step one: Two hydrogen atoms are removed from the alcohol molecule to create an entirely different substance, acetaldehyde. Ironically (and unfortunately), acetaldehyde is much more destructive to the cells than alcohol itself. Even tiny amounts of this toxic molecule can make a drinker violently ill. The drug Antabuse, which is sometimes used in alcoholism treatment, blocks metabolism at this stage, causing considerable misery for anyone who drinks while using the drug. Symptoms of the Antabuse (acetaldehyde) reaction include flushing, rapid pulse, pounding headache, difficulty breathing, nausea, vomiting, sweating, and blurred vision.

Step two: The liver cells quickly initiate the second step in alcohol metabolism, sending the enzyme aldehyde dehydrogenase (ALDH), NAD+, and water to the rescue. An extra oxygen atom is attached to acetaldehyde, transforming the Mr. Hyde monster into the gentle Dr. Jekyll of acetate, a salt of acetic acid (the acidic component of vinegar). Acetate is then broken down into carbon dioxide and water, both useful, nourishing substances the body can use for its vital functions. This final metabolic step proceeds at a slower pace and occurs in virtually every cell and tissue of the body.

A Word About NAD+

NAD+ provides the necessary energetic spark for metabolism to occur; it's the match that ignites the pilot light in the liver cell's furnace. In the process of converting alcohol to acetaldehyde and then to acetate, NAD+ is reduced to the nonfunctional NADH. As more NAD+ is used up and NADH accumulates, the pilot light flickers and threatens to go out. To keep the metabolic furnaces fired up, the liver must use oxygen to change NADH back into NAD+.

One or at most two drinks per day will not injure, in most cases, a normal, healthy liver. (The National Council on Alcoholism and Drug Dependence publishes guidelines suggesting no more than one drink per day for women and no more than two drinks per day for men; see References section for more information on these guidelines.) However, if you drink heavily, either periodically or chronically, NADH will begin to accumulate and the liver will gradually deplete its stores of oxygen to create more NAD+. Less oxygen will be available for other important cellular functions, and this can, over time, cause liver damage.

Excess NADH can also contribute to a slowdown in gluconeogenesis, the formation of sugar within the cell. This slowdown can lead, in turn, to hypoglycemia (low blood sugar). (For more information on alcohol-induced hypoglycemia, see pages 166–167.) Too much NADH lying around can also increase lactic acid levels, which can result, over the long term, in increased uric acid levels. Uric acid buildup can contribute to painful swelling or inflammation of the joints (gout), the development of kidney stones, and in some cases, kidney damage. (Jack London, whom we mentioned earlier in this chapter, died of kidney failure.)

Variations in ADH and ALDH

Each step in the metabolism of alcohol is controlled by different enzymes, which are responsible for initiating and accelerating chemical reactions throughout the body. Enzymes exist in different forms called isoenzymes (or isozymes), and the properties and activities of these isoenzymes differ from one individual to the next. Genetically determined enzyme abnormalities (polymorphisms) are fairly common. Alcohol dehydrogenase (ADH), for example, is actually a family of closely related enzymes, of which more than twenty have been identified so far. Class 1 ADH enzymes, for example, are regulated by three genes: ADH*1, ADH*2, and ADH*3, all located next to each other on the fourth chromosome. Thus, your individual genetic makeup will influence to a significant degree the number and relative percentage of these enzymes, and this in turn has a direct and often dramatic effect on your uniquely individual reaction to alcohol.

The following chart shows the occurrence of the ADH genes in different populations:

Occurrence of ADH Alleles in Different Populations

	$ADH_2{}^1$(%)	$ADH_2{}^2$(%)	$ADH_2{}^3$(%)	$ADH_3{}^1$(%)	$ADH_3{}^2$(%)
White Americans	>95	<5	<5	50	50
White Europeans	90	10	<5	60	40
Japanese	35	65	<5	95	5
Blacks	85	<5	15	85	15

This chart tells an amazing story. For these five different isoenzymes (and remember, there are dozens of enzymes and isoenzymes involved in alcohol metabolism), remarkable differences exist between different ethnic and racial groups. Let's look at the ADH2*1 isoenzyme as an example. Ninety-five percent of white Americans inherit this isoenzyme, compared to 35 percent of Japanese. The ADH2*2 isoenzyme, on the other hand, is found in 65 percent of Japanese but less than five percent of black and white Americans. And ADH3*2 is found in 50 percent of white Americans, 15 percent of black Americans, and only 5 percent of Japanese.

Similar differences exist for the ALDH (aldehyde dehydrogenase) enzyme. A study compared Asians with an inherited mutant form of the ALDH2*2 isoenzyme to Asians who did not have this mutation. The Asians with the mutation experienced significantly higher blood acetaldehyde levels after drinking alcohol, even though their blood alcohol concentrations were similar. Since acetaldehyde is an extremely toxic, reactive substance that creates immediate, unpleasant physical reactions for the drinker, Asians with the mutant gene are considered more "sensitive" to alcohol—the abnormal enzyme actually works to protect them against excessive drinking and alcoholism.

What do we mean by "sensitive"? Because of their particular enzyme configurations, approximately half of all Asians are more vulnerable to alcohol's negative effects, a vulnerability that is controlled not by their reaction to alcohol itself but by an enzyme abnormality that leads to a buildup of alcohol's metabolic by-product, acetaldehyde. That ultra-sensitivity ironically bestows a protective effect, at least in terms of alcoholism. When Asian people with the mutant ALDH2*2 isoenzyme drink, they experience such unpleasant reactions (flushing, nausea, dizziness) that they typically have no desire to repeat the experience.

MICROSOMAL ENZYME OXIDIZING SYSTEM (MEOS)

The MEOS is a backup enzyme system, somewhat like an emergency generator that can be used when the normal circuits are overloaded. When you drink large quantities of alcohol, your ADH pathway eventually reaches its limit and the MEOS kicks in to help. The MEOS consists of a family of enzymes operating in an area of the cell known as the smooth endoplasmic reticulum; in alcohol metabolism the most important of these enzymes is P-4502E1, also known by the nickname 2E1.

Just as there are genetically determined variations in the ADH and ALDH enzymes, 2E1 also exists in different, genetically determined forms (polymorphisms) that vary from one ethnic population to another. For example, a rare mutant or "wild-type" variation of 2E1 is found relatively frequently in Taiwanese and Japanese people, but is much less common in African-Americans, European-Americans, and Scandinavians.

Researchers believe that genetic variations in 2E1 may influence susceptibility to alcoholism. Charles Lieber, chief of the research program on liver disease and nutrition at the Bronx Veterans Administration Hospital, found that the same amount of alcohol produced much higher blood acetaldehyde levels in alcoholics when compared to nonalcoholics. Lieber theorizes that intensified MEOS activity is responsible for the higher blood acetaldehyde levels, since 2E1 results in "strikingly increased oxidation of alcohol to acetaldehyde, leading to high acetaldehyde levels." Thus, any drinker with a superefficient genetic variation of 2E1 will experience a buildup of the highly toxic chemical acetaldehyde.

Acetaldehyde is a nasty troublemaker, creating all sorts of damage to the body's cells. The far-ranging toxic effects of acetaldehyde are due, in large part, to its ability to bind to other substances the body uses for cellular growth and repair. Latching on to liver proteins, hemoglobin, red blood cells, and substances such as collagen, acetaldehyde can lead to numerous destructive reactions and interactions, including antibody responses, inactivation of enzymes, decreased ability to repair enzymes, and striking impairments in the liver's ability to utilize oxygen. In short, acetaldehyde buildup can damage the liver and other vital organs. Acetaldehyde's parasitic ability to bind to various proteins and red blood cells also gives it a free ride to the brain, where it interacts with diverse brain chemicals, paving the way for neurological addiction; see pages 46–52 for a description of acetaldehyde's interactions with neurotransmitters.

Although considered a minor pathway for metabolizing alcohol, the MEOS is nevertheless extremely important in understanding the pervasive toxic and addictive effects of the drug alcohol. Because the MEOS is an adaptive system that responds to the finite capacities of the ADH pathway, if you drink heavily, either periodically or chronically, you will most likely be metabolizing some of the alcohol through this secondary enzyme system. Once the MEOS gears up, you can't turn it off—the adaptations are permanent.

One potential problem area for heavy drinkers is the development of *metabolic tolerance*. When the MEOS adapts and intensifies its actions, the drinker is able to quickly and efficiently metabolize alcohol. Someone with an efficient metabolism can drink more alcohol than most people and at the same time feel and act less affected. Because they are less affected by the drug, people with a high metabolic tolerance tend to drink greater quantities of alcohol.

An adaptive increase in the MEOS is also associated with *cross-tolerance*. When the MEOS fires up 2E1 in response to alcohol ingestion, other related enzymes are automatically called into action at the same time. These additional enzymes work to accelerate the metabolism of various prescription and nonprescription drugs. Thus, if you develop a high metabolic tolerance for alcohol, you will also automatically have a high metabolic tolerance for a number of other drugs that act on the central nervous system including sedatives and hypnotics (sleeping pills) such as diazepam (Valium) and lorazepam (Ativan). (Alcohol's influence on the effectiveness of various drugs is extremely complex. See our explanation in the References.) If you take more than one drug at a time, however, the effects can be disastrous. Alcohol is always first in line for metabolism, and while the MEOS is preoccupied with alcohol, other drugs accumulate in the bloodstream. Because these drugs are present in the body for longer periods of time, their effects are magnified, and complications may include dizziness, difficulty breathing, respiratory failure, coma, or death.

The supercharged 2E1 system, it appears, works too efficiently. 2E1 has "an extraordinary capacity," in researcher Charles Lieber's words, to activate various drugs and chemicals to highly toxic by-products, a metabolic quirk that makes heavy drinkers vulnerable to liver injury when they are exposed to various anesthetics, certain prescription and nonprescription drugs, industrial solvents, and carcinogenic substances. The nonprescription pain reliever acetaminophen (the active ingredient in Tylenol) offers an interesting example: When an alcoholic stops drinking heavily, the MEOS is still operating in high gear even though alcohol is no longer present in the system. If the alcoholic repeatedly takes acetaminophen in therapeutic doses (2.5 to 4 grams) for headaches or gastrointestinal distress, the revved-up 2E1 system transforms acetaminophen into highly toxic chemicals that can cause liver damage.

We could fill a small library with articles and texts about the ADH pathway, MEOS, and all the enzyme variations, abnormalities, and eccentricities involved in the metabolism of alcohol, but here are the most important facts to keep in mind:

- In the liver, the metabolism (breakdown and elimination) of alcohol is controlled by dozens of different enzymes and isoenzymes.

- These enzymes and isoenzymes are under genetic control—specific genes or combinations of genes will determine the enzymes and isoenzymes you will have and in what relative proportion.

- Each of these enzymes directly affects the way you metabolize alcohol, which in turn controls your subjective experience of drinking.

Thus your individual reaction to alcohol is determined in large part by your enzymes, which are in turn controlled by the genes you inherit from your parents.

In the next chapter we will answer the question "Is alcohol a drug?" and offer surprising insights into exactly what kind of a drug this "simple" chemical turns out to be.

3

The Drug Called
Alcohol

Everyone in Oceana County, Michigan, was talking about the billboard.

Some people were shocked at the graphic link between alcohol and "hard" drugs. Others were relieved; finally, they thought, someone is willing to get out the message that alcohol—even in drinks such as beer, with its relatively low alcohol content—is a powerful drug capable of causing addiction just like heroin. Just about everyone agreed that the billboard did what it was intended to do: raise awareness of the deadly nature of alcohol problems and addiction.

At least one person was deeply offended, however, by the giant, highly visible hypodermic beer bottle. This beer wholesaler was proud to earn his living selling beer, and he didn't want anyone confusing him with a drug pusher. So he complained to the Michigan Beer and Wine Wholesalers Association, a powerful lobby group that demanded a meeting with the community health planners who sponsored the billboard.

The beer and wine merchants' argument went something like this: "Look, we're part of the community, and we think we ought to be consulted when you put up billboards about products we sell with pride. Let's work out a compromise. We'll sponsor an art contest in the local high school, the students can come up with ideas for a billboard, and we'll even help you judge the entries."

Community leaders figured that was a fair compromise. The hypodermic beer bottle billboard came down.

Try to imagine, if you can, public health officials sitting down with heroin or cocaine traffickers who are fuming about an antidrug campaign. Sipping coffee and passing the doughnuts, the two groups work out a compromise, toning down the antidrug message so as not to offend any of the parties involved.

That wouldn't happen, of course, because heroin and cocaine are illegal drugs. Alcohol is a legal drug and therefore afforded special status. Most people don't even think of alcohol as inherently dangerous or addictive or even, for that matter, a drug. How many times, in news programs, political speeches, or DARE (Drug Awareness Resistance Education) classes, have we heard the phrase "alcohol and drugs," as if they were two completely separate entities? Alcohol isn't really a drug, the thinking goes, because it won't hurt you unless you overindulge. Only when you "abuse" alcohol over and over again will you get in big trouble. Right?

Wrong. In this chapter we will explain exactly what kind of a drug this simple chemical happens to be. Given the fact that beer, wine, and distilled liquors are available in grocery and convenience stores, sold by the drink in bars, restaurants, bowling alleys, and even some movie theaters, can alcohol really be a "hard" drug like heroin, cocaine, or methamphetamine? What kind of a drug is it, exactly? Is it addictive for everyone or just a select few? And is it true that alcohol is beneficial to your health, actually protecting your cardiovascular system?

In the United States, approximately 120 million people of legal drinking age use alcohol at least occasionally, yet most drinkers have no idea what kind of a drug they're taking. Answer this questionnaire to see how much you know about the drug alcohol:

1. Alcohol is a stimulant.   True or False?
2. Alcohol is a sedative.   True or False?
3. Alcohol is a tranquilizer.   True or False?
4. Alcohol is an anesthetic.   True or False?
5. Alcohol is beneficial to health.   True or False?
6. Alcohol is an addictive drug.   True or False?

The answers to these questions do not fit into simple yes-or-no categories, because alcohol has different effects depending on the amount ingested and the individual drinker's sensitivity to the drug. This is the complicated story we will detail in the remainder of this chapter.

IS ALCOHOL A STIMULANT?

Most people answer false to this question, but the right answer is true—in low doses. In low to moderate doses, alcohol is indeed a stimulant, increasing blood flow, accelerating heart rate, and stimulating brain cells to speed up the conduction and transmission of nerve impulses. The impact of these physiologically stimulating effects on the drinker's behavior is obvious and immediate.

Psychologist James Milam liked to tell this story to patients at the treatment center he founded in Kirkland, Washington:

> Imagine a cocktail party. The host tells you not to bring any booze; he'll supply everything needed for a great time. So you get to the party, and your host hands you a bottle of sleeping pills. "Take three or four of these," he says with a wink, "and in half an hour this party will really start to roll!"

Week after week, every time Milam told this anecdote to recovering alcoholics and their families, the audience howled with laughter. They knew full well the truth about alcohol: The great majority of people, both alcoholics and nonalcoholics, do not drink to become heavily sedated and fall asleep—they drink to get high, to feel a rush of energy and euphoria that loosens the tongue, opens the heart, stimulates the imagination, and cranks up the noise level.

Most of us don't drink to turn *off*; we drink to turn *on*. We turn to alcohol for relaxation and stress reduction, and the drug delivers almost immediately by making us feel happy, energetic, and at peace with ourselves. Yet, ironically, these pleasurable, tension-relieving sensations are due to alcohol's stimulating effects on the body, particularly the brain and the heart. Research conducted over the last five decades confirms the stimulating properties of alcohol in low doses. "Most studies of nerve conduction and transmission, EEG records, and behavioral performance indicate stimulant actions of low doses," note H. Wallgren and H. Barry in their classic reference text *Actions of Alcohol*.

The important phrase to keep in mind is "low doses." If you continue to drink, the stimulating effects of alcohol will soon be overshadowed by its sedative effects.

IS ALCOHOL A SEDATIVE?

The answer, once again, is yes and no. Alcohol is a drug with a biphasic effect, meaning that it creates different effects at varying doses. In low doses alcohol acts as a stimulant; the sedative or depressant effects generally occur only at moderate to high doses. When you drink a 5-ounce glass of wine or a 12-ounce beer before dinner, for example, you will most likely experience a pleasant, mildly euphoric glow. Nerve cells are firing, ideas are multiplying, creative juices are flowing. The world, for a brief interval of time, may seem like a brighter, more pleasant place to be.

If you have another beer or two or toss down a few more glasses of wine, however, the initial stimulation quickly fades. Your thoughts slow down, your logic gets a little screwy, you lose your train of thought, your memory develops little gaps and even some gaping holes, and you feel dizzy, clumsy, and tongue-tied. Depending on your individual metabolism and temperament, you may enjoy the feeling of sedation or you may experience it as an uncomfortable loss of control.

When are the stimulant effects of alcohol overshadowed by the sedative effects? It all depends on the drinker. If you are a woman who weighs 110 pounds, the sedative effects may set in after one glass of wine. If you are a man weighing 180 pounds, you may be able to drink a six-pack of beer and still feel the energizing, euphoric kick. Early- and middle-stage alcoholics of all sizes, shapes, and genders are well known for their ability to stay lucid after drinking enough alcohol to topple a nonalcoholic giant.

In an interview on CNN's *Larry King Live*, actor and recovering alcoholic John Larroquette (sober for sixteen years) reminisced about an evening spent in a Mexican bar when he drank several dozen bottles of beer along with a bottle of tequila. At the evening's end, Larroquette was undoubtedly heavily sedated (it's a wonder he wasn't comatose), but the really interesting question is: When did the stimulant effects wear off? Was it after ten beers and two shots of tequila (unlikely, since he continued to drink prodigious amounts)? Fifteen beers and six shots (again unlikely, considering the final tally)? Or thirty beers and only the worm left inside the bottle of tequila?

For alcoholics the sedative effects generally take longer to set in because their brain cells have adapted to alcohol and can function normally even under the influence of large amounts of the drug. (For an in-depth discussion of central nervous system tolerance, see pages 57–59.) Still, whether you are an alcoholic or not, you will eventually begin to feel the sedative effects of alcohol if you continue to drink. As your blood alcohol level rises, you will experience a noticeable impairment in mental and physical reactions caused by the depressant actions of alcohol on the central nervous system. You may stumble around, slur your speech, and have difficulty grasping the thread of a conversation. If you continue to drink, your mental sluggishness and lack of physical coordination will intensify.

Your judgment will also be impaired, which creates a big problem because you may think your behavior is unaffected by alcohol. You may even believe that drinking a bottle of wine improves your performance. "Alcohol does not make us do things better; it just makes us less ashamed of doing them badly," noted Sir William Osler (1849–1919), a physician and professor of medicine at the Johns Hopkins School of Medicine.

Researchers have conducted numerous experiments with taxi, truck, and race car drivers who are regular drinkers as well as expert drivers. Without fail the research shows that performance deteriorates as the drinker's blood alcohol concentration rises. Alcohol adversely affects vision (visual acuity, glare resistance, tracking, visual recognition tasks, and eye movement activity), psychomotor responses (reaction time and manual dexterity), and cognitive functions (selective attention, information processing, memory, mood, and emotion). Yet despite the obvious impairment in their performance, most drivers insist they are in complete control; some even rate their driving as "improved" under the influence of alcohol.

In *Alcoholism and Other Drug Problems*, James E. Royce and David Scratchley summarize the research on alcohol and driving:

It is said that alcohol attacks judgment before skill, and then attacks the most recently learned skill. Driving is a skill learned much later in life than walking and talking. There are many specific ways in which driving is affected by alcohol, never fully appreciated by the driver because judgment is first dulled. Reaction time is slowed an extra fraction of a second in switching from accelerator to brake. With alcohol things seem to happen too fast and one does not plan ahead as good driving demands. Deep muscle sense, a feel for the car's position and movement, on which racing drivers rely a great deal ("driving by the seat of one's pants") is impaired. Depth or space perception of relative position to another car is less accurate, as are estimates of relative speed. Narrowing of the visual field ("tunnel vision"), blurred or double vision, and poorer discrimination between hues and between lights of different intensities have been reported. Night vision and resistance to glare (ability to readjust after exposure to bright lights) are notably impaired.

Poor motor coordination, faulty judgment, and lowered inhibitions are further complicated by a most important factor: emotional mood and personality change. Under the influence of alcohol, some people become very aggressive and impatient when they get behind the wheel, careless of others' rights and much more willing to take risks. Drowsiness and shortened attention span are dangers, as is a decreased ability to react to an unfamiliar situation; many alcoholics can drive home from their favorite bar or tavern while quite inebriated, as long as they know what to expect, but don't make it when something occurs that requires a new reaction.

Complicating the situation is the fact that the sedative effects of alcohol may be exacerbated by alcohol-induced hypoglycemia. If you drink enough to become intoxicated (and again, the amount will depend on the individual), your autonomic nervous system kicks into gear and releases the hormone epinephrine (adrenaline), which sends a message to the liver to break down glycogen into glucose. During glycogen breakdown, blood sugar levels initially increase; however, as the liver's glycogen reserves are gradually depleted, blood glucose levels drop, leading to low blood sugar (alcohol-induced hypoglycemia).

Since glucose is the brain's most important source of energy, the most obvious symptoms of low blood sugar are mental—irritability, emotional instability, mood swings, sudden fatigue, mental confusion, light-headedness, and dizziness. As the body responds to the falling blood sugar levels by releasing additional adrenaline, the drinker may experience distressing physical symptoms such as an increased pulse rate, sweating, rapid heartbeat, and intense anxiety or panic attacks. (See Chapter 14 for an in-depth discussion of alcohol-induced hypoglycemia.)

IS ALCOHOL A TRANQUILIZER?

The surprising answer is a categorical no. Tranquilizers relieve intense anxiety but are different from sedatives in that they do not significantly depress the central nervous system. A person who has taken a tranquilizer may feel drowsy but, unlike someone who has taken a sedative, can be aroused easily and respond to stimuli in the environment.

Alcohol fails as a tranquilizer in every sense of the word. While alcohol in low doses can relieve the muscle tension and even the guilt so often associated with anxiety, the effects are fleeting; with continued drinking, tension, anxiety, and guilt are increased. The truth is that excessive drinking will not relieve your anxiety; it will *increase* it. If you're a heavy drinker and experience intense anxiety when drinking or sober, it is a safe bet that your anxiety is caused by the drug alcohol.

Psychiatrist George Vaillant describes the relationship between alcohol and anxiety in *The Natural History of Alcoholism Revisited:*

> If alcoholism were just a symptom of emotional distress, we might expect that alcohol would be a good tranquilizer. Alcohol should achieve what the alcoholic insists that it does achieve; heavy alcohol ingestion should raise self-esteem, alleviate depression, reduce social isolation, and abolish anxiety. However, work by many investigators suggests that despite what alcoholics tell us, objective observation in the laboratory reveals that chronic use of alcohol makes alcoholic subjects more withdrawn, less self-confident, often more anxious, and commonly more depressed with increased suicidal ideation. . . . Most often the "anxiety" that alcohol is most effective in relieving is the tremulousness, fearfulness, and dysphoria [restlessness, uneasiness] produced by brief abstinence in an alcohol-dependent individual.

In a 1991 study, researchers tested 171 hospitalized male alcoholics, 40 percent of whom reported significant anxiety on admission. When questioned about their psychological state, the alcoholics perceived themselves as chronically prone to anxiety and described their drinking as a means of self-medicating their discomfort. After two weeks of abstinence, however, their anxiety levels returned to normal. At a three-month follow-up, anxiety declined still further in the men who remained abstinent. In those who relapsed, anxiety levels shot back up again.

Perhaps the most enduring myth about alcohol is that anxious, unhappy, shy, fearful, or depressed people drink in order to alleviate their discomfort and relieve their tension. Many heavy drinkers and alcoholics will tell you just that, pointing a shaky finger of blame at the specter of stress in their lives. "I'm a tense and anxious person," says one person, "and a few martinis always give me some relief." "When I'm stressed out, nothing works better than alcohol to make me forget my problems," says another. And then there's always this one: "I work too damn hard; I deserve a drink!"

Yet drinking heavily causes anxiety rather than relieves it. In *The Courage to Change*, a collection of stories by recovering alcoholics, actor and novelist Tom Tryon describes the anxiety he experienced when he was drinking:

> *I thought I had all these problems and the way I could handle them best was to drink. It greased the skids. It made everything easier. When I stopped drinking, the majority of my problems stopped. I was a victim of the worst anxiety attacks imaginable. I mean, they would put me to bed in a darkened room for hours. I would have to stop whatever I was doing and get into a bed—anybody's bed, anywhere—to deal with them. . . . God, what a shock it was later to find out that by stopping this one thing, drinking, all the other things suddenly ironed out. . . . No one told me. Goddamn it, no one ever told me the problem was alcohol.*

It's clear that alcohol is *not* an effective self-medication for chronic anxiety, stress, or tension. In fact, chronic heavy use of alcohol creates a heightened state of anxiety that can persist long after the last drink.

IS ALCOHOL AN ANESTHETIC?

You probably answered yes because you've heard some of the gruesome stories about Civil War soldiers and sturdy frontiersmen who gulp down half a bottle of whiskey before the surgeon starts sawing away at their gangrenous limbs. In truth, however, alcohol is a lousy anesthetic because by the time the drug numbs you to pain, it is perilously close to killing you.

Moderate and high doses of alcohol will make you drowsy, but they will not numb you to sensation or feeling. Only when you have had so much to drink that you are in danger of paralyzing your respiratory center, shutting down your breathing apparatus, and putting yourself in a coma can alcohol truly be called an anesthetic. "In higher doses [alcohol] possesses analgesic [pain-killing] properties, but the dose required for surgical anesthesia carries the real danger of failure of the respiratory center," explains alcohol researcher Joseph N. Santamaria.

IS ALCOHOL BENEFICIAL TO YOUR HEALTH?

In certain circumstances, for some people, the answer is yes; in most circumstances, for most people, however, the answer is no. As always with alcohol, it depends on the dose and the individual.

In a study involving five hundred thousand middle-aged to elderly Americans, researchers found that men and women who consume one drink a day of beer, wine, or distilled spirits had a 20 percent lower overall death rate than nondrinkers and a 30 to 40 percent reduction in death from heart attacks and other circulatory diseases. While those are significant benefits, we need to keep two very important facts in mind: The beneficial effects of alcohol depend on *low doses*, and they are experienced only by *people over the age of forty-five*.

What do we mean by low doses? For women a low dose is generally defined as no more than 4 to 5 ounces of wine, one 12-ounce beer, or 1.25 ounces of 80-proof alcohol per day. In men, a low dose is no more than 8 to 10 ounces of wine, two 12-ounce beers, or two mixed drinks containing a total of 2.5 ounces of 80-proof alcohol per day. (Whenever we talk about amounts, it is important to remember that a generously poured glass of wine may contain 6 to 10 ounces of the beverage rather than the suggested "low dose" of 4 or 5 ounces; a strong mixed drink generally consists of 2 or more ounces of 80-proof alcohol.)

In low doses alcohol may benefit your cardiovascular health, but only if you are over the age of forty-five, have no family history of alcoholism, and have never experienced any of the signs or symptoms associated with problem drinking or alcoholism. Teens and young adults experience no health benefits whatsoever from drinking low doses of alcohol; in fact, even low doses of alcohol significantly increase a young person's risk of death from injury or violence. For people between the ages of thirty and forty-five, the health benefits of alcohol are unclear, and researchers strongly caution this age group against drinking for "health" reasons.

As a further caution, having more than one or two drinks a day will cancel out any protective effect alcohol may have on coronary heart disease by increasing the risk of hypertension (high blood pressure), arrhythmia (irregular heartbeat), and cardiomyopathy (heart muscle damage). In addition, even low doses of alcohol may have an adverse effect on other organs and body systems. In a 1990 study comparing drinkers and nondrinkers, the researchers conclude:

> Nondrinkers enjoyed many health advantages over moderate drinkers. Compared to no drinking at all, even one drink a day led to increased esophageal cancer, two drinks a day increased the risk of liver cirrhosis, three drinks a day increased the risk of cancer of the oral cavity, and six drinks a day increased the risk of accidental death.

For women, even low to moderate doses of alcohol are associated with a sharply increased risk of breast cancer. Researchers at Harvard University pooled the results of various studies detailing the connection between alcohol and breast cancer. Their conclusions are enough to shake any woman's confidence in the health benefits of low-dose alcohol: Just one drink a day increases a woman's risk of contracting breast cancer by 9 percent. The risk increases by another 9 percent for *each* additional drink up to five drinks a day.

Whatever benefits the drug alcohol may bestow in low doses, the health risks of even moderate drinking appear to outweigh them. Harvard psychiatrist George Vaillant summarizes the research on the health benefits of alcohol in *The Natural History of Alcoholism Revisited:*

> It must be borne in mind that any increase in alcohol use by a population increases the risk of other alcohol-related problems. Therefore, increasing the number of social drinkers is unlikely to increase a nation's overall health.

IS ALCOHOL AN ADDICTIVE DRUG?

Yes—for the approximately 10 to 15 percent of its users who are genetically predisposed to alcohol addiction.

Imagine this sadistic experiment: A randomly selected group of men and women are forced to drink a bottle of whiskey every day for a year. At the end of the research period, the alcohol supply is abruptly cut off and the subjects are observed for signs of physiological withdrawal, a clear indication of addiction to the drug. What happens to the subjects? Do they all become addicted?

While no one has ever conducted such an experiment with humans, researchers have subjected mice and rats to chronic drunkenness. The conclusions reached from this line of research are clear and unequivocal: If you force rodents to drink enough alcohol over a long enough period of time, their central nervous systems will adapt to the drug, leading to increased tolerance for alcohol, physiological dependence on the drug, and symptoms such as tremors, insomnia, nausea, vomiting, anxiety, and seizures when it is withdrawn.

Can experiments with rats and mice be applied to humans? Do they offer proof for the theory that people who drink too much risk becoming alcoholics or for the corollary theory, which holds that if you don't drink to excess, you won't become an alcoholic? Is physiological dependence on alcohol merely a process of drinking so much that your central nervous system adapts to the drug and eventually needs it to function normally?

Here is a piece of the truth, and it is critically important for understanding the difference between alcoholics and nonalcoholics: For the great majority of human beings, you would indeed have to force-feed alcohol to them because they don't like the taste, they don't enjoy the feeling of being drunk and out of control, and/or they simply cannot drink large amounts because their bodies reject the drug by vomiting it back up again or passing out.

Given the unpleasant effects of intoxication (nausea, dizziness, loss of control, impaired judgment, memory lapses) and the aftereffects of excessive drinking (headaches, hangovers, excessive thirst, guilt, shame, and self-loathing), the great majority of us choose not to drink excessively. The wisdom of our bodies protects us; we want to feel good, not bad. We want to be in control of our bodies and our minds, maintain our health, and be able to think of ourselves as kind, considerate, logical, and intelligent human beings.

All these basic human needs are violated when we drink too much. No matter how good we feel after one or two drinks, most of us do not enjoy the feeling of being intoxicated and out of control. No matter how much fun we might have had the night before, the next day's pain far outweighs the pleasure. Sensitive to alcohol's immediate adverse effects and punishing aftereffects, we find it easy to moderate our drinking. If you tied us down and injected quarts of the stuff into our veins, maybe you could make addicts of us—but while we still had our wits about us, we would be kicking and screaming most of the way.

The desire to feel good is a natural human urge, common to drinkers and nondrinkers alike. Most of us are blessed with an ability to drink low doses of alcohol and feel the pleasures of the drug, yet we experience no physical or psychological need to drink more or more often.

However, for a minority of people (again, an estimated 10 to 15 percent) alcohol does something different. Alcohol makes these drinkers feel good—so good that even if the taste is repulsive and the consequences are unpleasant, they want to repeat the experiment.

For these drinkers, the same internal restraints don't apply. The next-day misery may be just as ferocious and the shame and guilt just as unbearable, but the deep-seated desire to drink again overwhelms the logical mind. "The physical loathing for alcohol I have never got over," Jack London wrote in his autobiographical memoir, *John Barleycorn*. "But I have conquered it. To this day I reconquer it every time I take a drink."

Alcohol did something magical for Jack London, just as it does something earthshaking for millions of drinkers in this country. No matter how desperately the rational mind wants to say no, the answer is always, inevitably, "Yes, *yes*, **yes**."

In the next chapter we will journey to the brain to unlock the mysteries underlying the reasons why certain people have so much difficulty saying no to the drug alcohol.

4

The Addicted
Brain

Toto, I have a feeling we're not in Kansas anymore.

— DOROTHY IN *THE WIZARD OF OZ*

For hundreds, even thousands of years, people have argued loud and long that alcoholism is a shameful personal weakness, a stubborn character defect, or a symptom of some underlying moral disorder. Alcoholics, because they "choose" their fate (unlike the innocent victims of epilepsy, heart disease, or cancer), rank low in the moral order. "Every human soul is worth saving," proclaimed J. E. Todd more than a hundred years ago in a tract titled *Drunkenness a Vice Not a Disease*, "but . . . if a choice is to be made, drunkards are about the last class to be taken hold of."

Despite stunning advances in our understanding of the genetics and neurophysiology of alcoholism, most people continue to believe that alcoholism is a disease of morals, a preventable psychological "weakness." In a 1979 survey, 67 percent of 2,187 respondents insisted that alcoholism is a sign of "personal emotional weakness"; only 19 percent believed that alcoholism is solely a health problem. A 1998 survey by the San Francisco–based Recovery Institute reveals that our attitudes toward alcoholics have not changed significantly over the years. The survey, which is based on telephone and one-on-one interviews with more than two thousand people, concludes:

> Most people see alcoholism as having elements of both disease and weakness. On average, fewer than one in four say it is 100 percent disease, while a majority of every group surveyed—except psychiatrists and counselors—say they consider alcoholism to be at least 25 percent due to personal or moral weakness.

Not surprisingly, counselors (70 percent disease, 20 percent weakness) and psychiatrists (77 percent disease, 19 percent weakness) are most likely to accept alcoholism as a medical condition while fundamentalist clergy (31 percent disease, 69 percent weakness) overwhelmingly report seeing alcoholism as a reflection of a shortcoming in character or morality.

When we dig even deeper and ask in effect whether, because alcoholism is a disease, we therefore can absolve the alcoholic of responsibility for the problem, the answer is a resounding "no" . . . when pressed, most [people] ascribe a very significant degree of volition to the condition of alcoholism.

The shame and stigma associated with alcoholism have persisted despite the fact that we know, from hundreds of studies conducted by thousands of researchers, that alcoholism is a progressive, physiological, genetically determined disease and not a moral or personal weakness. Over the past sixty years, roughly dating from the foundation of the Yale Center of Alcohol Studies in 1942, neurologists, pharmacologists, geneticists, biochemists, psychologists, psychiatrists, and, most recently, addiction medicine specialists (sometimes called "addictionologists"), have amassed a broad assortment of research projects confirming the hereditary, biochemical, and neurophysiological nature of alcoholism.

One of these researchers is pharmacologist Kenneth Blum, who became interested in alcoholism in the late 1960s when he was working as an assistant research scientist at the Southwest Foundation for Research and Education in San Antonio, Texas. Teaming up with psychopharmacologist Irving Geller, Blum began a series of experiments focusing on the nature of alcohol's actions on the nervous system. These early experiments, published in the 1970s, convinced Blum that specific neurotransmitters such as serotonin, GABA, and dopamine are involved in alcohol preference. As the years went by, he became increasingly interested in the actions of alcohol on specific opiate receptor sites in the brain and the neurochemical mechanisms underlying addiction to alcohol.

For the next decade Blum teamed up with researchers all over the world to conduct experiments designed to tease apart the mysteries of neurological addiction. By the mid-1980s Blum found himself powerfully drawn to a field of research in which he had no direct training: molecular genetics. Convinced that genes are involved in the craving for alcohol and the predisposition to alcoholism, he wanted to find out which specific genes were causing the problem. With newly discovered techniques such as "pulsed field gel electrophoresis" and "southern blot analysis," researchers were able to identify specific chromosomal markers for certain neurogenetic diseases, including Huntington's disease. Using these same tools, Blum hoped to find specific genetic markers for the neurogenetic disease of alcoholism.

There was no doubt in Blum's mind—or the minds of the men and women he collaborated with in laboratories ranging from California to Colorado, New York, England, and Italy—that alcoholism is a hereditary disease. All you had to do was look at the hundreds of experiments, conducted over more than five decades, confirming the genetic link. Tampering with the genetic code of rodents, researchers were able to breed strains of rats and mice that loved the taste of alcohol and others that couldn't stand the stuff. The DBA and C3H strains of mice, for example, consistently prefer water over alcohol when given a choice, while the C57 and C58 strains will choose alcohol over water almost every time. The offspring of the alcohol-loving rodents inherit this fondness for booze, while the offspring of the alcohol-hating mice simply don't like the stuff.

Adoption studies in humans also provided strong confirmation of the genetic link. In the early 1970s University of Kansas psychiatrist Donald Goodwin and colleagues in America and Denmark published studies conducted with adopted children of alcoholics and nonalcoholics. Children with at least one alcoholic natural parent were three to four times more likely to become alcoholics when adopted into nonalcoholic families than children whose natural parents were nonalcoholics. The old argument that alcoholics have underlying psychological or emotional disturbances (the so-called alcoholic personality) was debunked in these studies by the finding that adopted children whose natural parents included one or more alcoholics were no more likely to have a psychiatric disturbance than adopted children whose natural parents were nonalcoholics. Subsequent adoption studies confirmed Goodwin's work.

Research pioneered by Henri Begleiter and colleagues at the State University of New York Health Science Center in Brooklyn in the late 1970s added further weight to the genetic argument. Begleiter compared sons of alcoholics, age seven to thirteen, with sons of nonalcoholics (neither group of children had ever been exposed to alcohol or other drugs) and found that a specific type of electrical activity that occurs in the brain in response to certain sensory stimuli (and which is measured by the amplitude of the P3 brain wave) was markedly reduced in the children of alcoholics. These electrophysiological marker studies suggest, in Begleiter's words, "that decrements in P3 activity are not a consequence of years of heavy drinking but are genetic antecedents of alcohol abuse."

These are just a few of several dozen studies confirming that alcoholism is one of the more than three thousand known genetically influenced diseases in the human population caused by variations in DNA and passed down from one generation to the next. Given the fact that human beings have more than a hundred thousand genes, Blum knew that he was in for a long and difficult search.

In January 1988 Blum called his friend and fellow researcher Ernest Noble, former director of the National Institute on Alcoholism and Alcohol Abuse. Now at the University of California, Los Angeles, conducting research on the brain electrophysiology of alcoholic fathers and their sons, Noble had access to a large collection of brains of deceased alcoholics and nonalcoholics, along with complete medical records. The alcoholic brains would be a perfect DNA source for Blum's experiment, Noble said, because they belonged to late-stage alcoholics who had experienced multiple relapses and died from alcohol-related pathologies. If there was indeed a genetic mutation causing alcoholism, these brains would have it.

Using more than fifty gene probes that allowed them to search inside the DNA, Blum and Noble looked for unusual or mutated genes associated with alcoholism. After a year, they were getting discouraged—the probes they were using were not able to penetrate the one area they suspected was directly linked to alcohol addiction: the genes controlling the actions of the neurotransmitter dopamine.

In July 1989 Blum read an article in the *Wall Street Journal* about a successful cloning of the human D2 receptor (DRD_2) gene on chromosome 11. With great excitement he called the lead researcher, Olivier Civelli at Oregon Health Sciences University in Portland; Civelli said he would be happy to send Blum the D2 gene probe.

Using Civelli's probe, Blum and Noble renewed their quest for the abnormal genes. What they discovered in 1990 took their collective breath away. In the q22-q23 region of chromosome 11, they found a genetic mutation, which they later dubbed the A1 allele. Sixty-nine percent of the alcoholic brains in their sample contained the A1 allele, while 80 percent of the nonalcoholic brain tissue did not. In other words, looking only at this one genetic variation in brain tissue, the researchers could predict with 75 percent accuracy whether the brain belonged to an alcoholic or a nonalcoholic.

Blum's and Noble's research teams knew they had discovered only one of the genes associated with alcoholism, for 31 percent of the alcoholic brains did not contain the genetic abnormality. The challenge now facing Blum was to find the additional genes involved and eventually map out their actions and potentials.

The stunning discovery in 1990 of a gene mutation associated with alcoholism provides an avenue of fertile investigation into the potential biochemical, neurophysiological, and genetic roots of alcoholism. Researchers haven't mapped out all the genes involved, nor do they know the precise pattern of genes that combine to create varying degrees of susceptibility to alcoholism. They do know, however, that certain genes or gene combinations determine whether or not a specific individual will be predisposed to the disease of alcoholism.

In this chapter we journey into the brain to explore the neurological underpinnings of addiction to alcohol. We explain why we need a new definition of alcoholism—one that is based on the most current neurological and biochemical research. We then examine the interactions between alcohol's metabolic by-product acetaldehyde and the "feel-good" neurotransmitters such as dopamine, serotonin, norepinephrine, and GABA. Finally, we introduce the chemicals known as tetrahydroisoquinolines (TIQs), detailing their devastating effects on the alcoholic's body and mind and their central role in neurological addiction.

ALCOHOLISM: A DEFINITION

We need a new definition of alcoholism. The old ones, to put it bluntly, don't work. Consider this definition from Wallgren and Barry's classic text, *Actions of Alcohol*, published in 1970:

> For a person to be considered alcoholic, these criteria must be present:
>
> 1. Large quantity of alcohol consumed over period of years
>
> 2. Abnormal, chronic loss of control over drinking, shown by an inability to refrain or inability to stop
>
> 3. The drinking causes chronic damage to physical health or social standing

This definition and its variations continue to influence the way we identify, diagnose, and treat alcoholism, with the classic signs and symptoms of alcoholism identified as chronic heavy drinking, loss of control over drinking, and noticeable deterioration in physical health and social status due to drinking. The problem is that these symptoms occur in the *final* stages of a progressive, deteriorative disease. If we diagnose alcoholism by these three standards, the disease is already well entrenched, and the victims are seriously and therefore visibly ill. Many alcoholics die of complications caused by drinking before they ever reach this stage of the disease.

We need a definition that will help us identify the disease before the alcoholic is nearly dead from it. We define cancer, for example, as the unregulated growth of abnormal cells, and we watch for various warning signs that can alert us to the disease in its early stages—loss of appetite, indigestion, changes in bowel habits, irregular or unexplained bleeding, and so on. Any definition of alcoholism should also convey the fact that alcoholism progresses from an early stage in which signs and symptoms are often absent to its middle and late stages, where observable changes in physical and mental health occur.

The latest version of the *Diagnostic and Statistic Manual* (DSM-IV), published by the American Psychiatric Association, includes alcoholism under the broad category of "substance dependence" and lists seven diagnostic criteria. To qualify as an alcoholic, a person must show three or more of the following symptoms within a twelve-month period:

1. Tolerance, defined as a need for increasingly larger amounts of alcohol to achieve intoxication (over time the drug produces less intense reactions at the same dose)

2. Withdrawal symptoms, which include hand tremor, sweating, elevated pulse rate, insomnia, nausea, or anxiety; these symptoms may develop into hallucinations, grand mal seizures, and/or psychotic symptoms

3. Drinking in larger amounts or over longer periods than intended

4. Persistent desire or unsuccessful attempts to cut down or control drinking

5. Spending a significant amount of time trying to obtain alcohol, drink alcohol, or recover from its effects

6. Giving up social, occupational, or recreational activities because of alcohol

7. Continuing to drink despite persistent or recurrent physical or psychological problems caused or exacerbated by alcohol use

While this more detailed definition represents a definite improvement over Wallgren and Barry's three-point synopsis, the emphasis on obvious, visible signs of physical dependence remains intact. Many early- and middle-stage alcoholics, for example, drink regularly and in relatively large amounts but experience mostly pleasure from drinking and relatively little pain. Withdrawal symptoms in the early stages of the disease are relatively minor and often go unnoticed; metabolic tolerance is frequently misidentified as a positive attribute, proof that you can "hold your liquor"; and attempts to control drinking by quitting or cutting down are often successful (and practiced by many nonalcoholics as well). Changes in social or recreational activities, psychological problems, and physical complications rarely occur until the middle or late stage of the disease.

Relying strictly on the DSM-IV criteria, we continue to misdiagnose "high-functioning" alcoholics as heavy social drinkers or problem drinkers. That's what happened with Bill Asbury, one of the coauthors of this book. He was a high-functioning alcoholic for nearly twenty-five years; not once in his drinking career was he ever even labeled a "problem drinker." A prize-winning journalist, editor, and publisher and a devoted husband and loving father of five children, he never missed a day of work, and on workdays he never drank until he got home. Still, alcohol was causing considerable havoc in his life, including a drunk-driving conviction, an enlarged liver ("You might consider cutting down on your drinking," his doctor advised), a painful case of gout, suicidal thoughts, chronic depression and anxiety, serious lapses in judgment, and marital conflicts over his drinking. Despite these alcohol-related problems, Bill escaped diagnosis for more than two decades of progressively alcoholic drinking.

We must not wait until alcoholics show obvious signs of physical and psychological deterioration before we step in and say: "Aha! Now that you look like and act like a drunk, we can, with full assurance, call you one!" For too many alcoholics, this delayed diagnosis, based on a late-stage definition of the disease, constitutes a death sentence.

In an effort to emphasize the progression of the disease from its early to middle and late stages, the following definition was approved in February 1990 by the Board of Directors of the National Council on Alcoholism and Drug Dependence and the American Society of Addiction Medicine:

> Alcoholism is a primary, chronic disease with genetic, psychosocial, and environmental factors influencing its development and manifestations. The disease is often progressive and fatal. It is characterized by continuous or periodic: impaired control over drinking, preoccupation with the drug alcohol, use of alcohol despite adverse consequences, and distortions in thinking, most notably denial.

This definition represents a valiant attempt to describe an extraordinarily complex disease. Emphasis is placed on genetic factors, the progressive nature of the disease, and early- and middle-stage symptoms including preoccupation with alcohol, distorted thinking patterns, and denial. Missing from this definition, however, is the recent evidence confirming the neurological underpinnings of alcohol addiction.

In hopes of stimulating further discussion, we offer the following definition of alcoholism, which focuses specifically on the neurophysiological roots of alcoholism and is based on the most current research by biochemists, neurophysiologists, pharmacologists, psychologists, psychiatrists, and addiction medicine specialists. This definition does not include a list of diagnostic criteria (the signs and symptoms of the disease) because we hope to emphasize here the causes of alcoholism rather than its enormously varied expressions. (For a detailed explanation of the progressive signs and symptoms of alcoholism, see Chapter 5.)

Alcoholism is a progressive neurological disease strongly influenced by genetic vulnerability. Inherited or acquired abnormalities in brain chemistry create an altered response to alcohol which in turn causes a wide array of physical, psychological, and behavioral problems. Although environmental and social factors will influence the progression and expression of the disease, they are not in any sense causes of addictive drinking.

Alcoholism is caused by biochemical/neurophysiological abnormalities that are passed down from one generation to the next or, in some cases, acquired through heavy or prolonged drinking.

A NEUROLOGICAL DISEASE

The human brain is composed of billions of nerve cells, or neurons, which are responsible for two major functions: (1) sending messages to other neurons and (2) receiving messages from other neurons. To send or receive messages, the brain relies on a system of specialized "messenger" chemicals called neurotransmitters. The most important neurotransmitters involved in alcoholism are dopamine, serotonin, norepinephrine, and GABA.

- Dopamine intensifies feelings of well-being, increases aggression, alertness, and sexual excitement, and reduces compulsive behavior.

- Serotonin promotes feelings of well-being, induces sleep, reduces aggressive and compulsive behavior, and elevates the pain threshold.

- Norepinephrine increases feelings of well-being and reduces compulsive behavior; in excess, norepinephrine may induce anxiety and increase heart rate and blood pressure.

- GABA reduces anxiety and compulsive behavior and raises the pain threshold.

When a neurotransmitter is released from the neuron—imagine a Federal Express truck loaded up with packages and a list of addresses—it searches for the receptor cells with the right shape and electrical charge to receive its information. When it finds the correct address, the neurotransmitter pulls into the driveway and unloads its packages into the open door of the receptor cell.

That's the short course on normal brain chemistry. Something different, however, happens in the alcoholic's brain. When an individual with a genetic predisposition to alcoholism drinks—and remember, by definition, a genetic predisposition exists *before* the person ever takes a drink—strange and unusual events occur in the brain. The first part of this story begins with acetaldehyde, the metabolic by-product of alcohol.

When alcohol is metabolized (broken down) in the liver, it is converted first to acetaldehyde. Most alcoholics, even in the very earliest stages of their drinking careers, experience a buildup of acetaldehyde, leading to levels approximately 50 percent higher than in nonalcoholics. This inherited metabolic quirk is attributed to intensified activity in an alternative metabolic pathway called the microsomal ethanol oxidating system (MEOS). (See pages 24–26 for a thorough discussion of the MEOS.) Although the liver works hard to eliminate acetaldehyde by breaking it down into nontoxic acetic acid, a significant amount of acetaldehyde "escapes" the liver by binding to various substances. Most notable among these are red blood cells—the primary transporters of oxygen to every organ in the body, including the brain. Grabbing a free ride on substances the brain requires for its normal functioning, acetaldehyde is able to slip right through the protective blood-brain barrier and circulate freely in the brain tissue. Recent research also suggests that brain cells may possess the necessary enzymes to create acetaldehyde directly during the metabolism of alcohol.

Acetaldehyde's actions in the brain are critically important for understanding the process of addiction. Rough, tough, quick, and dirty, acetaldehyde is the ultimate party crasher. The brain's elegant waltz of chemicals is rudely interrupted when acetaldehyde enters uninvited, cutting in on the enzymes that normally dance with the neurotransmitters. Acetaldehyde has no manners; scientists call it "reactive," which in this context can be interpreted to mean that it acts like a testosterone-crazed adolescent, charged up and eager for action, highly attracted to the opposite sex, and willing to do just about anything to get its way.

In the fiercely productive orgy that ensues between the neurotransmitters and acetaldehyde, a new generation of chemicals is created. Scientists call these chemicals tetrahydroisoquinolines, or TIQs. In terms of personality, the happy, fun-loving TIQs are much more like their feel-good neurotransmitter mothers than their bullish acetaldehyde fathers. The brain likes having the TIQs around and rearranges its chemical furniture to make sure they can pull up a chair whenever they're in the neighborhood.

No wonder the brain cells are so accommodating to the TIQs—chemically, they're almost the spitting image of a family of sleep-inducing, pain-relieving addictive compounds known as the opiates.

Fig. 4-1 THP and Morphine

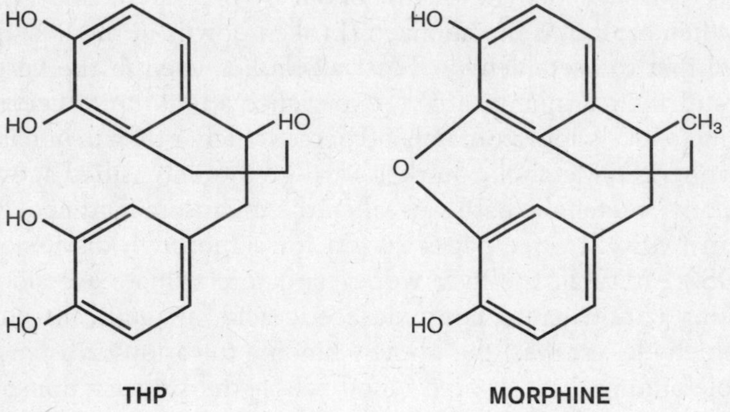

THP   MORPHINE

Chemical structure of tetrahydropapaveroline (THP), a known precursor of morphine in the poppy plant. From *Alcohol and the Addictive Brain* by Kenneth Blum, Ph.D., with James Payne (The Free Press).

Like the naturally occurring opiates (the endorphins and enkephalins) and the synthetic opiates morphine and heroin, TIQs are addictive substances that can induce excessive drinking behavior. How addictive are they? Over twenty years ago Purdue University researcher Robert D. Myers set up an experiment based on a hunch that the opiate-like TIQs would substitute for the need to drink alcohol in rats bred to prefer alcohol. Injecting TIQs directly into the animals' brains, Myers expected to see the rats, doped up on TIQs, contentedly refusing alcohol.

What happened stunned Myers and his graduate student assistant, Christine Melchior. The rats began to drink enormous amounts of alcohol; they couldn't get enough of the stuff. When Myers and Melchior forced the animals to go on the wagon, the rats suffered serious withdrawal symptoms, similar to the violent withdrawal symptoms experienced by animals repeatedly injected with morphine.

Myers repeated the experiment, using different families of TIQs and substituting rats and monkeys selectively bred to "hate" alcohol for the alcohol-loving animals. It didn't matter which TIQ was used or whether or not the animals initially were teetotalers or barflies—after three to six days of TIQ injections, the animals drank more and more alcohol, refused water, and once again suffered serious withdrawal symptoms when forced to go on the wagon.

What was happening to these animals? Myers explains:

We already knew that the brain produces TIQs following alcohol intake. We had now demonstrated that large amounts of TIQs injected directly into the brain stimulate an abnormal intake of alcohol. It seemed clear, therefore, that what we had done was simulate the overproduction of TIQs in the brain, as might be found in cases of chronic alcoholism.

It seemed reasonable to conclude, therefore, that if TIQs are formed in sufficient quantities in certain crucial areas of the brain, they may induce changes in brain chemistry that will generate a pathological craving for alcohol, despite its bad aftereffects. This may well be the pattern that creates human alcoholism.

DEFICIENCIES IN
DOPAMINE RECEPTORS

Nothing, as we have said, is simple in alcoholism, and the addictive potential of TIQs is only one piece in the complicated puzzle of addiction. Another piece of the puzzle fell into place when researchers Kenneth Blum and Ernest Noble discovered in 1991 that individuals with the A1 allele had approximately 30 percent *fewer* dopamine receptor sites than a comparison group. Blum and Noble theorize that the A1 gene mutation causes a reduction in the number of dopamine receptors—and a shortage of dopamine receptor sites is implicated in craving for alcohol.

Animal studies appear to confirm the connection between a deficiency in dopamine receptor sites and a craving for alcohol. In a 1981 experiment with mice, researchers found that "alcohol-loving" C57 black mice have 50 percent fewer dopamine D2 receptor sites than the "alcohol-hating" DBA strain of mice. And in a 1987 study with rats, researchers discovered that the number of dopamine D2 receptor sites in alcohol-preferring rats was significantly lower than in rats who didn't like alcohol.

Researcher Ken Blum explains what might be happening in humans who have a deficiency in dopamine D2 receptor sites:

> Individuals born with a dopamine D2 receptor defect may not respond normally to dopamine release, which goes on continuously in the brain. They may be inclined to attempt to increase dopamine activity by taking substances such as alcohol that stimulate dopamine release. These individuals would be at risk of becoming alcoholics.

A shortage of dopamine receptors helps explain why alcoholics experience, almost from the very first drink, that euphoric "Wow!" reaction to alcohol. Here's a quick, step-by-step version of what Blum has dubbed "the reward deficiency syndrome":

1. Most people are born with a relatively equitable balance between the pleasure-creating neurotransmitter dopamine and the dopamine receptors available to receive it. Thus if you have, say, ten "doses" of dopamine matched up with ten available receptors, everything works as it should. Sufficient dopamine is produced, and the receptors are ready and waiting to receive the dopamine so it can do what it's supposed to do—increase feelings of well-being.

2. Some people—for example, alcoholics who inherit the A1 form of the dopamine D2 receptor (DRD2) gene—have fewer dopamine receptors available to receive the pleasure-creating dopamine.

3. When alcoholics drink, alcohol and acetaldehyde interact with neurotransmitters to create TIQs, which open the dopamine faucet and flood the brain with pleasure molecules. The extra dopamine directly stimulates the available receptors, creating intensely pleasurable sensations.

4. TIQs, however, are less potent than dopamine and, in Blum's words, "eventually gum up the system," leading to a proliferation of both opioid and dopamine receptors.

5.   As the brain increases the number of receptor sites, the "Wow!" experience eventually fades (once again, too many receptors and too little dopamine) and craving for alcohol increases.

Researchers have disagreed with this theory, since a fairly sizable percentage (20 percent in Blum's and Noble's studies) of nonalcoholics also have the A1 allele. If this genetic mutation controls alcoholic drinking behavior, why don't the nonalcoholics with the A1 genetic defect drink addictively? The answer, proposed by Blum and other researchers, is intriguing: Alcoholism may be only one of the consequences of a dopamine D2 genetic defect. Other genetic mutations in combination with the A1 mutation influence whether or not a specific individual becomes addicted to alcohol, cocaine, heroin, or nicotine, engages in compulsive or pleasure-seeking behaviors such as compulsive gambling, abnormal sexual activity, or carbohydrate bingeing, or displays behaviors associated with Tourette's syndrome or attention deficit/hyperactivity disorder. That is why researchers are careful to call the DRD2 gene a reward or reinforcement gene rather than an "alcogene," which would imply that the gene was connected only to alcohol-seeking behavior.

The dopamine D2 receptor gene defect is clearly only one of the genetic abnormalities involved in an individual's predisposition to alcoholism. There are, in all likelihood, dozens of genes that play major and supporting roles. Genes that control liver enzyme activities and the metabolism of acetaldehyde are undoubtedly involved, as are genes that regulate the actions of serotonin, norepinephrine, GABA, and other neurotransmitters that we haven't yet identified.

For every neurotransmitter pinpointed so far, there may be five, ten, or twenty more that scientists have not yet discovered. Each neurotransmitter is governed by enzymes, which are in turn influenced by hormones and other circulating chemicals. The interactions between all these genetically controlled molecules create endless possibilities and help explain why the progression of alcoholism varies from one person to the next. With hundreds, even thousands, of possible gene-enzyme-hormone combinations, each individual with a genetic predisposition to alcoholism will react in uniquely individual ways to the drug alcohol.

This journey into brain chemistry can be dizzyingly complex. Any gene that encodes (governs the body's production of) a protein or enzyme capable of influencing alcohol's actions in the body may be involved in susceptibility to alcohol addiction. The recent discovery of a genetically determined brain enzyme, for example, provides surprising new insights into how alcohol affects brain neurons and why some people may be more susceptible to alcoholism. In a series of experiments conducted at the Riken Brain Science Institute in Wako City, Japan, researchers studied mice who lack a gene for an enzyme called Fyn tyrosine kinase. This enzyme counteracts alcohol's depressive effects on brain cells, causing a marked increase in tolerance to alcohol. In other words, the mice with higher amounts of this enzyme are relatively *insensitive* to alcohol, meaning that they can drink more alcohol without suffering ill effects from the drug.

The researchers injected alcohol into two sets of mice—one with the enzyme and one genetically altered group without the enzyme. They then placed the mice on their backs and measured how long it took for the animals to roll over and get back on their feet. The mice with the Fyn tyrosine kinase took anywhere from three to forty minutes to stand up, while the mice without the enzyme took twice as long to get off their backs.

The researchers concluded that mice and humans with large amounts of Fyn tyrosine kinase are more susceptible to alcohol addiction than those with relatively smaller amounts because the enzyme counteracts alcohol's effects on the brain, making the individual less sensitive to the drug's effects. "Initial insensitivity [to alcohol] seems to be a strong predictor of alcoholism later in life," notes pharmacologist Adron Harris of the University of Colorado Health Sciences Center in Denver.

The Human Genome Project, involving a worldwide consortium of universities, is currently mapping out the approximately one hundred thousand human genes. Tens of thousands of human genes fragments have been identified, and over 7,600 genes have been mapped to specific chromosomes; within the next decade we will have many of the answers to our questions about alcoholism and other genetically transmitted diseases. Nevertheless, what we have discovered in the last decade of the twentieth century about the genetically determined brain abnormalities of alcoholics gives us confidence that our definition of alcoholism as a progressive neurological disease with a genetic basis (see page 46) is correct.

One of the most important facts to remember about alcoholism is its *progression*. Alcoholism begins in an early stage that looks nothing at all like a life-threatening disease, proceeds into a middle stage where problems begin to appear and intensify, and gradually advances into the late, degenerative stages of obvious physiological dependence, physical and psychological deterioration, and loss of control. In the next chapters we will focus on the progressive stages of the disease and the signs and symptoms associated with each stage.

5

Alcoholism:
The Early and Middle Stages

First man takes the drink. Then drink takes the
drink. Then drink takes the man.

— JAPANESE PROVERB

On one occasion Welsh poet Dylan Thomas (who died of alcoholism at the age of thirty-nine) was drinking and talking a blue streak. He suddenly stopped in midsentence. "Somebody's boring me," he said. "I think it's me."

Once you understand the basic neurological mechanisms that underlie alcoholism, the symptoms associated with the disease begin to make sense. Why are alcoholics often irritable and oversensitive? Because their brain chemistry is disordered by alcohol. Why are alcoholics depressed and despondent? Because their brain cells are malfunctioning. Why do they behave in self-destructive ways? It's all in the brain.

All diseases are identified by a cluster of symptoms (what the patient subjectively reports) and signs (what the observer can visibly see or measure). The characteristic signs and symptoms of alcoholism are directly linked to alcohol's effects on the central nervous system. As time goes by and the disease progresses, the symptoms and signs increase in number and severity as virtually every organ system in the body is progressively damaged.

In alcoholism, as in other chronic, progressive diseases such as cancer, diabetes, multiple sclerosis, and heart disease, the symptoms are initially mild, with little indication of serious trouble. Over a period of months or years, however, the early- and middle-stage symptoms intensify, and obvious signs of disease begin to appear. Like all diseases, the symptoms and signs of alcoholism follow a more or less predictable course.

In this chapter we will detail the telltale symptoms of early-stage and middle-stage alcoholism, paying close attention to the underlying adaptations and transformations in brain chemistry. In the next chapter we will describe the symptoms and signs of the late, deteriorative stages of the disease.

THE EARLY STAGE

Alcoholism differs from virtually every other disease process in that it begins with symptoms indicating an *improvement* in functioning. These early-stage symptoms make sense only when you understand that the disease is characterized by neurological adaptations, which enhance the pleasurable sensations of drinking while mitigating the unpleasant effects. Only later (typically over a period of years or decades) do these adaptations lead to physical and mental deterioration.

EARLY-STAGE SYMPTOMS

- Intense pleasure associated with drinking
- Lower-intensity reaction (metabolic tolerance)
- Acquired (central nervous system) tolerance
- Preoccupation with alcohol

INTENSE PLEASURE

Most people who drink alcohol feel good after the first glass of beer, wine, or hard liquor. Alcohol creates a warm glow, a melting, freeing sensation captured in the rapturous phrase often muttered after a few drinks, "Ah, isn't life good?" In *The Liar's Club*, Mary Kerr describes the sensation she had when, as a child, she drank red wine mixed with 7UP: "Something like a big sunflower was opening at the very center of my being." Most drinkers, alcoholic and nonalcoholic alike, will identify immediately with that description of an inner unfolding, as if being warmed by some liquid, internal sun.

Underlying this feel-good response is alcohol's ability to raise, through a series of complex neurochemical interactions, the levels of dopamine, serotonin, norepinephrine, GABA, and other neurotransmitters in the brain. When alcohol opens the neurotransmitter faucets, the drinker is flooded with pleasurable sensations. Early-stage alcoholics experience the same euphoric feelings, but with a twist: The neurotransmitter rush is more intense, the warm glow persists for a longer period of time, and the state of well-being is quite unlike anything the novice drinker has experienced before. Looking back on their early drinking, many alcoholics describe the experience this way: "So this is what's been missing all my life!"

The intensity of this alcohol-induced rapture cannot be objectively measured, but it is common enough. In his memoir *A Monk Swimming*, Malachy McCourt remembers his first serious drinking episode, when he was an eleven-year-old boy guzzling beer in a Limerick pub: "A great feeling of peace and contentment floated out of the heavens and wrapped itself around my being, softly and lovingly clothing me in spiritual finery and the understanding that I was the best boy in the whole wide world, and there wasn't anything I couldn't be or do in this life."

In another testimonial to alcohol-induced bliss, Jean Kirkpatrick, founder and executive director of Women for Sobriety, describes her early experiences with the drug during her teenage years:

> *Before drinking I felt unloved, unpopular, undesirable, and a hundred other un's that one can think of. I wanted to be popular. I wanted to be the "life of the party." And when I first had a few drinks, it seemed as if I had found the nectar of the gods. Just a few drinks, and I began to believe I was all those things I wanted to be. I felt as if I were oozing charisma. My personality changed, and I had the dynamic feelings I had longed for. And all this happened with so little effort. Just a few drinks!*

LOWER-INTENSITY REACTION

Early-stage alcoholics typically experience "a lower-intensity reaction to alcohol's effects," reports Marc Schuckit, professor of psychiatry at the University of California, San Diego, School of Medicine and director of the Alcohol Research Center at San Diego Veterans Affairs Medical Center. In a ten-year study conducted between 1978 and 1988, Schuckit evaluated the effect of three to five drinks (the amount depended on the subject's weight) on the behavioral and perceptual reactions of 453 college-age men. Half of the men had severely impaired alcoholic fathers while the other half (the control group) had no known alcoholic biological relatives.

Reactions were measured by subjective feelings of intoxication, measures of brain activity, hormone levels, and standing steadiness tests that calculated body sway when under the influence. As compared to 10 percent of the control group, 40 percent of the men with a positive family history of alcoholism demonstrated "remarkably" low levels of reaction to alcohol. From his research Schuckit concluded that "reduced sensitivity to lower doses of alcohol makes it more likely that excessive alcohol consumption and subsequent alcohol-related difficulties will occur in about half of the children of alcoholics."

Those speculative conclusions were confirmed in a follow-up study conducted ten years later. Fifty-six percent of the group with a family history of alcoholism and low levels of alcohol response were diagnosed alcoholics compared to 14 percent of the men with high levels of sensitivity to alcohol and no family history of alcoholism. Thus, an individual's initial level of response to alcohol appears to be a potent predictor of future alcoholism risk. "Some people may therefore develop alcohol-related problems because they seek a response to alcohol that they can only perceive at higher levels of alcohol intake," Schuckit concludes. (The risk of alcoholism for these young men was *not* correlated with any higher risk for psychiatric disorders such as severe depression or anxiety.)

A lower-intensity reaction is directly related to enhanced metabolic activity in the liver and is synonymous with what researchers call metabolic tolerance or initial tolerance. The liver has two basic pathways for metabolizing alcohol: the well-paved, often-used ADH pathway, which relies on the enzymes alcohol dehydrogenase (ADH), aldehyde dehydrogenase (ALDH), and NAD+, and the less frequently used microsomal ethanol oxidizing system (MEOS). (See Chapter 2 for an in-depth discussion of these enzymes and metabolic pathways.)

In heavy drinkers and people genetically predisposed to alcoholism, the MEOS adapts to the presence of alcohol by increasing its activity, which leads to an ability to metabolize alcohol more quickly than normal. If your metabolism is speeded up, you get rid of alcohol faster, which means that alcohol does not build up in your bloodstream as quickly, which in turn means you will not feel as intoxicated as someone with a slower metabolic capability. It also means that you will need to drink more alcohol to get the same feelings of relaxation and euphoria.

In an earlier experiment Schuckit evaluated acetaldehyde levels in forty male college students. None of the students experienced any symptoms or signs of alcoholism; their average intake was two to four drinks per drinking day. The main difference between the students was that twenty came from nonalcoholic families while the other twenty had an alcoholic parent. Blood samples were taken before the students drank sugar-free soda spiked with alcohol, fifteen minutes after they drank alcohol, and at thirty-minute intervals over the next three hours. In the men from alcoholic families the blood acetaldehyde level was more than 50 percent higher than in men from nonalcoholic families. This is significant because acetaldehyde journeys to the brain, where it interacts with various neurotransmitters to create the addictive compounds known as TIQs (tetrahydroisoquinolines), paving the way for neurological addiction (see pages 48–50).

While some researchers challenged the methodology of Schuckit's experiment, many believed that his conclusions paralleled the findings of other researchers investigating the genetic factors underlying a predisposition to alcoholism. In *Alcohol and the Addicted Brain* pharmacologist Kenneth Blum discusses Schuckit's experiment and concludes that "his findings fit in with other data to suggest that these higher levels of acetaldehyde are, indeed, found in the sons of alcoholics and are a genetic characteristic . . . it seemed reasonable to conclude that there is a metabolic anomaly in the sons of alcoholics that puts them at risk of becoming, in their turn, alcoholics."

ACQUIRED (CENTRAL NERVOUS SYSTEM) TOLERANCE

Researchers estimate that metabolic tolerance is responsible for approximately 20 percent of the early- and middle-stage alcoholic's ability to consume relatively large amounts of alcohol without feeling intoxicated, while acquired tolerance accounts for the remaining 80 percent. Acquired tolerance is a symptom of central nervous system adaptation to alcohol and represents actual physical alterations in the nervous system leading to an improvement of functioning when under the influence of alcohol.

The ability to drink a lot of alcohol without feeling or showing the effects is a common symptom of early- and early-middle-stage alcoholism. "I could drink everybody under the table. I took everyone else home," recalled Marty Mann, the first woman to remain sober in Alcoholics Anonymous and the founder of the National Council on Alcoholism. Author Jack London had the same experience. In *John Barleycorn* he describes the "pride" he felt when, at age fourteen, he drank "cheap rotgut" with a seventeen-year-old sailor and a nineteen-year-old harpooner and was able to stand upright after his comrades had fallen into drunken stupors:

> *I had a splendid constitution, a stomach that would digest scrap-iron, and I was still running my Marathon in full vigor when Scotty began to fall and fade. . . . Scotty's reeling brain could not control his*

muscles. All his correlations were breaking down. He strove to take another drink, and feebly dropped the tumbler on the floor. Then, to my amazement, weeping bitterly, he rolled into a bunk on his back and immediately snored off to sleep.

The harpooner and I drank on, grinning in a superior way to each other over Scotty's plight. The last flask was opened, and we drank it between us, to the accompaniment of Scotty's stertorous breathing. Then the harpooner faded away into his bunk, and I was left alone, unthrown on the field of battle.

I was very proud, and John Barleycorn was proud with me. I could carry my drink. I was a man. I had drunk two men, drink for drink, into unconsciousness. And I was still on my two feet, upright, making my way on deck to get air into my scorching lungs.

London's pride in his capacity to consume large amounts of alcohol was tempered in later years by the realization that his high tolerance was a curse and not a blessing:

It was in this bout . . . that I discovered what a good stomach and a strong head I had for drink—a bit of knowledge that was to be a source of pride in succeeding years, and that ultimately I was to come to consider a great affliction. The fortunate man is the one who cannot take more than a couple of drinks without becoming intoxicated. The unfortunate wight is the one who can take many glasses without betraying a sign; who must take numerous glasses in order to get the "kick."

Not all alcoholics share the same early experiences with alcohol, but many report a remarkably high tolerance for alcohol and a marked absence of aftereffects following a night of heavy drinking. It is perhaps ironic that many alcoholics in their early drinking careers report less-negative side effects to alcohol than do normal drinkers. High tolerance for alcohol is a clear sign of the brain's early, adaptive responses to alcohol. For the individual genetically predisposed to alcoholism, alcohol literally fills a gap, latching on to the neurotransmitter receptors to create a feel-good rush that in truth is a sign of addiction. Many early-stage alcoholics take great pride in their high tolerance for alcohol, boasting about their ability to drink everyone else under the table. Like so many people, they have not been informed about the neurological adaptations underlying addiction.

Co-author Bill Asbury worked as a freelance foreign correspondent stationed in Korea and Tokyo during the Korean War. He was given full military privileges, including unlimited access to the officers club, where martinis cost 17 cents and a bottle of wine was 70 cents. Several times a week Bill joined his friends at the bar, where he started out the evening with six or seven martinis. "After a few generously poured martinis," Bill recalls, "I was feeling good and loose." After several more, Bill or one of his drinking cronies would look at his watch—this was a well-oiled routine, and all participants adopted a conspiratorial grin—note that it was after 7 P.M., and suggest that perhaps it was time to switch to stingers, a potent concoction consisting of brandy and crème de menthe. After three or four stingers and a shared bottle or two of wine—and often no dinner—Bill would call it a night.

He rarely suffered any noticeable aftereffects from these alcohol-saturated evenings. "Some mornings I'd feel a little slow," Bill recalls, "but by nine A.M. I was always up and running, feeling good and looking forward to the end of the day, when I could enjoy my well-earned respite from the pressures of the workday and enjoy 'just a few' with my friends." Bill was twenty-eight years old at the time.

PREOCCUPATION WITH ALCOHOL

As the months and years go by, the early-stage alcoholic begins to experience a preoccupation with alcohol. Everything feels so good, so right when you're drinking that the desire to repeat the experience seems perfectly sensible. Since drinking is so much fun and makes you feel on top of the world, how can it possibly be bad for you? In *Drinking: A Love Story*, Caroline Knapp describes the way alcohol made her feel when she used to drink with a friend at the Ritz Hotel bar in Boston:

> *I loved those moments, that sense that the world had boiled down to such simple elements: me and Sam and the two glasses on the table; everything else—the clink of waiters clearing tables, the low buzz of talk from others around us—just background music. Drinking was the best way I knew, the fastest and simplest, to let my feelings out and to connect, just sit there and connect with another human being. The comfort was enormous: I was an easier, stronger version of myself, as though I'd been coated from the inside out with a warm liquid armor. . . .*
>
> *The amazing thing was how effective the drink was, how easily you could uncork a sense of well-being, how magical it was—magical! You could open a bottle and build yourself a liquid bridge.*

It is not hard to imagine why early-stage alcoholics like that feeling or why they want to repeat it. Alcohol makes the early-stage alcoholic feel real, warm, open, *alive*. With such intense pleasure and so little pain, who could imagine the misery to come?

THE MIDDLE STAGE

In the middle stage of alcoholism, the predictable euphoria associated with drinking gradually begins to dissipate. The clouds of pain begin to gather, partially obscuring the light and heat of the early-stage alcoholic's pleasure. Wispy at first, the clouds gather in force until by the end of the middle stage the landscape is heavily shadowed and the thunderheads begin to roll in, one right after the other.

Middle-stage alcoholics still feel good when they drink, no doubt about that, but life in general is not quite so easy or simple as it used to be. Nobody really wonders or worries about that fact—after all, the average middle-stage alcoholic is in his or her thirties and forties, a time when work and family pressures often build up and become overwhelming. Who would think to connect the periodic angry outbursts, recurring anxiety, persistent depression, and general emotional instability with alcohol? Much more likely targets are the demanding boss, the complaining spouse, the self-centered kids, or the unrelieved stress of everyday life. Alcohol is a friend, not the enemy—the well-earned reward after a stressful day.

The problems, when they do begin to appear, seem relatively minor, with no apparent cause-and-effect relationship to drinking. Heated words with the boss, ongoing arguments with the spouse, constant irritation with the kids—so what's new? Headaches, memory lapses, shaky hands—clear evidence of the nerve-jangling pace of everyday life, right? A strong desire (not yet experienced as a compelling need) for a drink— well, jeez, look around you, isn't everyone downing a few these days?

Alcohol is considered the hard-earned compensation for a stress-filled existence. Who would deny the busy executive his three martinis after a fifteen-hour workday? Who could argue with the working mother when she says she deserves a few drinks (maybe four or five) after a harried day at work and with the kids? Why shouldn't the exhausted carpenter, the stressed-out stockbroker, and the brain-fatigued professor celebrate the end of the day with a few strong belts at the local watering spot?

Middle-stage alcoholics don't miss work because of drinking, they don't go home early because of a hangover, and they don't neglect their family obligations—at least not very often. They don't drink a quart a day, they don't drink in the morning (or even necessarily at lunch), and they don't drink cheap, rotgut booze wrapped up in a paper bag. They don't get drunk every night, pick fights at taverns, beat up on their kids when they're loaded, or complain about pink elephants dancing around the room. Sure, they get hangovers, sometimes they don't feel like getting out of bed for work, and every once in a while they go overboard and drink too much—but, really, how abnormal is that?

MIDDLE-STAGE SYMPTOMS

- Withdrawal

- Blackouts

- Personality disintegration

- Denial

WITHDRAWAL

"It is as if a coiled spring were suddenly released," says Jerome Levin, Ph.D., of the withdrawal syndrome (also called abstinence syndrome). The syndrome begins when the blood alcohol concentration begins to descend. Most people think that withdrawal occurs when alcohol is completely eliminated from the bloodstream, but the addicted brain begins to call out its misery long before its alcohol bath is completely drained. The brain cells require a specific amount of the drug to feel good; when that level begins to drop, the pain and misery of withdrawal begins. Thus, you can be in withdrawal while you are still intoxicated—even when your blood alcohol level is high enough to qualify you as legally drunk.

In the early and middle stages, withdrawal is often subtle and the symptoms seem to bear little or no relationship to excess drinking:

- Anxiety

- Irritability

- Tremors (involuntary trembling of the body or limbs)

- Nervousness

- Weakness

- Insomnia

- Gastrointestinal distress

- Loss of appetite

- Elevated blood pressure

- Elevated temperature

- Exaggerated reflexes (hyperreflexia)

Henri Paul, the driver of the Mercedes that crashed in Paris in August 1997, killing Princess Diana and Dodi Fayed, was legally drunk when he got behind the wheel. Three separate blood tests confirmed that his blood alcohol concentration was more than triple the legal limit. Yet it also seems clear that Paul was in withdrawal, for he had been called back to work two hours before he got into the Mercedes and for much of that time he was under the surveillance of the hotel's security cameras. Although an employee at the Ritz allegedly told reporters that Paul had a few drinks in the hotel's Hemingway bar that night, there seems to be little doubt that Paul did most of his drinking in the period before he returned to the hotel, at least two or three hours before he started driving. Paul was drunk *and* he was in withdrawal—both facts sealed his doom and the fate of his passengers.

The strange truth that alcoholics are often in worse shape when their blood alcohol concentration is descending than when it is at its highest level is an extremely difficult point to grasp. After all, isn't alcohol itself the culprit? Logically it would seem that the higher your blood alcohol concentration, the worse off you should be. Although this is typically the case for nonalcoholics, in alcoholics different physiological reactions occur. The cells of the central nervous system have adapted to alcohol, leading to the ability to function "normally" even in the presence of large amounts of the drug. With these adaptations the addicted cells literally need alcohol to carry on their normal duties. When alcohol is withdrawn, the cells become fragile and unbalanced.

The withdrawal syndrome represents a state of hyperexcitability, or extreme agitation, in the central nervous system. The brain cells, which have reached a state of equilibrium when alcohol is present in sufficient quantities, cry out for more when alcohol is withdrawn. The withdrawal syndrome is proof positive that you are physically dependent on (addicted to) alcohol.

BLACKOUTS

When you drink to the point of intoxication—whether you are alcoholic or not—alcohol and its metabolic by-product acetaldehyde destroy cells in the hippocampus, the long-term memory storage areas of your brain. Cell destruction is usually associated with a rising blood alcohol level and may be related to oxygen deprivation in certain crucial areas of the brain. While patchy memories are a common after-effect of heavy drinking, blackouts—total wipeouts of moments, hours, or even days of your life—are less common. They are always, however, terrifying.

Bill Asbury suffered from periodic blackouts during his twenty-five years of alcoholic drinking. This one was his worst:

> *I was in Spokane, Washington, for a job interview. After the interview I celebrated (I didn't get the job) with three double martinis, a bottle of good red wine, and two after-dinner snifters of brandy. Somewhere in there I think I ate a steak and a potato. Sufficiently tanked up, I got in my car and started driving back home. Three hours later, when I became conscious of what I was doing, I discovered that I was sixty miles past my destination. My speedometer told me I was going 100 mph. To this day, twenty-seven years later, I have no memory, not a single trace, of that three-hour drive.*

Blackouts are often listed as a telltale symptom in checklists for diagnosing alcoholism. While anyone who drinks too much at a given time (or who mixes alcohol with other drugs that affect the central nervous system) can experience memory loss, true drug amnesia due to hippocampal changes is diagnostic of alcoholism. Still, an estimated 50 percent of alcoholics do not have blackouts—or at least they don't remember having them. Since a blackout is defined as total memory loss for moments, hours, or even days, alcoholics often won't remember having one unless someone or something (like a crumpled fender, a broken nose, or a friend's blow-by-blow description) calls attention to the missing event.

PERSONALITY DISINTEGRATION

Somewhere in the middle stage, which can last for many years and even decades, the alcoholic's personality begins to undergo dramatic changes. At first the symptoms are subtle, and the alcoholic seems only slightly more irritable, nervous, anxious, or depressed. "You're on edge these days," a coworker might comment, while the alcoholic's spouse might say, "You're working too hard," or the kids might complain about Mom's short temper. No one thinks to connect last night's half case of beer or pint of gin with today's touchy nerves.

Irritating or annoying events such as a traffic jam, the neighbor's barking dog, a child's piercing scream, or a bounced check get blown out of proportion. Psychologist James Milam calls this emotional explosiveness "augmentation." When the brain cells are hyperactive, having been bathed in alcohol for a period of time and then left to dry out, even a slight provocation will set the nerves on fire.

"When I had a bad hangover and the phone rang," one recovering alcoholic recalls, "it felt like World War Three was going off in my head." Another alcoholic recalls how she would curl up into a ball and start to cry when her children fought with each other. Only after several months of recovery was she able to deal with loud noises and intense emotional displays.

When a situation that would normally rate low on the irritability scale gets an extreme response, it's obvious that something else is going on. That's augmentation: The brain is agitated by alcohol, and any stimulus moving through its hyperactive cells is going to seem bigger, stronger, louder, and more emotionally jarring than it actually is. Augmentation is a process that happens to everyone, alcoholic and non-alcoholic alike. If you're exhausted from lack of sleep and a friend looks at you cross-eyed, you might feel like bursting into tears or punching him in the nose. When you have the flu, you might be extremely sensitive to loud noises or certain smells. A week or so before their menstrual periods, many women experience a heightened sensitivity, created by hormonal shifts, to physical and emotional stimuli.

In alcoholism, however, the process of augmentation feeds into the idea that alcoholics are somehow emotionally unstable, nervous, anxious, or depressed. Everyone seems to miss the alcohol connection because from all outward appearances the middle-stage alcoholic doesn't seem to be in any big trouble with booze. The middle-stage alcoholic is equally confused (that's the addicted brain at work again) because alcohol is still, at least 70 or 80 percent of the time, friend, not foe.

Later, when alcoholism seems obvious to just about everyone, people will say, "She was always a nervous person," or "He was born an angry son of a bitch," in the belief that the personality disorder predated the alcohol problem and contributed somehow to its development. Even the great pioneering alcohol researcher E. M. Jellinek, author of *The Disease Concept of Alcoholism*, expressed some confusion about the psychological state of alcoholics. "In spite of a great diversity in personality structure among alcoholics," Jellinek wrote in 1960, "there appears in a large proportion of them a low tolerance for tension coupled with an inability to cope with psychological stresses."

The idea of a preexisting "alcoholic personality" has been debunked, however, by numerous prospective studies, which follow a given population through time, carefully recording changes in behavior and drinking patterns. (Most alcoholism studies are retrospective, which means that they look back over time in an attempt to reconstruct events, thoughts, feelings, and behaviors.) In *The Natural History of Alcoholism Revisited* Harvard psychiatrist George Vaillant presents the results of six prospective studies, each of which confirms that the alcoholic personality is a consequence, not a cause, of alcoholism.

In a landmark prospective study published in 1960, for example, researchers reviewed the predisease personality characteristics of 325 antisocial grammar-school boys. The boys who later became alcoholics were no more likely to have inferiority feelings, phobias, "feminine" feelings, or oral dependencies than the boys who did not become alcoholics. In fact, the boys who eventually became addicted to alcohol were outwardly more confident, aggressive, hyperactive, and heterosexual and less disturbed by normal fears than the boys who did not become alcoholic.

In another prospective study published in 1973, researchers compared the psychological test results on the Minnesota Multiphasic Personality Inventory (MMPI) of 38 college students who later developed alcoholism with the MMPIs of 148 classmates. The MMPI profiles for all thirty-eight men who later became alcoholics were within the normal range. Years later, when the men were hospitalized for alcoholism, they scored in the pathological range on the test's depression, psychopathic deviancy, and paranoia scales. Their personality profiles at this time revealed, in the words of the researchers, "the neurotic patterns consistent with self-centered, immature, dependent, resentful, irresponsible people who are unable to face reality."

George Vaillant's fifty-two-year prospective study, originally published in 1983 and updated in 1995, provides the most compelling evidence currently available to show that the "alcoholic personality" is actually caused by the disease of alcoholism. Although many alcoholics in Vaillant's study rationalized their loss of control over drinking by citing psychological trauma (divorce, sexual abuse, job loss, and so on), excessive drinking typically predated the alleged trauma. Summarizing his results, Vaillant concludes that "alcoholics are selectively personality disordered as a consequence, not as a cause, of their alcohol abuse.

Although the conscience may be soluble in alcohol, heavy alcohol use does not relieve anxiety and depression as much as alcohol abuse induces depression and anxiety." Vaillant is careful to point out that while unhappy childhoods, serious family problems, depression, and anxiety do not cause alcoholism, "these factors will make any chronic disease worse."

The conclusion is unmistakable: A normal personality is warped by addiction to alcohol into an abnormal, pathological personality. The "alcoholic personality" is the consequence, not the cause, of alcoholism. "Just as light passing through water confounds our perceptions, the ill-ness of alcoholism profoundly distorts the individual's personality, his social stability, and his own recollection of relevant childhood variables," Vaillant writes.

DENIAL

In a society where alcoholism is associated with "abuse" and alco-holics are depicted as morally depraved, physically unfit, mentally unsound social outcasts, it is not difficult to figure out why middle-stage alcoholics practice denial. They simply don't fit the stereotype. And besides, everyone else around them is practicing denial, too. When you look back and hear the stories of all the missed opportunities to diag-nose alcoholism in the early stages, when you consider all the misery that could have been prevented, it breaks your heart.

Take the case of Terry McGovern. When Terry was twenty years old, she was drinking an average of five or six beers, three or four shots of hard liquor, or a bottle of wine every day. Despite continued drinking, occasional use of marijuana and amphetamines, and persistent, unre-lieved depression, Terry's psychoanalyst did not believe that she was an alcoholic; her basic, underlying problems were depression and unre-solved psychological conflicts. Terry "progressed very well" in therapy, he insisted, even though she continued to drink and use drugs.

This is a clear case of "professional denial," which is rampant in our society. Thousands of recovering alcoholics can tell you stories about how their doctors mentioned their swollen, enlarged livers but sug-gested only that they might perhaps want to cut down on their drink-ing. (To which the typical middle-stage alcoholic responds by temporarily cutting back from a daily average of, say, six mixed drinks to four or five.) Tens of thousands of alcoholics like Terry McGovern consult psychiatrists and psychotherapists who are ignorant of the neu-rochemistry of alcoholism and who view heavy drinking as a symptom of deeper emotional problems. Months or years pass—and thousands of the patient's dollars are spent—searching for the "real" cause, thought to be buried deep somewhere in the multilayered psyche.

On a recent PBS debate titled "Is Abstinence the Answer to Alcoholism?" a psychotherapist explained his approach to the subject of alcoholism. This description, in our opinion, is a classic example of professional denial based on ignorance about the neurophysiological nature of alcoholism. "I don't treat people for addiction or alcoholism," the psychotherapist emphatically stated. "I don't focus on the drinking at all, or very little. I focus on the other life problems. And interestingly, when these people tackle the real issues going on in their life, perhaps three months, six months later I ask them, 'Well, how are the drinking problems?' and they say there aren't any problems. So I think it's a real mistake right off the bat to focus on drinking as a problem. Drinking excessively is a symptom of some other life problem, and I think it's a mistake to focus on the symptom alone."

Family denial is as common as professional denial. When Terry McGovern was twenty-six years old and a student at the University of South Dakota, her brother, Steve, began to worry about her drinking. One Sunday, when there was no liquor in the house and all the bars were closed, he watched in amazement as his sister systematically searched the kitchen cabinets, took out all the cooking extracts containing alcohol, and drank them one right after the other. Still, he rationalized away his fears: It was the 1970s, Terry was in her mid-twenties, and most of her friends were also drinking too much. "In those days," Steve McGovern recalled, "we thought that alcoholism was something that happened to someone's dad or uncle or grandfather. Students might drink too much—but alcoholism, no way."

That's classic denial. Think about it: Why would a young woman guzzle bottles of vanilla, almond, and orange extract if she didn't have a drinking problem?

In our society denial is a symptom of confused thinking, brought on by years of arguments about the deep-seated psychological problems and emotional instability of alcoholics. After all, the thinking goes, alcoholism is a shameful weakness, something that happens to emotionally unstable people from dysfunctional families, or to people who have been severely traumatized by life experiences—how could it happen to someone like Terry McGovern, the daughter of a U.S. senator, for heaven's sake?

Alcoholics practice the same sort of denial in rationalizing why they can't possibly be alcoholics. No self-respecting human being wants to be considered "one of *them*." Denial helps the alcoholic assert with confidence: "I'm not weak or screwed up or self-destructive, so I can't be one of *them*." In alcoholics, however, denial goes deeper than basic ignorance or wishful thinking—it is a symptom of their addicted brain. Addicted brains do not think or react logically.

• A middle-stage alcoholic sits at his favorite table in his favorite tavern, getting good and tight on pitcher after pitcher of beer, but comforts himself with the thought that he's not like the poor, red-nosed souse at the end of the bar who keeps falling off his stool. "Sure," he thinks, "sometimes I drink too much, but I'm nowhere near *that* bad."

• A middle-stage alcoholic reasons that alcoholism isn't something to worry about because she's the chief executive officer of a major corporation and grosses $500,000 a year.

• A thirty-five-year-old figures he's not an alcoholic because he drinks only beer, and everyone knows that most alcoholics get drunk on wine or whiskey.

• "I never drink before noon! I can quit whenever I want! My husband and kids love me! I'm a good mother! I can't be an alcoholic."

In the alcoholic, denial is a symptom of a brain addled by addiction. In the early stage of the disease, alcohol is a source of intense physical pleasure, and the alcoholic has good reason to practice denial. Sure, she may be drinking a lot, but alcohol makes her feel awfully good, and it isn't doing her any apparent harm. Why stop? As the disease progresses and the brain cells continue to adapt their functioning to the presence of alcohol, the addicted brain begins to mastermind the alcoholic's denial. When the neurons get agitated and start crying out for alcohol, the brain isn't going to deep-six their need by conveying the message to cut down or stop. When you're hungry, your brain says, *"Eat!"* When you're addicted to alcohol, your brain says, *"Drink!"*

Alcoholics in denial have been called stupid, stubborn, selfish, and pigheaded (to list only a few of the pejorative terms used), but in reality they are simply following the dictates of their addicted brains. This is why they can't accurately judge what's happening to them, why they stubbornly refuse to look at reality, and why they can't "just say no." Their brains are urging them on, using all sorts of physical and emotional prods: "Go ahead and take a drink, it won't hurt you!" the brain cajoles. "And, by the way, don't listen to those fools telling you to cut down. They don't know what they're talking about."

The truly astonishing fact is that alcoholics can and do talk back to their brains, calling on reserves of inner strength and willpower that few nonalcoholics ever have reason to summon. These brief skirmishes inevitably end in defeat, however, for the sword of willpower is soon rendered defenseless against the mighty cannons of the addictive brain. In her journal Terry McGovern described the ongoing struggle between her body and her mind, when her mind would tell her to stop and her body cried out, "Just one more!" This journal entry was written on November 13, 1993, thirteen months before Terry died of alcoholism:

I need to write this as tears well up in my eyes . . . how it feels after three drinks to have to stop.

1. *Depression*
2. *Anxiety*
3. *Some fear*
4. *Agitation*

My body and mind do not feel relaxed, even though a nonalcoholic's mind and body would be relaxed after 3 drinks. My body is telling my mind, just one more really strong one would do it—coat the nerves and they'd stay coated and numbed. With all my being I would like to have been like the man who could drink a shot of whiskey every morning—like a cup of coffee—and leave it be. But what happens is that shot gives me a feeling of wholeness, and when it starts to go away there is artificial emptiness just as there was artificial wholeness. . . . I could weep and weep that the lie is still alive. How could I want to keep company with the same agent that has snatched from my grasp all that I have loved. God forgive me. Teresa forgive Teresa.

As strong as the denial system must be to protect the needs of the addicted brain, it cannot defend the alcoholic against her own self-hatred. As the addiction strengthens its hold and makes a mockery of the individual's willpower and strength of character, depression, anxiety, and fear deepen. Terry McGovern's request for forgiveness—from God, from herself—is heartbreaking. She reaches for the bottle, knowing the devastation it will cause, and it is that seemingly willing alliance with the devil that creates the fierce, unending tortures of shame, guilt, and self-loathing. Of all the unrelenting horrors that occur as alcoholism progresses into its late and final stages, the most agonizing of all is the belief that if death or insanity does come, it is not undeserved.

6

Late-Stage
Alcoholism

At no point in my life did it occur to me that my
many accidents (including fights), failed relationships, medical problems, and depression were a
consequence of my drinking. It was only after my
alcoholism had been identified and treated that I
was able to clearly see the path of carnage that
alcoholism had cut through my life.

— JOSEPH BEASLEY, M.D.

In the late, deteriorative stage of alcoholism, the thunderclouds of pain
gather in force and intensity, and the forecast begins to look grim indeed.
This is the stage we imagine when we think about this disease—a dark,
dreary world inhabited by lonely human beings who have lost everything of value in their lives and can think about only one thing: their
next drink. Alcoholism is a progressive disease, and as the following story
illustrates, the descent into its late stages is sometimes much faster than
we would anticipate. Late-stage alcoholics are not just career drunks or
oldtimers down on their luck—they are just as likely to be talented,
intelligent human beings in the prime of their lives.

*Jeff Jay had everything: good looks, academic talent, close friends, lov-
ing parents. In high school he was a National Merit Scholar and president of his student association. It was during those happy, productive
years that Jay discovered alcohol, and from the first time he took a drink,
he called the drug "the love of my life." In college alcohol became an essential part of his daily life. As he began to drink more and more often, his
grades dropped; as his relationship with alcohol replaced his connections
with family and friends, he became more isolated and depressed. In his
senior year of college, he dropped out.*
It was a spectacularly fast downhill slide from there, filled with all the

signs and symptoms of rapidly progressing alcoholism—car accidents, lost jobs, broken friendships, estrangement from his family, financial problems, mental and physical deterioration. In his mid-twenties Jay was a homeless drunk, panhandling enough spare change to buy the cheap wine that would fuel his brain addiction and forestall the agony of withdrawal. He couldn't eat solid food because of a bleeding ulcer and bleeding colon. Nerve damage from years of heavy drinking and associated nutritional deficiencies made it difficult for him to walk. By the time his parents finally found him in a flop house in San Francisco, he was near death.

He was twenty-six years old.

For the late-stage alcoholic the balance of pleasure and pain, so carefully maintained in the middle stage, tips precariously. Pleasure becomes short-lived; pain is ever-present. "By this time, drinking was no fun for me anymore," recalls Doc Severinsen, a jazz musician and the leader of Johnny Carson's *Tonight Show* band. "There was no more yah ha and paper hats and climbing up on furniture. I never felt good when I drank. Never. There was never a pleasant moment of it." As the disease progresses, the pleasures associated with drinking continue to diminish until the only gratification is the reduction, for just a few moments, of the physical, emotional, and spiritual agony that accompanies every waking moment of every day.

Yet even at this stage, when the disease seems to have progressed into irreversible physical and mental deterioration, hope is not lost. Hope is never lost, for alcoholism is that rare disease for which there is a miraculous, fast-acting end to the misery: abstinence. Late-stage alcoholics who are physically incapacitated and mentally deranged can and do recover their health and sanity when they stop drinking. Go to an AA meeting anywhere in the world and you will hear bright-eyed, energetic, intelligent human beings in fine physical shape telling stories of a past life that can only be described as a living hell.

Jeff Jay, the young man in our opening story, tells one of those stories. When his parents finally found him in 1981 in a San Francisco flop house, they brought him back home to Michigan, where he was hospitalized and cared for around the clock. As the months went by, his mental confusion cleared and his body healed. He stayed sober, completed college, and became a professional alcoholism counselor. Today, fifteen years after his last drink, he is the director of program development for Michigan's Brighton Hospital, an alcoholism treatment facility, and president of the Terry McGovern Foundation in Washington, D.C.

SYMPTOMS OF LATE-STAGE ALCOHOLISM

- Late-stage withdrawal
- Craving
- Medical complications
- Loss of control

LATE-STAGE WITHDRAWAL

In the final stages of alcoholism, the drive to drink is so ferociously demanding that alcoholics often feel they have no choice but to obey the addicted brain's commands. Getting alcohol to the cells is the first priority; over time, it becomes the only priority. When late-stage alcoholics stop drinking or cut down on the amount they normally drink, the real misery begins.

When the drinker's blood alcohol concentration begins to descend, the blood vessels constrict, cutting down on the flow of blood and oxygen to the cells. Blood glucose levels drop sharply and remain unstable, and levels of neurotransmitters such as dopamine, serotonin, and norepinephrine decrease dramatically. The end result is widespread cell distress and panic. Imagine a room full of starving infants, screaming their lungs out for food, and you'll have a fairly accurate picture of the cells' distress. "Feed me!" they wail, and the incessant clamor for alcohol doesn't let up. The brain cells are starving for alcohol; they're literally dying for it.

The alcoholic sees no choice but to obey the command, and within moments alcohol quiets the cells. As long as the cells are adequately nursed with alcohol, they are content. Take the drug away, however, and the cells once again become agitated and hyperactive. "The drinker's position," writes clinical psychologist Jerome Levin, "is the reverse of that of the man who banged his head against the wall because it felt so good when he stopped; the physiologically dependent drinker drinks because it feels so awful when he stops."

If late-stage alcoholics could perfectly regulate the amount of alcohol supplied to the cells (through an alcohol IV drip, for example), they could save themselves a lot of misery. Hard as they might try, however, they cannot maintain forever the blood alcohol levels required to stave off withdrawal. They have to sleep, for one thing, and while they're sleeping (and not drinking), the blood alcohol level is descending, which leads to withdrawal symptoms.

General deterioration in physical health also figures into withdrawal. The alcoholic's body, ravaged by liver disease, gastrointestinal problems, brain cell destruction, or malnutrition, may physically reject alcohol through vomiting, hemorrhaging, or passing out. When alcoholics are physically unable to keep alcohol in their systems, their blood alcohol concentration will descend. In addition, the mental confusion brought about by widespread brain cell destruction clouds the late-stage alcoholic's judgment and makes it extremely difficult to decide when enough is enough. A three-day binge may lead to two days of sleeping it off, which in turn leads to severe withdrawal symptoms.

The more serious late-stage withdrawal symptoms—elevated pulse, heart rate, respiration, and blood pressure; extreme agitation; disorientation; high fever; hallucinations; seizures; and delirium tremens (DTs)—generally occur within several days after prolonged, heavy drinking. A general rule is that alcoholics are at risk for serious withdrawal if they consume more than a pint of whiskey (approximately ten drinks) every day for at least ten days. Of course, there are exceptions to every rule, and alcoholics who drink more than a pint a day for weeks at a time may not go through serious withdrawal, while alcoholics who drink less than a pint a day may have seizures or even go into DTs.

The withdrawal syndrome usually begins several hours to several days after the last drink; symptoms tend to peak around the third day and abate within a week. In the first (mildest) stage of withdrawal, symptoms include tremulousness, restlessness, anxiety, apprehension, appetite loss, and insomnia. Physical signs include rapid pulse and heartbeat. For most early- and middle-stage alcoholics, withdrawal ends here. Late-stage alcoholics may advance into second-stage withdrawal, which is marked by an intensification of first-stage symptoms. Hallucinations, which are a sign of a hyperactive nervous system, and seizures ("rum fits") may occur during the first forty-eight hours of withdrawal after prolonged, heavy drinking.

In the third and most dangerous stage of withdrawal the late-stage alcoholic may experience delirium tremens (DTs). Symptoms include severe tremors, anxiety, paranoia, profuse sweating, agitation, rapid pulse, fever, and diarrhea. Hallucinations are tactile as well as visual and auditory—the alcoholic actually feels, hears, and sees things that are not there. In *Huckleberry Finn* Mark Twain depicts the horrors of such a state:

> I don't know how long I was asleep [Huck Finn confides] but all of a sudden there was an awful scream and I was up. There was pap looking wild, and skipping around every which way and yelling about

snakes. He said they was crawling up his legs; and then he would give a jump and scream, and say one had bit him on the cheek—but I couldn't see no snakes. He started to run round and round the cabin, hollering "Take him off! take him off; he's biting me in the neck!" I never see a man look so wild in the eyes. Pretty soon he was all fagged out, and fell down panting; then he rolled over and over wonderful fast, kicking things every which way, and striking and grabbing at the air with his hands, and screaming and saying there was devils a-hold of him. He wore out by and by, and laid still awhile, moaning. Then he laid stiller, and didn't make a sound. I could hear the owls and wolves away off in the woods, and it seemed terrible still. He was laying over by the corner. By and by he raised up part way and listened, with his head to one side. He says, very low: "Tramp—tramp—tramp; that's the dead; tramp—tramp—tramp; they're coming after me, but I won't go. Oh, they're here! don't touch me—don't! hands off—they're cold; let go. Oh, let a poor devil alone!" Then he went down on all fours and crawled off, begging them to let him alone, and he rolled himself up in his blanket and wallowed in under the old pine table, still a-begging; and then he went to crying.

Years ago, before alcoholics received adequate medical treatment during acute withdrawal, the mortality rate of patients suffering from DTs was 20 to 25 percent. Today, even with proper medical care, an estimated 5 percent of alcoholics will go into DTs; of these, approximately 10 percent will die during the episode.

CRAVING

"I *need* a drink." Every middle- and late-stage alcoholic understands the imperious demand in that statement. The craving for alcohol represents a physiological imperative created by millions of addicted cells clamoring for their fix. In *The American Alcoholic*, William Madsen compares the craving for alcohol to the demands of the bowel or bladder—you can ignore it for a while, but sooner or later you'll be obliged to do something about it.

The early American physician Dr. Benjamin Rush vividly described the nature of craving:

When strongly urged, by one of his friends, to leave off drinking [an habitual drunkard] said, "Were a keg of rum in one corner of a room, and a cannon constantly discharging balls between me and it,

I could not refrain from passing before that cannon, in order to get at the rum.

Craving, like so many of the symptoms associated with alcoholism, can be understood as a complicated series of actions and reactions in the addicted brain. Pharmacologist Kenneth Blum, Ph.D., author of *Alcohol and the Addictive Brain*, believes that the complex neurological events underlying irresistible craving go a long way toward explaining the very nature of addictive disease. Blum's theory of the "reward cascade" underlying craving is complicated; we briefly reviewed the theory in Chapter 4, but because of its importance in understanding the phenomenon of craving, we'll go over it in more detail:

1.   In alcoholics a genetically transmitted defect (the A1 form of the dopamine D2 receptor gene) leads to inadequate functioning of the dopamine reward system, which is responsible for creating feelings of pleasure and euphoria.

2.   The brain, ever an adaptive organ, compensates by increasing the number of dopamine receptor sites; with more receptors available, the brain hopes to capture more of the available (but in short supply) dopamine, thereby increasing feelings of joy and elation.

3.   The brain's adaptive response backfires, however, for now the cells are in a double-whammy situation, with a short supply of dopamine and an overabundance of dopamine receptors. In other words, there's not enough "food" and too many mouths to feed. The supply is low, while the demand is high.

4.   Deprived of their feel-good chemical food, the brain cells send out distress signals, and the body responds by searching for substitute pleasure-creating substances.

5.   Alcohol works almost instantaneously to open up the dopamine faucets, and so those individuals with the genetic profile for alcoholism turn to alcohol for pleasure and euphoria. (Heroin, cocaine, marijuana, sugar, nicotine, gambling, and sex also release various pleasure-creating neurotransmitters; researchers are in the process of identifying the specific genetic profiles that will lead one person to seek out alcohol while another turns to cocaine or nicotine.)

6.   Alcohol and its metabolite acetaldehyde interact with various neurotransmitters to produce tetrahydroisoquinolines (TIQs), chemical substances that imitate the actions of dopamine and other feel-good neurotransmitters.

7.   The TIQs fit like a key into the lock of the opiate receptors, stimulating the release of pleasure-creating chemicals, which in turn creates feelings of well-being and euphoria.

8.   When alcoholics stop drinking, the dopamine supply is abruptly cut off, withdrawal may ensue, and the craving for alcohol returns.

9.   The solution: Drink more alcohol!

As Blum sums it up: "Forty years of research into the causes of alcoholism and other addictions have led to one conclusion: Irresistible craving is a malfunction of the reward centers of the brain involving the neurotransmitters and the enzymes that control them. Genetic research . . . indicates that the malfunction begins in the gene. Psychological and sociological research indicates that the environment can trigger, worsen, or to some degree alleviate the genetic predisposition, but the determining factors are biogenetic and biochemical."

MEDICAL COMPLICATIONS

Heavy, prolonged use of alcohol eventually threatens every cell in the body. The organs most likely to be affected are the heart, liver, stomach, pancreas, and central nervous system. The most common cause of death for alcoholics is cardiovascular disease (heart attacks and strokes), followed by cancer, suicide, accidents, and cirrhosis of the liver. Death certificates rarely list alcoholism as the cause of death, a fact that leads many alcoholism experts to conclude that statistics about the prevalence of alcoholism (ten million to fifteen million cases is the ballpark figure) are grossly underestimated.

HEART

Alcohol and its metabolite acetaldehyde directly injure cell membranes and damage the mitochondria in the heart muscle (myocardium), disrupting heart muscle activity and reducing the effectiveness of muscle contractions. Drinking moderately or excessively also contributes to increased triglyceride (blood fat) levels and decreased amounts of high-density lipoproteins ("good" cholesterol); both events can lead to fatty deposits in the arteries. As a result, high blood pressure, cardiac arrhythmia, and alcoholic cardiomyopathy are common in middle- and late-stage alcoholics and contribute to approximately 30 percent of alcoholic deaths. High blood pressure also increases the demand on blood vessels in the brain, leading to a greater risk of stroke.

Most alcoholic heart problems are reversible if treated in the early stages of the disease.

LIVER

One of every ten or twenty alcoholics (5 to 10 percent) will develop liver disease. Virtually every drinker, alcoholic and nonalcoholic, experiences some buildup of fat in the liver because alcohol interferes with the liver's ability to process fat. As fat is deposited in the liver cells, the liver enlarges. A swollen, tender liver, considered the first stage of alcoholic liver disease, is a clear sign of alcohol-induced liver damage.

The second stage of liver disease is alcoholic hepatitis (as distinguished from serum and infectious hepatitis); only a minority of alcoholics develop this condition, which is characterized by active inflammation of the liver, cell destruction, and some degree of permanent liver damage. Symptoms include liver swelling, pain, tenderness, nausea, fatigue, fever, and jaundice. A telltale sign of a diseased liver, jaundice is caused by the liver's inability to eliminate dead red blood cells, which leads to a yellowing of the skin and the whites of the eyes.

A sick liver is unable to produce sufficient amounts of proteins and blood-clotting factors, nor can it adequately control levels of cholesterol, fatty acids, and triglycerides. In men, a diseased liver is unable to detoxify female sex hormones; this fact, combined with direct alcohol-related damage to testicular tissue, may result in loss of hair on the chest and upper body, loss of facial hair, enlarged breasts, and shrunken testicles. (Alcoholism is also the second leading cause of impotence in men.) In women, alcoholism disrupts the balance of sex hormones and is a major cause of amenorrhea (loss of normal menstrual cycles).

Because alcohol interferes with the liver's ability to convert glycogen into glucose, prolonged heavy drinking can lead to blood sugar fluctuations, hypoglycemia (low blood sugar), and serious complications of diabetes. The liver also plays an important role in immunity, manufacturing proteins essential for antibody production and a vigorous immune system. As a result, heavy drinkers are more susceptible to viral and bacterial infections, pneumonia, skin diseases such as psoriasis and acne rosacea, cancer, and AIDS.

As liver disease advances, the liver cells, which normally line up in neat rows to allow blood to flow uninterruptedly, randomly clump together. Like boulders clogging up a river, the disorganized cells obstruct the free flow of blood and other body fluids, which can back up into the abdomen and create the classic "beer belly." A swollen, tender abdomen in a heavy drinker is not a symptom of weight gain from drinking too much beer—in all likelihood, a heavy drinker's bloated belly is due to abnormal accumulation of fluid in the abdominal cavity (called ascites), which is a clear sign of alcoholic liver disease. Blood can also back up into the paper-thin veins of the esophagus, leading to a condition called esophageal varices. If the veins burst and the hemorrhage is not stopped immediately, the patient will die.

If the alcoholic continues to drink, more liver cells become inflamed and die, and healthy liver tissue is gradually replaced with fiber and scar tissue; this condition, called alcoholic cirrhosis or Laennec's cirrhosis, is considered the third stage of alcoholic liver disease. Blood flow is dramatically reduced, the blood becomes saturated with toxins, and over time the liver begins to resemble a moonscape: dusty, dry, and incapable of sustaining life. Cirrhosis of the liver occurs in an estimated 8 percent of alcoholics, about seven times as often as in nonalcoholics. An estimated two-thirds of alcoholics with cirrhosis will survive if they stop drinking. If drinking continues, death typically results from liver failure or esophageal hemorrhage.

GASTROINTESTINAL SYSTEM

Alcohol directly irritates and inflames the stomach lining, causing gastritis. Symptoms of gastritis include gas, bloating, heartburn, nausea, headaches, abnormal increase or decrease in appetite, and internal bleeding, which can vary from minimal to significant blood loss. Ironically, the most immediate cure for gastritis is alcohol. Before-and-after photographs show a stomach raw and inflamed after a prolonged drinking bout restored to "normal" after just one or two drinks. The long-term effect of drinking, however, is continued irritation and inflammation of the stomach. The poison is the cure is the poison.

Ulcers are relatively common in early and middle-stage alcoholics. A high tolerance for alcohol leads to excessive consumption, which increases the secretion of hydrochloric acid and can contribute to ulcers. Because of the progressive damage to their livers, late-stage alcoholics have a lower tolerance for alcohol, which leads to reduced hydrochloric acid secretion and fewer problems with ulcers.

PANCREAS

The pancreas secretes digestive enzymes and the hormone insulin, which regulates the body's use of carbohydrates. Heavy, prolonged drinking can cause both acute pancreatitis, with symptoms of severe abdominal pain, vomiting, and fever, and a condition called chronic relapsing pancreatitis. Alcohol is the direct cause of approximately one-third of all pancreatitis cases.

CENTRAL NERVOUS SYSTEM

Alcohol interferes with the supply of oxygen and glucose (blood sugar) to the brain, leading to cell suffocation, cell death, and, in many late-stage alcoholics, brain damage. Oxygen levels are notably diminished even at 0.1 percent blood alcohol concentration (the legal limit for drunkenness). At 0.3 percent blood alcohol concentration (the level where most people would appear obviously drunk, staggering around and slurring their speech), the amount of oxygen reaching the brain cells is decreased by 30 percent; at 0.5 percent blood alcohol concentration (a dangerously high, potentially fatal level), the oxygen available to the brain is diminished by 60 to 80 percent.

Young people's brains are particularly vulnerable to alcohol's toxic effects. A 1998 study by the National Institute of Alcohol Abuse and Alcoholism found that children who begin drinking at age thirteen face a 47 percent risk of becoming an alcoholic during their lifetime. The risk falls to 25 percent for adolescents who start drinking at age seventeen, and 10 percent for those who have their first drink at age twenty-one.

The NIAAA research has profound implications: There are people who will become alcoholics due to drinking at an early age who would not be so afflicted if they postponed alcohol exposure until after the biological and developmental changes that take place during adolescence. In other words, young men and women who may not have a high genetic risk for alcoholism may acquire a susceptibility to addiction based on the interaction between alcohol and their rapidly developing bodies and brains.

This study also reinforces the genetic link to alcoholism: Adolescents with a family history of alcoholism who began drinking at age thirteen have a 60 percent risk of becoming alcoholics compared with a 30 percent risk in those with no family history of the disease. Researchers believe that early drinking, particularly in children genetically predisposed to alcoholism, may cause irreversible changes in the brain leading to a much higher risk of developing alcoholism.

In drinkers of any age, prolonged heavy drinking may result in damage to the cerebral cortex, causing a condition known as alcoholic chronic brain syndrome or alcoholic dementia. Long-lasting deficits may occur in four basic areas of brain functioning: abstract thinking and problem solving, verbal skills and/or memory, fine and gross motor movements, and visiospatial skills. Personality changes associated with brain damage include emotional instability, paranoia, and mood swings.

As alcoholism progresses, the brain's ventricles (hollow spaces) enlarge and the cortex shrinks. Brain shrinkage occurs in women after shorter periods of exposure to alcohol; the most likely reason is differences in the way women metabolize alcohol (see page 16). In elderly drinkers, much smaller amounts of alcohol can lead to cognitive impairments, such as mental confusion, memory loss, and perceptual problems, and difficulties with problem solving. In one study conducted at the University of Maryland, 10 percent of patients over age sixty diagnosed with Alzheimer's disease actually suffer from brain toxicity and/or brain damage due to prolonged heavy drinking. In alcoholic patients the brain begins to clear after two months of abstinence; in patients with Alzheimer's, the brain damage is irreversible.

SUICIDE

Suicide has been described as a permanent solution to a temporary problem. For late-stage alcoholics, whose brain cells cry out day and night for alcohol, suicide may seem like the only solution to a permanent problem. The lifetime risk for death by suicide among alcoholics exceeds 15 percent, while the suicide rate in the general population is less than 1 percent. Because alcohol is a mind-altering drug, anyone who drinks alcohol is at high risk for suicide—as many as 70 percent of men and 40 percent of women who attempt suicide have blood alcohol concentrations exceeding the legal limit. An estimated 40 percent of all alcoholics attempt suicide at least once.

The risk of suicide does not disappear with sobriety; according to one estimate, suicide is also the cause of death for an estimated 25 percent of *treated* alcoholics. The addicted brain requires months and often years of abstinence, nutritional therapy, and tender loving care to recover from the extensive damage caused by chronic alcoholism. When cravings for alcohol return, which they invariably will, often at unexpected times; when the guilt and shame connected with the label "alcoholic" overwhelm the recovering alcoholic's vulnerable defenses; or when depression, anxiety, and fear linger on, suicide may once again seem like the only way out.

Chronic depression and suicidal thoughts are a direct consequence of alcohol's widespread disruption of brain chemistry. Early psychological theories held that alcoholics suffer from severe anxiety and depression that predate and contribute to heavy drinking. But numerous recent studies have shown that this is *not* true for most alcoholics. Although many drinking alcoholics are anxious, depressed, and paranoid, their psychological problems are most likely caused by the toxic effects of alcohol on the brain. In two studies published in 1988 and 1994, researchers reported that in 90 to 95 percent of men and women given general supportive care (but with no specific medications or psychotherapy aimed at the psychological problems), the depression, anxiety, and paranoia disappeared with abstinence.

In *Educating Yourself About Alcohol and Drugs: A People's Primer*, psychiatrist Marc Schuckit summarizes the results of various studies on the psychological symptoms of alcoholics. "The conclusion from all of these studies is basically the same," Schuckit writes. "There is no evidence that people who later go on to develop severe alcohol and drug problems are more likely than others in the general population to have had severe depressions, severe anxiety conditions, or psychotic conditions prior to the development of their alcohol and drug disorders."

To understand why alcohol causes anxiety, depression, paranoia, and general emotional instability, all of which can lead to suicidal tendencies, we need to look once again at the dramatic effects alcohol has on neurotransmitters and other brain chemicals.

- *Serotonin* is a neurotransmitter that promotes feelings of well-being, induces sleep, and reduces aggression and compulsive behavior. A study funded by the National Institute of Mental Health found that serotonin was almost completely depleted in the brains of people who had committed suicide. Chronic alcohol ingestion drains the brain's supply of serotonin by reducing the neurotransmitter's activity at the synapse and accelerating the conversion from its active form to its nonactive form.

- *Dopamine* is a neurotransmitter that increases feelings of well-being, alertness, and sexual excitement and reduces compulsive behavior. Chronic alcohol ingestion reduces the amount of dopamine in the brain by inhibiting dopamine release in the reward center of the brain, and increasing its metabolism, which in turn decreases the supply at the synapse.

• *GABA* is an inhibitory neurotransmitter that reduces anxiety and compulsive behavior, elevates the pain threshold, lowers the heart rate and blood pressure, and reduces the risk of convulsions during withdrawal. Heavy, prolonged drinking modifies the sensitive GABA receptors; when alcohol is withdrawn, the receptors are no longer able to inhibit brain signaling. These disruptions can contribute to strong feelings of anxiety and increase the risk of seizures.

• *Opioid peptides*, including endorphins, enkephalins, and dynorphins, function as natural opiates to balance the emotions, stimulate feelings of well-being, and increase the pain threshold. Chronic alcohol ingestion leads to decreased activity of the natural opioids, alterations in their structure and bonding capabilities, and increased enzyme activity, which reduces their supply.

• *DNA and RNA* are proteins that oversee the construction of amino acids, the building blocks of neurotransmitters and enzymes. Alcohol disrupts the formation of DNA and RNA proteins, which leads to abnormalities and deficiencies in neurotransmitters.

• *Cofactors* allow enzymes to function properly; many vitamins function as cofactors. Chronic alcohol consumption blocks the absorption of numerous vitamins and minerals, leading to widespread nutritional deficiencies. Common vitamin deficiencies in alcoholics include vitamin B_1 (thiamine), vitamin B_6 (pyridoxine), and vitamin C. Vitamin B_1 is necessary for the manufacture of glutamine, an amino acid essential for synthesizing the neurotransmitter GABA. Deficiencies in vitamin B_6, which is needed for the formation of fifty different enzymes, interfere with the conversion of certain amino acids into neurotransmitters. Too-low levels of vitamin C interfere with the conversion of dopamine to its metabolite norepinephrine.

Chronic depression, anxiety, fear, and suicidal thoughts in alcoholics may also be related to alcohol's interference with blood sugar (glucose) regulation. We will talk more about alcohol-induced hypoglycemia in Part II, but here's a quick synopsis: Alcohol and its metabolite acetaldehyde play havoc with the body's intricate and complex blood sugar control system. Continued heavy drinking damages cells and tissues in the liver, pancreas, intestinal tract, adrenal glands, and central nervous system; these are the primary organs responsible for controlling and monitoring blood sugar levels. Low blood sugar levels, common in both drinking and recovering alcoholics, contribute to such distressing symptoms as nervousness, exhaustion, depression, insomnia, anxiety, irritability, phobias, mental confusion, and suicidal tendencies.

Profound disruptions of brain chemistry, neurotransmission, enzymes, hormones, and blood glucose levels combine to make chronic depression and suicidal thoughts a reality for both drinking and recovering alcoholics. Mark, who is coauthor Dr. Arthur Ciaramicoli's patient, is a case in point. At age forty, Mark was diagnosed as an alcoholic and admitted to a detox ward. Although Mark remained abstinent and regularly attended AA meetings, he became increasingly moody, depressed, and suicidal. Dr. Ciaramicoli was convinced that Mark's diet was directly affecting his emotional state—he ate doughnuts or muffins for breakfast, drank six to ten cups of coffee with three sugars in each cup, and relied on fast food, soda pop, and candy snacks to get him through the day—but Mark refused to cut back on his sugar intake. "At least I'm not drinking," Mark kept telling himself.

One day, after almost a year of sobriety, Mark walked into a hospital emergency room, told a nurse he was thinking about killing himself, and asked to be admitted to the psych ward. After he was released from the hospital, Mark was finally willing to look at the effect of his high-sugar diet on his emotional stability and mental state. He cut back drastically on sugar, gradually increased his protein intake, and started exercising regularly. His moods leveled out, the sugar cravings disappeared, and the anxiety and depression eased significantly. (See Chapter 14 for more on the relationship between diet and recovery.)

Mark's story has a happy ending, but many such stories do not. In her book *Seven Weeks to Sobriety*, Joan Mathews Larson describes what happened to her adolescent son, Rob. A typical teenager who loved junk food and liked to party, Rob began to complain of shakiness, mood swings, irritability, emotional instability, sudden fatigue, and mental confusion. Suspecting a blood sugar problem, Larson took her son for a six-hour glucose tolerance test. The results showed that he was seriously hypoglycemic. "At the time, much of his life revolved around ingesting sugars," Larson writes, "particularly alcohol, a sugar that reaches the brain quite rapidly. Drinking gave him energy and made him feel great, and he never followed the doctor's advice to cut down on alcohol, or on colas and sweets."

Rob's mood swings continued, his drinking intensified, and his grades began to drop. The summer before Rob's senior year of high school, his mother enrolled him in a hospital inpatient treatment program for adolescent alcoholics. "The program focused on identifying the underlying psychological reasons for Rob's drinking," Larson writes. "The counselors fixed on his relationship with his father and assumed that Rob's drinking problems stemmed from feelings of guilt—all the things he had or hadn't said to his father in the months before my husband's death."

After completing the inpatient program, Rob was admitted to a halfway house, where he spent the next six months. His mood swings returned, his depression deepened, and in many ways he seemed to be getting worse, not better. Just a few months after he left the halfway house, in the middle of his senior year in high school, Rob walked into his family's garage, shut the door, turned on the car, and lay down under the exhaust pipe. His mother and younger brother found him hours later and rushed him to the hospital. He was declared dead on arrival.

Rob's treatment, which consisted of psychological counseling focusing on his guilt, shame, and emotional instability, may have sealed his doom. His counselors didn't know enough about alcoholism, the process of neurological adaptation and addiction, or hypoglycemia to help him understand how his mood swings were connected to disruptions in his brain chemistry. Because they did not have accurate or sufficient knowledge about the drug or the disease, they could not educate Rob adequately, and he was left with no way of protecting himself against the ongoing anxiety, fear, depression, and craving for alcohol.

In a heartbreaking epilogue to this story, Larson writes, "If I had known then what I know now about the chemical relationship between heavy alcohol use and [hypoglycemia-induced] depression, I might have been able to save my son."

LOSS OF CONTROL

> Of over 100 alcoholics that I queried . . . only three
> percent said they could not quit drinking after one
> drink if other circumstances warranted the discom-
> fort they would suffer.
>
> — WILLIAM MADSEN

"One drink from a drunk," the AA saying goes. That adage is not meant to be taken literally, for alcoholics can and often do exercise amazing control over their drinking. Control is, in fact, an integral part of the disease of alcoholism, and repeated attempts to control drinking are a common symptom of alcoholism. When alcoholics wait until 5 P.M. (or noon or 3 P.M.) to start drinking, they're practicing control. When they quit drinking for a day, a week, or a month, that's control. When they force themselves to stop drinking after only two or three drinks, that's control, and when they choose to drink orange juice instead of champagne at a Mother's Day brunch, that is also control.

Early- and middle-stage alcoholics spend a good part of their drinking careers trying (and often succeeding) to control when, where, how much, and how often they drink. What they lose as the disease progresses is the ability to *consistently* control their drinking. Nonalcoholics do not have difficulty limiting themselves to two or three drinks a day; in fact, most nonalcoholics would agree that two or three drinks is too much booze to handle on a daily basis.

Alcoholics, on the other hand, can control their drinking by limiting themselves to two, three, or four drinks a day, but at some point—and despite their best efforts—they will start to drink more and more often. On Wednesdays and Thursdays Patrick can limit his drinking to a six-pack of beer, but on Fridays he drinks a whole case. Honoring her New Year's resolution, Janet successfully avoids drinking before 5 P.M. for the entire month of January. Then on February 1 (and February 5, February 20, March 1, and so on) she celebrates with a bottle of wine in the afternoon. Dennis stops drinking Sunday night and does not start again until Friday afternoon, when the work week is over; on Saturday and Sunday he downs half a gallon of Scotch. And then, of course, there's the inimitable W. C. Fields, who once said, "Don't say you can't swear off drinking. It's easy—I've done it a hundred times."

Alcoholics are not the only drinkers who try to control their drinking. Social drinkers might feel tempted to have another beer at a party but make a conscious decision to stop, knowing that they have to go to work in the morning. Problem drinkers who have been convicted of drunk driving and know that they will lose their job if they get another citation have a strong incentive to keep their drinking under control; the threat of losing your job is enough to keep most people off the sauce.

The difference is that in alcoholics, trying to control drinking requires intense mental and physical effort; as the disease progresses, the effort involved in control increases. While a social drinker might quit for a month and then have a couple of beers once or twice a week, an alcoholic might quit drinking for a month and then immediately start guzzling five or six drinks every night of the week. A heavy social drinker may drink two or three beers every night and only rarely (say once a month) overindulge by drinking six or seven beers at a party. An alcoholic may drink two or three beers one night, six the next, then ten or fifteen or twenty the next; over the years, the number increases and the days of drinking just "two or three" dwindle. Loss of control in alcoholics has a wild unpredictability about it.

Fully aware of the shame and stigma associated with the label "alcoholic," and terrified of losing control, alcoholics devise many different experiments to prove that they can drink like "normal" people. In *Alcoholics Anonymous* (the "Big Book") Bill Wilson lists some of the ways alcoholics conduct research on themselves. The list is fifty-five years old, but some things never change:

> Here are some of the methods we have tried. Drinking beer only, limiting the number of drinks, never drinking alone, never drinking in the morning, drinking only at home, never having it in the house, never drinking during business hours, drinking only at parties, switching from scotch to brandy, drinking only natural wines, agreeing to resign if ever drunk on the job, taking a trip, not taking a trip, swearing off forever (with and without a solemn oath), taking more physical exercise, reading inspirational books, going to health farms and sanitariums, accepting voluntary commitment to asylums—we could increase the list ad infinitum.

Every alcoholic—and there are no exceptions—has tried at one point or another to drink "normally." They may succeed for a week or a month or even for a few years, only to fail over the long haul. "Controlled-drinking" experiments have been going on for a very long time, with alcoholics placing themselves in the position of both researcher and subject. Only recently have scientists gotten into the act, conducting research studies designed to determine whether alcoholics can, in fact, learn how to drink "like normal people." Here's the basic theory: Since alcoholics can and do control their drinking, it should be possible to teach them how to drink in control all (or most) of the time.

This theory inspired Mark and Linda Sobell, both graduate students at the University of California, Riverside, to embark on a controversial experiment to teach "severe" alcoholics how to drink in moderation. In a study originally released in 1972, the Sobells reported that nineteen of the twenty alcoholic subjects were successfully practicing controlled drinking. Ten years later, in a careful follow-up study conducted by clinical psychologist Mary Pendery and behavioral psychologist Irving Maltzman, it became clear that the experiment was not a "success," as originally claimed. In fact, it was a disastrous failure.

Thirteen of the twenty patients, it turns out, were hospitalized within the first year of the study. Three others drank heavily and experienced alcohol-related problems during the Sobells' two-year follow-up. Three of the four remaining subjects had a record of repeated arrests or drunk driving charges. By 1983 five of the twenty patients (25 percent of the sample) were dead from alcohol-related causes; all were under age forty-two at the time of death. Only one subject continued to drink in "control," and after carefully assessing the patient's medical and social history, Pendery and Maltzman concluded that the patient was probably misdiagnosed as an alcoholic.

Despite the known facts about the genetics, neurophysiology, and biochemistry of alcoholism, some people still insist that alcoholics can be taught how to drink moderately. Philosopher Herbert Fingarette claims that there is no scientific evidence for the existence of physical dependence in the sense of needing or intensely desiring a drink. "In no known respect," Fingarette proclaims, "does a person who experiences the physical symptoms of alcohol dependence require—either subjectively or objectively—a drink of alcohol."

To buttress his point Fingarette offers the case of an alcoholic convicted of drunk driving. While on probation, this individual was able to show up sober for his meetings with probation officers, even while he (in Fingarette's words) "had not curtailed his overall drinking." Fingarette concludes his anecdote with the comment: "This sensible self-control by a diagnosed alcoholic is not an unusual phenomenon."

Indeed, it is not an unusual phenomenon. In fact, as every alcoholism expert knows, one of the telltale symptoms of alcoholism is the attempt to exert "sensible self-control" by cutting down or quitting. To make the leap from the uncontested fact that alcoholics can and do successfully control or curtail their drinking to the notion that alcoholics can be successfully taught to return to social drinking in the community is worse than wishful thinking—it is a dangerous, unsupported theory that if put into practice can destroy people's lives. "If those who advocate that alcoholics return to drink have guessed wrong, an immense amount of suffering and death will be the result," writes William Madsen in *The American Alcoholic*. "If they are wrong, history may look back on their experiments with the same horror with which we today view the U.S. Public Health Service's study which 'induced' 655 syphilitics to go without treatment to 'determine the disease's effect on the human body.' I do not doubt the sincerity of those involved in trying to condition alcoholics to drink socially. I do question their judgment."

Yet despite such cautions, controlled-drinking programs are gaining in popularity even as the scientific evidence supporting the need for total abstinence accumulates. Programs such as DrinkWise and Moderation Management explicitly warn that their strategies are not designed for alcoholics; however, because alcoholism is typically defined in terms of late-stage symptoms, early- and middle-stage alcoholics are often confused with problem drinkers and considered prime candidates for controlled drinking. (The problem is clearly one of diagnosis—how to differentiate between problem drinkers and alcoholics in the early stages of the disease. This is the subject of our next chapter.)

Teaching people how to control their drinking is not inherently a bad idea. Alcohol is a drug, and anyone who drinks is susceptible to the toxic and potentially fatal effects of this drug. Teaching elementary, middle-school, and high-school students about the dangerous effects of the drug alcohol and the health risks associated with excessive drinking or binge drinking is essential. Any talk about "control," however, must acknowledge the differences between nonalcoholics, who are not physically addicted, and alcoholics, whose behavior is governed by a neurological addiction to alcohol.

The mistake controlled-drinking proponents make is to assume that every drinker, alcoholic and nonalcoholic alike, can permanently moderate his or her drinking. To support their theories, Fingarette and other advocates of controlled drinking must ignore decades of thoroughly documented, methodologically sound research studies outlining the genetic, biochemical, neurophysiological nature of alcohol addiction. They must also ignore the fact that virtually all alcoholics try and ultimately fail to control their drinking. Such blind ignorance is forgivable in the untutored but unconscionable in men and women who devote their careers to understanding the disease of alcoholism and conveying their knowledge to the public at large.

For nearly four decades researchers have been trying to prove that alcoholics can drink in control. The end result can be summed up in two words: *They can't.* Given the facts about brain addiction, this should come as no surprise. Alcoholism is not a psychological habit, a sign of collapsed willpower or emotional weakness, or a learned response to psychological, emotional, or physical trauma. Alcoholism is a genetically transmitted neurological disease.

When we understand and accept the truth about alcoholism, we have no choice but to accept the futility of trying to teach an addicted brain how to circumvent its own chemistry. We might as well try to teach a butterfly how to turn back into a caterpillar.

The controversy over controlled drinking points to the need to clearly define the differences between problem drinking (often referred to as "alcohol abuse") and alcoholism. How can you tell when someone is crossing the line from social drinking into problem drinking, or from problem drinking into alcoholism? Are all problem drinkers potential alcoholics? What is the difference between use and excessive use, and when does excessive use become addiction?

Distinguishing between social drinkers, problem drinkers, and alcoholics is critically important. We live in a society where our attitudes about the drug alcohol and the disease of alcoholism are based on black-and-white categories with little appreciation for shades of gray. If we all just drink in moderation, the thinking goes, we won't have any alcohol problems. Social drinkers are praised for their self-control, problem drinkers are considered prime candidates for psychological counseling or "moderation management" courses, and alcoholics are regarded as moral degenerates who "abuse" alcohol with no regard for the consequences to themselves or others.

These stereotypes, based on ignorance and misconception, prevent us from understanding the complexity of the alcohol problems we face in our society. Only when we look at drinking behavior in all its dimensions can we begin to understand why some people drink moderately all their lives while others descend, slowly but surely, into the living hell of alcoholism.

The Social Drinker,
the Problem Drinker,
and the Drunk

I drank for happiness and became unhappy.

I drank for joy and became miserable.

I drank for sociability and became argumentative.

I drank for sophistication and became obnoxious.

I drank for friendship and made enemies.

I drank for sleep and woke up tired.

I drank for strength and felt weak.

I drank for relaxation and got the shakes.

I drank for courage and became afraid.

I drank for confidence and became doubtful.

I drank to make conversation easier and slurred my
speech.

I drank to feel heavenly and ended up feeling like
hell.

— AUTHOR UNKNOWN

A forty-one-year-old bespectacled, balding bachelor whose favorite hobby was flying airplanes, Henri Paul took his job as assistant chief of security at the Ritz Hotel in Paris very seriously. Paul's employers knew they could depend on him; they never suspected he had a drinking problem. "If Mr. Paul had ever betrayed a taste for drink, he would have been summarily fired," said a spokesman for his employer.

At 7:30 P.M. on August 30, 1997, Henri Paul left work after being told he would not be needed again that day. Two hours and twenty-two minutes later, at 9:52 P.M., he was summoned back to the hotel; two and a half hours later, at 12:20 A.M., he got behind the wheel of a Mercedes S-280 sedan with three passengers: Diana, Princess of Wales; her companion, Dodi Fayed; and Fayed's bodyguard, Trevor Rees-Jones.

Fifteen minutes after the Mercedes left the Ritz Hotel, it crashed into a support pillar of a bridge underpass at a speed estimated between 90 and 110 mph. Blood tests revealed that Paul's blood alcohol concentration was 1.75 grams per liter, three times the French legal limit. To reach that level, someone Paul's size would have to drink the rough equivalent of one and a half bottles of wine or nine quick shots of 86 proof whiskey.

The blood tests also revealed that Paul was taking two prescription medications: the antidepressant Prozac and tiapride, a major tranquilizer sold in Europe and often prescribed for alcoholism. His blood alcohol concentration was so high, however, that one physician described these medications as "innocent bystanders."

Henri Paul didn't look or act like an alcoholic. Friends and family members insisted, even as the evidence accumulated, that Paul was a social drinker and not an alcoholic. His employer claimed that if he'd even suspected Paul had a drinking problem, he would have fired him without question. Acquaintances and coworkers told the media that Paul recently had gone on the wagon. Even the impartial Ritz Hotel videotapes showed a smiling middle-aged man looking relaxed, confident, and in perfect control.

The proof, however, was in the blood tests, and they showed that Paul wasn't just tipsy or tight—he was drunk. So then everyone was left to wonder: Was Henri Paul a social drinker who had had too much to drink after a hard day's work and then made a tragic error in judgment by getting behind the wheel? Was he a problem drinker who sometimes drank too much and, under the influence, got himself into difficult situations? Or was he an alcoholic who kept his drinking a secret from virtually everyone who knew him, even family members and intimate friends?

Henri Paul was certainly a social drinker. According to his friends and colleagues, he drank socially in bars, at parties, and in intimate gatherings with friends. He liked to drink champagne, clearly a "social" type of beverage. (A bottle of unopened champagne was found in his refrigerator.) Sometimes, like many social drinkers, he partied without drinking, sipping orange juice or Perrier instead of alcoholic beverages.

Henri Paul was also a problem drinker. A friend told reporters that Paul would sit in the same corner of Willi's Bar most evenings, quietly getting drunk on whiskey. Paul began drinking heavily after a love affair ended, said another friend. Staff members at the Ritz privately told reporters that Paul was well known to have a fondness for the bottle. And after he was called back to work on August 30, Paul had a few drinks in one of the hotel bars, even though it was against hotel rules for employees to drink in the bars.

Henri Paul was also, it seems, an alcoholic. He could drink a lot of alcohol and hide it from everyone, even from himself, for he clearly judged himself capable of getting behind the wheel of the Mercedes. His high blood alcohol concentration at the time of his death, combined with his ability to walk around looking and acting as if he were sober, indicates a high tolerance for alcohol; high tolerance, as discussed on pages 57–59, is a sign of central nervous system adaptation to alcohol. Like many undiagnosed alcoholics, Paul was taking antidepressants for symptoms that were undoubtedly caused or intensified by his drinking. He was also taking a prescription drug widely used in Europe for treating alcoholism.

"His life was a series of watertight compartments," said one of Paul's friends. "Everyone saw a separate bit of him. But nobody saw it all."

Henri Paul's story teaches us an important lesson: You can look and act like a social drinker and be an alcoholic. You can look and act like a problem drinker and be an alcoholic. And you can look and act nothing at all like an alcoholic and be an alcoholic. No one around you will guess the truth unless and until circumstances conspire to place you in a position where you can do harm to yourself or others. Then and only then, in ninety-nine out of a hundred cases, do the rest of us scratch our heads and ask: "Why didn't anybody notice?"

WHO DRINKS ALCOHOL?

One of the most surprising statistics about drinking behavior in this country is that most people either don't drink or drink only occasionally and always in moderate amounts. Researchers who study drinking patterns report that one-third of the adult population in the U.S. completely abstains from drinking alcohol and approximately 55 percent drinks less than three drinks per week. That leaves only 10 to 11 percent of the adult population who can be classified as daily, heavy, or excessive drinkers. Of these drinkers, an even smaller percentage consumes the most alcohol. According to the National Institute on Alcoholism and Alcohol Abuse, 10 percent of all drinkers (those who drink most heavily) drink 50 percent of all the alcohol consumed in this country.

The prevalence of drinking is highest (and abstinence rates are lowest) among men and women between eighteen and twenty-nine years old; young white males, on the whole, drink more than any other group. Alcohol problems among the elderly appear to be increasing. According to data released by the NIAAA in 1998, surveys indicate that 6 to 11 percent of elderly patients admitted to hospitals exhibit symptoms of alcoholism, as do 20 percent of elderly patients in psychiatric wards and 14 percent of elderly patients in emergency rooms. The prevalence of problem drinking in nursing homes is as high as 49 percent in some studies.

While surveys of different age groups indicate that the elderly consume less alcohol and have fewer alcohol-related problems than younger people, it is important to keep in mind that alcoholism and problem drinking have already taken their toll on this population. In Harvard psychiatrist George Vaillant's classic study, summarized in *The Natural History of Alcoholism Revisited,* nearly one-third of the alcoholics were, as Vaillant puts it, "no longer at risk for alcohol abuse because they were dead." Another one-third of the alcoholics elected to give up alcohol completely and were described as "stably abstinent." That's an attrition rate of almost two-thirds.

These statistics reveal an astonishing truth about drinking in the U.S. Contrary to the images that bombard us from television, radio, and magazine advertisements, which imply that everyone (at least everyone who is cool and beautiful) drinks to have fun, most adult Americans either don't drink at all or drink only occasionally and in small amounts. A truthful liquor advertisement would show a beer-guzzling college student throwing up on the front lawn of a fraternity or sorority, a twenty-five-year-old early-stage alcoholic who drinks too much at a dinner meeting and then gets behind the wheel to drive home to the family, or a thirty-year-old mother of three small children guzzling vodka as she changes her baby's diapers. Those are the drinkers who fill up the coffers of the booze merchants so they can spend millions of dollars a year trying to win over new converts to their products. (See Part III for an in-depth discussion of the liquor industry.)

THE SOCIAL DRINKER

> If you need a drink to be social, it's not social drinking.
>
> — NIAAA PUBLIC AWARENESS CAMPAIGN, 1973–74

Travis, thirty-six, is a social drinker. He drinks one, at the most two, glasses of wine a week, and he never drinks more than two drinks in one evening. He enjoys fine wines and buys "splits" or half bottles because he and his wife don't drink enough at one time to justify opening a full bottle. In college Travis got drunk a few times, but that was all it took to convince him that alcohol is a beverage of moderation. He doesn't enjoy the feeling of being intoxicated, and when given a choice, he usually drinks nonalcoholic beverages. Travis can be classified as a light social drinker.

Laurie, forty-seven, is a heavy social drinker. Every night, almost without fail, she drinks two or three 6-ounce glasses of wine. Every Friday night she replaces one of those glasses of wine with a Manhattan containing approximately 2 ounces of 80-proof alcohol. Only rarely, and always on social occasions, does she drink more than her usual amount.

In twenty-five years of drinking, Laurie has had several unpleasant experiences. A few years ago at a fancy dinner party, she drank too much champagne and threw up before she could make it to the bathroom. She sometimes has trouble sleeping and worries that alcohol might be a factor; she read in a magazine that alcohol interferes with REM sleep. She also wonders if alcohol contributes to her infrequent but severe migraine headaches.

Travis and Laurie represent the two extremes of social drinking, which is defined as "asymptomatic" drinking, or drinking without experiencing any serious or recurring problems. While Travis's drinking is clearly social and asymptomatic, Laurie's drinking is more complicated. Although it could certainly be argued that Laurie has experienced problems—sleep disturbances, headaches, occasional drunkenness—she has never suffered from any of the symptoms typically used to assess "problem drinking." Her family and friends have never complained about her drinking, her marriage is solid, she is a loving and attentive mother, she's never had a blackout, and she's never experienced loss of control over her drinking. Because her drinking has not created any serious, recurring problems, Laurie can be classified as a heavy social drinker.

This is not to say that Laurie will always be a heavy social drinker. She may eventually cut down on her drinking, recognizing that even though it doesn't cause any obvious harm, it is definitely not doing her any good; or she may begin to drink more and more often and experience serious physical, emotional, or social problems when she drinks. Because Laurie has no family history of alcoholism and her drinking has not progressed (in fact, she drinks significantly less than she did in her single years), she is probably not at risk for alcoholism.

A PLASTIC CATEGORY

Most people believe (because that's what we've been told) that social drinkers and problem drinkers are two fundamentally different types of people. Social drinkers supposedly are able to control their drinking and thus are relatively invulnerable to problems, while problem drinkers and alcoholics lack self-esteem and self-discipline and thus are prone to problems when they drink.

"Alcoholics and social drinkers are two different kinds of people," writes sociologist Dan Beauchamp, author of *Beyond Alcoholism*. Beauchamp is wrong—and he's right. He's wrong because in the very beginning of their drinking careers, alcoholics and social drinkers are the same kind of people in that they start drinking for exactly the same reasons—to get high, to turn on, to relax, to instill liquid courage, to overcome shyness or fear.

Beauchamp is right, however, in the sense that once an alcoholic starts drinking, something different happens. The alcoholic's brain is hard-wired for addiction; when the brain cells respond to their genetic programming by adapting to alcohol, the addiction process begins. Over a period of several years and sometimes decades, the social drinker is irreversibly transformed into an alcoholic. (For an in-depth discussion of the chemical interactions and neurological adaptations that underlie alcohol addiction, see Chapter 4.)

Unaware of the physiological differences between alcoholics and nonalcoholics, social drinkers tend to turn up their noses at problem drinkers and alcoholics. Travis, the light social drinker we described in the beginning of this section, has been known to swirl the very expensive wine in his glass and question the moral character of his younger cousin, who started drinking at eleven, showed signs of physiological addiction at fourteen, and went into treatment at seventeen. "She's basically a good person," Travis says, "but I will never understand why she can't drink moderately like I do."

Travis, who is protected by an inborn sensitivity to the drug alcohol that makes excessive drinking an unpleasant experience, believes that it all comes down to the decision to drink moderately so the addiction process can't begin. He doesn't understand (and he is certainly not alone in his ignorance) that for most alcoholics the process of becoming an addict is an inborn response to the drug alcohol.

THE PROBLEM DRINKER

Taking a deep breath, we plunge into one of the most complicated and hotly contested areas in the study of the drug alcohol—problem drinking.

It should be simple, right? Problem drinkers experience problems when they drink. But what kinds of problems, exactly, and how many, and how often? How much do you have to drink to cause problems? If a social drinker has a few problems related to drinking, is he or she automatically relegated to the category "problem drinker"? How do you distinguish problem drinkers from alcoholics, since both experience problems when they drink? Is problem drinking simply the midpoint on the continuum between social drinking and alcoholism?

Alcohol researchers agree that problem drinking should be defined not by how much or how often you drink, but by the negative consequences that occur and, more important, recur when you drink. When drinking causes *recurring* problems in your life or in the lives of people around you, you qualify as a problem drinker.

Problem drinking can be assessed in different ways, using criteria that reflect the negative impact of the drug alcohol on family and social life, work or school performance, problems with the legal system, and physical health. In the American Psychiatric Association's 1994 revision of the *Diagnostic and Statistical Manual*, problem drinking is described as "a maladaptive pattern of substance use leading to clinically significant impairment or distress." One or more of the following symptoms occurring within a twelve-month period is sufficient to diagnose problem drinking:

1. Recurrent use of alcohol resulting in problems at work, school, or home, such as child neglect, suspension or expulsion from school, repeated absences from work, deteriorating work performance, and so on

2. Recurrent use in situations that put your life or other people's lives at risk, such as driving a car or operating machinery while under the influence

3. Recurrent legal problems such as drunk driving citations or disorderly conduct arrests

4. Continued drinking despite recurrent interpersonal problems directly caused or intensified by alcohol such as barroom brawls, arguments with friends and family over drinking behavior, and so on

The most important word in the DSM-IV list, included in all four criteria, is *recurrent*. Problem drinking is identified when a "maladaptive pattern" of drinking causes repeated problems at home, on the job, at school, in social situations, and/or with the legal system. The DSM is careful to point out that problem drinkers are not physically dependent on alcohol and do not experience tolerance changes, withdrawal symptoms, and/or periodic loss of control over drinking.

Other so-called problem drinking scales are more specific about the precise nature of the drinker's problems. The Cahalan Scale, which was devised nearly thirty years ago, describes problem drinking largely in terms of social deviance and relies heavily on problems identified by others. The scale (which we have edited slightly for clarity) is scored in the following way: Give yourself one point for each item that describes your drinking. If you experience seven or more of these problems, you are considered a "problem drinker." If one or more of these problems are severe, problem drinking can be diagnosed with fewer than seven symptoms.

CAHALAN SCALE

1. *Frequent intoxication:* five or more drinks once a week; or eight or more drinks on one of the most recent two drinking occasions and twice in the last two months; or twelve or more drinks on one of the last two occasions and twice in the last year; or currently getting high or tight at least once a week

2. *Binge drinking:* being intoxicated for at least several days at one time or for two days or more on more than one occasion

3. *Symptomatic drinking:* more than one of the following: drinking to get rid of a hangover; having difficulty in stopping drinking; blackouts or lapses of memory; skipping meals while on a drinking bout; tossing down drinks for a quicker effect; sneaking drinks; taking quick drinks in advance of a party to make sure you get enough

4. *Psychological dependence:* drinking to alleviate depression or nervousness or to escape from the problems of everyday living, that is, a drink is helpful when you are depressed, tense, or nervous; an important reason for drinking is to forget everything, to help you forget your worries, or to cheer yourself up when you're in a bad mood

5. *Problems with spouse or relatives:* your spouse leaves or threatens to leave, is chronically angry or concerned over your drinking; your spouse or a relative asks you to cut down on your

drinking; you feel your drinking has had a harmful effect on your home life

6. *Problems with friends or neighbors:*   friends or neighbors have suggested you cut down on drinking; you feel that drinking has been harmful to friendships and social life

7. *Job problems:*   you lost or nearly lost a job because of drinking; people at work have suggested that you cut down on drinking; drinking has been harmful to work and employment opportunities

8. *Problems with law, police, accidents:*   trouble with law over driving after drinking; drunkenness; drinking contributed to an accident in which there was a personal injury

9. *Health:*   you feel that drinking is harmful to your health, and your doctor has advised cutting down

10. *Financial problems*

11. *Belligerence:*   you have felt aggressive or cross after drinking; you got into a fight or a heated argument

Harvard psychiatrist George Vaillant designed his Problem Drinking Scale as a sort of hybrid medical-sociological scale to identify problem drinkers and alcoholics; the scale was first published in a scholarly article in 1980. If you experience four or more of the problems identified on this scale, you are considered a problem drinker.

VAILLANT'S PROBLEM-DRINKING SCALE

- Employer complains
- Multiple job losses
- Family/friends complain
- Marital problems
- Medical problems
- Multiple medical problems
- Diagnosis by clinician
- Alcohol-related arrests

- Three or more alcohol-related arrests

- Single hospital, clinic, or AA visit

- Three or more visits to clinics

- Two or more blackouts

- Going on the wagon

- Morning tremulousness/drinking

- Tardiness or sick leave

- Admits problem with control

PROBLEM DRINKING OR ALCOHOLISM?

As useful as these different scales can be in identifying the severity of problems associated with drinking alcohol, confusion sets in when we try to differentiate between problem drinkers and alcoholics in the early or middle stages of the disease. How severe does problem drinking have to be before it crosses the line into alcoholism? Suppose, for example, that you checked off seven of the eleven items on the Cahalan Scale and thus qualify as a "problem drinker." Most experts would consider any combination of seven symptoms on that scale as indicating a problem serious enough to warrant heavy suspicion, if not an outright diagnosis, of alcoholism.

Or take the four most commonly reported symptoms on Vaillant's Problem Drinking Scale: "family/friends complain," "marital problems," "going on the wagon," and "admits problem with control." If you answer yes to these four problems, you would certainly qualify as a problem drinker (particularly if the problems recur), but how do you know that you're not, in truth, an early- or middle-stage alcoholic? "Admits problem with control," for example, corresponds with the "periodic loss of control" criterion described in the DSM-IV for alcohol dependence (that is, alcoholism).

Labeling someone a "problem drinker" based on any of these problem drinking scales may actually divert attention from the proper diagnosis of early- or middle-stage alcoholism. When you label someone a problem drinker, you're implying that with time, therapy, or increased self-control, the problems should go away. Only when the problems stick around year after year does the problem drinker begin to look like a probable candidate for alcoholism. At that point, unfortunately and often tragically, the problems have shredded the very fabric of the alcoholic's life. George Vaillant makes this point when he bemoans the fact that alcoholism is often diagnosed too late: "Conservatively, the average . . . 'alcohol abuser' experienced 15 to 30 times as many alcohol-related problems as the average man . . . who did not abuse alcohol. The pity is still that we diagnose alcoholism too late, not too early."

We believe all three scales—the DSM-IV criteria for "substance abuse," the Cahalan Scale, and Vaillant's Problem Drinking Scale—are useful for detecting problem drinking (as opposed to alcoholism) if the number of problems is set low rather than high. Instead of diagnosing problem drinking from seven yes answers on the Cahalan Scale, for example, we believe that two or three yes answers are sufficient to indicate problem drinking. On Vaillant's scale, two or three recurring problems would be enough to diagnose problem drinking.

A problem drinker is not simply a social drinker who drinks too much at a wedding reception, trips on a table, and breaks her leg, never to repeat the episode. A problem drinker has recurring problems when he or she drinks.

- If a high-school student regularly skips classes in order to join his older brother and friends for an early afternoon beer (or two), that's problem drinking.

- If a college student never drinks during the week but gets drunk every Saturday and spends every Sunday sick as a dog, that's problem drinking.

- If a thirty-year-old joins his friends after work every day for a few beers, ignoring his family obligations and inevitably upsetting his wife, that's problem drinking.

- If a forty-year-old continues to drink straight whiskey at his Friday night poker party despite the serious gastrointestinal distress he inevitably experiences the next morning, that's problem drinking.

- If a fifty-year-old gets belligerent and fights with her husband every time she drinks, even though she only drinks once a week, that's problem drinking.

- If a sixty-year-old continues to enjoy her evening routine of two gin and tonics, even after her doctor warns her of potentially adverse interactions between alcohol and her prescription medications, that's problem drinking.

As a society, we're under the misconception (born and bred by the liquor industry) that "just a few" won't hurt anyone, that if you restrict yourself to one or two drinks, you're drinking "responsibly," and that if you don't drink every day, you can't possibly be a "problem drinker." In truth, it isn't how often you drink or even how much you drink that determines whether or not you're a problem drinker. What matters is what happens to you when you drink. If you keep having the same problems when you drink, even if it's only once or twice a month, you're a problem drinker.

THE "TYPICAL" PROBLEM DRINKER

"The modal [average] 'problem drinker' is aged 25 to 35 and is married and working," writes George Vaillant in *The Natural History of Alcoholism Revisited*. "He (or she) has never been treated for alcoholism; and his use is markedly responsive to environmental factors and can, over time, become either more or less symptomatic."

The great majority of problem drinkers are teenagers and young adults in their twenties and early thirties. A 1995 study, "Binge Drinking on American College Campuses," conducted by the Harvard University School of Public Health shows how serious and widespread problem drinking is among college students. From a random sample of nearly eighteen thousand students at 140 American colleges located in forty states and the District of Columbia, the researchers report the following statistics:

- Eighty-four percent of students drank during the school year surveyed.

- Nearly half (44 percent) of all students could be classified as binge drinkers. Binge drinking is defined as five or more drinks in a row one or more times during a two-week period for men, and four or more drinks during the same period for women.

- Nineteen percent were frequent binge drinkers, bingeing three or more times in the previous two weeks.

- Forty-seven percent of the frequent binge drinkers experienced five or more different problems as a result of their drinking.

- Fourteen percent of binge drinkers (compared to only 3 percent of students who drank but didn't binge) experienced five or more drinking-related problems.

Problems Caused by Drinking

	Non–binge drinkers	Bingers	Frequent Bingers
Had a hangover	39%	75%	90%
Did something they regretted later	14%	37%	63%
Missed a class	8%	30%	61%
Forgot where they were or what they did	8%	26%	54%
Got behind in schoolwork	6%	21%	46%
Argued with friends	8%	22%	42%
Engaged in unplanned sexual activity	8%	20%	41%
Had unprotected sex	4%	10%	22%
Got hurt or injured	2%	9%	23%
Damaged property	2%	8%	22%
Got into trouble with campus/ local police	1%	4%	11%
Required treatment for alcohol overdose	<1%	<1%	1%

The researchers also make the important point that problem drinking is not just a problem for the drinker. Approximately 75 percent of students surveyed had experienced one or more problems as the result of *other* students' drinking. These secondhand binge effects include being insulted or humiliated; getting into a serious argument or quarrel; being pushed, hit, or assaulted; having their sleep or studying interrupted; having to baby-sit a drunken student; and damage to personal property. Women faced two additional problems: unwanted sexual advances and sexual assault (date rape).

Given the number of problems they experienced and the overall negative impact of binge drinking, the most shocking statistic of all is that 91 percent of the women and 78 percent of the men who were frequent bingers considered themselves to be moderate or light drinkers and perceived their drinking to be within acceptable limits.

A 1998 report by the CORE Institute at Southern Illinois University at Carbondale based on surveys from 89,874 students confirms the ongoing problem of binge drinking on our college campuses:

- Forty-three percent of students report that they experienced various forms of violence in the previous year, including threats of violence, actual physical violence, theft involving force or threat of force, forced sexual touching, unwanted intercourse, and ethnic or racial harassment. A high percentage of students were under the influence of alcohol or other drugs during these episodes, especially in incidents of unwanted sexual intercourse (79 percent), forced sexual touching (71 percent), actual physical violence (64 percent), and threats of physical violence (51 percent).

- Students who engaged in binge drinking were three and a half times more likely to endure unwanted sexual intercourse than non-bingers and more than twice as likely to have experienced forced sexual touching.

- Half the students (49 percent) reported that alcohol and drug use by fellow students interfered with the quality of life on campus by interrupting studying (29 percent), "messing up" their space (25 percent), making them feel unsafe (22 percent), preventing enjoyment of events (19 percent), and adversely affecting group activities (12 percent).

Despite the high percentage of students who experienced problems as a result of other people's drinking, the majority of students surveyed insist that alcohol has an overall beneficial effect on their college experience:

- Two-thirds of the students claim that alcohol breaks the ice, enhances social activity, and gives people something to do.

- Fifty percent believe alcohol contributes to having fun, facilitates male bonding, and enhances connections with peers.

- Fifty-seven percent of males and 41 percent of females believe that drinking facilitates sexual opportunities.

Reflecting on these sobering statistics, you cannot help but wonder what happens to these young men and women as they continue on their way through life. Do most of them continue to experience problems when they drink? Is problem drinking in college an accurate predictor of alcohol-related problems later in life?

The surprising answer to these questions is no. In one study involving a twenty-year follow-up of college students, researchers found that only 20 percent of fifty students identified as serious problem drinkers in college still had problems twenty years later. And in George Vaillant's landmark prospective study, which followed 660 men over a fifty-two-year period (from 1940 to 1992), heavy college drinking turned out to be a relatively poor predictor of problem drinking later in life.

The point is—and we cannot overemphasize its importance—problem drinking can change dramatically over time. Many people in their teens, twenties, and thirties who are classified as problem drinkers eventually cut back on their drinking or stop drinking altogether. A large majority of those who continue to drink and experience recurring problems into their twenties, thirties, and forties are not, in all likelihood, problem drinkers—they are alcoholics.

Time will tell, then, whether people who experience recurring problems when they drink are nonaddicted problem drinkers or alcoholics in the early or middle stages of the disease. But we don't have to wait to diagnose alcoholism until problem drinkers reach middle age and experience so many problems that their careers, marriages, emotional stability, and physical health are threatened. As we explained in previous chapters, alcoholism is a progressive disease that begins with subtle, unremarkable, seemingly benign symptoms such as increased tolerance for alcohol, intense pleasure associated with drinking, lower sensitivity to alcohol, and preoccupation with drinking. While these early-stage symptoms are rarely recognized as evidence of alcoholism, they offer the careful observer a clear picture of what the future holds.

If you experience recurring problems when you drink and answer yes to *any* of the questions below, you should consider yourself at high risk for alcoholism:

• Do you have a family history (parents, grandparents, aunts, uncles, brothers, sisters) of alcoholism?

• Do you have a high tolerance for alcohol, meaning that you can drink more than most people and still function normally?

• Are you preoccupied with alcohol, looking forward with great anticipation to drinking occasions, keeping a considerable supply of alcohol in your home, and/or feeling uncomfortable about social events that don't involve alcohol?

• Have you experienced a change in your drinking patterns over a period of several years? Do you drink faster, gulping down your first drinks? Do you drink more, and more often? Do you periodically try to quit or cut down on your drinking?

THE MYTHS AND REALITIES OF PROBLEM DRINKING

Myth: Problem drinking is defined by how much you drink.

Reality: Problem drinking is determined by the problems you experience when you drink.

Myth: "Responsible" drinkers don't have problems with alcohol.

Reality: Many "responsible" drinkers experience problems when they drink. Alcohol is a drug that affects different people in different ways. Even "just a few" can cause serious problems for certain drinkers.

Myth: Problem drinking is somewhere on the midpoint of the continuum between social drinking and alcoholism.

Reality: Problem drinking can change over time. Many problem drinkers revert to social drinking when they realize the negative effect of alcohol on their lives; others continue to drink and experience problems but are not physically dependent on alcohol; and still others are not problem drinkers at all but early- or middle-stage alcoholics.

Myth: Problem drinkers and alcoholics are the same thing—it is just a matter of degree.

Reality: While it's true that most (if not all) alcoholics can also be described as problem drinkers, not all (or even, perhaps, most) problem drinkers are alcoholics.

THE DRUNK

Hundreds of thousands of alcoholics look and act just like social drinkers or problem drinkers. Nobody suspects they are alcoholics because the word *alcoholic* brings to mind images of lurching, drooling, rheumy-eyed, slurring, stubble-faced winos with brown paper bags in hand, panhandling on a city street or sleeping it off in some dark alleyway.

Most people, for example, would have described journalist Caroline Knapp as a social drinker. A heavy social drinker? Sure. Problem drinker? Nah. Alcoholic? No way! Yet Knapp is, in fact, an alcoholic. In *Drinking: A Love Story* Knapp describes the striking discrepancy between the appearance and the reality of the "high-functioning" drunk:

> *The fact is, nobody would have known from looking. An outsider walking past my cubicle that morning would have seen a petite woman of thirty-four with long, light brown hair pulled back in a barrette, neat and orderly-looking. . . . Colleagues saw me as smart and introspective, a little reserved maybe, and a paragon of efficiency at work: organized, professional, productive. . . .*
>
> *I wrote a book during my last, most active year of alcoholism. I wrote several award-winning columns. I spent my days in a bustle of focused, highly concentrated activity—editing stories, working with designers, meeting with writers and editors—and only a very particular sort of person (probably another alcoholic) could have peered into that cubicle and realized that, in fact, I was clicking away at my computer with a pounding hangover, or sitting there at the end of the day, my body screaming for a drink. . . .*
>
> *Perception versus reality. Outside versus inside. I never missed a day of work because of drinking, never called in sick, never called it quits and went home early because of a hangover. But inside I was falling apart.*

When Knapp got loaded, she did it "quietly, politely." She knew she was drinking too much, but she told herself that a "real alcoholic" would be drinking in the morning (which she never did), or be so hung over that she'd miss work (which she never did), or get fired (which she never was). Knapp would look at the tiny burst blood vessels on her nose and cheeks and think she'd just gotten too much sun, even though her sister, a physician, suspected they were alcohol-related and told her so. She would go to a party and solemnly swear to herself that she would stop after three or four glasses of wine; a few hours later, after five, seven, or ten glasses of wine, she'd be smashed. Lying in bed on a Saturday morning with a jackhammer headache, she would try to remember what she had said or done the night before and pray that she hadn't embarrassed herself or hurt someone else.

Some days she would wake up in the morning still drunk. She hid a bottle of brandy behind an old refrigerator on the back porch of her boyfriend's apartment, kept a bottle of Old Grand-Dad in the bathroom of her parents' house, and stashed a fifth of Dewar's in her purse. On her way to work she sometimes got the dry heaves. A noticeable tremor in her hands lasted for days. She worried about her drinking, but always there was comfort to be found in that image of the "real" alcoholic, like the woman at Knapp's favorite Boston bar who would drink gin and watch TV until closing:

> *She was a very reassuring presence to me, this strange woman at the Aku, so obviously a drunk. When a group of us sat at a table near her barstool, we'd glance over at her once in a while and whistle softly:* What a life, huh? *She was far worse than my friend Elaine and far, far worse than me, and so she was very helpful to me for a very long time, symbolizing not what I feared I might become but what, for the moment, I wasn't. My drinking was so social by comparison, so normal. Wasn't it?*

When a high-functioning middle-stage alcoholic looks at the sad antics and desperate cravings of a late-stage alcoholic, the difference between the two drinkers can be so pronounced that even a casual observer would insist there is no comparison. But as the disease progresses and the brain addiction tightens its grip, the persistent protest that "I can't be an alcoholic because they're all far worse than I am" becomes increasingly difficult to maintain.

In *A Monk Swimming* the Irish actor and writer Malachy McCourt ends his own story of alcoholic drinking with a sad tale of his alcoholic father's reunion with his family after a twenty-five-year separation. Hoping his father would now be sober and contrite, McCourt went to greet him when his ship arrived in New York City after the long trip from Belfast. Too drunk to walk, the old man was carried off the boat; he had spent most of the trip in leg irons, the captain told McCourt, definitely a nuisance to all aboard.

A few weeks later McCourt dragged his father to an AA meeting. The speaker that night told a horrifying story about his descent into the hell of alcoholism and the final night of his drinking career, when he swigged kerosene. Father turned to son at that point and said, "Ah, I'm not an alcoholic. I don't drink kerosene."

The power of a neurological addiction is such that it blinds even the late-stage drunk to its inexorable progression, making willing partners of its ill-fated victims. Putting an end to this deadly march before it destroys the alcoholic's body, mind, and spirit is the story we will tell in Part II.

PART II

The Solution

8

Am I an
Alcoholic?

Formula for longevity: Have a chronic disease and
take care of it.

— OLIVER WENDELL HOLMES

When you experience a crushing pain in your chest, you go to your doctor, who puts you through a series of tests and then, with a reliable degree of certainty, tells you whether you had a heart attack or a bad case of indigestion. When you have difficulty breathing accompanied by a high fever and exhaustion, you don't sit around in bed thinking nothing is wrong with you—you go to the doctor, who probes and pokes at your vital organs, sends you to the lab for blood work, and then offers you a firm diagnosis and several prescriptions. If you are experiencing serious gastrointestinal distress that lasts for weeks on end, your doctor uses scopes and probes to look inside you and figure out what is wrong.

The addicted brain does not reveal its secrets so readily. Scientists have not yet figured out how to design a test that will positively identify neurological addiction to alcohol or other drugs. (Someday, without a doubt, they will.) While certain laboratory profiles are indicative of alcoholism, even the most highly sensitive tests cannot detect the disease in its early stages. In the liver, for example, fully one-third of the cells must be damaged before a liver function test shows up as abnormal. Thus, the symptoms and signs of alcoholism (see lists on pages 124–31) are often missed or misdiagnosed.

The sad truth is that you cannot diagnose alcoholism unless you recognize it, and few people are knowledgeable enough about brain addiction and the early stages of neurological adaptation to alcohol to recognize alcoholism in its early and middle stages. We all know what the late-stage drunk looks like; even a ten-year-old child can diagnose alcoholism at that stage. Early- and middle-stage alcoholics, however, go unrecognized and untreated, or they are mistakenly diagnosed as "problem drinkers" and advised to cut down on their drinking.

At this very moment, hundreds of thousands of early- and middle-stage alcoholics are carrying on their daily business as if nothing were wrong with them. Because of the stigma associated with the label "alcoholic," the fact that the disease affects logic and reasoning capabilities, and the prevailing confusion about early-stage symptoms, these "high-functioning" alcoholics will continue to drink, and their addiction will become more firmly entrenched.

Diagnosing alcoholism is still, unfortunately, more of an art than a science—although, as we have explained, there is plenty of science to support the fact that alcoholism is a progressive neurological disease with widespread effects on all vital organs and systems. The "art" of diagnosis rests in the ability to discern through the drinker's symptoms—psychological, behavioral, spiritual, and (the least important in the early stages) physical—whether or not the brain is addicted to the drug.

We can recognize the disease, in other words, by its effects on the drinker's life, and the way we find out about its negative impact is to ask questions. Studies show that paper-and-pencil tests are much more consistent and accurate than even the most sophisticated lab tests available. A laboratory test is likely to diagnose alcoholism in approximately 50 percent of alcoholics who have advanced into the later stages of the disease; simple questionnaires can diagnose 80 to 90 percent of alcoholics even in the early stages of the disease.

In this chapter we include five questionnaires commonly used to diagnose alcoholism. Why so many? Each test is slightly different; by including several, the reader will learn a great deal about the nature and progression of the disease. That is the purpose of these tests: to inform, not to frighten or intimidate, and certainly not to pass judgment on your drinking behavior. Designed by experts, these yes-or-no tests focus on the psychological, behavioral, spiritual, and physical problems created by alcohol. In each test you will learn a little more about alcoholism and the potentially devastating effect of alcohol on your life.

THE NATIONAL COUNCIL ON ALCOHOLISM AND DRUG DEPENDENCE (NCADD) QUESTIONNAIRE

The following 10 questions are part of a 26-question self-test designed by the National Council on Alcoholism, the first nationwide volunteer agency in the field of alcoholism. Answer the questions with yes or no; if your answer is sometimes (and this applies to all the questionnaires in this chapter), put down yes. Be sure to answer all the questions before you look at the explanation that follows.

1. Can you handle more alcohol now than when you first started to drink?

2. Do you sometimes feel a little guilty about your drinking?

3. Has a family member or close friend ever expressed concern or complained about your drinking?

4. Do you often want to continue drinking after your friends say they've had enough?

5. Have you tried switching brands or drinks, or following different plans to control your drinking?

6. Have you ever had a DWI (driving while intoxicated) or DUI (driving under the influence of alcohol) violation, or any other legal problem related to your drinking?

7. Are you having more financial, work, school, and/or family problems as a result of your drinking?

8. Have you recently noticed that you can't drink as much as you used to?

9. Do you ever feel depressed or anxious before, during, or after periods of heavy drinking?

10. Have any of your blood relatives ever had a problem with alcohol?

Scoring: According to the NCADD, any yes answer indicates you may be at greater risk for alcoholism. More than one yes answer may indicate the presence of an alcohol-related problem or alcoholism, and the need for consultation with an alcoholism professional.

THE JOHNS HOPKINS UNIVERSITY DRINKING SCALE

Another questionnaire that many experts consider an effective tool for diagnosing alcoholism, even in its early and middle stages, is the Johns Hopkins University Drinking Scale.

Ask yourself the following questions and answer them as honestly as you can:

1. Do you lose time from work due to drinking?

2. Is drinking making your home life unhappy?

3. Do you drink because you are shy with other people?

4. Is drinking affecting your reputation?

5. Have you ever felt remorse after drinking?

6. Have you gotten into financial difficulties as a result of your drinking?

7. Do you turn to lower companions and an inferior environment when drinking?

8. Does your drinking make you careless of your family's welfare?

9. Has your ambition decreased since drinking?

10. Do you crave a drink at a definite time daily?

11. Do you want a drink the next morning?

12. Does your drinking cause you to have difficulties in sleeping?

13. Has your efficiency decreased since drinking?

14. Is your drinking jeopardizing your job or business?

15. Do you drink to escape from worries or troubles?

16. Do you drink alone?

17. Have you ever had a complete loss of memory?

18. Has your physician ever treated you for drinking?

19. Do you drink to build your self-confidence?

20. Have you ever been in a hospital or institution on account of drinking?

Scoring: Three yes answers indicates a probable drinking problem, according to the designers of this scale. Four to seven yes answers indicates early-stage alcoholism; seven to ten yes answers indicates middle-stage alcoholism; and more than ten yes answers indicates late-stage alcoholism.

MICHIGAN ALCOHOLISM SCREENING TEST (MAST)

Perhaps the most widely used screening test for detecting alcoholism is the Michigan Alcoholism Screening Test (MAST), designed in 1971 by psychiatrist M. L. Selzer. The MAST is considered a self-screening test but is often used by physicians, psychologists, psychiatrists, and alcoholism treatment professionals in diagnosing alcoholism.

1. Do you feel you are a normal drinker? (By "normal," we mean you drink less than or as much as most other people.)

   (No, 2 points)

2. Have you ever awakened the morning after some drinking the night before and found that you could not remember a part of the evening?

   (Yes, 2 points)

3. Does your wife, husband, parent, or other near relative ever worry or complain about your drinking?

   (Yes, 1 point)

4. Can you stop drinking without a struggle after one or two drinks?

   (No, 2 points)

5. Do you ever feel guilty about your drinking?

   (Yes, 1 point)

6. Do friends or relatives think you are a normal drinker?

   (No, 2 points)

7. Are you able to stop drinking when you want to?

   (No, 2 points)

8. Have you ever attended a meeting of Alcoholics Anonymous?

   (Yes, 5 points)

9. Have you ever gotten into physical fights when drinking?

(Yes, 1 point)

10. Has drinking ever created problems between you and your wife, husband, parent, or other near relative?

(Yes, 2 points)

11. Has your wife, husband, parent, or other near relative ever gone to anyone for help about your drinking?

(Yes, 2 points)

12. Have you ever lost friends, girlfriends, or boyfriends because of your drinking?

(Yes, 2 points)

13. Have you ever got into trouble at work because of your drinking?

(Yes, 2 points)

14. Have you ever lost a job because of drinking?

(Yes, 2 points)

15. Have you ever neglected your obligations, your family, or your work for two or more days in a row because you were drinking?

(Yes, 2 points)

16. Do you drink before noon fairly often?

(Yes, 1 point)

17. Have you ever been told you have liver trouble? Cirrhosis?

(Yes, 2 points)

18. After heavy drinking, have you ever had delirium tremens (DTs) or severe shaking, or heard voices or seen things that weren't really there?

(Yes, 2 points)

19.   Have you ever gone to anyone for help about your drinking?

(Yes, 5 points)

20.   Have you ever been in a hospital because of drinking?

(Yes, 5 points)

21.   Have you ever been a patient in a psychiatric hospital or on a psychiatric ward of a general hospital where drinking was part of the problem that resulted in hospitalization?

(Yes, 2 points)

22.   Have you ever been at a psychiatric or mental health clinic or gone to any doctor, social worker, or clergyman for help with any emotional problem, where drinking was part of the problem?

(Yes, 2 points)

23.   Have you ever been arrested for drunken driving, driving while intoxicated, or driving under the influence of alcoholic beverages?

(Yes, 2 points)

24.   Have you ever been arrested, even for a few hours, because of other drunken behavior?

(Yes, 2 points)

Scoring: Add up the points from your answers. A total score of 0–3 points indicates no alcoholism; 4 points is suggestive of alcoholism (except for a positive response to questions 8, 19, or 20, which are considered sufficient by themselves to diagnose alcoholism); and 5 points or more indicates alcoholism. The authors of the MAST admit that this scoring system is "sensitive," meaning that it may produce a fairly high number of false positives—nonalcoholics who score in the alcoholic range. To screen out false positives, the scoring system can be adjusted to 0–4 points for no alcoholism; 5 or 6 points as suggestive of alcoholism; and 7 or more points as indicating alcoholism.

SHORT MICHIGAN ALCOHOLISM SCREENING TEST—(SMAST)

The longer, more detailed questionnaires are valuable because they educate the person taking the tests about the progressive symptoms of the disease. Short screening tests, however, are often extremely accurate at identifying alcoholism. The Short Michigan Alcoholism Screening Test (SMAST) consists of questions 1, 3, 5, 6, 7, 8, 10, 13, 15, 19, 20, 23, and 24 on the MAST.

The reliability of the thirteen-item SMAST is almost as high as the twenty-four-item MAST. A total score of 0 or 1 points on the SMAST indicates no alcoholism; 2 points, possible alcoholism; and 3 or more points, alcoholism. Once again, questions 8, 19, and 20 are considered diagnostic.

MICHIGAN ALCOHOL SCREENING TEST— GERIATRIC VERSION (MAST-G)

Questionnaires used to screen for alcoholism are often inappropriate for the elderly, who frequently do not experience the social, legal, and occupational problems that are commonly used to diagnose the disease in younger drinkers. Alcohol-related consequences of heavy drinking such as depression, insomnia, poor nutrition, congestive heart failure, and frequent falls are often mistakenly diagnosed as the primary medical or psychiatric condition and treated with drugs or psychological counseling. The average person older than sixty-five takes between two and seven prescription drugs daily; when mixed with alcohol, the risk of serious drug interactions is high.

For these reasons, alcoholism experts have devised the MAST-G, a questionnaire specifically designed to diagnose alcohol-related problems in the elderly population.

1. After drinking have you ever noticed an increase in your heart rate or beating in your chest?

2. When talking with others, do you ever underestimate how much you actually drink?

3. Does alcohol make you sleepy so that you often fall asleep in your chair?

4. After a few drinks, have you sometimes not eaten, or been able to skip a meal, because you didn't feel hungry?

5.   Does having a few drinks help decrease your shakiness or tremors?

6.   Does alcohol sometimes make it hard for you to remember parts of the day or night?

7.   Do you have rules for yourself that you won't drink before a certain time of the day?

8.   Have you lost interest in hobbies or activities you used to enjoy?

9.   When you wake up in the morning, do you ever have trouble remembering part of the night before?

10.   Does a drink help you sleep?

11.   Do you hide your alcohol bottles from family members?

12.   After a social gathering, have you ever felt embarrassed because you drank too much?

13.   Have you ever been concerned that drinking might be harmful to your health?

14.   Do you like to end an evening with a night cap?

15.   Did you find your drinking increased after someone close to you died?

16.   In general, would you prefer to have a few drinks at home rather than go out to social events?

17.   Are you drinking more now than in the past?

18.   Do you usually take a drink to relax or calm your nerves?

19.   Do you drink to take your mind off your problems?

20.   Have you ever increased your drinking after experiencing a loss in your life?

21.   Do you sometimes drive when you have had too much to drink?

22.   Has a doctor or nurse ever said they were worried or concerned about your drinking?

23.   Have you ever made rules to manage your drinking?

24.   When you feel lonely does having a drink help?

Scoring: Five or more yes responses is considered indicative of alcohol problems.

THE CAGE QUESTIONNAIRE

The CAGE questionnaire, designed by John Ewing, M.D., is a simpler test used by many health care practitioners to make a quick assessment of their patients' drinking problems.

CAGE

• Have you ever tried to Cut down on your drinking?

• Do you get Angry when people discuss your drinking?

• Do you feel Guilty about things you have done while drinking?

• Do you ever have an Eye-opener (that is, do you ever take a drink to get rid of a hangover or to start the day)?

The questionnaires in this chapter are extremely useful in determining whether or not you have a drinking problem. A questionnaire as simple and straightforward as the CAGE, for example, correctly identifies more than 85 percent of people with alcohol problems. If a four-question test can identify four out of five people with a drinking problem, why do alcoholics continue to cycle in and out of doctors' offices and hospital emergency rooms without ever being identified as alcoholics?

In a landmark study conducted at Seattle's Harborview Medical Center (see pages 280–281 for more details on this study), researchers discovered that half of patients admitted to the emergency room had alcohol in their bloodstream, and nearly one-third were intoxicated on admission. Of the acutely intoxicated patients, 75 percent were chronic alcoholics. Yet in the great majority of emergency-room admissions, the researchers point out, no alcohol screening is conducted on patients. They are simply treated and released in the proverbial revolving door of alcoholism.

A big part of the problem, of course, is denial. The addicted brain, unlike the diseased heart, the inflamed stomach, or the infected lungs, is instrumental in its own downfall. That's because the drug responsible for creating neurological addiction is also the substance that relieves the pain associated with addiction. The poison is the antidote, for the addicted neurons actually need the drug to function. Alcohol makes the brain cells feel good, not bad, and this is particularly true in the early and middle stages of the disease. Thus the brain follows what seems to be the pathway of good health and smart living—avoiding pain whenever possible.

The denial system created by the addicted brain to protect its access to alcohol is not invulnerable, but it is incredibly stubborn. In *Introduction to Alcoholism Counseling*, psychiatrist Jerome Levin recalls a patient who was finally able to recognize the death-dealing consequences of addiction after more than twenty hospitalizations:

> He told me how de-humanized he felt when he was first restrained during DTs. But he went on to say, "You know it was funny, Doctor, after a while I looked forward to being put into a straitjacket on the 'flight deck' [AA slang for closed psychiatric ward]. When the cops brought me in they all knew me. An aide would say, "Shit, Jack, you back again? You better get in the jacket before you get too bad like you always do," and I would feel kind of warm and safe and secure when they laced me in.

For this late-stage alcoholic, and for many other alcoholics in earlier stages of the disease, recovery begins with a gradual and often grudging acceptance of reality. Every time Jack got strapped into the straitjacket he felt safe and warm. The cops knew him and cared for him, and the hospital staff was kind to him. After more than twenty such experiences, he was finally ready to admit that life might be better without the booze. What if someone—a police officer, a doctor or nurse, his insurance company or managed-care provider—had given up on Jack after his fifth hospitalization or even after his fifteenth? Is there ever a good place or a good reason to give up on an alcoholic? Knowing the nature of the addicted brain, there can be only one answer to that question. Never.

Other questions require more complicated answers. If an alcoholic progresses into late-stage alcoholism before he or she is finally diagnosed, whose fault is that? Where were the missed opportunities, and who will take responsibility for the damage incurred by the disease— economic, social, legal, and health costs that must be borne by all of us, not just alcoholics and their families? If a simple yes-or-no test can diagnose this devastating disease in its early stages, why do the great majority of alcoholics escape detection? Where, exactly, does the fault lie? And who will remedy it?

THE PHYSICIAN'S ROLE
IN DIAGNOSIS

Because early- and middle-stage alcoholics cycle in and out of doctors' offices with alcohol-related complaints such as gastritis, ulcers, broken bones, impotence, depression, anxiety, and insomnia, primary-care physicians are in an ideal position to diagnose the disease in its early stages. Relatives, friends, and employers can also diagnose alcoholism (as long as they know what to look for), but physicians have the credentials needed to impress the patient with the gravity of the situation and the emotional distance needed to cut through the alcoholic's denial.

In order to accurately diagnose alcoholism, however, physicians must be properly educated about the nature of addictive disease. The sad truth is that most physicians lack adequate training and knowledge about alcoholism, and many have not escaped the common prejudices, born of ignorance and misconception, against alcoholics. To further complicate matters, an estimated 10 percent of physicians in this country are drinking alcoholics themselves. (Many experts believe the number is much higher.) It is highly unlikely that these addicted doctors will accurately diagnose a drinking problem in their patients when they cannot recognize one in themselves.

And so it is that more than half the alcoholics seen by physicians go undiagnosed. Doctors, like the rest of us, are accustomed to thinking about alcoholism in terms of its later stages. If physicians are looking for a red-nosed drunk with liver disease, a string of arrests and hospitalizations, financial difficulties, family problems, and obvious mental confusion, they're going to overlook nine out of ten alcoholics who walk into their offices.

Even if doctors recognize the fact that alcoholism is progressive and begins with relatively benign and unremarkable symptoms, they will miss the diagnosis if they get diverted by the "psychological" symptoms of depression, anxiety, and irritability. Treating these symptoms as primary rather than secondary to the disease of alcoholism creates all kinds of additional problems, particularly when sedative or tranquilizing drugs are used. Any drug that affects the central nervous system will accelerate the addiction process, leading to cross-tolerance (the need for higher doses of the new drug to achieve the desired effect) and cross-addiction (rapid or immediate physical dependence on the new drug).

Asking the suspected alcoholic how much he or she drinks isn't going to work because the alcoholic will deny any problems; denial, as we discussed on pages 66–69, is a telltale symptom of an addicted brain. Experts agree that alcoholics consistently underreport their drinking by about 50 percent. Thus, if Joe tells his doctor that he drinks, at most, "four or five" beers a night, in all likelihood he's drinking twice that much. Alcoholics don't deny they have a drinking problem because they're lying, deceitful, self-destructive cowards or louts; they hide the truth because their addicted brains are working hard to make sure the alcohol supply keeps flowing without interruption. When doctors ask alcoholics how much they drink, the addicted brain quickly sniffs out the threat hidden in the question and offers all sorts of lies and prevarications to obscure the truth.

Diagnosing early- and middle-stage alcoholism requires accurate knowledge about the addicted brain and the skill, developed through wisdom and experience, to see through the alcoholic's denial. As George Vaillant writes:

> To overcome their own myopia and the alcoholic's denial both relative and clinician must learn to conceive of alcoholism as a disease that *causes* depression, marital breakup, and unemployment, not as a symptom that *results from* such distressing events. In other words, to decide if a person is drinking alcoholically, the clinician should ask diagnostic questions of the form, "Was your use of alcohol one of the reasons your wife left you?" rather than merely accepting the patient's explanation, "I did not drink really heavily until my wife ran off with another man."

To assist in the diagnostic process, Vaillant recommends that physicians use the questionnaire put together by the National Council on Alcoholism (see pages 112–113). These indirect questions are specifically designed to minimize guilt and maximize self-awareness, and they provide, in Vaillant's words, "the most useful guide I know to the clinical interview."

Whether or not physicians choose to use a detailed questionnaire to help diagnose alcoholism, they should always, with every adult patient, be sure to ask (1) if the patient drinks, (2) if he or she has any problems caused by the use of alcohol and/or other drugs, and (3) if any relatives have problems with alcohol and/or other drugs. One way of opening up the subject would be to say, "Now I'd like to find out about your use of alcoholic beverages. Do you drink?" If the patient seems embarrassed, hostile, evasive, or defensive, the physician should note these reactions. In all interactions, however, the physician should try to avoid threatening or frightening the patient. Kindness, caring, and compassion have always been the most effective means of breaking through denial.

While taking the medical history and conducting a physical examination, the following symptoms and signs of alcoholism may be noted. Symptoms are what the patient feels or reports; signs are what the physician observes.

WARNING SYMPTOMS OF ALCOHOLISM

Physical

- Head injuries
- Headaches
- Loss of memory or blackouts (partial or total memory loss of events surrounding a drinking event)
- Morning nausea
- Impotence, inability to achieve orgasm
- Past ulcer operations
- Multiple GI complaints: nausea, cramping, vomiting (especially early morning), diarrhea with no cause
- Indigestion
- Unexplained seizures
- Vomiting of blood
- Frequent infections
- Frequent pancreatitis
- Withdrawal symptoms (tremors, seizures, abnormally rapid heart beat)

Behavioral

- Mood swings
- Depression
- Irritability
- Aggressive behavior
- Suicide threats or attempts
- Anxiety
- Insomnia
- Regular or prolonged use of tranquilizers or sedatives
- Overdose of pills
- Repeated attempts to stop drinking
- History of increased tolerance to large amounts of alcohol; loss of such tolerance
- Craving for sweets
- Fatigue

Family

- Divorce (often multiple)
- Children with behavior problems
- "Bad nerves," depression, anxiety, neuroses in spouse
- Decreased sexual relations
- Decreased social life
- Financial difficulties
- Child or spouse abuse
- Few friends
- Rarely goes out
- Few outside activities or hobbies
- Inappropriate use of telephone (late-night calls, long monologues, rambling conversations)
- Frequent canceled appointments
- Complaints from neighbors, friends

Occupational   (*these problems generally develop in the late-middle to late stage of the disease*)

- Absenteeism
- Tardiness
- Job-related accidents
- Increased insurance claims
- Poor performance
- Loss of job
- Complaints from superiors, coworkers
- Periods of unemployment
- Early retirement
- Frequent job changes
- Moving toward job where there is freedom to drink (house painter, traveling sales representative, freelance work, realtor, etc.)

Legal

- Frequent auto accidents
- Citations for driving while under the influence (two or more DUIs are highly indicative of alcoholism)
- Assault charges
- Disorderly conduct, resisting arrest, public drunkenness citations

PHYSICAL SIGNS OF ALCOHOLISM

Skin

- Cigarette burns
- Decrease in hair
- Gynecomastia (overdevelopment of the mammary glands in the male)
- Increased presence of blood vessels in the face
- Flushing
- Multiple contusions, abrasions, and cuts in various stages of healing
- Nicotine stains on fingers
- Palmar erythema (reddened skin on the palms)
- Livedo reticularis (permanent reddish blue mottling of the skin of the extremities)
- Poor personal hygiene
- Spider angiomas (tiny spiderlike patterns of broken blood vessels)
- Unexplained edema (abnormal accumulation of fluid)
- Minor trauma (bruises on legs or arms, small burns)

Eyes

- Toxic amblyopia (partial loss of vision, due to nerve damage; particularly night blindness)
- Conjunctival infections
- Lateral nystagmus (horizontal jerking movement of the eyes with gaze to the right or left)

Mouth

- "Green tongue" (from breath fresheners)
- Increased gag reflex
- Odor of alcohol at inappropriate times
- Poor oral hygiene

Chest

- Frequent pneumonia, bronchitis, unexplained rapid heart beat, arrhythmia, myocardiopathy, congestive heart failure

Abdomen

- Enlarged liver (tender or nontender)
- Jaundice
- Ascites (swelling with fluid)
- GI bleeding
- Nonhealing ulcers

Gonads

- Atrophic testes (decrease in size)

Extremities

- Myopathies (any disease of a muscle)
- Palmar erythema (reddened skin on the palms)
- Thin in proportion to trunk
- Unexplained edema (abnormal accumulation of fluids)

Neurologic

- Hallucinosis (altered perception in which awareness consists primarily of hallucinations)
- Hyper- or hyporeflexia (increased or decreased reflexes)
- Neuropathies (diseases of the nervous system)
- Seizures ("rum fits," DTs)
- Tremors

ALCOHOL-RELATED DISORDERS AND DISEASES

Gastrointestinal

- Esophagitis (inflammation of the esophagus)
- Esophageal carcinoma
- Gastritis
- Malabsorption
- Chronic diarrhea
- Pancreatitis
- Fatty liver
- Hepatitis
- Cirrhosis
- Ulcers
- GI bleeding
- Cancer of liver or bladder

Cardiac

- Myocardiopathy
- Beriberi
- Hypertension
- Palpitations

Skin
- Rosacea
- Telangiectasia of face and upper chest (dilated capillaries causing dark red blotches on the skin)
- Rhinophyma (an enlarged, red nose as might be seen in a heavy drinker)
- Cutaneous ulcers

Neurologic and Psychiatric

- Peripheral neuropathy
- Convulsive disorders
- Hallucinations
- Delirium tremens
- Wernicke's encephalopathy (a chronic brain syndrome associated with long-term alcoholism and caused in part by B_1 [thiamine] deficiency; marked by loss of memory, disorientation, agitation, and confusion)
- Korsakoff's syndrome (a psychosis associated with chronic alcoholism and caused in part by vitamin B_1 deficiency; characterized by memory failure, imaginary reminiscences, hallucinations, and agitation)

Muscle

- Myopathy

Joints

- Gout

Hematologic

- Megaloblastic anemia (a deficiency of red blood cells characterized by enlarged red blood cells)

Vitamin Deficiency Diseases

- Peripheral neuritis
- Toxic amblyopia
- Beriberi
- Pellagra (caused by a deficiency of B_3)
- Scurvy

Metabolic

- Hypoglycemia
- Diabetes

LABORATORY TESTS

A number of common laboratory tests offer information that may help in the diagnostic process. Because lab tests are highly variable, however, the absence of abnormalities should not be used to rule out alcoholism—many middle-stage alcoholics have absolutely normal laboratory tests. Also, the absence of abnormal results does not indicate normal functioning; as we have said, fully one-third of the liver's cells may be damaged before abnormalities show up on the tests.

The most common laboratory tests for alcoholism include liver tests, blood count, and blood fats.

Liver Tests

SGOT, SGPT, GGTP, and alkaline phosphatase are cellular enzymes concentrated in liver cells. High blood levels indicate that the enzyme has leaked out of the cells into the bloodstream; thus, it can be assumed that the liver cells have been damaged.

Elevated liver enzyme levels do not tell what the specific cause of the damage is, but only that damage exists. In addition to injuries induced by alcohol, other possible causes are viral hepatitis, cancer, exposure to toxic chemicals, infections, or abscesses. In a heavy drinker, the most likely cause is alcohol.

The two liver function tests most indicative of alcoholism check levels of GGTP (gamma-glutamyl transpeptidase) and SGOT (serum glutamine oxaloacetic transaminase). If these two enzymes are elevated along with the MCV (mean corpuscular volume) in the blood count, alcoholism definitely should be suspected.

With abstinence and good nutrition, abnormal results on liver tests usually improve progressively over the first few weeks, resolving to normal by around four weeks. If the tests are still abnormal after several weeks of abstinence, other causes should be investigated.

Blood Count

In many alcoholics the number of red blood cells per unit of blood is reduced. Furthermore, the size of the cell, as indicated by the MCV, is often abnormally large. This indicates that the blood cell manufacturing system is faulty and is producing large, immature red blood cells, which are inefficient in their oxygen-carrying capacity. Enlarged red blood cells are commonly caused by alcohol's direct toxic effect on the bone marrow (the red blood cell manufacturing plant) and/or decreased levels of folic acid (a B vitamin that is needed for normal production of red blood cells).

LABORATORY PROFILE

40 IU/L	52 IU/L	38 U/L	100 IU/L	1.0 mg/dl	6.2 mill/mcl	6.2 mill/mcl	100/FL	37g/dl	10.5 x 10
SGOT	SGOT	GGTP	ALK PHOS	BILIRUBIN	MALE RBC	FEMALE RBC	MCV	MCHC	
8	0	9	30	0.1	4.6	4.1	80/FL	33g/di	

———— Liver Test ————   ———— Blood Count ————

This chart shows the range of normal lab values commonly seen in men and tests. Anything ouside this normal range—either higher or lower—could lem. Alcoholics in the middle-late and late stages of the disease tend to range on these tests. Liver tests and blood fats tend to be elevated in alcoholics tests, the RBC, WBC, and platelet counts are generally lower in late-stage alcoholics MCHC indices are typically higher than normal.

Blood Fats

Triglycerides (blood fats) are frequently elevated in people who drink excessive amounts of alcohol because alcohol interferes with the normal processing of fats and sugars in the liver.

THE NEXT STEP

When physicians suspect a patient is an alcoholic, based on information gleaned from the medical history, physical exam, questionnaires, and/or lab tests, they should initiate a series of actions designed to help the alcoholic stop drinking.

1. *Involve the family.* The physician should make an appointment with the alcoholic's spouse, parents, or children and at this meeting discuss openly and honestly the evidence supporting a diagnosis of alcoholism. Physicians should offer assurance that they are available to help and will do everything within their power to assist the alcoholic and/or the family in the recovery process. (See References for information on resources for family members.)

2. *Suggest a treatment regimen.* Outpatient treatment is often very successful with early-stage alcoholics; middle- and late-stage alcoholics who experience problems with control and/or serious withdrawal symptoms may require inpatient treatment. In selecting a treatment program, the family will need to investigate any restrictions imposed by their insurance company or managed-care provider.

3. *Endorse Alcoholics Anonymous and family support groups.* The physician should strongly recommend regular AA meetings for the alcoholic, Al-Anon meetings for the spouse, and Alateen meetings for the alcoholic's children. Offering phone numbers and AA or Al-Anon contacts is a great help to the family.

4. *Emphasize the need for quick action.* The physician can help the family understand that alcoholism is a chronic and progressive disease that will only get worse if the alcoholic continues to drink. Acting immediately will save the family a lot of heartbreak; it may also save the alcoholic's life.

In the next chapter we discuss intervention, a process of education and enlightenment designed to outsmart the addicted brain and break through the denial system that keeps the alcoholic imprisoned by the disease. The sole purpose of intervention is to halt the progression of the disease before it destroys everything of value in the alcoholic's life.

9

Intervention

To understand is to forgive, even oneself.
— ALEXANDER CHASE

Nan Robertson, a *New York Times* reporter who was later to win the Pulitzer Prize, was drinking too much, and she knew it. She tried to hide how much she was drinking by sneaking drinks and leaving out the soda in her scotch and soda. She needed alcohol to sleep, and so she slept a lot. When she was lonely or anxious, she drank to make things better; when things got worse, she drank to numb the pain. When she realized she might kill someone by driving drunk, she didn't stop drinking—she stopped driving.

One morning at work she suddenly doubled over with excruciating pain. A coworker rushed her to the doctor's office. In *Getting Better*, she describes what happened next:

> Our family doctor was on vacation. A physician I had never seen before, Dr. Charles Thompson, was covering for him. The waiting room was jammed. Dr. Thompson, a baldish man with a blunt, pugnacious manner that I instinctively felt masked great compassion, put me on the table in the examining cubicle. The door was wide open. He took up my hands and began scrutinizing the palms. In the center of each was a deep red rash about the size and shape of a quarter. He gazed intensely at me, questioned me and stared again at the palms, thoughtfully running a thumb over the rash. He asked me if the pain in my belly had begun to travel up my right side. Yes, it had.
>
> Then Dr. Thompson put me on my back on the table and poked and prodded around my abdomen and looked at my reddened palms once more. He bent over with his nose almost on mine and

asked in a husky whisper, "Do you know what's wrong with you, my dear?"

I looked up meekly, nose to nose, and said, "No, Dr. Thompson, I don't."

"BOOZE!!!" he bellowed. "BOOOOOOZE!!!"

The sound boomed out through the open door and echoed around the crowded waiting room, where all those people, including Laura, my very proper colleague, were hearing the ghastly truth about me. I was rigid with mortification.

"STOP IT!" roared Dr. Thompson.

Having captured my total attention, he proceeded to tell me that I had acute pancreatitis—an inflammation of the pancreas—and that my deeply reddened palms were a serious early warning sign of alcoholic damage. I would have to stop drinking at once and entirely. I promised.

Despite the scare and the promise, Nan Robertson continued to drink. Although she couldn't quite forget Dr. Thompson's warning, the need to drink was too immediate and overpowering. The disease progressed, affecting her work, her relationships, and her health. Over the years as friends voiced their concern, colleagues offered to help, and more doctors advised her to stop drinking, she finally came to accept the truth.

Four and a half years after Dr. Thompson's nose-to-nose confrontation and command to stop drinking, Nan Robertson agreed to enter treatment. At the treatment center a kindly nurse asked her several questions. Did she have memory blackouts? Did she sneak drinks? Did she find it difficult to talk to people about her drinking, drink in the morning to still her shaky hands, neglect eating, spend a lot of time thinking about drinking?

She answered yes to every question. "The truth dawned that I was *really* an alcoholic," she writes. "I did not feel shattered. I grinned at the nurse. 'Yep,' I said. 'I sure am an alcoholic.' There, I had said it. I was overwhelmed with relief."

Nan Robertson was a lucky woman. In her book she describes four separate interventions with four different physicians, all knowledgeable about the disease of alcoholism. Openly and honestly, with no sense of judgment or censure, they told her the truth: Alcohol was destroying her body, her mind, and her spirit. If she wanted to live a good, long life, she would have to quit drinking.

Many alcoholics are not so fortunate. Alcohol creates serious problems in their lives, but family members, friends, and health care practitioners hesitate to mention the dreaded word *alcoholism*. The disease progresses, the alcoholic's problems worsen, and still no one makes a move to help. Even when the alcoholic's problems are obvious to all close observers, people stand by and watch, unsure about what they can do to help, concerned that anything they might say or do will eventually backfire.

According to the old theory, which still guides the way many people think about alcoholism, alcoholics have to hit bottom before they can accept the reality that alcohol is destroying their lives. That theory, based on the misguided notion that alcoholics have to want to get help before they can commit themselves to lifelong sobriety, has ruled alcoholism theory and treatment for years.

If someone forces you into treatment, the hit-bottom theorists argue, you are being coerced against your will and denied the opportunity to use your willpower and self-control to seek help for your problems. Misgivings about intervention (often referred to as coercion) arise from the difficult-to-uproot idea that willpower is essential in the battle against a brain addiction—a misconception that is grounded in the belief that a failure in willpower leads to excessive drinking in the first place. Alcoholism, as we have emphasized, is a progressive neurological disease strongly influenced by genetic vulnerability. Willpower is as powerless to alter the neurochemical changes in alcoholics as it is to stabilize blood sugar fluctuations in diabetics or heart fibrillations in coronary patients.

The idea of forcing someone into treatment against their will bothers many people, but, as the authors of *Healing the Healer* point out, the disease itself exerts one of the most potent coercive forces:

> Chemical dependency forces an individual to suffer significantly through a series of losses (both financial and interpersonal), and ultimately through loss of control associated with drug use. In this way, the greatest degree of coercion really comes from the disease process. Complete surrender to the treatment process is essential for long-term recovery. Coercion, both from the law and from the disease, can clearly act as an impetus.

Waiting until the alcoholic is ready to quit drinking is a dangerous strategy. Over the years the hit-bottom theory has cost many alcoholics their lives—for every alcoholic who hits bottom and sees the light, dozens more are destroyed on the way down. Even if you hit bottom, there's no guarantee that you will automatically come back up again. Many years ago when co-author Arthur Ciaramicoli was fresh out of graduate school, he counseled an alcoholic who expressed deep concern about his fast downhill slide. "I'm afraid I'm going to hit bottom," he said.

"What will happen to me if I do?" Hoping to reassure the patient that help would be available to him at all times, Dr. Ciaramicoli responded, "You'll come back up again."

Several years later doctor and patient ran into each other at a grocery store.

"Hey, Doc, remember me?" a disheveled man called out.

"You sure look familiar," Dr. Ciaramicoli responded.

"Well, maybe you'll remember telling me that if I hit bottom, I'd come back up again."

"That sounds like something I might have said."

"You were wrong, as you can see," the man said, holding his arms out, palms up, in humble acceptance of his destitute state. "Some of us, Doc, hit bottom and just start sliding sideways."

Dr. Ciaramicoli sums up the story this way: "He was right. From that point on I have taken a much more aggressive approach with alcoholics in every stage of the disease, doing everything within my power to help them into treatment and long-term recovery."

Intervention is a technique designed to help alcoholics before they hit bottom or start "sliding sideways." More than twenty-five years ago Vernon Johnson detailed the concept and process of intervention in the now-classic *I'll Quit Tomorrow.* Intended to "bring the bottom up" before alcohol destroys everything of value in the alcoholic's life, intervention is a process of education and enlightenment in which family members, friends, and coworkers learn about the disease of alcoholism and the symptoms associated with its early, middle, and late stages. Once the alcoholic's family and friends understand the true nature of the disease, they are able to see that the addiction—not the alcoholic—is the true enemy.

When family members understand that the alcoholic is sick and will get sicker if the drinking continues, they realize the importance of getting help for both the alcoholic and themselves. Creating a treatment plan—inpatient or outpatient treatment, ninety AA meetings in ninety days, regular sessions with an addiction medicine specialist or clinical psychologist who understands the neurophysiological nature of the disease—is an essential part of the intervention. Making all the practical arrangements to carry through with that plan is critically important; creating a support system for the family is equally essential. (See Reference section for information on family issues.)

Intervention happens in different ways. Nan Robertson's drinking problem, for example, was brought to light by several *informal interventions,* in which physicians, friends, and colleagues offered their concern and support. Over the years those brief interventions made a difference. The turning point for Robertson came slowly, as the disease gradually replaced optimism with pessimism, joy with despair, feeling with numbness. Seven months before Robertson entered treatment, she told her doctor that "the world looked unrelievedly grim" and she "felt numb, anesthetized." When she finally decided to enter treatment, it was less a leap than a final, weary step on a long journey. Her doctor showed her a brochure of Smithers intensive inpatient treatment center in Manhattan. "My gloom and despair lightened," Robertson recalls. "It looked like a lovely place. I said I would go."

A *crisis intervention* is more immediate and forceful. When an alcoholic or family member is in crisis—an emergency-room admission for a heart attack, for acute hepatitis, or for a bone-breaking fall while intoxicated; a drunk-driving charge; a potentially violent child custody situation; a suicide attempt—an intervention can be arranged to provide immediate emergency assistance. The purpose of a crisis intervention is to focus attention on the underlying cause of the emergency—neurological addiction to the drug alcohol—and then direct the alcoholic into treatment for the primary problem rather than get sidetracked by mistaken diagnoses, legal entanglements, or court battles.

Deferred prosecution is an extremely effective form of crisis intervention. The alcoholic who is convicted of driving under the influence is given a choice: either prosecution for the crime with the possibility of stiff fines and/or imprisonment, or referral to treatment. Most alcoholics choose treatment, of course, and a high percentage of those who are referred to a disease-model, abstinence-based program get sober and return to active, productive lives.

A *formal intervention* generally involves several weeks of planning and preparation. The first step is to find a counselor who will guide the family members through the intervention process, educate them, encourage them to build up a support system, and act as a clearinghouse for various resources, including information about successful, disease-based treatment centers and programs in the community that are specifically designed to help families cope with alcohol-related problems. Of all the steps involved in a formal intervention, education is the most critical, for only when friends and family members understand the neurophysiological nature of this disease can they also grasp the often complicated nature of treatment and recovery. (See References for resources on intervention and help for the family.)

Formal interventions generally culminate in a face-to-face meeting with the alcoholic, where family members, friends, and concerned others confront the alcoholic with specific facts pointing to the devastating impact of alcohol on the drinker's life. Here are the essential elements involved in the actual intervention:

1.   The facts and data must be presented by people who are close to the alcoholic or exert a powerful influence on the alcoholic's life—family members, friends, bosses, supervisors, coworkers, physicians, clergy members, and so on.

2.   Specific firsthand evidence is especially convincing. The most powerful evidence is, in alcoholism expert Vernon Johnson's words, "descriptive of events *which have happened* or conditions *which exist.*" Opinions and generalizations ("You drink too much," "You have to quit") should be avoided.

3.   Everyone involved in the intervention should avoid moral judgments and any tone of censure. All the facts presented should be used to support the reasons why the family members and friends are concerned. Here is an example: "Jane, three weeks ago this Saturday you insisted on driving Alison and her friend to a slumber party. You had been drinking wine all afternoon. I tried to take your keys away, but you became very upset, yelled at the kids to get in the car, and drove off. I waited in agony for you to come home, scared to death that you would all be killed in a car wreck. I know how much you love your children and how devastated you would be if anything happened to them. I want you to get well. We all want you to be healthy again."

4.   Whenever possible, the facts should center around the use of alcohol; highlighting the contradictions or conflicts in values caused by drinking makes your point even stronger. Here's an example: "You are so gracious and loving when you're sober, Mom, but when you drink, you're a completely different person. I know you would never even think of hitting me when you're sober. Last Wednesday, though, you got so drunk that you slapped me several times. I still have bruises on my face."

5.   Vivid details are particularly effective, for they give the alcoholic a wide-screen view of his or her behavior at a particular point in time. Videotapes and home movies taken when the alcoholic is drinking and intoxicated are very convincing, for they leave no room for denial.

When family and friends are properly educated and the facts are carefully gathered and lovingly presented, a formal intervention can be extremely effective. In *The Times of My Life* former First Lady Betty Ford describes what happened when her family and a physician and nurse from an alcoholism treatment center confronted her about her addiction to alcohol and prescription drugs:

For some reason, I can tell you where every single person in that room was sitting; the floor plan is burned in my brain. Besides Jerry and the boys and Susan and Gayle, Captain Joe Pursch, the Navy doctor who's head of the Alcohol and Drug Rehabilitation Service at Long Beach, was there, and so was a Navy nurse. . . . They'd met together, and with Captain Pursch's guidance, the family had prepared what they were going to say.

I can't remember the words. I was in shock. I've been told that Susan harked back to the days before I'd stopped drinking the first time, and said she'd had to turn to Clara when I wasn't available, and Mike and Gayle spoke of wanting children, and wanting those children's grandmother to be healthy and in charge of her own life, and Jerry mentioned times when I'd fallen asleep in the chair at night, and times when my speech had slurred, and Steve brought up a recent weekend when he and a girlfriend had cooked dinner for me and I wouldn't come to the table on time. "You just sat in front of the TV," Steve said, "and you had one drink, two drinks, three drinks. You hurt me."

Well, he hurt me back. All of them hurt me. I collapsed into tears. But I still had enough sense to realize they hadn't come around just to make me cry; they were there because they loved me and wanted to help me.

As mentioned earlier, intervention is sometimes equated with coercion and criticized, often severely, for forcing alcoholics into treatment against their will. The idea that alcoholics are sick, irrational, and incapable of giving up alcohol by themselves and thus need an external force to break through their denial offends many people, while others insist that alcoholics need to assume full responsibility for getting and staying sober.

In a thoughtful essay on AA, Ernest Kurtz and William Miller argue that "the idea of externally coercing an alcoholic to do *anything* is utterly foreign to A.A.'s way." Referring to a section in *Alcoholics Anonymous* (the Big Book), they quote the advice of Bill Wilson, cofounder of AA, to would-be helpers:

If he [sic] does not want to stop drinking, don't waste time trying to persuade him. You may spoil a later opportunity. . . . If he does not want to see you, never force yourself upon him. . . . Be careful not to brand him an alcoholic. Let him draw his own conclusion. . . . He should not be pushed or prodded by you, his wife, or his friends.

This advice appears in Chapter 7, titled "Working with Others," in which AA's twelfth and final step ("Having had a spiritual awakening as a result of these steps, we tried to carry this message to alcoholics and to practice these principles in all our affairs") is elaborated. We believe that the very act of twelve-stepping—carrying the message to other alcoholics—constitutes an intervention, however informal and non-directive it may be. Other passages in the Big Book could be used as models for modern-day interventions:

- "Call on him while he is still jittery. He may be more receptive when depressed."

- "Continue to speak of alcoholism as an illness, a fatal malady. Talk about the conditions of body and mind which accompany it."

- "Outline the program of action."

- "If your talk has been sane, quiet and full of human understanding, you have perhaps made a friend. Maybe you have disturbed him about the question of alcoholism. This is all to the good."

- "Never talk down to an alcoholic from any moral or spiritual hilltop. . . . Offer him friendship and fellowship. Tell him that if he wants to get well you will do anything to help."

- "Burn the idea into the consciousness of every man that he can get well regardless of anyone."

The ultimate goal of intervention is to initiate a process of internal coercion, characterized by an inner voice that repeats phrases like "I'm sick and tired of being sick and tired" and "There's help available if I'm willing to consider it." Without that ongoing process of internal coercion—often brought about by persuading and even, in some cases, forcing the alcoholic to attend AA meetings or enter a formal treatment program—it is probably safe to say that the alcoholic's chances of long-term recovery are not good.

Whether intervention consists of the informal act of telling an alcoholic that you care about her and are concerned about her drinking, or the formal act of family, friends, and treatment professionals meeting with the alcoholic to outline their concerns and present a step-by-step course of action, the goal should always be to give a gentle but firm push to the process of internal coercion. Once that inner voice starts talking, it is extremely difficult to keep it quiet.

Perhaps, in the not-so-distant future, we will not need to coerce alcoholics into treatment. When the facts about alcoholism are well known and widely accepted, the misconceptions will fade away and the shame associated with the label *alcoholic* will disappear. Understanding the genetic predisposition to alcohol and informed about the progressive stages of the addiction, early-stage alcoholics will make the decision to quit drinking before the disease becomes firmly entrenched. Family members and friends will support this decision wholeheartedly. The word *abuse* will be recognized as pejorative and inappropriate when used in the context of a neurological addiction.

This, we hope and believe, is the way we will approach the disease of alcoholism in the future. Among people who are educated and enlightened about the hereditary, biochemical nature of alcoholism, it is happening already.

This story, told by Katherine Ketcham, describes what happened when her husband, Patrick Spencer, decided to stop drinking.

Pat and I were married in 1979 when I was researching Under the Influence. *I was reading all the literature on heredity and at the same time listening to Pat's stories about alcoholic relatives on both sides of his family. We often talked about the genetic and metabolic aspects of alcoholism and the early-stage symptoms that could serve as warning signs.*

Pat never had any obvious problems with alcohol; in fact, he had an unusually high tolerance, and he rarely suffered from hangovers. He loved to drink—he used to say that it made him feel on top of the world—and his friends enjoyed watching this normally quiet, introverted man loosen up and become the life of the party after a few beers. I knew, however, that high tolerance and preoccupation with drinking were signs of early-stage alcoholism, and I was concerned.

One evening, when Pat was thirty-four years old and our children were still toddlers, we went to a party at a neighbor's house. Pat had a lot of fun and drank a lot of beer, and on the walk home he stumbled a few times. On our front lawn he staggered and almost fell. I remember that we stopped and just looked at each other; for several moments neither of us said a word. "Okay," he said after a long silence. "That's it. I'm not drinking anymore."

The next morning Pat turned to me and said, "I meant what I said last night." He hasn't had a drink in fifteen years. He often tells me that of all the accomplishments in his life, he is most proud of the fact that he gave up alcohol. When we go to a party and someone asks him why he doesn't drink, he says, simply, confidently, "Because I'm an alcoholic."

10

Treatment

One that hath wine as a chain about his wits, such
a one lives no life at all.

— ALCAEUS, 600 B.C.

Never give up on anybody.

— SENATOR HUBERT H. HUMPHREY

On a warm summer evening in a quiet suburban neighborhood east of
Seattle, Mary and Keith Johnsen walked hand in hand. Safely off to the
side of the road, they were engaged in conversation about their busy
lives as working parents of two children. Neither of them heard the vehicle approaching from behind.

Traveling at an estimated speed of 50 mph, the 1994 Dodge Caravan
veered onto the shoulder of the two-lane asphalt roadway, struck Mary
square in the back, and hurled her 146 feet, half the length of a football
field. When Keith Johnsen reached his wife's body, he kneeled down
beside her and sobbed, "My sweet girl, oh my sweet girl."

Mary Johnsen, thirty-eight years old, was dead. She died of "catastrophic injuries," according to the police report. Her spine and aorta
were both severed.

The driver of the van was Susan West, a thirty-nine-year-old mother
of two young children. West was also an alcoholic with a history of drunk
driving arrests and convictions. In March 1978, when West was a nineteen-year-old student at Washington State University, she was arrested
for drunk driving. In 1985, in Seattle, she was convicted of driving under
the influence and placed on probation. Four years later, in 1989, West
made an illegal U-turn and her vehicle collided with another; in that
incident her blood alcohol concentration was 0.24, more than double
the Washington limit of 0.10. In exchange for a deferred prosecution,
West admitted she was an alcoholic and agreed to court-ordered treatment, which consisted of regular sessions with a psychiatrist.

In 1991, two years after she began her psychiatric counseling, West drove her car over an embankment into a stranger's front yard. Once again, police were summoned; once again, West's blood alcohol level was 0.24; and once again, her attorney succeeded in getting the prosecution deferred. Washington state law at that time allowed for only one deferred prosecution every five years, but since the second case was handled by a different court, the judge wasn't aware of the 1989 conviction.

West continued to see the psychiatrist, who filed periodic reports with two different judges in two different courts attesting to West's "progress" in treatment. According to the psychiatrist's reports, West drank excessively because she was having difficulty balancing the stress of family and work.

On July 26, 1997, the day she killed Mary Johnsen, Susan West's blood alcohol level was 0.34, more than three times the .10 legal limit. To reach that level, experts estimate that a woman her size (120 pounds) would have to consume nine 1-ounce shots of 80-proof alcohol or twelve beers in one hour or less.

For weeks after Mary Johnsen's death, friends, neighbors, citizen activists, and state legislators expressed their outrage and clamored for tougher drunk driving laws. Why, people wondered, hadn't Susan West's license been taken away after her second conviction? Why was she granted two deferred prosecutions in violation of state law? One letter writer fumed that he was fed up with drunk drivers and their "selfish and destructive behaviors."

Amidst all the expressions of anger and grief, no one asked the most important question of all: Why was Susan West offered psychiatric treatment focusing on stress as the cause of her drinking when, as a diagnosed alcoholic, she suffered from a primary neurological addiction to alcohol? How could anyone suggest that West was "progressing" in treatment when she continued to drink and drive?

No one thought to point out that if Susan West had received appropriate treatment for her disease—if, in fact, her disease had been recognized as a physiological addiction requiring abstinence and adequate followup to prevent relapse—she would not be serving a nine-year prison sentence at the Washington Corrections Center for Women. And Mary Johnsen, wife and mother of two young boys, would be alive today.

For decades our society has blamed alcoholics for the failures of treatment, concluding that they are stubborn, self-destructive, willful, and immature. During Susan West's trial her attorney asked that she be allowed to enter treatment. The judge's response: "It's too late for that." Alcoholics don't really want to stop drinking, we're told, because they're hell-bent on destroying themselves. One therapist described his repeated failures with alcoholics in this way: "They simply find drunkenness too attractive a way of life to abandon."

Anyone who has lived the life of a drinking alcoholic can testify to the fact that being a drunk is anything but "attractive." Drunkenness is not a way of life anyone in his or her right mind would willingly choose. Surely Susan West, who was married, had two young children, and held a management position with clothing outfitter Eddie Bauer, did not choose to kill someone and then spend nine years in prison for her crime. Why, then, did she continue to drink after she had been diagnosed an alcoholic and went through treatment with a psychiatrist? The answer to that question may seem complicated, but it is actually surprisingly simple: If alcoholics are given the wrong treatment, focusing on psychological and emotional symptoms as the primary causes of excessive drinking, most will continue to drink and progress in their disease. This is what happened to Susan West, and it's happening right now to many thousands of alcoholics who are seeking help for their addiction to alcohol.

Alcoholism treatment *does* work, and the great majority of alcoholics *do* recover from their disease—*if* they're offered the right treatment. It really is that simple: With the right treatment, most alcoholics can recover. With the wrong treatment, most alcoholics will relapse and return to drinking. So when people tell you that "treatment doesn't work" or claim that the "success rates are the same for alcoholics who go through treatment and those who don't," ask them what kind of treatment they are talking about. Treating Susan West with psychological counseling focusing on work and family stress as the primary cause of excessive drinking and claiming that she was "progressing in treatment" even as she continued to drink and drive does not qualify as treatment. In our book it qualifies as malpractice.

A SUCCESS STORY

William F. Asbury, our coauthor, is a recovered alcoholic. Before he got sober at the age of fifty-one, Bill had been the editor and/or publisher of six daily newspapers and the owner of a successful weekly in California. During his drinking days he won the best editorial award for the state of California, one of the most competitive newspaper arenas in the nation. He was happily married and the loving father of five children.

How could a man of such fine accomplishments be an alcoholic? Alcohol is an equal-opportunity disease. It strikes down U.S. senators,

Air Force colonels, chief executive officers of Fortune 500 companies, and editors in chief of newspapers as surely as it destroys the lives of working mothers like Susan West. In fact, Bill's story of alcoholic drinking and all its varied and assorted miseries is not so very different from Susan West's experiences. When Bill was a college student, he drove drunk and sideswiped a parked car; the damage to both vehicles was serious, but he never reported the accident. In his late twenties, when he was a news correspondent in Tokyo, Bill got rip-roaring drunk one night and smashed his car into a taxicab in a busy intersection; the force of the collision flipped the cab over so that it rested on its roof.

When he was fifty-one years old, Bill was convicted of drunk driving. That was the first and only time he was caught, which is too bad because Bill counts that drunk driving arrest as one of the crucial factors propelling him into treatment. (He entered an inpatient treatment program just a few months later.) Bill figures that in his thirty-five-year drinking career he drove drunk more than one hundred times.

After he was arrested for drinking and driving, Bill was handcuffed and escorted to the county jail. With great embarrassment, he used his one phone call to call his editorial page editor who bailed him out. He spent the next day (and countless other "days after") filled with shame and self-loathing. His drinking caused terrible fights with his wife and almost led to a divorce.

His children suffered, too. One beautiful summer afternoon while his wife and one son were out of town, Bill was in his backyard getting drunk on cheap red wine and watching his elder children toss his youngest child high into the air. Someone missed the catch, and his six-year-old lay facedown on the cement, her arm twisted at a grotesque angle. Too drunk to drive, he forced his fifteen-year-old daughter, who had no license and had never driven a car, to drive to the emergency room.

The stories go on and on, of course; all alcoholics can tell many such tales. The difference between Susan West's case and Bill Asbury's, however, is that Bill was referred to an abstinence-based inpatient treatment center. He got sober. He's been sober for 25 years (and in those years he was named editor in chief of a major metropolitan newspaper, ranked in the top 35 nationally).

Bill's story differs from Susan West's in one more respect—he never killed anybody. That last fact explains why stories like Susan West's are so painful for so many alcoholics. "For there," Bill quotes a phrase heard over and over again at AA meetings, "but for the Grace of God, go I."

Here is the story of Bill's recovery, told in his words, with the deepest gratitude for all who contributed to saving his life.

My wife, Janet, and all five of our children accompanied me on the six-hour trip from our home in eastern Washington to Alcenas Hospital in Kirkland, Washington, near Seattle. Janet walked with me to the small front office, while the kids stayed in the car. I remember my shame and grief as I looked back to see Sarah, my gentle, smart, beautiful sixteen-year-old, sobbing as if her heart would break. I had caused this pain. I didn't think I would ever be able to forgive myself.

"Give me all your keys and your shaving kit," the admissions person said. Later I found out that she was looking for mouthwash, aftershave lotion, cough syrup, and other items that might contain alcohol. I would also discover that the frisking I got that first day was intended to establish the dead-serious tone of treatment. "You have a disease that can kill you," staff members said in every possible way they could say it, "and we're serious about keeping you alive."

Was this to be like prison? Or like the navy boot camp I had to endure as an apprentice seaman during World War II? I had trouble formulating sensible questions, and at that point I couldn't believe I would ever discover any answers. The only question I should have been asking was: "Can you help me stop drinking?" But I didn't want to ask that question because down deep I really didn't want to stop drinking.

Alcenas was an ancient barracks of some kind; I remember thinking that the building had died years ago and no one had the decency to bury it. The carpets were in tatters. Sofas and chairs would not have qualified as donations to Goodwill. Because it was a new treatment center (new in the sense of recently established), money was tight and all available resources were directed to what mattered the most—getting people sober.

I was assigned a room and a roommate, an elderly dairy farmer of Swedish heritage who had sold his farm for lots of money and had been drunk since the deal closed. I was also assigned a counselor. Her name was Millie, and she was a large woman, fierce and dictatorial, with a thick Norwegian accent. In the twenty-eight days I spent with Millie, I never once saw her smile. But I was soon to learn that her seriousness of purpose and her stern enforcement of discipline would help get me sober and keep me that way. Millie was a recovered alcoholic, as were all the counselors and administrators at Alcenas.

Alcenas was founded and directed by James R. Milam, Ph.D., a decorated World War II fighter pilot, research psychologist, and (not the least of his notable accomplishments) recovered alcoholic. In one of his weekly lectures, Dr. Milam explained with great sadness that he decided to devote his life to helping alcoholics recover from their disease because "when I arrived at middle age I became aware that I had spent half of my life drunk." All the alcoholics in the audience nodded knowingly; most of us had wasted much of our lives, too.

Treatment consisted of a few simple procedures. We attended daily lectures to learn about the disease that threatened to destroy our bodies, minds, and spirits. "Alcoholism is a physiological, inherited disease," we were told, "and alcohol is the drug that causes that disease." We learned about the progression of alcoholism and the psychological symptoms caused by the underlying neurological addiction. We also learned about malnutrition, hypoglycemia, the withdrawal syndrome, relapse, Alcoholics Anonymous, and the spiritual aspects of recovery.

Freewheeling group counseling sessions preceded and followed the daily lectures. The purpose of the counseling sessions was to get to know each other—and, even more important, to get to know ourselves. Millie and other counselors were always there to keep these groups on track—I'm not sure there is anything quite as volatile as a group of six or seven recovering drunks gathered in one small space trying to figure themselves and each other out. There was never a dull moment.

At that time there were thirty-three of us at Alcenas, and friendships developed that would last a lifetime. We had all been in that same boozy, sinking boat. As time went by we grew comfortable with one another, and we told our drinking stories honestly, refusing to withhold even the most painful, sordid details. Most of us were telling these stories for the first time, for up until this point we had done everything we could to avoid telling the truth about our drinking days.

I remember many of the stories, but one in particular has stuck with me for all these years. One of my fellow drunks was a handsome, soft-spoken twenty-one-year-old named John. John told the group that for the last five years he had consumed a full case of beer every day. One day he drank his requisite case of beer, got into his car, drove through a stop sign, and smashed into the driver's door of a small sedan. He killed the mother of three young children. At his trial, the judge agreed to defer John's prosecution if he went to treatment and never touched alcohol again. I have never heard what happened to John. I hope he stayed sober.

We began every day with exercises and calisthenics. Those who were fit enough to walk or jog were encouraged to do so. Some of my fellow patients arrived at the treatment center in such bad shape, they had difficulty walking at all for several days. One day a flight attendant for a major airline (she was in her mid-thirties) arrived by ambulance and was wheeled into the clinic on a gurney, comatose. She was in detox for several days before she was able to join our morning exercises, and even then she had to be pushed around the track in a wheelchair. Insisting that she join the group no matter how bad her condition was part of the discipline we were taught in treatment. I remember thinking that those walks around the track by the halt and the maimed resembled the Bataan Death March.

Meals at Alcenas were nutritious, high in protein, low in fat and sugar. Coffee was decaffeinated. We were taught how to prepare our own meals and design menu plans, concentrating always on foods that would continue the healing of our alcohol-damaged bodies. After every meal we lined up for vitamin and mineral supplements.

Once a week we were taken to an AA meeting in town. Those meetings were mandatory. Dr. Milam, his wife, Dorris Hutchison, and every staff member at Alcenas knew from their own experience that without the supportive community of Alcoholics Anonymous, many of us would relapse. I know now that without AA, particularly in those first years of recovery, I would not have made it.

Every Saturday we listened to a two-hour lecture by Dr. Milam. After we had been in treatment for two weeks, our families were allowed a brief Saturday visit. Family members were encouraged to sit in on Milam's educational (and always entertaining) lectures.

No phone calls were allowed to disrupt the daily regimen except in emergencies. Lectures were mandatory, as were meals and nutritional supplements. All events started on time. This discipline was to help establish a pattern of living and habits we would need in the real world.

The most memorable part of my treatment came on the Saturday of my first week. In his lecture, Dr. Milam talked about how we alcoholics (and he always made sure the audience knew he was one, too) "had been chosen" to become drunks. We were not willful violators of decency, law, or common sense, Milam said; we were the unlucky 10 to 15 percent of drinkers who had a special body chemistry and genetic vulnerability to the drug alcohol, and this physiological inheritance paved the way for addiction. Milam spoke eloquently and persuasively as a scientist, a researcher, and a good, decent human being. Most important, he spoke as one of us—a fellow drunk.

Sitting in the lecture hall that day, I felt as if I had been turned inside out. For the first time, I "got" it. I understood that I wasn't an alcohol "abuser." I was addicted to the stuff, and I could get well if I stayed sober. It was that simple and that profound.

I finished the twenty-eight-day treatment program in September 1975. I took the weekend off and then reported Monday morning for my new job as news editor at the Seattle Post-Intelligencer, a daily newspaper read by approximately four hundred thousand readers. I eventually became editor in chief of that newspaper, a position I held until I retired from journalism and began a new career in Washington State government.

I haven't had a drink in twenty-five years.

THE MINNESOTA MODEL*

The techniques used by James Milam at Alcenas Hospital twenty-five years ago are similar to those used today at such successful clinics as the Betty Ford Center in California, Hazelden in Minnesota, Sundown M Ranch in Washington State, and scores of comparable treatment centers across the land. These addiction treatment programs are organized under the general principles of a treatment system called the "Minnesota model." The state of Minnesota recognized alcoholism as a disease very early, just after the American Civil War. As early as 1873 Minnesota imposed a tax on saloons and used the proceeds to build and operate a "treatment center for inebriates" in Rochester. After its founding in the early 1930s, Alcoholics Anonymous flourished in Minnesota, and AA members were instrumental in spreading the word about the physiological nature of the disease. Minnesota eventually became known as the "land of ten thousand treatment centers."

The earliest examples of the Minnesota model were found in three

---

* It is important to note that within the alcoholism treatment field itself there exists an enormous diversity of treatment philosophies and techniques; outside the field, of course, alcoholics are exposed to an even broader arena of treatments offered by disciplines ranging from medicine to psychiatry, psychology, social work, and pastoral counseling. In the remainder of this chapter we describe the approaches and basic principles that we believe—from experience, research, and discussions with experts in the field—offer the greatest chance of successful treatment to the greatest number of alcoholics.

treatment centers in the state: Willmar State Hospital, which opened in 1912 as an "inebriate asylum"; Pioneer House, which opened in 1948; and Hazelden, which officially opened on May 1, 1949. In *Slaying the Dragon*, which traces the long and colorful history of addiction treatment in this country, researcher and author William White summarizes the basic tenets of the Minnesota model:

1.   Alcoholism is an involuntary, primary disease that is describable and diagnosable.

2.   Alcoholism is a chronic and progressive disease. Barring intervention, the signs and symptoms of alcoholism self-accelerate.

3.   Alcoholism is not curable, but the disease may be arrested.

4.   The nature of the alcoholic's initial motivation for treatment—its presence or absence—is not a predictor of treatment outcome.

5.   The treatment of alcoholism includes physical, psychological, social, and spiritual dimensions.

6.   The successful treatment of alcoholism requires an environment in which the alcoholic is treated with dignity and respect.

7.   Alcoholics and addicts are vulnerable to the "abuse" of a wide spectrum of mood-altering drugs. This whole cluster of mood-altering drugs can be addressed through treatment that defines the problem as one of *chemical dependency*.

8.   Chemical dependency is best treated by a multidisciplinary team whose members develop close, less-formal relationships with their clients and whose activities are integrated within an individualized treatment plan developed for each client.

9.   The focal point for implementing the treatment plan is an assigned primary counselor, usually recovered, of the same sex and age group as the client, who promotes an atmosphere that enhances emotional self-disclosure, mutual identification, and mutual support.

10.   The most effective treatment for alcoholism includes an orientation to A.A., an expectation of "Step work," groups that combine confrontation and support, lectures, one-to-one counseling, and the creation of a dynamic "learning environment."

11.   The most viable, ongoing, sobriety-based support structure for clients following treatment is Alcoholics Anonymous.

GETTING SOBER AT SUNDOWN

The Minnesota model, with its eleven basic tenets, forms the heart and soul of most good treatment programs in this country. In this section we will describe one of those treatment programs: Sundown M Ranch in Selah, Washington, the oldest freestanding nonmedical chemical dependency treatment center in Washington State. Since 1968 Sundown has served more than thirty thousand chemically dependent people and their families.

We selected Sundown for several reasons. First, it is representative of many thriving, low-profile treatment programs that offer high quality at low cost. While Hazelden and the Betty Ford Center receive a great deal of media attention, places such as Sundown are less well known but equally successful in helping alcoholics to long-term recovery.

Our second reason for featuring Sundown is its down-to-basics, no-frills approach to treatment. Managed-care providers, which determine the need for treatment and decide whether or not to pay for it, are always looking for cost-cutting alternatives to expensive rehabilitation centers. The program at Sundown provides a working model of a solid, successful abstinence-based program offered at a low price tag.

COSTS

For adults, an average stay of 21 days costs approximately $3,000 in the year 2000. The fee includes room, board, and laundry. It also includes a three-day, two-night inpatient family treatment program for two family members, with individual and group counseling sessions, lectures, and general education about the disease.

For adolescents, the average treatment is around twenty-eight days for a total cost of approximately $5,000. The tuition includes room, board, laundry, and five days of residential family counseling for two family members.

Outpatient treatment is also an option at Sundown. (See page 160 for a description of this three-phase program.)

Sundown is able to keep its fees low because it is a nonprofit organization located on inexpensive land in an area with a low cost of living. It also operates as a nonmedical program with no nurses or physicians on the full-time staff. Each incoming patient is given a medical screening, however, and any previously prescribed drugs or other medical needs are administered by Sundown's medical director, Frederick A. Montgomery, M.D., a psychiatrist and addiction specialist with a private practice in nearby Yakima who visits Sundown at least once a week. Dr. Montgomery has been the medical director at Sundown since 1975.

LOCATION AND FACILITIES

Sundown's thirty-acre ranch is located just north of Yakima, Washington, in a quiet, undeveloped part of the Yakima River Valley. Cows graze the pastures, which extend for miles, eventually sloping upward into the foothills of the majestic Cascade Mountains.

Sundown consists of five separate buildings: an administration/office building, the adult inpatient and outpatient building, the adolescent inpatient and outpatient quarters, a residential unit for families, and a seven-thousand-square-foot gymnasium with a full basketball court, weight room, and running track.

All the buildings are clean and tastefully decorated, and the grounds are carefully tended. The director of treatment, H. Charles Buttrey, explains why the staff insists on cleanliness and order. "We want our patients to have respect—respect for this place, and more important, respect for themselves." If a gum wrapper or cigarette butt is seen on the grounds, the counselors and administrators make sure to pick it up. The patients soon learn to follow their example—and are reminded, often, to do so.

STAFF

Like so many treatment centers, Sundown was organized by alcoholics who got sober and then committed their lives to helping others who are suffering as they once did. Three decades after its founding, Sundown is still managed by recovered people. Most of the staff are recovering alcoholics, and many staff members (such as executive director Scott Munson) got sober through the treatment program at Sundown.

Sundown's staff is made up mostly of young people, ranging in age from twenty-five to forty-five. Forty-six counselors care for 156 patients (96 adults and 60 adolescents) when the clinic is full; Sundown is always running near capacity. Staff turnover is low, around 10 percent. Most of the counselors and staff have been at Sundown for years, with the average being six to seven years. Sundown is unusual in this respect, for many other treatment centers around the country are having difficulty keeping their staff and finding qualified replacements. The field as a whole is experiencing a counselor shortage. According to Scott Munson, the demands of managed-care providers have decreased patient contact and increased paperwork to the point that some people are leaving the field. "Counselors are attracted to the field because they want to work with people, not spend their days filling out paperwork," Munson comments. To alleviate the paperwork demands on its counselors, Sundown hired extra staff and devoted an entire wing of offices in the administration building to processing the paperwork required by insurance and managed-care providers.

PATIENTS

The population at Sundown includes men and women, the very young and the very old, members of all ethnic groups, the rich and the poor, alcoholics who have spent many years drinking heavily and those fortunate few who are diagnosed early in the disease.

Half of Sundown's 156 beds are reserved for women. Sundown's staff believes there are as many women in this country suffering from the disease of alcoholism as there are men, but women traditionally have escaped diagnosis because they did their drinking at home and were not as likely to be referred to treatment because of problems at work or drunk driving charges. That picture is rapidly changing as society begins to accept the fact that alcoholism is an equal-opportunity addiction.

The drug picture itself is also changing. Not so very long ago, perhaps fifteen or twenty years, most people at Sundown were addicted to just one drug: alcohol. Now a majority of adult patients and nearly all adolescent patients are polyaddicted (addicted to two or more drugs), with the most common drug pattern among adolescents being combined use of alcohol, marijuana, and methamphetamines, an addictive stimulant. Methamphetamine use and addiction is a growing problem, particularly on the West Coast; in California, for example, methamphetamine-related emergency room admissions increased 460 percent from 1984 to 1994.

Despite the rise in polyaddiction, the one drug used by every adult and adolescent who checks into Sundown is alcohol. Alcohol may not be their "drug of choice" (although in most cases it is), but it's the constant in every drug user's life. Many patients claim that other drugs such as marijuana, cocaine, or methamphetamine are their "primary drug," but Munson says that when you ask them which drug they use most often, they invariably cite alcohol.

DETOXIFICATION

Most of us have seen the movie versions of the far-gone drunks who are forced to stop drinking suddenly. When the alcoholic's magic elixir is taken away, Hollywood shows us a helpless wretch suffering with the sweats and the shakes, besieged by visions of snakes or pink elephants, and in the throes of gut-wrenching physical and emotional agony. While the moviemakers tend to exaggerate, late-stage alcoholics left to dry out on their own can and often do experience serious, even life-threatening withdrawal symptoms such as hallucinations, seizures, and delirium tremens (DTs).

Like all competent hospitals, clinics, and treatment centers that care for alcoholics and other drug addicts, Sundown has established a carefully designed process for identifying and treating patients who are at risk for painful or potentially serious withdrawal symptoms. This care and the hours or days it occupies at the beginning of treatment is called detoxification or, simply, "detox."

How does detox work? Addictive drugs come in different families. Alcohol belongs to the most popular family of drugs, known as sedative-hypnotics, which have primarily depressant effects, especially in large doses. Besides alcohol, this kind of drug includes most sleeping pills as well as the Valium-type benzodiazepine drugs. The stimulant family includes cocaine, crack, and methamphetamine. Heroin, morphine, codeine, and a variety of prescription painkillers belong to the opioid family.

Each family of drugs produces its own type of withdrawal syndrome. Removal of a depressant drug such as alcohol causes agitation, sometimes intense, in the central nervous system, which in turn causes nervousness, insomnia, anxiety, and, in more severe cases of withdrawal, fever, sweating, and increased pulse rate and blood pressure. In certain patients, particularly those who have been drinking large amounts of alcohol over a long period of time, the overexcited nerves can lead to hallucinations, seizures, or DTs.

In the process of determining whether or not a patient will need medical attention during withdrawal, Sundown's staff interviews family members about the patient's drinking, drug use, medical history, and prior withdrawal problems or seizures. This information is crucial in designing a treatment plan. The family's participation in this process is critically important because the patient may not be willing or able to reveal these facts at the time of admission.

Sundown relies on specially trained addiction counselors and staff who monitor each patient, keeping a careful watch for any signs or symptoms that might indicate the need for medical attention. Fewer than 10 percent of Sundown's patients require medical care or intervention for withdrawal; if a problem arises, however, the patient is referred immediately for treatment, which generally consists of medicating the agitated nervous system with sedative-type drugs. Many detox centers also use vitamin and mineral therapies and auricular (outer ear) acupuncture to ease the discomfort of withdrawal. (See pages 234–236 for an in-depth discussion of acupuncture in treatment and recovery.)

THE ADULT FACILITY

The rooms in the adult units are actually suites. Each suite has two single bedrooms, connected by a shared bath. A sliding door in each unit leads to a grassy area where patients can sit in lawn chairs, read, play cards, or just talk. The rooms are spacious, well lit, and tastefully decorated, in accordance with tenet number six of the Minnesota model: "The successful treatment of alcoholism requires an environment in which the alcoholic is treated with dignity and respect." Looking at the rooms, it is easy to imagine that you are staying in a Marriott hotel room rather than an alcoholism treatment facility. At Sundown, however, patients are expected to make their beds and clean up after themselves.

Adult Program Basics

The adult program features the following basics:

Abstinence. "We are an abstinence-based program," Scott Munson explains. "Our philosophy, supported by decades of research, is that patients have to stay off all mood- and mind-altering drugs. We are not a harm-reduction facility. Our measure for success is abstinence."

Education. This is really a process of reeducation because alcoholics need to *un*learn all the false and misleading information they have accumulated over the years before they can start to absorb the facts about their disease. In assigned readings, lectures, and individual and group therapy sessions, alcoholics learn to replace the myths and misconceptions about alcoholism and other drug addictions with research-supported facts.

Alcoholics Anonymous. "Without Alcoholics Anonymous, our work at Sundown would go unfinished," explains Chuck Buttrey, the director of treatment at Sundown; Buttrey has been at Sundown for more than twenty-three years. "When our patients leave here, they would have no place to go. From our patients' experiences we know that AA attendance is the greatest predictor of long-term abstinence." Sundown's insistence

Sundown M Ranch Weekly Schedule

TIME	MONDAY	TUESDAY	WEDNESDAY
7:30 A.M. 8:00 A.M.	Breakfast	Breakfast	Breakfast
8:00 A.M. 9:00 A.M.	Bed and Room Cleanup	Bed and Room Cleanup	Bed and Room Cleanup
9:00 A.M. 10:00 A.M.	Lecture	Lecture	Lecture
10:00 A.M. 11:30 A.M.	Group Therapy	Group Therapy	Group Therapy
11:30 A.M. 11:45 A.M.	Free Time	Free Time	Free Time
11:45 A.M. 12:30 P.M.	Lunch	Lunch	Lunch
12:30 P.M. 1:00 P.M.	Free Time	Free Time	Free Time
1:00 P.M. 2:00 P.M.	Lecture	Lecture	Discussion Groups
2:00 P.M. 3:00 P.M.	Group Therapy	Group Therapy	Group Therapy
3:00 P.M. 5:30 P.M.	Study Time	Study Time	Study Time
3:15 P.M. 4:00 P.M.	Women's Exercise	Men's Exercise	Women's Exercise
5:30 P.M. 6:00 P.M.	Dinner	Dinner	Dinner
6:00 P.M. 6:30 P.M.	Free Time	Free Time	Free Time
6:30 P.M. 7:30 P.M.	Video	Video	Video
8:00 P.M. 8:30 P.M.	AA Meeting Al-Anon Meeting	Film: First-Week Clients and Ranch Orientation	Recreation
8:30 P.M. 12 Midnight	Free/Study Time	Free/Study Time	Free/Study Time

THURSDAY	FRIDAY	SATURDAY	SUNDAY
Breakfast	Breakfast	Breakfast	Breakfast
Bed and Room Cleanup	Bed and Room Cleanup	Bed and Room Cleanup	Bed and Room Cleanup
Lecture	Lecture	Lecture	Lecture
Group Therapy	Group Therapy	Group Therapy	Group Therapy
Free Time	Free Time	Free Time	Free Time
Lunch	Lunch	Lunch	Lunch
Free Time	Free Time	Free Time	Free Time
Lecture	Lecture	Lecture	Lecture
Group Therapy	Group Therapy	Group Therapy	Group Therapy
Study Time	Study Time	Study Time	Study Time
Men's Exercise	Open	Open	Open
Dinner	Dinner	Dinner	Dinner
Free Time	Free Time	Free Time	Free Time
Video	Video	Group Discussion	Video
Recreation	Film: Third-Week Clients, "Disease Concept II"	AA Meeting	
Free/Study Time	Free/Study Time	Free/Study Time	Free/Study Time

on AA involvement is supported by recent research. In a study of sixty-five thousand patients followed after completing treatment, AA attendance proved to be the most powerful predictor of sustained sobriety. Of patients who attended AA at least weekly for one year, 73 percent stayed sober. Of those who attended AA only occasionally, 53 percent stayed sober, and of those who never went to AA or who quit going, 44 percent stayed sober.

Psychological Counseling. Every patient is required to participate in daily individual and group therapy sessions.

Family participation and treatment. Recovery for family members is a process, just as it is for the chemically dependent individual. "Alcoholism/chemical dependency is an illness that never affects just one person," Scott Munson says. "Because this disease affects everyone around the chemically dependent individual, often in very profound ways, it is extremely important to help family members address their needs and find appropriate, ongoing sources of help."

As part of the cost of treatment, Sundown offers a mandatory three-day residential family program. Two family members stay in the 54-bed family lodging facility, which is located in a separate building from the adult and adolescent inpatient treatment centers. The first day involves general education and interviews with the counselors. Education and counseling continue on the second day, which also includes a "conjoint" session involving the counselor, the alcoholic, and family members. The third day is set aside for "debriefing," in which the family members discuss any problems or concerns they might have with the treatment staff and administrators.

THE ADOLESCENT UNIT

The Sundown youth program, which was started in 1993, is located approximately a football field's distance from the adult facility. (Adolescents and adults do not share activities.) The youth facility has sixty beds, thirty each for males and females. Although the program is designed for youths between the ages of twelve and eighteen, occasionally an eleven-year-old or nineteen-year-old will be accepted for treatment.

Most of the activities in the adolescent facility are gender-specific; the staff find that keeping young men and women away from each other has a definite positive effect on their attention span. Breakfast and dinner are segregated as are the classrooms, and gym hours are restricted to either boys or girls. Counseling sessions are gender-specific as well. The daily lectures are coed, although females sit on one side of the lecture hall and males sit on the other.

The youth program begins with a forty-eight-hour trial treatment period and screening process. Every patient and at least one family member are required to participate in this two-day trial period, which is designed as an orientation to treatment and a time for the family and adolescent to make an informed decision about treatment options.

After the two-day screening process, adolescent patients are assigned to a primary chemical dependency counselor, who is supported by a multidisciplinary team of educational, psychological, and recreational specialists. Discharge planning, which the Sundown staff considers the most important part of the adolescent program, begins the moment the patient is admitted. In the first days of treatment, Sundown's youth director, James Barth, and his staff begin to contact the patient's school counselors, teachers, clergy, and extended family members in an effort to establish a network of caring people who will be available and involved with the patient when he or she returns home.

Each adolescent is assigned a case manager, who oversees exchanges of information between Sundown and the community to which the young person will return. As a result, after adolescents leave treatment, they enter a well-established community treatment plan with supportive therapy, scheduled activities, and a preestablished supportive system of interpersonal relationships. Making sure the patients are hooked up with a sponsor and suitable AA or NA program in their hometown is considered a high priority and a primary element of relapse prevention.

Adolescent Program Basics

Sundown's youth program consists of six basics:

Primary group therapy. Separate male and female therapy groups are led by two counselors each. During the average twenty-eight-day program, each adolescent will have eighty-four hours of group therapy.

Chemical dependency education. This consists of eighty-two lectures, selected films, and assigned readings.

Recreational therapy. Males and females are separated during recreation times.

Schooling. Adolescents continue their education while in treatment. Sundown is accredited through a nearby school district, and two certified teachers are assigned to the youth program.

AA or NA Involvement. Sundown staff talk at length with adolescent patients about AA's history, traditions, twelve steps, and significance in treatment and recovery. During treatment patients attend AA meetings at Sundown and in the community.

Residential family therapy. At the beginning of the adolescent's treatment, one or more parents/caretakers spend two days at Sundown's residential family facility learning about the disease of chemical dependency, intervention techniques, the demands of recovery, and available resources in the community. At the end of the treatment period, family members check into the family lodging facility for a three-day program of education and counseling sessions.

OUTPATIENT TREATMENT

At Sundown, outpatient treatment is presented in a three-phase treatment plan. The first phase is called "intensive outpatient care" and requires seventy-two hours of lectures, group therapy, and counseling over a six-week period. Patients come to Sundown four days a week, Monday through Thursday, from 5:30 to 9:00 P.M. for an hour-long educational session and two hours of group therapy. The intensive outpatient course content and therapy are modeled on the residential treatment program.

Phase Two of outpatient treatment is called "continuing care" and consists of once-a-week sessions for twelve continuous weeks. The continuing-care patients discuss the real-life problems they experience when they return to their families, jobs, peer groups, and communities where they once used alcohol and/or other drugs. In these continuing-care sessions, the patients get help from their counselors, often in one-on-one sessions, and benefit from being with other newly recovered men and women who are trying to find ways to cope with similar posttreatment realities at home or on the job. Phase Two is also available for those individuals who have completed intensive inpatient treatment.

Phase Three is an extended course of once-a-month lectures and group therapy in meetings that last between an hour and a half and two hours. Phase Three is used for monitoring by the Sundown staff and to help satisfy the terms of Washington State's deferred-prosecution laws, which allow drunk drivers to avoid jail, fines, and/or driver's license suspensions by agreeing to treatment for alcoholism or other drug addictions. The Phase Three patients must go through both the intensive outpatient and continuing-care phases as well as the long-term monthly meetings to meet their legal obligations. The total time required for Phase Three clients is two years, which includes a special twenty-four-week continuing-care program (versus twelve weeks for non-deferred-prosecution outpatients).

The cost of the intensive outpatient care and continuing care combined is under $2,000. The cost of the three-phase course for deferred-prosecution drunk drivers is approximately $2,000.

Sundown M Ranch is similar in design to hundreds of other successful treatment centers, including such highly visible programs as the Betty Ford Center in Rancho Mirage, California. Both programs follow the basic tenets of the Minnesota model of addiction treatment, insisting on lifelong abstinence and emphasizing the importance of education, involvement in AA and other twelve-step groups, individual and group counseling sessions, and family therapy.

The Betty Ford Center differs from Sundown in one major respect— it offers sophisticated medical facilities with physicians, nurses, and dietitians on staff. While many if not most recovering alcoholics do not require medical attention during treatment, some alcoholics (particularly those in the later stages of the disease) will have physical injuries or limitations that require twenty-four-hour nursing care for acute medical problems. Pregnant women and alcoholics who have coexisting medical problems like heart disease or cancer may also require intensive medical care during treatment.

Treatment programs that offer on-site medical services are necessarily more expensive than nonmedical programs such as Sundown's. At the Betty Ford Center, for example, a twenty-eight-day inpatient program costs approximately $13,000. This is considered "mid-range" in terms of the cost of inpatient treatment nationwide. Many insurance companies cover a percentage of these costs, and scholarships are available for those patients who cannot afford treatment.

The fundamental guiding principle at Sundown M Ranch, the Betty Ford Center, and hundreds of other abstinence-based, disease-model treatment centers in this country and other countries all around the world is the same: care, compassion, and respect for the individual who is trying to recover from addiction to alcohol or other drugs. Prominently displayed in Sundown's centrally located office building is an oak-framed document titled simply "Creed." This creed (on page 162) is universal and can be found in treatment centers all around the world.

CREED

Patients are the most important people to enter this facility; in person, by mail, or by telephone.

Patients are not dependent upon us; on the contrary, we are dependent upon them.

Patients are not an interruption of our work; they are the purpose of it.

We are not doing them a favor by serving them; they do us a favor by permitting us to do so.

Patients are not outsiders to our work; they are our work.

Patients are not cold statistics; they are concerned human beings with feelings and emotions like our own.

Patients are persons who bring us their problems; our job is to handle those problems with understanding, fairness, and professional skill.

Our work begins and ends with our patients and is measured by how well we serve them.

11

Relapse Prevention

Stopping isn't hard. Not starting again is.

—ROBERT DOWNEY JR.

I have come to realize that the name of the game is not so much to stop drinking as to stay sober.

—CITED IN *ALCOHOLICS ANONYMOUS*

I've been sober for a few months, but my brain just feels numb—I don't know how to think or what to think or even if I want to think.

I haven't had a drink in seven weeks, but I feel like I'm going nuts. When my kids yell at each other, I want to curl up into a ball and die. Bright lights, loud noises, intense emotions—I can't be around them. I feel like they are frying my brain.

I'm sober, but my memory is shot, and I'm afraid I have permanent brain damage or maybe even Alzheimer's.

I can't figure it out. I've got eight months of sobriety under my belt, but the anxiety and the fear just don't quit. Once or twice a week I wake up in a sweat, dreaming about the time I ran over my son's bicycle when I was drunk and imagining that I killed him.

Some days I feel great, happy, solidly sober, but then the next day I feel just plain awful. My mood swings are like flash floods—there's never any warning.

I cry all the time. I'm always overreacting to everything—a pile of dirty clothes in the hallway is enough to make me want to scream.

I'm telling you—alcoholism was hell. But what is this, purgatory?

If recovery is viewed as a lifelong adventure, the most difficult terrain to traverse is encountered in the first leg of the journey. Adjusting to a life without alcohol requires a major shift in the way the brain goes about its daily activities. Under the influence of alcohol, the neurotransmitters know what they're doing, where they're going, and why they're in such a hurry to get there. As long as the drug is around, everything works according to plan, and the feel-good chemical rush is predictable.

Take alcohol away for any length of time, however, and all those well-traveled neural pathways are hit with the equivalent of a major earthquake. Bridges collapse, roads buckle under the strain, huge mountains of earth are bulldozed directly into the path of oncoming traffic. New construction begins soon after the quake strikes, but while the mess is being cleared away you can expect plenty of traffic jams and all the attendant problems of stalled rush-hour traffic.

While your brain tries to regain its balance, you'll need to make adjustments in your schedule and your expectations. "So I'm sober," one recovering alcoholic says. "All my expectations have come to nothing. What's the use?" Another recovering alcoholic looks at the difficulties encountered in sobriety from a perspective that engenders hope, not despair. "The less I expect, the more humility I have, the more serene and happy I am, and the more I feel that life is on my side and not out to get me."

Understanding the long-term effects of alcohol on your central nervous system will help protect your sobriety and guard you against relapses. Rather than assume that you are a weak, confused, hypersensitive person who can't enjoy life without alcohol, you will gain a deeper appreciation for the devastating, slow-to-fade effects of the drug on diverse brain functions. You will see that "emotional" symptoms are directly linked to disruptions in neurochemistry. And you will understand that time is your friend, not your enemy. This knowledge will protect you and keep you safe.

Given time to heal, the addicted brain will return to its "normal," nonaddicted (sober) state. *Time* is the key word, however, for years of damage and destruction cannot be undone in a few days, weeks, or even months. Researchers estimate that 75 to 95 percent of recovering alcoholics experience some form of lingering dysfunction related to the damage alcohol has inflicted on the body and mind; many alcoholics continue to have long-term withdrawal symptoms—also known as protracted withdrawal or postacute withdrawal—for months and even years after their last drink.

The protracted withdrawal syndrome offers clear evidence of the power of neurological addiction and the toxic, long-term effects of alcohol on the body and mind. Recovery, like addiction, is a period of adaptation, in which the body needs time to heal its wounds and restore balance. In the meantime recovering alcoholics must be reminded—over and over again—that these lingering symptoms are *not* signs of emotional weakness or proof of an inability to maintain sobriety, but evidence of the body's ongoing efforts to restore balance. Relatives, friends, coworkers, and health care professionals also need to be educated about the nature of the protracted withdrawal syndrome in order to avoid misinterpreting the symptoms as evidence that alcoholics are "neurotic," "anxiety-prone," "chronically depressed," or simply "immature."

The Protracted Withdrawal Syndrome

• *Disrupted thought patterns* are common among recovering alcoholics, who may express concern about their "foggy" brains and symptoms such as difficulty concentrating, inability to pay attention, problems with abstract (theoretical) reasoning, and circular or obsessive thoughts.

• *Memory gaps* are characterized by short-term memory loss, the inability to remember significant events from the past, and/or difficulty learning new skills.

• *Emotional hypersensitivity* is evident when an event that would normally evoke a minor emotional reaction stimulates an extraordinarily intense response. Emotional overreactions are common in early recovery, and many alcoholics find themselves constantly on the verge of tears, ready to explode in anger, prone to temper tantrums, and so on. Hypersensitivity can eventually lead to emotional exhaustion or a sense that one is "numb" and does not care anymore what happens. The recovering alcoholic may say, "I can't feel anything," "Nothing seems to matter," or "I just don't care what happens."

• *Sleep problems*, which typically show up in disturbing dreams or nightmares, general restlessness, fragmented sleep, and multiple awakenings, are common.

• *Physical coordination problems* may include dizziness, problems with balance and hand-eye coordination, and slow reflexes, often leading to physical clumsiness and accident-proneness.

MAJOR CAUSES OF PROTRACTED WITHDRAWAL

NEUROTRANSMITTER DEPLETION

In Chapter 4 we explained that alcoholics inherit a defective gene (or, more accurately, genes) that interferes with the synthesis of serotonin, dopamine, GABA, and other "feel-good" neurotransmitters. These neurotransmitter imbalances may lead to general feelings of anxiety, irritability, depression, sleep disturbances, and craving for alcohol. Complicating the alcoholic's genetic legacy is the fact that chronic heavy drinking creates neurotransmitter imbalances that can persist for months or even years after the alcoholic's last drink, further exacerbating anxiety and depression.

MALNUTRITION

Chronically excessive use of alcohol interferes with the absorption, digestion, and utilization of nutrients in the body, leading to widespread vitamin and mineral deficiencies. Many middle- and late-stage alcoholics consume 50 percent or more of their calories as alcohol, the only drug that is also a substantial source of calories. Alcohol also severely damages the organs responsible for processing, utilizing, and distributing nutrients, most notably the liver and the pancreas.

HYPOGLYCEMIA

Alcohol disrupts blood sugar (glucose) mechanisms, leading to steep spikes and sudden drops in glucose levels. When the blood sugar level drops below a certain point, the body releases epinephrine (adrenaline), an emergency hormone that instructs the liver to release glucose into the bloodstream. As adrenaline surges through your body, your heartbeat speeds up, your blood pressure rises, and you may experience symptoms such as anxiety, fear, nausea, intense hunger, shakes, sweats, and a pounding heart.

The brain depends on glucose as its primary energy source, and when blood glucose levels drop abruptly, the brain signals its distress through symptoms such as mental confusion, headaches, irritability, nervousness, depression, and an intense craving for alcohol or high-sugar foods. When blood sugar levels begin to rise in response to the liver's release of glucose or the ingestion of alcohol, these hypoglycemic symptoms are quickly relieved. But what goes up must come down, and as the blood sugar drops again, the symptoms return.

Abstinence from alcohol does not automatically relieve hypoglycemia. Some researchers theorize that hypoglycemia *precedes* alcoholic drinking and may, in fact, contribute to the craving for alcohol as a quick, effective remedy for low blood sugar. The old saying "Candy is dandy, but liquor is quicker" is, unfortunately for alcoholics, the literal truth.

Here, too, is the danger for recovering alcoholics who rely on sweets and high-sugar foods to quell their craving for alcohol. While sugar-laden foods and beverages produce a quick rise in blood sugar, the blood sugar soon drops like a rock, generating a desire for more sweets—or for alcohol, which works better than anything to relieve the low-blood-sugar blues.

AUTONOMIC NERVOUS SYSTEM DYSFUNCTION

The more serious and long-lasting symptoms of protracted withdrawal generally occur in late-stage alcoholics who have been drinking excessively for many years, even decades. One cause of these symptoms is alcohol-related damage to the autonomic nervous system, which governs the glands, the cardiac muscle, and the smooth muscles of the digestive and respiratory systems, controlling such functions as blood pressure, pulse, temperature, sweating response, tremor, and muscle tone. Symptoms of autonomic nervous system dysfunction include excessive perspiration, rapid pulse, tremor, and increased heart rate. Although these symptoms generally lessen as sobriety lengthens, it is not uncommon for alcoholics sober for two or three years to experience lingering problems.

CORTICAL ATROPHY

Another cause of more serious withdrawal symptoms is cortical atrophy. The brain is blanketed with an outer layer of gray matter, called the cortex, which is involved in a number of functions, including reasoning, memory, regulation of the five senses (sight, hearing, touch, taste, and smell), and supervision of the body's conscious movements. Alcohol acts as a direct poison to brain cells, killing them off by the millions and leaving many more millions severely damaged. Approximately half of all late-stage alcoholics have a measurable decline of cortical function and may experience symptoms such as memory lapses, difficulties with abstract reasoning, sensory deficits, muscle weakness, and lack of physical coordination. In the great majority of cases, normal functioning gradually returns as sobriety continues and the body heals itself.

Cognitive dysfunctions, especially the subtler forms such as memory lapses and problems with abstract reasoning, can help us understand why some alcoholics appear so resistant to change and difficult to rehabilitate. Even after months of abstinence, many recovering alcoholics continue to experience problems with circular thinking, irrational thought patterns, and forgetfulness. Rather than label alcoholics weak, stubborn, or uncooperative, we can learn to appreciate the underlying physiological changes that make recovery such a challenge and understand the need for patience as the body works to heal the damage inflicted by the drug alcohol.

STAYING SOBER

The protracted-withdrawal syndrome and the experience of countless alcoholics put the lie to the common myth that if an alcoholic gets sober, everything else will fall into place. The idea that sobriety will cure all your ills is one of the most dangerous falsehoods in the myth-laden world of alcoholism. After two months or two years of sobriety, when everything hasn't fallen into place as promised, recovering alcoholics may find themselves thinking: "Something must be wrong with me because I'm sober, but I'm definitely not enjoying myself."

Family members, friends, and coworkers can't quite figure out why the alcoholic continues to experience problems after months of sobriety, and they often conclude that the ongoing symptoms are evidence of underlying psychological or emotional problems. Continued cravings for alcohol appear to confirm psychological theories about the alcoholic's lack of willpower and moral resolve.

The danger, of course, is relapse. If the recovering alcoholic is anxious, frustrated, and emotionally unstable, has trouble thinking or sleeping, and continues to crave alcohol—and if he or she is surrounded by people who misinterpret the symptoms of protracted withdrawal as evidence of immaturity, irresponsibility, or inability to cope with stress—the risk of relapse rises dramatically.

Relapses must not be interpreted as a symptom of weakness or inability to stay sober. All chronic (incurable) illnesses that have some behavioral component—even socially acceptable, nonstigmatized illnesses such as cardiovascular disease, diabetes, and asthma—are characterized by relapses. The patient, in other words, doesn't always follow the treatment plan. Diabetics relapse when they eat too many sweets or ignore blood sugar fluctuations; heart attack victims relapse when they stray from their diet or sneak cigarettes; asthmatics relapse when they forget to use their medication; and alcoholics relapse when they let down their defenses and experience an overpowering craving for a drink. Research shows that alcoholics actually have relatively high compliance rates (meaning they follow the prescribed recovery guidelines) when compared to individuals with other chronic diseases.

Understanding why relapses occur can help prevent them. Staying sober requires a steady mind-set—a way of thinking and behaving in which you remain ever conscious of the powerful influence the drug alcohol has on your body, mind, and spirit. The craving for alcohol does not suddenly disappear after a few days or weeks of sobriety, and it can return at any time, even after many years. Recovering alcoholic Bob Welch, formerly a pitcher for the Los Angeles Dodgers, describes the situations in his life that automatically elicit a craving for alcohol:

> There are three times I still really have a craving to drink. One of them is on an airplane. I associate it with getting drunk. When I first started flying, I always drank. Another time is after I play golf. Last, when I'm done pitching. My body at times still says, "All right, where's the fucking booze?" I'm flying after a game. My body is thinking, Where is the booze at, man? We've got to go to sleep. In those three areas it pops out like, "Am I going to drink or am I not going to drink?" But as long as I know what is going on, I can prepare myself.

A sudden craving for alcohol usually has a basis in some prior behavior or experience, or in some physiological change such as illness or injury. If you know where these craving attacks come from and what situations are likely to create them, you can anticipate and protect yourself against them. At the very least you can understand them. When recovering alcoholics are taught and then continually reminded about the neurological nature of craving and the mind-set needed to combat the sudden urge for a drink, they can begin to think and act in ways that will protect them against the sudden, powerful, seemingly irrational urge for a drink.

BUILDING UP TO DRINK (BUD)

Experts have identified a process known as BUD, or "building up to drink," that sometimes occurs in recovery. At the beginning of the buildup, which generally lasts about 72 hours, you might feel slightly irritated, bored, restless, or anxious. Instead of gradually fading away, these feelings gain momentum until you feel as if you are losing control over your life, your emotions, and even your sanity.

A return to the alcoholic state of mind is only the first step in the progression toward relapse. In the second step your behavior mirrors this subtle inward change, and you begin to withdraw from those people, places, and activities that work to support your sobriety—AA meetings, your AA sponsor, treatment staff, sober friends or neighbors, and others. You may find yourself resenting your family and friends and thinking back with fondness and regret to "the good old drinking days" (a strange sort of selective memory, that).

Sometime during this second stage of the BUD process, your body may give a clear warning that all is not well—your hands tremble, you perspire profusely, your heart pounds, and you feel anxious, fearful, or exhausted. When the emotional and physical symptoms reach their peak, you may feel depressed, miserably unhappy, and in despair—after all, you're sober, but you feel worse (or at least it seems right now that you do) than when you were drinking. This is the point where many recovering alcoholics experience a powerful craving for alcohol.

As soon as you begin to experience a build-up of physical and emotional symptoms, you can recognize the danger of relapse and guard yourself against it. Call your AA sponsor, go to an AA meeting, talk to a family member or a close, sober friend who understands alcoholism and the process of relapse. Notice what you are eating; pay particular attention to your sugar intake. Assess the level of stress in your life and give yourself time and space to relax. Keep a close watch for the four danger signals included in the acronym HALT: Hungry, Angry, Lonely, or Tired. A nutritious meal, a long walk, a heart-to-heart conversation with a friend or counselor, or a good night's sleep may help you through a particularly rough period.

Follow AA's advice to "live one day at a time." For many alcoholics the key to a stable recovery is discovered in the ability to live in the present moment. Jean Kirkpatrick, a recovered alcoholic and founder of Women for Sobriety, Inc., writes about the need to learn how to live in the immediate present in *Goodbye Hangovers, Hello Life*:

We must learn to live in the present. We must learn to live today. As we begin to move away from our negative period of depression, loneliness, overcoming guilt, we will begin to cherish each day and our sobriety and our new feelings of good health. We will begin to have energy that we haven't had recently. We will begin to have some enthusiasm as we come into a period of self-knowledge.

All these good feelings come to us as we recognize the futility of reacting to our past, which is over and done and must be put where it belongs, behind us. There is not a single thing we can change about our past except the way we think about it: that it is over and we are changing.

"Life isn't fair," writes William Goldman in his novel *The Princess Bride*. "It's just fairer than death, that's all." Recovery could be said to begin with the acceptance of that simple summing up of the unfairness of both life and death. From there recovery becomes a process of investigating what life, difficult as it is at times, holds for you as a sober human being. Learning the truth about the drug and the disease is only the beginning of your journey. Learning the truth about yourself—who you are, what you want to do with your life, how to become a better human being—constitutes the real adventure and exhilaration of recovery.

CAN DRUGS HELP ME STAY SOBER?

In early recovery, treatment professionals sometimes prescribe "maintenance pharmacotherapy," drugs to help alcoholics stay sober. These drugs include Antabuse (disulfiram) and Revia (naltrexone); Campral (acamprosate) is widely used in Europe and may be available for use in the United States later this year. Another class of drugs known as the SSRIs (selective serotonin reuptake inhibitors) are not specifically used for relapse prevention but are thought to help many recovering alcoholics who suffer from depression, anxiety or panic attacks, or obsessive-compulsive disorder.

While a few of these drugs show promise in alcoholism treatment, long-term controlled studies are needed to confirm early reports of encouraging results. Antabuse, which was first introduced in 1951, is the only sobriety-maintenance drug that has been studied over a long period; yet even with this drug, the number of controlled clinical trials is limited and reveals mixed findings. Naltrexone has been on the market since 1994; studies of the drug's effectiveness over long periods of time are not yet available. Acamprosate has been extensively studied in Europe, and studies are currently under way in the United States; once again, however, long-term research has not been conducted on this drug.

Researchers who believe that maintenance pharmacotherapy drugs show promise in alcoholism treatment are careful to point out that long-term studies lasting several years, with follow-up extended for five or even ten years, are needed before any conclusions can be reached about the long-term effects and potential benefits of these drugs. Our general recommendation, based on past experience with drugs that seemed to show great promise but over longer periods created serious, even life-threatening problems for users, is to approach all drug therapies with caution, including drugs that are specifically designed to help you stay sober.

DISULFIRAM (ANTABUSE)

Disulfiram (Antabuse) interferes with the metabolism of alcohol, leading to a buildup of the highly toxic substance called acetaldehyde. If an alcoholic drinks while taking Antabuse, acetaldehyde accumulates in the bloodstream, producing an extremely unpleasant reaction, with symptoms such as flushing, violent headaches, nausea, vomiting, sweating, extreme thirst, chest pain, heart palpitations, difficulty breathing, abnormally rapid heart rate, weakness, blurred vision, and mental confusion.

As long as recovering alcoholics continue to take Antabuse, they know they can't drink without suffering the consequences. The problem most often cited with Antabuse (in addition to the fact that it must be used with caution in alcoholics with known liver disease) is that the drug does not eliminate the craving for alcohol. If the craving continues, all the alcoholic has to do is stop taking the daily Antabuse pill, wait several days, and start drinking again.

We believe there is a bigger problem with Antabuse, however, and it may account for the extremely high dropout rates seen with this drug. In an experiment conducted in 1987, nondrinking rats were injected with cyanamide, a substance that acts like Antabuse to stall the metabolism of acetaldehyde. The rats experienced a significant increase in their craving for alcohol. Why? The researchers theorize that Antabuse may increase the craving for alcohol because the accumulating acetaldehyde interacts with neurotransmitters in the brain to create an overabundance of the addictive compounds known as TIQs. (For a full explanation of the interactions between acetaldehyde and the TIQs, see pages 46–49.)

As so often happens with drug therapies, the long-term negative effects of Antabuse may far outweigh any potential short-term gains.

NALTREXONE (ReVia or Trexan)

Naltrexone is a narcotic antagonist that was originally used to treat heroin addicts. Unlike Antabuse, which makes people violently ill when they drink, naltrexone blocks the craving for alcohol and is sometimes used to help alcoholics "unlearn" the positive, reinforcing effects of the drug.

How does the drug work? Naltrexone stands like a three-hundred-pound bodyguard in front of the opiate receptors, refusing entry to alcohol and other opiate-type drugs such as heroin. Thus, when you take naltrexone and drink alcohol, you won't get the rewarding euphoric kick because naltrexone blocks alcohol from entering the opiate receptor, which in turn prevents the release of the feel-good chemicals that create the euphoric high. Alcohol loses its buzz; in fact, many alcoholics who take naltrexone claim that it makes alcohol taste repulsive.

Does naltrexone keep recovering alcoholics from relapsing? The answer is qualified: According to the relatively few studies available, the drug seems to work in a limited way for some alcoholics, dulling the craving for alcohol. Two short-term studies published in 1992 showed that naltrexone reduced alcohol drinking in alcoholics; in one of these studies, the relapse rate for patients treated with naltrexone was 23 percent compared to 54 percent for a control group treated with a placebo. In a 1997 study involving ninety-seven alcoholics the investigators concluded that "naltrexone showed only modest effects in reducing alcohol drinking for the 12 weeks of treatment." However, for those subjects who completed the research study and were "highly compliant" with taking the medication, improvement was noted in a variety of outcome measures. Patient compliance appears to be a key issue with naltrexone and other pharmaceutical approaches to alcoholism treatment.

Joseph Volpicelli, a psychiatrist and psychologist at the Center for the Study of Addictions at the University of Pennsylvania in Philadelphia and the author of several studies on naltrexone, believes that naltrexone can "stop the vicious cycle of alcohol addiction in which one drink nearly always leads to a full blown relapse." He prescribes naltrexone for recovering alcoholics "whose alcohol drinking has not irrevocably impaired their social relationships or occupational functioning and who are not profoundly depressed."

While naltrexone may be useful for preventing relapses in some alcoholics, it appears to have a downside. In a 1997 study designed to test the drug's safety, 9.8 percent of patients reported nausea, while 6.6 percent reported mild to moderate headaches; 15 percent of patients discontinued the drug because of negative side effects. If prescribed in too high a dose, naltrexone can cause liver damage.

Some researchers are concerned that naltrexone may have a long-term negative effect on the recovering alcoholic's psychological health. Not only does naltrexone block alcohol from creating a high, it also appears to block the actions of the natural (endogenous) opiates that create normal feelings of well-being. According to Avram Goldstein, a pharmacologist, neurobiologist, and physician who teaches at Stanford University, "studies have shown a subtle but measurable dysphoric effect of naltrexone, even in normal volunteers." *Dysphoria* is a technical term for restlessness, uneasiness, and a general sense of discomfort, despair, or depression.

Naltrexone is not in any sense a treatment for alcoholism, nor can it be considered a cure, because it does nothing to dismantle the neurological scaffolding that supports addiction. If alcoholics want to feel the magic again, all they have to do is stop taking naltrexone; the bully guarding the opiate door disappears, and the euphoric high returns. Until more studies are available and the long-term impact of naltrexone on the alcoholic's emotional state and craving for alcohol is fully assessed, we recommend that this drug be used with caution.

ACAMPROSATE (CAMPRAL)

Acamprosate (Campral) has a similar structure to GABA (gamma-aminobutyric acid), one of the brain's most widely distributed neurotransmitters and a key chemical involved in alcohol addiction. GABA helps quiet down the brain cells, decreasing brain activity. Valium and other benzodiazepine drugs exert their sedative effect on the brain through their interactions with GABA.

Researchers believe that acamprosate may stimulate inhibitory GABA receptors, allowing more of the neurotransmitter to collect in the synapse and exert its calming, sedating influence on the mind and body. Acamprosate also appears to restrain certain excitatory amino acids such as glutamate.

In laboratory experiments, alcoholic rats given acamprosate voluntarily decreased their alcohol consumption. A number of studies with alcoholics show that acamprosate reduces alcohol intake and appears to reduce craving. In a 1996 article in the *Archives of General Psychiatry* researchers reported that patients who received acamprosate were continuously abstinent for longer periods of time and less likely to drop out of treatment than patients who received placebos.

In a 1996 article that appeared in the prestigious British medical journal *Lancet*, researchers randomly assigned 455 alcoholics between the ages of eighteen and sixty-five to different treatment groups. One group was given 2 grams of acamprosate daily while the other group was given a placebo. Subjects were followed after one, three, six, nine, and twelve months. At the study's end, 18 percent of the patients on acamprosate had been continuously abstinent compared to 7 percent on the placebo. After a further year of follow-up, twenty-seven acamprosate-treated patients remained abstinent compared to eleven in the placebo group.

The researchers observed:

The results are very encouraging suggesting a more than three times increase in abstinence at one year for those who took acamprosate, with effects persisting for at least a year after treatment. Unfortunately less than a fifth of the patients can be considered as treatment successes, so acamprosate is clearly not going to be useful in all cases. It remains to be established if a subgroup of alcoholic patients can be identified in whom treatment with acamprosate would be a particularly beneficial adjunct to normal psychosocial rehabilitation programs.

Of all the maintenance psychotherapeutic drugs available for recovering alcoholics, acamprosate may have the greatest potential. The drug is well tolerated and has no sedative, hypnotic, anxiety-reducing, antidepressant, or muscle-relaxant properties that could lead to physical or psychological dependence. The only side effect appears to be mild to moderate diarrhea. Studies suggest that acamprosate "enhances abstinence" and reduces drinking days, although only minimal evidence exists that the drug diminishes craving or relapse rates.

Still, the biggest problem with acamprosate (as with naltrexone) appears to be one of patient compliance. Dropout rates in acamprosate studies are high. Forty-one percent of subjects dropped out in one study; in another, 50 percent of patients dropped out in the first ninety days of treatment and only one-third of the patients completed the entire 360 days of treatment.

Our optimism for this drug is also tempered by experience with drugs such as Antabuse and naltrexone. These products may help certain individuals stay sober, but they are, at best, only a partial answer. As always, continuing research and clinical trials with recovering alcoholics will clarify the usefulness of these drugs and help target the specific individuals who might benefit from them.

SELECTIVE SEROTONIN REUPTAKE INHIBITORS (SSRIs)

Selective serotonin reuptake inhibitors, or SSRIs (Prozac, Zoloft, Serzone, Paxil, Effexor) are nonaddictive and may be useful for some alcoholics who suffer from severe depression, chronic anxiety, recurrent panic attacks, or persistent sleep disturbances that are unrelated to drinking alcohol or withdrawal from alcohol. SSRIs alter the synthesis of serotonin and other neurotransmitters in the brain; since alcoholism is related to a genetic defect that contributes to neurotransmitter deficiencies, it makes sense that these drugs might help correct those imbalances.

We are concerned, however, by the fact that many treatment centers hand out these drugs "by the truckload," in the words of one treatment professional, without careful individual assessment of each patient. Although depression and chronic anxiety may exist independently of alcoholism, in the great majority of cases these disorders disappear after several months of sobriety. Ongoing emotional or psychological problems may be a symptom of protracted withdrawal (see pages 164–168) rather than a sign of a "dual disorder," the current lingo for serious psychological problems that coexist with alcoholism.

A number of research studies conducted in the last decade indicate that SSRIs do indeed help alcoholics reduce their drinking—from an average 6.0 daily drinks to 5.5 drinks in one study, and from 25 to 19 ounces of whiskey daily in another study. The goal of treatment and recovery, however, is not to assist alcoholics in their efforts to cut down on their drinking but to help the alcoholic stop drinking and stay sober. While some people might consider a 6-ounce reduction in alcohol intake a significant improvement, 19 ounces of whiskey a day is a heck of a lot of booze and more than enough to fuel the fires of the alcoholic's addicted brain.

SSRIs are not considered addictive, for they work on different brain pathways than the addiction-causing drugs such as alcohol, cocaine, and the benzodiazepines. That does not mean, however, that these drugs cannot cause problems. Psychiatrist Marc Schuckit comments:

> The antidepressant drugs, including the serotonin re-uptake inhibiting agents, are not totally safe. They have effects on diverse parts of the brain, many patients complain of side effects with some agents including anxiety and tremor, and all of these drugs are dangerous when mixed with large amounts of alcohol.

That last point is particularly crucial to keep in mind if there is a danger of relapse.

The bottom line is that SSRIs should never be considered a standard part of alcoholism treatment. Recovering alcoholics who report chronic depression, sleep disturbances, anxiety, or panic attacks may be good candidates for SSRIs, but in most cases we recommend waiting six to twelve months to see if these problems disappear as the alcoholic's body heals itself and balance is restored. However, if depression, anxiety, or sleep disorders are having a profound effect on the recovering alcoholic's ability to stay sober, SSRIs may help in the transition from early sobriety to a stable, secure recovery.

National Institute on Alcohol Abuse and Alcoholism (NIAAA) director Enoch Gordis, M.D., emphasizes the need for ongoing research specifically designed to understand the complicated effects of sobriety maintenance drugs:

> NIAAA places a high priority on neuroscience research that will form the basis for the development of medications to treat alcoholism. . . . Further neuroscience research is needed to characterize the biological processes in the brain that lead to the development of alcoholism, and to apply that information to the development of medications that act on specific brain mechanisms associated with the pathophysiological processes involved in this disease.

At this point we don't fully understand the neurochemistry of addiction to alcohol, nor do we have sufficient research available to judge the long-term effects of recently introduced drugs such as naltrexone and acamprosate. In the next decade our knowledge will expand exponentially. In the meantime, we have many proven ways to help alcoholics stay sober, including basic education about neurological addiction, Alcoholics Anonymous, psychological counseling, and nutritional therapy. If we stick to what works, we can help the great majority of alcoholics to a stable, long-lasting recovery. And we can remain confident that science will provide the information we need to guide treatment choices in the future.

Psychological Counseling

The name of the game is to replace rum with relationships.

—JEROME LEVIN, PH.D.

I'm sober, have been for two years," says Grant, age forty-four. "I attend AA meetings faithfully and get a lot out of them, but I definitely have problems to work out. My wife is struggling with her weight and feels ashamed of her body; we haven't been intimate for years. I work long hours, which adds to the problems in my marriage. And my ten-year-old son was recently diagnosed with asthma. As much as I love Alcoholics Anonymous, the structure and methods of the program can't help me deal with all these problems and the stress they create in my life."

Grant is physically healthy, intelligent, and financially secure. He owns a very successful business, exercises regularly, enjoys his close-knit family and many solid friendships, and embraces life's challenges with energy and enthusiasm. He is also prone to depression and suffers from chronic anxiety and full-blown panic attacks.

Two years ago, when Grant completed an eight-week outpatient treatment program, he consulted a psychiatrist. The psychiatrist concluded that Grant's primary problem was anxiety; he prescribed Xanax and referred Grant to a psychotherapist. The psychotherapist agreed that Grant's primary problem was psychological and concluded from Grant's history that he was probably not an alcoholic after all but a problem drinker who needed help controlling his drinking. With encouragement from his psychiatrist and psychotherapist, Grant enrolled in a controlled-drinking program; two weeks later, frustrated and distraught, he was readmitted to the outpatient alcoholism treatment program.

At the end of his second treatment, Grant asked his addiction counselor for a referral to a psychotherapist who understood the disease of alcoholism. "I'm not worried about staying sober," he explained. "I know that I have a disease, and I know I have to stay away from the booze. But I need to find a way to control my anxiety, and I'd like to work on my relationship skills." The addiction counselor referred Grant to our coauthor, clinical psychologist Arthur Ciaramicoli, for individual therapy.

After meeting with Grant in individual therapy for several months, Dr. Ciaramicoli asked him if he might be interested in joining a weekly group session. "Once alcoholics have stabilized in recovery and begin to feel more comfortable with their ability to handle emotions and diverse relationships," Dr. Ciaramicoli explained to Grant, "their energy for greater health in all areas grows. The brain regains its balance, moods even out, sleep patterns stabilize, and anxiety recedes. You have told me many times over the past few months that you feel the need to be challenged, expand your boundaries, learn more about yourself, and test your relationship skills in different situations. I think you would do very well in this group."

Grant now attends both individual and group sessions weekly. He also goes to AA meetings at least once a week. In AA, Grant benefits from close association with other recovering alcoholics, sharing in the triumphs and struggles of sober life. In individual and group therapy sessions, he is learning how to manage conflict, clearly express his emotions, and develop his interpersonal skills. "AA has been extremely helpful for me," Grant says. "In fact, I owe my life to the program. But I am equally convinced that without the group and individual therapy sessions, I would not have made it."

Grant's journey from active alcoholism into long-term recovery is typical of many alcoholics. The disease affected his life in many diverse areas; as time went on and his recovery solidified, he began to feel better, both physically and emotionally, but his problems did not simply disappear. Like all human beings, Grant faces daily stresses at work, at home, and in his everyday encounters with family, friends, coworkers, and strangers. His ability to handle emotional situations and manage periodic problems in his personal relationships is complicated by the fact that he started drinking when he was fourteen; from that point on, alcohol became the most important relationship in his life. Over the next thirty years he learned a lot about how to pretend that nothing was wrong with him and how to avoid dealing with people who might confront him about his drinking, but he never learned how to manage stress or tension without picking up a drink, nor did he learn the fine art of creating and maintaining intimate relationships.

Individual and group counseling sessions represent an opportunity for Grant to discover lost parts of himself—elements of his personality and character that he didn't even know existed. He is learning how to honestly and openly express his feelings, avoid impulsive actions and reactions, and empathize with others who are struggling with their own limitations and crises. In therapy Grant believes he is discovering how to become a better—more tolerant, more empathic, more forgiving—human being.

When the subject of psychological counseling comes up in the context of long-term recovery, the question is invariably raised: If psychological and emotional problems don't cause alcoholism, why does a recovering alcoholic need psychotherapy? We have at least four convincing answers to that question.

The first and most obvious answer is discovered in the very nature of the alcoholic's disease. A neurological addiction is characterized by widespread changes in brain chemistry. Over a period of many months or years, the brain adapts to alcohol, eventually needing the drug in order to function normally. Recovery is a gradual process of allowing the brain to restore normal functioning in the absence of alcohol. For most alcoholics this process requires several months, and in some cases several years, of reorganization and healing. (See Chapter 11, particularly the discussion of protracted-withdrawal syndrome on pages 164–168.) Psychological counseling with a competent professional who understands the subtle and profound ways in which a brain addiction disrupts thoughts, moods, emotions, and behaviors will help alcoholics understand why their thoughts and emotions are disrupted and how to cope with any ongoing problems.

The second reason for recommending psychological counseling is related to the alcoholic's undeveloped relational skills. It doesn't matter whether the alcoholic starts drinking at age fourteen, twenty-five, or forty—once addiction is established, the alcoholic's relationship with alcohol soon comes to mean more than anything else. Time and time again, when push comes to shove, the alcoholic chooses alcohol over friendships, marriage, and, most painful of all, children.

This "choice" is predetermined by the needs of the addicted brain, which also provides the alcoholic with plenty of reasons to rationalize the act of reaching out for the bottle. Human beings, after all, are difficult, demanding, and frequently disappointing; alcohol, on the other hand, is always available to soothe the hurts and frustrations of life, and it always, without fail, works. Alcohol is "magic"; alcoholics sometimes refer to the drug as "the love of my life." Mere human beings, with all their flaws and limitations, simply can't measure up. When human relationships fail, the bottle heals all wounds.

At the point when alcohol becomes the central relationship of the alcoholic's life, the development of interpersonal skills slows down. Because most alcoholics start drinking early in life, usually in their teens or early twenties, many of the insights and competencies involved in what *New York Times* science reporter Daniel Goleman calls "emotional intelligence"—self-awareness, the ability to control one's emotions and bounce back from life's setbacks, accurately understanding what other people are thinking and feeling, responding with tact and sensitivity to another person's needs—remain undeveloped. The years spent with the beer can or the bottle rob alcoholics of countless opportunities to learn how to maintain intimacy and resolve interpersonal conflicts without reaching for the booze. (It is interesting, however, that while intimate relationships with friends, family, and lovers suffer during those years of active alcoholism, many if not most middle-stage alcoholics continue to perform at high levels in their professional careers. They may earn a reputation as a no-good son of a bitch, but it is not until the deteriorative stage, when the disease profoundly affects physical health and mental functioning, that things at work begin to fall apart.)

A third reason for recommending psychological counseling relates to a minority of recovering alcoholics. An estimated 20 to 30 percent of alcoholics—the same percentage found in the nonalcoholic population—suffer from ongoing or preexisting psychological disturbances such as chronic depression, anxiety disorders, panic attacks, manic-depressive illness, obsessive-compulsive disorder, and major psychiatric disorders such as schizophrenia or mania. When the psychological problems predate the alcohol problem and/or continue for months or years after the alcoholic stops drinking, medications may be needed to subdue the symptoms associated with these disorders. Referral to a competent psychologist or psychiatrist who understands the neurophysiological nature of alcoholism is essential.

We must emphasize once again that alcoholism is not a *symptom* of a psychological disturbance or an ill-fated attempt to self-medicate depression or anxiety. In *Educating Yourself About Alcohol and Drugs*, Psychiatrist Marc Schuckit summarizes the extensive research into the connection between psychological problems and alcoholism:

> There is no evidence that people who later go on to develop severe alcohol and drug problems are more likely than others in the gen-

eral population to have had severe depressions, severe anxiety conditions, or psychotic conditions prior to the development of their alcohol and drug disorders.

And here is our final reason for recommending psychological counseling: Alcoholics are part of a larger society that, because of misconceptions and widespread ignorance about the causes of alcoholism, continues to view them as morally depraved, self-centered, pleasure-obsessed individuals. Learning how to live in a world that considers you somehow abnormal or deficient in character is an ongoing process full of conflict and challenge. Retreating from that larger world does not work. In fact, this may be one of the most valuable lessons learned from years of alcoholic drinking: Disengaging from the outside world can only increase your loneliness and intensify your despair. Isolation from others destroys the body, the mind, and the spirit—and greatly increases the risk of relapse.

Recovery consists of a gradual reintroduction to the inevitably complex and often painful domain of interpersonal relationships. Learning how to defend and take care of yourself is the first priority. As time goes by, however, it becomes just as important to learn how to reach out to others whom you might initially label intolerant or incapable of understanding your life as an alcoholic. If we connect only with those people who are "just like us," then we miss out on one of the most exhilarating adventures of life—getting to know, understand, and appreciate the great diversity of life on this planet. The more we interact with others, the more we realize the fundamental truth that despite differences in "diagnosis," gender, upbringing, ethnic or racial background, education, personal wealth, or choice of career, we are all more alike than we are different.

In the book *Portraits of Recovery*, an alcoholic identified only as Michael describes his transformation from "the token black gay person in recovery" to "100 percent human":

> *It took me a long time to realize that I am 100 percent human and everything in my life is meant to be—including my mistakes. For years I thought that I had to be something else. It finally dawned on me a few years ago when this old redneck, who was about sixty years old, was yelling at the top of his lungs that his name was such-and-such and that he was an alcoholic and a human being. That touched a nerve in me, and I realized that I am first and foremost, regardless of where I came from, a human being. It doesn't matter what anyone else thinks of me. It doesn't matter what clothes I wear*

or what I own, I'm not better or worse than anybody else. That is the greatest gift of my life, and my sobriety. To be positive, to be negative, but whatever it is, feel what I need to feel, do as I need to do, but above all to be human.

A GRADUAL PROCESS

The recovering alcoholic's need for psychological counseling changes as the months and years of sobriety continue. In early recovery—which should be defined in terms of the alcoholic's physical and emotional stability rather than by how many months or years have elapsed—individual and group counseling sessions generally focus on educating the alcoholic about the nature of the addiction and basic ways of protecting and caring for the self. When alcoholics are treated with empathy and understanding, trust develops, anxiety and fear begin to lessen, and confidence in the ability to manage stressful situations increases. As sobriety lengthens and the alcoholic's sense of self stabilizes, other options such as theme-oriented group therapy and "mixed" interactive groups can be considered.

In the remainder of this chapter we will briefly explore the possibilities available to the recovering alcoholic. There is one situation, however, that recovering alcoholics must avoid at all costs: treatment with a counselor or psychotherapist who is ignorant about the nature of alcoholism. How do you go about finding a competent, enlightened therapist? Word of mouth from respected members of the alcoholism treatment community may be your most reliable guide. In the best of all worlds, you will be referred to a therapist in treatment as part of your outpatient planning and relapse prevention program; it is particularly important that you meet with the therapist before you leave treatment so that the relationship is established early on in sobriety.

If you never went through a formal treatment program or if you have been out of treatment for some time, you can call a reputable treatment center in your area, ask to speak to an addiction counselor or staff member, and request a referral. You may also want to ask around at AA meetings. AA members, particularly the old-timers, have heard enough horror stories (mostly true) about disastrous treatment at the hands of psychiatrists and psychotherapists that they may warn you away from anyone with the prefix *psych* as part of his or her title. Others may tell you that "all that psychology stuff is for the birds" and that AA will give you everything you need. But a growing number of people who love AA and credit the program with saving their lives also recognize that some individuals have needs that cannot be fulfilled or problems that cannot be solved in AA. Ask around at AA meetings, and you may get some good referrals.

Be sure to schedule an initial consultation with the therapist. During this interview, ask the therapist to explain his or her beliefs about alcoholism. Listen carefully to the answer. Here is the general answer you are most likely to get: "I believe alcoholism is a disease." At that point, ask: "What exactly do you mean by the word *disease*?" If you hear something along the lines of "Alcoholism is a symptom of other life problems" or "Alcoholism is a maladaptive behavior rooted in psychological conflict," say, "Thank you very much for your time," and schedule an interview with another therapist. What if the therapist says something like, "Alcoholism is a disease, I have no question about that fact. Still, it seems to me that you might also be depressed—have you ever considered taking medication for your depression?" This happens often, and here's how you should respond: "Do you think that my depression is caused by alcoholism or that it is an independent problem?" The answer to this question will tell you whether or not the therapist is considering a dual diagnosis.

Dual diagnosis is an extremely controversial topic in alcoholism treatment circles. In many treatment centers the majority of alcoholics are labeled dual-diagnosis patients and treated for both alcoholism and, say, chronic depression or chronic anxiety; treatment for psychological disturbances often involves the use of various medications including antidepressants, sleeping pills, mood elevators, or sedatives. Too often the diagnosis is made on the basis of the patient's presenting symptoms—the recovering alcoholic is clearly anxious, depressed, or suicidal—and no effort is made to review the patient's history to determine if the anxiety or depression existed prior to the use of alcohol and/or other drugs.

When the primary problem is alcoholism, it is highly likely that the secondary symptoms of depression, suicidal thoughts, anxiety, and panic attacks will improve rapidly over a period of several days or weeks of abstinence, eventually disappearing without the need for medication. A dual diagnosis, in these cases, would constitute a misdiagnosis, for the disruptions in thought, mood, and behavior are not separate disorders at all but consequences of alcoholism. In most cases these symptoms will abate after several weeks of abstinence and disappear after several months. If the psychological symptoms continue unabated or worsen as time goes on, the need for medication can be reevaluated.

Some recovering alcoholics do benefit from antidepressant medication in the early stages of recovery, but in determining who is a candidate for medication, this essential question must be asked: Is the recovering alcoholic's depression related to the lingering effects of the disease and thus destined to lift over time, or is the depression a separate disorder that predated the drinking and will continue despite abstinence? If the depression is not severe or debilitating, many alcoholism experts and clinicians will advise you to wait three or four months (or longer, in some cases) before taking medication. They don't want you to suffer unnecessarily, but they also don't want to jump to conclusions or suggest therapies that might jeopardize your sobriety.

Although many recovering alcoholics have experienced relief from depression, anxiety, insomnia, and obsessive-compulsive disorders by taking the class of antidepressants known as SSRIs, these drugs are not, unfortunately, without their problems (see Chapter 11). Our general recommendation is to approach *all* long-term drug treatments with caution.

COUNSELING APPROACHES AND TECHNIQUES

EARLY SOBRIETY: THEME-ORIENTED GROUPS

During treatment and in the first months of sobriety, theme-oriented group therapy is particularly effective and therefore the most popular counseling approach. In a theme-oriented early recovery group all members are alcoholics in a similar stage of recovery. The group is generally led by someone who has firsthand knowledge of or experience with the disease; often the leader is a recovering alcoholic with "time," meaning that he or she has been stably sober for several years.

The purpose of a theme-oriented group is to provide ongoing education about alcoholism, discuss relapse prevention techniques, and offer information about Alcoholics Anonymous and how to "work the program." The group meetings are generally supportive and inspirational, offering hope and help to the newly sober alcoholic. Group members discuss problems with self-esteem and interpersonal relationships, and efforts are made to help the alcoholic develop the necessary skills to get by "one day at a time."

Theme-oriented groups complement AA membership, and group members often spend a lot of time discussing the program—how to choose a sponsor, problems with "letting go," questions or concerns about the "higher power" concept, conflicts or close friendships (sometimes sexual) with other AA members, and so on.

Research supports the clinical observation that alcoholics in the early stages of recovery benefit most from groups that emphasize education, basic self-care skills, group cohesiveness, and a hopeful, supportive atmosphere. Focusing on interpersonal interactions or "psychodynamic" issues such as helping alcoholics dismantle their defenses is generally not considered helpful at this stage. In fact, research by several investigators shows that confrontational, insight-oriented groups that encourage active emotional expression can lead to feelings of inadequacy and frustration in newly recovering alcoholics, which can in turn lead to a relapse.

Many alcoholics in early recovery are simply fighting to hang on and need to protect rather than expose themselves. Alcoholics are usually so filled with guilt and shame at this stage of recovery that the last thing they need is conflict or confrontation.

STAGE-TWO GROUPS

As recovery continues and the group members begin to feel more stable and secure, a theme-oriented group may gradually shift focus. Providing support and mutual identification remains an important goal of the group, but members are also encouraged to express their feelings and explore the defenses they use to protect themselves. Often called stage-two groups, these recovery groups are still homogeneous, meaning that every member is an alcoholic. In large cities, you can find stage-two groups specifically created for women alcoholics, gay alcoholics, black alcoholics, alcoholic police officers, teenage alcoholics, and so on; members frequently share many common experiences and emotions.

These groups begin to branch out to explore the individual members' emotions and the relationships between different members, using group interactions as learning experiences and employing problem-solving strategies to help resolve any disagreements that might arise. The cohesiveness of the group depends to a large extent on the skills of the leader, who must consistently maintain firm boundaries, skillfully manage anger and aggression, and respond with empathy to every member of the group.

STAGE THREE: HETEROGENEOUS OR MIXED GROUPS

Many recovering alcoholics are not aware that another choice is available to them: a stage-three heterogeneous or "mixed" group. In a mixed group, diversity among the group members is both tolerated and, eventually, welcomed. Indeed, it is the mixture of people from different backgrounds with varying experiences that is thought to create the greatest opportunities for self-awareness and growth in these groups.

A typical mixed group consists of six to eight members of varying diagnoses, genders, ages, educational backgrounds, and economic status. Here's an example of a mixed group: Alice, forty-eight, is a college administrator who was married to a drinking alcoholic for fifteen years. Now divorced, she suffers from chronic depression. Helen, thirty-six, is a certified public accountant, married, with two teenage daughters. Her parents are both alcoholics. She suffers from depression and has struggled with obesity for years. Henry, fifty-six, works in an administrative capacity for the state government; separated with two adult children, he suffers from anxiety and depression and was recently hospitalized for suicidal ideation. Richard, forty-one, is a contractor who is single but has been living with a woman for a year; he suffers from anxiety and panic attacks. Rob, forty-four, works for the telephone company; a recovering alcoholic who has been sober for eight months, he lost both his parents in the last year and is having difficulty dealing with his grief. Peter, thirty-nine, an Ivy League graduate who is married and has two teenage sons, runs a very successful computer technology business. He has been sober for eighteen months; both his parents are drinking alcoholics, and his son recently completed treatment for a cocaine addiction. April, fifty-four, is a schoolteacher with one adult son; her husband is terminally ill with cancer, and she suffers from depression and obsessive-compulsive tendencies.

In a mixed group, men and women gain experience working through conflicts with others; they learn how to cope with aggressive and impulsive behaviors and develop close relationships while maintaining an individual identity. Group therapy, in short, mimics real-life situations because it involves several individuals who may, on the surface, have little in common with each other and do not always see eye to eye. Under the guidance of a skilled therapist who encourages the group members to empathize with each other, recognizing that every person in the room is human and therefore imperfect, alcoholics discover how and where they fit into the larger world. As their perspective expands, so does their tolerance for difference and their ability to understand the experiences of others who are struggling with their own unique problems.

Mixed groups are not for everyone, and the question of who can benefit from them is of paramount importance. Grant, who appears in this chapter's opening story, was emotionally prepared for a mixed group after just six months of sobriety. Rick, a police officer who has been sober for three years, is not ready at this point for mixed-group therapy. Rick faithfully attends AA, sees a psychotherapist for individual counseling once a week, and is firmly committed to staying sober. Yet he also takes great comfort in a set routine, he does not feel safe in situations where he feels out of control, and he is easily provoked to anger and highly sensitive to criticism. At this point in his recovery Rick could not tolerate the close, personal interactions and direct feedback that take place in a mixed group. By "direct feedback" we do not mean aggressive, hostile, or angry confrontations between group members, but honest, clear interactions handled with tact and sensitivity.

The point is that while Grant and Rick are both recovering alcoholics committed to maintaining their sobriety, they are also unique human beings. As clinical psychologist Jerome Levin puts it:

> Different alcoholics have different needs and the same alcoholic will have different needs at different times. . . . Treatment deals first with maintaining sobriety and only later, if at all, with unconscious motivations.

As sobriety progresses, your needs will change. Will you, at some point, need therapy to help you adapt to difficulties or address ongoing problems in your life? Maybe, maybe not. Like all human beings, however, you can almost certainly benefit from interactions with compassionate, caring individuals who are good listeners and can teach you how to handle conflict, tolerate anxiety, and express your feelings openly and honestly.

Recovery is a gradual process of reentering the world. Many recovering alcoholics find that ongoing psychological counseling helps them to see that world not as a hostile, frightening place where they don't really belong, but as a diverse, ever-changing universe filled with challenges but also offering warmth, humor, and love. As part of that world, they learn that they can handle their problems and grow through their relationships, becoming more tolerant and forgiving human beings.

WHAT ABOUT COMPULSIONS?

When does a behavior warrant the label "compulsive"? It is, as always, a highly individual affair. For recovering alcoholics a long-term point of view is essential. When a particular way of thinking or behaving creates intense short-term pleasure but invariably leads to long-term pain, it can be considered dangerous and self-defeating. The problem isn't with the behavior itself—whether it's exercise, eating, shopping, or AA attendance—but with the intense attachment to the activity that threatens other essential parts of life.

If you become so addicted to candy or ice cream that you stop eating nutritious foods and in two months gain ten pounds, that's a self-defeating behavior. Purchasing a new dress or business suit every month won't strain most budgets, but buying one or two new outfits every week could have a disastrous effect on finances. Running fifteen miles a week is not the same as running fifteen miles a day.

The line between normal and compulsive shifts according to the individual, but here's one way to assess the negative impact of compulsive behaviors. Ask yourself: "Is this way of thinking or behaving damaging my relationships with the people who mean the most to me?" A compulsion becomes self-defeating when it draws you away from others into a more narrowly focused world. That's what addiction to alcohol does, and that's one reason why compulsions can be so dangerous for alcoholics. By their very nature compulsions can become psychologically addictive, and for alcoholics any addictive behavior can serve as a painful reminder of the master addiction, the substance that always worked, the key that never failed to unlock the door of intense and immediate pleasure: alcohol.

That said, we need to look at the positive side of compulsions. In early recovery, alcoholics often need their compulsions and obsessions. Working out at the gym two hours a day every day, drinking five cups of coffee every morning, chain-smoking cigarettes, or attending twenty AA meetings in one week might seem compulsive, but these behaviors could also be interpreted as adaptive responses to the stress of recovery and creative approaches to directing pent-up energy into activities that do not involve drinking.

Compulsions can serve to temporarily hide unresolved sadness and grief. Since alcoholics have not had a whole lot of practice learning how to tolerate these emotions without reaching for the bottle to dilute the pain, a compulsion can offer an emotional reprieve, a cooling-off period that directs energy outward rather than inward. Forcing an alcoholic to strip away the compulsion in order to reveal underlying emotions can be unbearably painful and, in the end, self-defeating.

Recovery is synonymous with change, and it is marked not by an external, authoritarian command that tells us we have to change, but by an inner voice that says, "I am willing to change." Over time, with the humility that sobriety so often engenders, that refrain becomes, "I am willing to *be* changed." The willingness to be changed is a mysterious process, a quiet transformation that involves the rediscovery of your identity as an ever-evolving human being rather than a personality carved in stone.

A personal story told by Jesuit spiritual director Anthony de Mello speaks to the change of heart that so often accompanies the desire for growth and transformation:

> *I was neurotic for years. I was anxious and depressed and self-ish. Everyone kept telling me to change. I resented them, and I agreed with them, and I wanted to change, but simply couldn't, no matter how hard I tried.*
>
> *What hurt the most was that, like the others, my best friend kept insisting that I change. So I felt powerless and trapped. Then, one day, another friend said to me, "Don't change. I love you just as you are."*
>
> *Those words were music to my ears. "Don't change. Don't change. Don't change . . . I love you as you are." I relaxed. I came alive. And suddenly I changed!*
>
> *Now I know that I couldn't really change until I found someone who would love me whether I changed or not.*

When we accept ourselves *as* ourselves, with all our flaws and imperfections, we discover that change is possible. The purpose of change is not to compete with others, proving that you are bigger, stronger, or better than someone else, but to become your own true self, the person you were meant to be . . . and, perhaps even more important, the person you would like to be. Transforming yourself means becoming yourself, which involves learning how to be comfortable in your own (sober) alcoholic skin.

In the next chapter we will look at the spiritual elements of recovery, which go beyond theory or technique to reveal the mystery and the miracle of life as a sober human being.

13

The Spiritual Connection

Sometimes people get the mistaken notion that spirituality is a separate compartment of life, the penthouse of our existence. But rightly understood, it is a vital awareness that pervades all realms of our being. Someone will say, "I come alive when I listen to music," or "I come to life when I garden," or "I come alive when I play golf." Wherever we come alive, that is the area in which we are spiritual. And then we can say, "I know at least how one is spiritual in that area." To be vital, awake, aware, in all areas of our lives, is the task that is never accomplished, but it remains the goal.

— BROTHER DAVID STEINDL-RAST

The disease of alcoholism is as toxic to the soul as it is to the liver or the brain. By "soul" we mean all those intangible realities that give meaning and value to human life—goodness, kindness, mercy, love, empathy, altruism, self-awareness, courage, willpower, heroism, honor, duty, truth, and simple human decency. These qualities are twisted and torn, bruised and bloodied by the disease of alcoholism. Tending to the needs of the soul takes time and patience, for while the body and mind heal relatively quickly, injuries to the soul can fester for a long, long time.

"We must find some spiritual basis for living, else we die," AA cofounder Bill Wilson insisted. Bill meant that literally, for he was convinced by his own experience that the only way to combat the thirst for alcoholic "spirits" was to develop an even stronger craving for a spiritual way of life. *Spiritus contra spiritum*—spirit against spirits—is the "helpful formula" devised by Swiss psychoanalyst Carl Jung, whom Bill

Wilson credits as one of the founders of Alcoholics Anonymous. In a letter to Bill Wilson written in 1961, Jung discusses the case of Rowland H., an alcoholic he had treated thirty years earlier, to emphasize his belief that the human spirit holds the key to release from alcoholism:

> [Rowland's] craving for alcohol was the equivalent, on a low level, of the spiritual thirst of our being for wholeness, expressed in medieval language, the union with God. . . .
> You see, "alcohol" in Latin is "spiritus" and you use the same word for the highest religious experience as well as for the most depraving poison. The helpful formula therefore is: *spiritus contra spiritum*.

Spirituality is experienced as a thirst for connection to others and to the world itself. When hope seems to be lost and despair closes in, you feel cut off, torn apart from the world, alone, and bereft. The yearning you experience is a spiritual longing for reconnection, a sick soul's response to a shattered existence combined with a fierce desire to put the broken pieces back together again and discover some semblance of wholeness.

The thirst for wholeness cannot be satisfied by a fleet of new cars or a factory full of gin, for it is a spiritual craving. Nobody knows that truth better than alcoholics, who have searched for God in the bottle and discovered hell on earth. Alcoholism is all about loneliness. The bottle gives, the bottle takes away, and in the end that's the nature and extent of the alcoholic's meaningful relationships. As the years go by, the bottle gives less and takes more, gradually stripping away everything of value in the alcoholic's life. G. Douglas Talbott, M.D., a recovered alcoholic, addiction medicine specialist, and founder and medical director of the Talbott Recovery Campus in Atlanta, Georgia, describes this peeling away as a "depeoplization" process:

> Alcoholics begin to peel off layers. First goes the activity in the church; second goes the activity in the community; third goes the activity with friends, the hobbies and leisure-time activity; fourth goes the activity with peers, people at work, fellow housewives, and so on—people the alcoholic interacts with during an average work day; fifth goes the distant family; sixth goes the nuclear family. Then, suddenly, the alcoholic is . . . completely isolated . . . completely depeoplized. He [sic] has layered off every person around like skins off an onion and he is alone.

In recovery those layers need to be stitched back on, layer by painful layer. Spirituality is the thread that mends our relationships with each other, with ourselves, and with the larger community. This spiritual stitching is a slow and painful process, for each seam must be sewn by hand, and the stitches often draw blood. Pride bleeds out, as does grief, shame, guilt, anger, and resentment. Yet for all the pain, there is healing, too, which comes in the reconnection to the living, breathing world and in the mending of relationships with other human beings who are also tending their wounds and seeking answers to their most anguished questions.

Alcoholic or nonalcoholic, we are all torn and broken. We all ache to be whole again. Wholeness comes in our relationships with each other and in our willingness to reach out, not with the desire to take something from the other person but with the need, growing all the time, to give something back. How do we fulfill that paradoxical need to give away what we don't have?

In all spiritual traditions, this question leads us directly to the age-old practice of storytelling, as stories show us how other people have dealt with hardship and suffering. Stories don't try to "fix" us with answers or solutions but seek only to help us see and understand, through the mirror of another person's experience, that the yearnings we feel are universal. Stories, in master storyteller Ernest Kurtz's words, "convey the mystery and the miracle—the adventure—of being alive," guiding us back into the circle of human relationships and allowing us to warm our hands and our hearts before a communal fire.

Here is a story that speaks to the distinctly human need for community:

Time before time, when the world was young, two brothers shared a field and a mill. Each night they divided evenly the grain they had ground together during the day. Now as it happened, one of the brothers lived alone; the other had a wife and a large family. One day the single brother thought to himself: "It isn't really fair that we divide the grain evenly. I have only myself to care for, but my brother has children to feed." So each night he secretly took some of his grain to his brother's granary to see that he was never without.

But the married brother said to himself one day, "It isn't really fair that we divide the grain evenly, because I have children to provide for me in my old age, but my brother has no one. What will he do when he is old?" So every night he secretly took some of *his* grain to his brother's granary. As a result, both of them always found their supply of grain mysteriously replenished each morning.

Then one night the brothers met each other halfway between their houses, suddenly realized what had been happening, and embraced each other in love. The story is that God witnessed their meeting, and proclaimed, "This is a holy place—a place of love—and here it is that my temple shall be built." And so it was. The holy place, where God is made known, is the place where human beings discover each other in love.

Human beings thrive on connection and communication. "The spiritual approach was as useless as any other if you soaked it up like a sponge and kept it to yourself," said AA's cofounder, Dr. Bob Smith, summing up the most important lesson he learned in his long association with Bill Wilson. The point is that *we need to give it away*. We can sit in our rooms forever, communing with the heavens, but where will that get us? What good will it do if we keep all that insight and enlightenment to ourselves? "Staying is nowhere," insisted German poet Rainer Maria Rilke. At some point—and the sooner the better—we have to go out and rejoin the human race.

Keeping spirituality to ourselves inevitably leads to stagnation, like a pond that is isolated from other bodies of water, its spring dried up, its surface covered with algae, its waters murky and thick with sludge. The spirit needs free-flowing contact with other human beings, for it is in the give-and-get of our relationships that we discover what it means to be human.

GIVING IT AWAY

In recovery many alcoholics discover this vital, spiritual lesson: You get what you give, and when you give something away, you will surely get something back. Let's consider for a moment the word *give* and all the different ways we use it in our language. When we give, we hand something over or pass it down. Giving consists of a yielding, a loosening, and a willingness to let go of both material possessions and the vision of the self as needy and grasping. Waiting to get before we give means that we are holding something back. Giving just for the sake of giving requires a detachment from the need to get something in return; the gift, we realize, has already been given to us.

Spirituality is discovered in that sense of giftedness. "The spiritual person is the one who is animated by the giftedness of the universe, fascinated by the giftedness of life, especially one's own life, and hence quickened by the holy urgency to respond to that giftedness," writes theologian Francis Baur. We respond to that giftedness by giving back in the following ways:

GIVE EAR

When we "give ear," we listen, heed, pay attention. Psychologist William James extolled this mode of giving as "the essential achievement of the will," because when you choose to "attend to a difficult object and hold it fast before the mind," you chart the course of your life. You have a choice—hundreds of choices, really—about where you can focus your attention. What will you choose, to which realities in life will you "give ear" and to which will you respond with a deaf ear?

These are not idle questions, as James emphasizes, for the choices you make will determine the experiences you create for yourself in life.

GIVE FORTH

When you give forth, you send something out into the world, as in expelling your breath, expressing an opinion, or giving voice to your innermost longings. Giving forth can connote pomposity; we all know teachers and sermon givers who like to pound the lectern as they offer detailed instructions about moral conduct or the "right" way to solve some complicated problem. In spiritual terms, however, giving forth signifies a letting go of the need to be right or perfect or perfectly in control; it's a way of stepping out of the self and into some other reality that is greater or larger or more powerful than the self.

"Every exit," playwright Tom Stoppard muses, "is an entry somewhere else."

GIVE BACK

We are all indebted to whoever or whatever has given us the gift of life, and it is through the way we live our lives that we pay back that debt. If you are an alcoholic, during your drinking days you only took in; if you are like most alcoholics, you took everything you could get from anyone who was willing to give it to you. Rarely did you give anything back. The anguished insight that so much was taken and so little was given in return is the source of the alcoholic's most profound spiritual distress.

"How can I make up for those years?" the alcoholic asks, a question that is always posed with great doubt that a satisfactory answer exists. This question is often misinterpreted as "I've lost so much of my life, I have to make it up," but the truth is discovered in this paradoxical insight: "I've taken so much and my debt is so massive that I cannot possibly ever pay it back."

The most difficult spiritual work in recovery is to understand that the source of your anguish is not the desire to get back what you have lost, but to give back what you have taken. Learning to hear that howl of pain—"I've lost so much!"—not as a self-centered request for more but as an appeal from the anguished soul, asking how and in what ways you can give back what you have been given *and* what you have taken from life, is the most important work you will do in recovery.

GIVE IN ✳

The surrender implied in the act of giving in indicates a willingness to give yourself over to something more powerful than your self. Giving in is akin to giving up, giving out, and giving way, as the rock crumbles under the steady pounding of the waves, or the earth yields to the raging river. As your boundaries bend and flex, the image of the self as fixed and immobile gives way to a sense of being stretchable, formable, impressionable. "I can change," you realize. This thought leads to another idea: "I can *be* changed," which in turn makes possible the surrender in the words "I am *willing* to be changed."

When you give in, you let go. In recovery you'll hear a lot about letting go, a simple concept that seems to confuse as often as it enlightens. "Let go of what, exactly?" the alcoholic wonders. "And why should I let go?" Letting go seems to imply some kind of weakness or incapacity, and many alcoholics rebel, hoping to maintain ultimate control and remain masters of their own fate. Relinquishing control is difficult for all human beings, alcoholic and nonalcoholic, for we don't like to think (or, even worse, admit) that we might not be in charge or that we're at the mercy of forces much larger and more powerful than our own will and desire. Pride works overtime to defeat that humbling notion.

Addiction to alcohol, of course, offers the illusion of control, even of magical control: a few sips, several deep gulps, and in moments your entire life is transformed. Letting go of the idea that you can do that whenever you want or that you can control what happens to you when you drink is the first and most difficult step in recovery. For with that admission of helplessness, you give up not only the substance you crave but the ultimate control over your life that all human beings desire.

A favorite story circulates around AA meetings all over the world:

Paul, an alcoholic, is bound and determined to swim three miles across a glacier-fed lake, carrying a thirty-pound anvil the whole way. Jumping into the ice-cold water, he begins to swim with one arm, holding on to that anvil as if for dear life. Less than halfway across, he is struggling mightily. The anvil, which seemed so easy to lift when he was back on shore, now feels like an anchor. His lungs are burning, his muscles are screaming, and he is beginning to panic.

On the opposite shore he can hear people yelling. A minister cries out, "Hang on! We're praying for you!" A doctor shouts, "Don't give up hope! We're doing research, and eventually we'll figure this out!" A psychiatrist loudly encourages the sinking swimmer to reflect on his childhood in order to lighten his load, while a philosopher holds up a huge banner printed with big letters: "Willpower! Ethics! Morals!"

Confused, gasping for breath, certain that he is about to die, Paul hears one clear, insistent voice rising above the others. It is the voice of an AA member: "Drop the damn anvil!"

This funny little story shows how simple it can be to get sober—all you have to do is drop the damn anvil. If you hold on to the anvil of alcohol, every stroke you take will require an effort of tremendous will and impossible strength; eventually even the strongest swimmers sink to the bottom. The process of letting go is not as easy as it sounds, however, for plenty of voices (the loudest being the constant whine inside the alcoholic's head) insist that there are other options.

Not until you give up your demand to be in control—a release that occurs when you finally accept the fact that you are definitely not in control—can you also liberate yourself from the self-centered conviction that you can do anything and everything you want. The surrender that occurs when you give in and give up opens your eyes to a whole new world. When you accept your limitations, you find peace. Triumph is discovered in defeat.

The paradox of being both bound and free—bound by what you cannot control and freed by the knowledge that you are bound—is captured in AA's Serenity Prayer: "God grant me the serenity to accept the things I cannot change, the courage to change the things I can, and the wisdom to know the difference."

GIVE CHASE

If you're going to give back, you've got to get up and get moving. Anyone can "talk the talk," as alcoholism educator Father Martin puts it, but "walking the walk" is an entirely different story. When you stand up, put one foot in front of the other, and start moving, you give chase. It doesn't matter if you're going sideways or even backward, as long as you're moving and keeping your mind and heart open to whatever it is that might present itself to you. No matter what, however, you have to keep "walking the walk."

A gently humorous story from the Buddhist tradition points to the folly of trying to find something without the willingness to get up and go look for it:

> The great master Mat-su, as a youth, was a fanatic about sitting in meditation for many hours at a time. One day, his patriarch's disciple, Huai-jang, asked him what on earth he hoped to attain by this compulsive cross-legged sitting.
>
> "Buddhahood," said Mat-su.
>
> Thereupon Huai-jang sat down, took a brick, and started to polish it assiduously. Perplexed, Mat-su asked his friend what he was doing.
>
> "Oh," said Huai-jang, "I am making a mirror out of my brick."
>
> "You can polish it till doomsday," scoffed Mat-su, "but you'll never make a mirror out of a brick!"
>
> "Aha!" said Huai-jang with a smile. "Maybe you are beginning to understand that you can sit until doomsday, but it won't make you into a Buddha."

In just the same way, you cannot achieve or keep your sobriety unless you are willing to give chase to a new way of life. When you give away alcohol, you get sobriety, but that's all you get. If you want more, you will have to go looking for it. Spirituality is something that you need to seek out, and then you have to keep after it with a fierce will and determination. "With all the earnestness at our command, we beg of you to be fearless and thorough from the very start," writes Bill Wilson in *Alcoholics Anonymous*.

The nineteenth-century philosopher William James used to talk about acting yourself into a new way of thinking, an ancient concept that finds new meaning in the AA motto "Bring the body, the mind will follow." AA's twelve steps put the body in a forward-moving position, allowing you to "give chase" to this new way of life. Sometimes newcomers to AA, after spending a month or two in the fellowship, will announce with pride that they have "finished" the steps. "Is that so?" an old-timer is likely to comment with a wink. "Well, if you've only taken twelve steps, you're not very far from where you started, are you?"

The steps don't lead automatically to a higher plane of existence; they are merely arrows pointing in a general direction. As long as you keep moving, the steps will guide you along the way, but the focus should always be on the journey itself rather than the final destination. "Spirituality is one of those realities that we have only so long as we seek it," write the authors of *The Spirituality of Imperfection*, a book about the ancient spiritual traditions that found modern expression in Alcoholics Anonymous. "As soon as we stop seeking, we stop finding; as soon as we think we've got it, we've most certainly lost it."

GIVE RISE TO

All these different ways of giving give rise to the birth of something new. In giving away—letting go, yielding, surrendering—you give up the demand for ultimate control. The very act of surrendering (giving up, giving in, giving out, giving way) creates an other-centered perspective on life. Why surrender, after all, if you can do it all by yourself? Acknowledging that you cannot do it all, or handle it all, or control it all, you also accept the fact that someone or something outside you has more power or influence than you do.

In the experiences of surrender and acceptance, you take the first tentative steps toward "a spiritual way of life." "First of all we had to quit playing God," explains Bill Wilson in the "Big Book." Why? His answer is, as always, wholly practical and related to real-life experience: "It didn't work." From that jumping-off point your task is to discover what *does* work. Released from a totally self-centered focus, you are free to look outside yourself for the answers to your questions.

Those answers may not give you perfect peace, however, as this story illustrates:

A long, long time ago there lived a woman named Sono, whose devotion and purity of heart were respected far and wide. One day a fellow Buddhist, having made a long trip to see her, asked, "What can I do to put my heart at rest?" Sono's answer was surprisingly simple: "Every morning and every evening, and whenever anything happens to you, keep on saying, 'Thanks for everything. I have no complaint whatsoever.' "

For an entire year, day after day, the man did as he was instructed, but still his heart was not at peace. He returned to Sono, deeply discouraged. "I've said your prayer over and over, and yet nothing in my life has changed; I'm still the same confused, selfish, uncertain person I was before. What should I do now?"

Sono immediately responded, "Keep on saying, 'Thanks for everything. I have no complaint whatsoever.' "

This time, on hearing those words, the man's spirit was released, and he returned home with a great joy.

Life is life in all its messy, complicated, chaotic uncertainty. Life is not certain. Life is not pure joy. Life is not just peace and serenity. Life suffocates us at the same time it forces oxygen into our lungs. Life has its hands around our throats while simultaneously jump-starting our hearts. In one moment we feel bowled over with rhapsodic bliss, in the next we are howling with pain. Paradox is the name of the game.

The Homeless Kodo, a famous Zen teacher, liked to say: "Pulled around by Zen, kicked and dragged around by Zen . . . ah, wonderful." Substitute *life* for *Zen*, and you've got the idea and the direction.

THE GIFTS OF THE SPIRIT

Spirituality bestows many gifts, but of all the little treasures to be discovered along its muddy banks the most precious are gratitude, humility, tolerance, and forgiveness.

Gratitude is experienced in the sudden awareness that everything is just as it should be, that the gift of life is enough all by itself. When we learn to see all of life's realities, tangible and intangible, as gifts that we have already been given, we discover gratitude, recognizing how many gifts we have been given without ever having to ask for them. Life is a gift, surely, and so are the sunrise and the sunset, the moon reflecting on water, the feel of a kiss, the fragrance of a rose.

In *Portraits of Recovery* a young man named Derrick speaks to his gratitude:

> *I try to keep things in perspective. Regardless of everything, Derrick is sober. Derrick has one day at a time done something he never thought he could do. And a higher power, if you will, has done for me what I could not do for myself. Now there is more or less a deep gratitude and a thrill about existence and life. When you come close to being dead and come to know years and years of not believ-*

ing that you can live for even twenty-four hours without chemicals, and can come to be productive, that is excitement. Life is never dull to me; it is a constant thrill. So that's what sobriety is for me. It's like, look what I've done . . . when I look at my life now, it's nothing but a miracle.

Gratitude leads to *humility*, for with the vision of giftedness comes the awareness that somehow, for some reason, something or someone has singled you out as the recipient of this gift. That's a humbling notion, for sure, and somewhere along the line it will require the admission that you are not in absolute control. For how can you get something if it has not been given to you? Humility is discovered in the realization that you do not have the power to alter the inalterable realities of life. Your heart will never be wholly at peace because you are human, which means that you are, by definition, incomplete and imperfect. You are, in other words, still under construction—a humbling notion, to be sure.

Sober for two and a half years, professional golfer Laura Baugh describes how humility saved her life:

The scary thing about being an alcoholic is you feel weak. You feel like you should be able to stop drinking, to use your willpower and your strength. I pride myself on my willpower, and I'll tell you what—alcohol slapped me around like I was an infant. It was only when I could admit to not being in control that I could, with God's help, become strong enough to stay sober.

Tolerance is unearthed in the understanding that you are not alone in your imperfections, for every other human being is also under construction. If you are not perfect and your heart is not at rest, how can you expect anyone else to be flawless or error-free? Humbly accepting the fact that you are merely human and therefore not God leads to tolerance for others who are also human and therefore imperfect, flawed, error-prone, and merely mortal.

There is not a human being on this earth who has not at one point singled out another human being for judgment. One of the more humbling gifts of sobriety is the realization that you have no right to sit in judgment of others. Bill Wilson liked to poke fun at alcoholics who considered themselves more honorable or virtuous than others: "The way our 'worthy' alcoholics have sometimes tried to judge the 'less worthy' is, as we look back on it, rather comical," Bill wrote in 1947 in the *AA Grapevine*. "Imagine, if you can, one alcoholic judging another."

Forgiveness is revealed in the willingness to let go of any lingering resentments that life hasn't given you everything you wanted. "Resentment is the 'number one' offender," Bill Wilson writes in *Alcoholics Anonymous*. "It destroys more alcoholics than anything else." Resentment is dangerous because it is a way of clinging to the past and holding on to the feeling that you didn't get something you desired, or perhaps that you got something you feel you did not deserve.

The word *give* is at the literal center of *forgiveness*. When you give away your resentments, you release yourself from the need to get more than has been given to you. The recovering alcoholic's approach to forgiveness can be greedy and grasping—the "I need it right now" entreaty that characterized so much of the drinking days. "Please forgive me," countless alcoholics have said to their families and friends. "I can't go on if you don't forgive me. Just say the words, please. I need you to say them right now. I can't live without them." That desperate plea sounds a lot like an alcoholic sidling up to a bar, plunking down some loose change, and saying, "Give me a drink right now, I can't live without it, I need it *right now*!"

Forgiveness is not coin-operated; it cannot offer you instant gratification. Forgiveness comes to you when you make room for it by clearing away the old resentments and accepting the fact that life can't give you everything, but what it has given you is more than enough. That thought, of course, leads back to gratitude for all the gifts that have been given, which leads in turn to humility and tolerance, circling back, again and again, to forgiveness.

WRESTLING WITH A HIGHER POWER

"Okay, okay," the alcoholic says, "I'm ready to seek out the spiritual way of life, and I'm willing to work on being grateful, humble, tolerant, and forgiving. But I am not prepared to accept this God stuff, this 'higher power' malarkey, or whatever you want to call it. Who needs it, anyway?"

It is the rare alcoholic who accepts "the 'higher power' malarkey" without any quibbling. All human beings like to think that they are in control; alcoholics, who have already lost control over their ability to drink like "normal" people, tend to think that they should at least have some control over their sobriety. For many alcoholics, relinquishing control to some nebulous notion of a higher power seems like too much to ask when they have already lost so much control over their lives.

In *Staying Sober*, Susan Powter tells the story of a discussion that occurred after her first AA meeting. Standing on the sidewalk talking to several AA members, Powter discussed her ambivalence about what she perceived to be the religious aspects of the program. Although genuinely moved by the stories people told and touched by the warmth and love she had been offered, Powter admitted that she was having a hard time swallowing "the Christian theme" and the refrain "I am powerless."

"But I'm really scared," she tearfully confessed to her new friends, "because I have the feeling that if I can't just come here and accept all this stuff without question, then I'll have nowhere to go and this thing will kill me."

"Then, sister," one of the listeners said, her voice raised, finger pointing at Powter, "you may as well go drink tonight because until you surrender and understand that you are powerless, you can't and won't ever get help—you'll never stay sober."

That brief encounter goes a long way toward explaining why some people avoid AA. They are either scared away or completely turned off by the idea of someone wagging a finger in their faces, warning them to follow the rules or else demon alcohol will gobble them up and spit them out before breakfast. The image of AA as self-righteously moralistic creates fear and disdain in many thousands of alcoholics and non-alcoholic observers, who use phrases such as "organized religion," "cult," and "systematic indoctrination" to describe the fellowship.

AA cofounder Bill Wilson would have shared Susan Powter's outrage at such tactics, for it is precisely that sense of moral self-righteousness that inspired Bill to break off from organized religion. One dreary November day in 1934, when Bill was still drinking, his old friend Ebby dropped by for a visit. Here's the story as Bill tells it in *Alcoholics Anonymous:*

> *I pushed a drink across the table. He refused it. Disappointed but curious, I wondered what had got into the fellow. He wasn't himself.*
>
> *"Come, what's all this about?" I queried.*
>
> *He looked straight at me. Simply, but smilingly, he said, "I've got religion."*
>
> *I was aghast. So that was it—last summer an alcoholic crackpot; now, I suspected, a little cracked about religion. He had that starry-eyed look. Yes, the old boy was on fire all right. But bless his heart, let him rant! Besides, my gin would last longer than his preaching.*

The notion of a vengeful God sitting on a heavenly throne tossing lightning bolts of judgment hither and yon aroused in Wilson "a certain antipathy":

I didn't like the idea. I could go for such conceptions as Creative Intelligence, Universal Mind or Spirit of Nature but I resisted the thought of a Czar of the Heavens, however loving His sway might be. . . .

My friend [Ebby] suggested what then seemed a novel idea. He said, "Why don't you choose your own conception of God?"

That was a lightning-bolt moment for Bill Wilson, who suddenly realized that he didn't have to buy into anyone else's ideas about God—he could create his own. Ever wary of religions and "their claim how confoundedly right all of them are," Bill worked hard to create a program that made no claim to be "right," and in fact found its deepest humility in the undeniable imperfections of its assorted members.

AA embodies a "spirituality of imperfection," which encourages alcoholics to look at themselves as they truly are and in that honest assessment discover not only humility but gratitude, tolerance, and forgiveness. Choose your own conception of God, and then let go of the demand for ultimate control: That philosophy forms the beating heart of AA. As long as you are willing to admit that something somewhere has more control than you do—as long as you accept the fact that you are not God—then you are free to think of God in any way that you please.

Wrestling with God, a "higher power," or, as one alcoholic puts it, "this great invisible something or someone" comes down to this one question: "Do I have all the answers?" If you think that you do, then you have nothing more to learn, and that is that. If, on the other hand, you are willing to admit that somewhere, somehow, there may be something or someone who knows more than you do, your world gently expands into spiritual territory.

"Is there a power greater than myself?" All of us, alcoholic and non-alcoholic, must answer that question for ourselves. For those who answer yes, there are countless individual variations on the theme. Some people believe in a real God, sitting in a real heaven. Others believe that there is something "out there" but have no idea what it looks or sounds or feels like. Many use terms such as *force* or *spirit* or *vital presence* to describe the indescribable.

Still others search for a concrete image in the world of nature to give weight and substance to the spiritual realm. One recovering alcoholic likes to look out at the clear blue sky and remind herself that the stars are out there, even though she cannot see them. Another sees the workings of an invisible, ever-present energy in the crashing of the waves against the shore. And still another takes a few minutes of every day to watch the Weather Channel, a daily reminder of powerful forces beyond human control.

What you believe in is significantly less important than living your life based on the conviction that you are not the one in ultimate control. "The spiritual life is not a theory," Bill Wilson insisted. *"We have to live it."* How do you live spirituality? How and where can you experience spirituality in your life? One of the best answers we have found to these questions is in the musings of an anonymous recovering alcoholic who emphasizes the practical, down-to-earth quality of spirituality. You won't find guardian angels or fiery visions in this description, which seeks to discover spirituality in the wonder of ordinary, everyday life.

"What is spirituality?" the writer asks.

> It's seeing a mystical power for good in each and every human being. It's patience in the face of stupidity. It's feeling that you want to knock somebody's head off—and walking away instead. It's when you're down past your last dime, and you know you still have something that money can't buy. It's wearing dungarees that feel like a tuxedo. It's wanting to go home, yet being there. It's a rocket ride that goes far beyond the world your eye can see. It's looking at something that superficially is ugly, but radiates beauty. It's a majestic skyline or a western desert. It's a young child. It's seeing a caterpillar turn into a butterfly. It's the awareness that survival is a savage fight between you and yourself. It's a magnetic pull toward those who are down and out. It's knowing that even the bad times are good.

The concluding paragraph in this passage (we have altered the language to speak for both men and women) contains the single most important message about the spiritual way of life:

> The singular thing that is spirituality cannot be given to a human being by word of mouth. If everyone is to have it, then everyone must earn it, in their own way, by their own hand, stamped by the seal of their own selves, in their own individual right.

Spirituality is just like life (and sobriety)—a gift, freely given, which we can nurture with care or squander through neglect. When we accept the gift, we see what we have never seen before, and we see, too, the handiwork of some power greater than ourselves. These visions come unbidden—we cannot command them to appear—but they do not last forever. Eventually we must return to everyday life with all its stresses, demands, and emotional upheavals. At some point, inevitably, we get lost in the practical details of our day-to-day existence.

Then one day—out of the blue, it seems—we sense that something has been lost. Something is missing. At that moment we understand that the thirst for spirituality is as strong as any craving we have ever experienced before. That's when we understand that there are no shortcuts, no final answers, and no end to the journey. That is the point when we "get" it, realizing that we must give in order to receive, for the spiritual way of life is earned moment by moment, inch by inch. And that is the time when, driven by a powerful longing for reconnection and inspired by the example of so many others who have walked this way before, we put one foot in front of the other and go searching for it.

A Diet for
Sobriety

Food can act as drugs, and we must be aware of
how our moods and physiology—mental and physical—are so inextricably intertwined that what and
how we eat can have an enormous impact on our
lives.

—CANDACE B. PERT, PH.D.

Frank had been sober for seven months. He didn't want to drink, he
didn't even crave alcohol like so many of his friends in AA, but he
couldn't seem to shake the depression that sometimes threatened to
engulf him. For years Frank had worked on the psychiatric ward of a
state hospital, and now he was beginning to see himself in some of the
patients—perhaps he, too, was manic-depressive, or even schizo-
phrenic? His mood swings were wild and unpredictable. He was anxious, irritable, and easily provoked to anger, and he had trouble sleeping.
Sometimes he even thought about suicide.

At first Frank's coworkers chided him about a midlife crisis, but
eventually they took their concerns about his emotional instability to his
supervisor. When his supervisor advised him to take a leave of absence
from his job and consider seeing a psychiatrist for his problems, Frank
knew he needed help. He was sober, but he was afraid he couldn't hang
on much longer. He called his AA sponsor, who told him about a highly
regarded inpatient treatment program, and Frank admitted himself a
few days later.

The staff doctor and nutritionist asked Frank detailed questions about
his diet and ordered various laboratory tests. A glucose tolerance test
revealed that Frank was hypoglycemic, and the staff prescribed a balanced diet of regular meals and between-meal snacks and daily vitamin
and mineral supplements. After five days of treatment, Frank's depression began to lift and his "foggy head," as he put it, cleared up. His

thoughts became more rational and orderly, his mood swings were less abrupt, and for the first time in years he was enjoying a good night's sleep.

The week before his discharge, Frank went out on a weekend pass to visit friends and family. He got caught up visiting and talking and after a few hours was overcome by the all-too-familiar symptoms: mood swings, mental confusion, intense anxiety, and feelings of panic. He realized he hadn't eaten anything in over six hours, and he immediately fixed himself a nutritious lunch. In less than an hour he was feeling refreshed, energetic, and clearheaded.

With that experience, Frank had all the proof he needed that his diet had a profound effect on his mood and emotions. After treatment he continued to watch what he ate and told friends he had never felt better in his life.

Long before nutritional therapy became a fad, respected scientists and alcohol researchers understood the pervasive nature of alcoholics' nutritional deficiencies and the need for long-term treatment to correct these imbalances. One problem, as we can see with Frank, is that alcohol blocks to some extent the formation of sugar by the liver, causing hypoglycemia. But alcohol also negatively affects how the body absorbs, stores, and uses nutrients.

All alcoholics have nutritional problems—even early- and middle-stage alcoholics. Men and women who drink heavily and eat poorly for many years will be more severely malnourished, but because alcohol interferes with the body's ability to process nutrients, even alcoholics who eat well during or between drinking bouts suffer from malnutrition.

DIRECT CAUSES OF NUTRITIONAL DISORDERS

APPETITE AND FOOD INTAKE

Alcohol works in a number of ways to cut down on food intake. First, when alcoholics drink regularly and in large amounts, they don't feel like eating nutritious foods, for the empty calories of alcohol satisfy their hunger. One ounce of pure alcohol contains about 170 calories, the equivalent of a glass of whole milk, a large baked potato, two large eggs, two bananas, or four fish sticks. As we've noted, for many middle- and late-stage alcoholics, alcohol supplies more than half their daily calories. (No other drug supplies calories, by the way.)

Alcoholics are also plagued with stomach and intestinal upsets that wreak havoc on their appetite. Nausea, vomiting, diarrhea, and stomach pain from gastritis, ulcers, a swollen liver, or pancreatitis make even the thought of eating nauseating, and any food that is eaten may be promptly expelled in one way or another.

Last but not least, alcoholics get trapped in a vicious cycle in which regular, heavy drinking causes a loss of certain nutrients essential for a healthy appetite. Vitamins B_1, B_3, and B_5, for example, work as appetite stimulants; all three of these vitamins are commonly deficient in drinking alcoholics. Many alcoholics also have low levels of zinc, which can cause a loss of taste and smell and therefore a lack of interest in food.

DIGESTION AND USE OF NUTRIENTS

Alcohol attacks every organ involved in digestion, creating nutritional disaster for the alcoholic. Large amounts of alcohol typically produce changes in the digestive system that interfere with the body's absorption and use of nutrients, as illustrated by the figure below.

This drawing shows that when alcoholism is a factor, the body's

TABLE 14-1 How Alcohol Works Against Nutrition

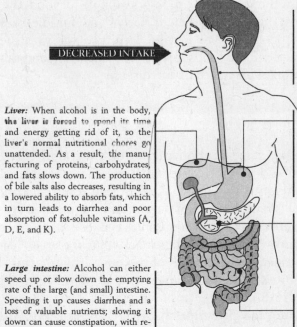

DECREASED INTAKE

Esophagus: Alcohol irritates and inflames the lining of the esophagus (causing esophagitis) and can interfere with swallowing. An inflamed esophagus will produce burning pain, nausea, vomiting, and loss of appetite—all of which contribute to nutritional problems.

Liver: When alcohol is in the body, the liver is forced to spend its time and energy getting rid of it, so the liver's normal nutritional chores go unattended. As a result, the manufacturing of proteins, carbohydrates, and fats slows down. The production of bile salts also decreases, resulting in a lowered ability to absorb fats, which in turn leads to diarrhea and poor absorption of fat-soluble vitamins (A, D, E, and K).

Stomach: Alcohol irritates stomach tissue, and prolonged, heavy drinking contributes to inflammation of this tissue (causing gastritis) and also contributes to ulcers. Alcohol also causes a decrease in digestive acids and enzymes. All of these effects lead to poor digestion, especially of proteins and minerals.

Pancreas: Excessive amounts of alcohol can disrupt the ability of the pancreas to produce the enzymes needed for protein and fat digestion. The pancreas may get plugged up with protein, leading to inflammation (pancreatitis).

Large intestine: Alcohol can either speed up or slow down the emptying rate of the large (and small) intestine. Speeding it up causes diarrhea and a loss of valuable nutrients; slowing it down can cause constipation, with reabsorption of toxins from the waste materials.

Small intestine: Excessive drinking causes damage to the lining cells and the cilia, which border them. This leads to poor absorption of nutrients as well as diarrhea and "flushing" of nutrients in the urine.

nutritional needs cannot be satisfied simply by eating a sufficient amount of nutritious foods. Chronic consumption of alcohol interferes with the body's ability to manufacture the necessary digestive enzymes and acids, prevents nutrients from getting into the cells, and damages the cells' ability to process various nutrients.

INDIRECT CAUSES OF NUTRITIONAL DISORDERS

Alcohol's direct, toxic effect on cells, tissues, and organs is only one way in which chronic heavy drinking disturbs the body's nutritional equilibrium. Indirect causes of nutritional disorders in alcoholics include other factors such as lifestyle, use of over-the-counter and prescription drugs, trauma, surgery, and infections.

LIFESTYLE FACTORS

The cost of nutritious foods, combined with lack of appetite for food and little motivation to eat, plays a role in the alcoholic's nutritional deficiencies. Late-stage alcoholics often live alone; many are destitute. Having no one to cook for them and little money available for food, they eat poorly and are inevitably malnourished. Early- and middle-stage alcoholics, like so many people in our fast-food culture, follow a diet consisting of processed and refined foods loaded with sugar, fat, and salt. Skipping meals is common in all stages of the disease.

DRUGS

Early-, middle-, and late-stage alcoholics use over-the-counter drugs for a myriad of physical and mental complaints, including headaches, nausea, insomnia, and anxiety. Visits to the doctor often result in a prescription for sleeping pills, antidepressants, tranquilizers, or sedatives. These drugs can be dangerous in and of themselves because many travel along the same brain pathways that alcohol uses, and regular use can lead to both cross-tolerance (needing high doses of the new drug to achieve the desired effect) and cross-addiction (rapid development of physiological need for the new drug).

Many over-the-counter and prescription drugs also interfere with the use and processing of nutrients in the body. Tranquilizers, for example, disrupt the metabolism of vitamin D and deplete folic acid levels in the body; the antibiotic tetracycline decreases the absorption of iron and depletes vitamin C levels; and broad-spectrum antibiotics deplete vitamin K and vitamin B_{12} levels.

Numerous over-the-counter medications also contain alcohol. Recovering alcoholics should learn to be suspicious of any and all liquid medications such as cough syrups, decongestants, and mouthwashes, which are usually alcohol-based. If you are still in doubt after reading the label, ask your pharmacist.

TRAUMA, SURGERY, INFECTIONS

Nutrients are the body's protectors, helping the cells to resist assault by various toxic substances. When assailed by stress or disease or subjected to great physical demands, the cells need extra nutritional protection. Trauma (bodily injury), surgery, and infections put great stress on the body and significantly deplete nutritional stores. Alcoholics, particularly late-stage alcoholics, are typically in and out of hospitals for accident-related injuries such as head injuries from falling down the stairs, broken jaws from barroom brawls, or fractured legs or arms from car accidents; respiratory ailments; cardiovascular disease; or alcohol-induced illnesses such as gastritis, hepatitis, cirrhosis, and pancreatitis.

THE CONSEQUENCES OF MALNUTRITION

Because so many different organs and systems are affected by alcohol, the symptoms of malnutrition are diverse and often mimic other disorders. Even slight deficiencies can have a dramatic effect on your thoughts, moods, emotions, and behaviors. The most common symptoms of marginal nutritional deficiencies are precisely those that plague many alcoholics during the protracted-withdrawal period: depression, irritability, mental confusion, memory loss, mood swings, nervousness, anxiety, inability to concentrate, insomnia, lethargy, and fatigue. (See pages 164–168 for an in-depth discussion of protracted withdrawal.) Moderate and severe alcohol-related nutritional disorders can cause or aggravate skin infections, respiratory infections, anemia, high blood pressure, arrhythmias (irregular heartbeat), heart failure, strokes, osteoporosis, Wernicke's syndrome, and Korsakoff's psychosis.

The following table lists the major body systems affected by alcohol-induced nutritional disorders and the symptoms associated with these disorders:

Body Systems Affected by Alcohol-induced Nutritional Disorders

SYSTEM	ASSOCIATED NUTRIENTS	SYMPTOMS
Central nervous	B vitamins Calcium Magnesium Zinc Cerebral amines and neurotransmitters	Depression, anxiety, irritability, mental confusion, insomnia, convulsions, personality disturbance
Respiratory	Vitamin C Vitamin A	Colds, respiratory infections, pneumonia
Cardiovascular	Vitamin B_1 Magnesium Potassium	High blood pressure, irregular heart rate, heart failure
Digestive	B vitamins Minerals	Diarrhea
Skeletal-muscle	Calcium Magnesium	Muscle inflammation (myositis), decreased bone density, propensity to fracture
Blood	Folic acid Iron Vitamin B_{12} Vitamin B_6	Anemia, lowered white-blood-cell count, fewer platelets
Skin	Zinc Vitamin A Vitamin C Vitamin E	Infections, poor healing ability, skin diseases and disorders (eczema, rashes, etc.)
Endocrine	B vitamins Vitamin C Vitamin E Pantothenic acid	Reduced sexual function, pancreatic malfunction, adrenal malfunction, thyroid malfunction

TREATING NUTRITIONAL
DEFICIENCIES

"All alcoholics are malnourished to some degree," writes Joseph Beasley, M.D., in *How to Defeat Alcoholism*. "Every alcoholic needs nutritional restoration, and every alcoholic should learn to live by the principles of good nutrition." Yet in the majority of alcoholism treatment centers throughout this country, nutritional assessment is not practiced, laboratory tests to determine biochemical abnormalities are not ordered, and the staff (which, in most cases, does not include a nutritionist or dietitian) is not encouraged to ask questions about diet or eating patterns. Alcoholism, in these treatment centers, is treated as if it had no effect at all on the alcoholic's nutritional health; the attitude seems to be that any nutritional problems an alcoholic might have will clear up after a week or two of sobriety.

Even if there are no visible signs or symptoms, marginal nutritional deficiencies (which typically do not show up on laboratory tests or in physical exams) can create great distress for the recovering alcoholic. Depression, insomnia, fatigue, headaches, and many other mental and physical complaints can be greatly relieved and even eliminated if the alcoholic's diet and eating patterns are carefully evaluated and a therapeutic program geared to individual needs is developed.

Since so many recovering alcoholics suffer from symptoms related to marginal nutritional deficiencies, and because these symptoms are often associated with a return to drinking, the continuing neglect of nutritional therapy in most treatment programs is unacceptable. Ignoring this vital aspect of recovery can undermine the alcoholic's most determined efforts to stay sober and make sobriety a hellish existence in which the urge to drink eventually becomes overpowering.

The dietary principles we suggest here are designed to help you feel healthy, energetic, and emotionally stable while sober. Unlike most diets, this nutritional program is not designed for weight loss (although that can be one of its additional benefits). Instead, this diet for sobriety concentrates primarily on gaining valuable nutrients by eating the right kinds of food while avoiding the physical and emotional distress associated with eating the wrong kinds of food.

This healthy, healing diet builds physical and mental strength by supplying those nutrients essential for stabilizing blood sugar and correcting nutritional deficiencies. If you want to be rid of the long-term hangover of alcoholism—the anxiety, depression, nervousness, irritability, and sudden cravings for alcohol—follow these general principles. Even alcoholics who do not suffer from any lingering symptoms can benefit from this nutritional program, for by eating right they can solidify their good health and avoid future problems.

GENERAL RULES FOR
GOOD NUTRITION

The principles of good nutrition are relatively straightforward. In treatment and recovery, alcoholics should follow these five general rules:

Rule 1:   Eat three nutritious meals every day. Concentrate on natural, whole, unprocessed, and unrefined foods such as fresh vegetables, fresh fruits, and whole grains. Avoid sugar, white flour, white bread, white pasta, white rice, fast foods, high-sugar foods, and high-fat foods whenever possible.

Rule 2:   Eat three nutritious snacks every day. Space the snacks several hours apart, one in midmorning, another in midafternoon, and a final snack in the evening, an hour or so before bedtime. Snacks will keep your blood sugar on an even keel, which will, in turn, keep your energy high, reduce cravings for alcohol, and prevent hypoglycemic reactions. Nutritious snacks include foods such as fresh fruit and vegetables, nonfat yogurt, and whole-grain bread or crackers in combination with a high-protein food such as peanut butter, cheese, nuts, or small portions of turkey or chicken.

Rule 3:   Cut back on sweets. High-sugar foods include desserts, candy, sugar-sweetened drinks such as soda pop, and most cereals. Sugar stresses the alcohol-weakened organs involved in controlling and regulating blood sugar. A high-sugar diet can cause fluctuations in blood sugar, and related symptoms such as depression, fatigue, anxiety, and mood swings.

Rule 4:   Cut back on caffeine. Caffeine is a powerful stimulant capable of upsetting blood sugar control and aggravating gastrointestinal disorders. Caffeine is found in caffeinated coffee and teas, cola beverages, chocolate, cocoa, many soda pops, and certain over-the-counter drugs such as Midol and No-Doz.

Rule 5:   Take vitamin and mineral supplements. Nutritional supplements will help speed up cellular repair, restore nutrients depleted by chronic heavy drinking, and provide immune system support. (In Chapter 15, "Alternative Therapies," we outline our specific recommendations for nutritional supplements.)

NOW FOR THE SPECIFICS . . .

A healthy diet needs to have the appropriate balance of protein, carbohydrates, and fats. *Protein* intake should be moderate, supplying around 12 percent of total calories. *Carbohydrates* should supply 55 percent or more of total calories. *Fat* intake should be at or below 30 percent of total calories, with saturated fat supplying less than one-third of those calories. We will look at these three major food groups, offering specific advice for you as a recovering alcoholic. We will also offer advice on fiber, beverages, sweeteners, and seasonings.

PROTEIN

Proteins are complex molecules consisting of different combinations of amino acids. Complete proteins supply all eight essential amino acids, which the body cannot synthesize on its own. Foods containing complete proteins include meat, poultry, fish, eggs, and dairy products. Incomplete proteins, which supply some but not all of the essential amino acids, are found in legumes (peas, beans, lentils), nuts, and seeds; these foods can be combined to create a complete-protein meal. For example, if you eat legumes with rice, corn, or barley, you increase the protein value significantly.

The body needs protein to make and repair cells and tissues, to form antibodies to fight infections, to spark various chemical reactions, and to manufacture hormones, enzymes, and red blood cells. Yet for all the good that proteins do for the body, they also require a lot of energy and fuss. The digestive system expends significant energy breaking down the complicated protein molecules so they can then be metabolized by the liver. In the process of metabolizing proteins, nitrogen-containing residues are released, and it's the liver's job to change these highly toxic substances into urea, another toxic chemical. The burden then falls on the kidneys, which are responsible for eliminating urea. Meanwhile, the immune system can be adversely affected by protein's toxic by-products.

Protein from meat and poultry creates its own unique set of problems. It is more difficult to digest than protein available from vegetables, dairy products, nuts, grains, and seeds. Many alcoholics have chronic digestive problems caused by years of drinking and thus have difficulty digesting heavy loads of meat protein. Also, red meats such as beef and pork are high in saturated fat, which contributes to the buildup of "bad" (low-density lipoprotein) cholesterol, hardening of the arteries, heart disease, strokes, and high blood pressure. Other foods high in saturated fat include butter and cream; products such as cheese, ice cream, and yogurt that are made with cream or whole milk instead of low-fat or nonfat milk also contain saturated fats. Tropical oils (coconut and palm) are very high in these unhealthy fats.

Meats generally contain a variety of toxic chemicals. Most of the animals we eat today receive antibiotics and growth-promoting hormones in their feed—every year an estimated twenty million pounds of antibiotics are fed to animals in the United States. And processed meats, such as hot dogs, sausage, salami, pepperoni, bologna, bacon, and various smoked meats, contain nitrates and nitrites, which are directly linked with stomach, colon, and esophageal cancers in humans. These foods are also very high in salt; excessive salt intake can lead to high blood pressure (see pages 226–227).

Here are some simple protein strategies:

1.   Replace meat and poultry protein with fish and soy protein. Soybeans are high in protein, contain significant amounts of "good" fat, and include chemicals called phytoestrogens, which may protect men from prostate cancer and women from estrogen-driven diseases including breast cancer, endometriosis, and uterine fibroids.

2.   Eat more fish, particularly deep-sea fish such as salmon, mackerel, herring, anchovies, canned sardines, and albacore (white meat) tuna. These fish are high in omega-3 fatty acids, which are essential to the health of every cell in the body and protect against many autoimmune diseases, such as allergies, asthma, lupus, cancer, eczema, and psoriasis.

3.   Substitute vegetable proteins—beans, grains, nuts, and seeds—for meat proteins; these foods are also important sources of fiber and nutrients.

4.   If you eat meat, restrict it to one meal a day and try to buy organic products.

CARBOHYDRATES

There are "good" carbohydrates and "bad" carbohydrates (see box on page 217). For example, compare a banana to a piece of fudge. Both foods deliver approximately the same calories, but the banana has twice as much protein, three times as much iron, ten times as much potassium and niacin, over two hundred times as much vitamin A, seven times as much thiamine, three times as much riboflavin, and fourteen times as

THE GOOD AND BAD CARBOHYDRATES

	Natural ("Good")	Refined/Processed ("Bad")
Sugars	Fruit Honey	Table sugar (white and brown) Molasses

Starches	Whole grain (wheat,
	   oats, barley, rye)
	Fresh vegetables
		White flour
		White-flour products
		   (bread and pastas)
		Processed grains (white
		   rice, pearl barley)
		Canned and frozen
		   vegetables

Cellulose	Fiber (roughage found
	   in skins or fruits
	   and vegetables)	

much vitamin C. Fudge, on the other hand, contains more than fifty times as much sodium as a banana, and more than ten times the fat.

The bad carbohydrates are usually easy to recognize: They're white or they're sweet. White sugar, white flour, white rice, and white pasta products are all "bad" in the sense that they have been stripped of important nutrients. In the refining process, the germ (which contains polyunsaturated fats, vitamin E, B vitamins, and protein) and the fibrous bran coating are removed. What is left is the endosperm, which is primarily starch. For example, 80 percent of the essential nutrients provided by whole wheat are missing in white bread.

Worst of all for the recovering alcoholic, refined carbohydrates contain simple chains of sugar that are readily broken down, flooding the body with a sudden surge of glucose. While the body's cells need glucose for energy, they do not cope well with large amounts all at once. The blood sugar shoots up, only to come crashing back down. This blood sugar roller coaster brings on many distressing symptoms.

HYPOGLYCEMIC SYMPTOMS

Psychological symptoms:

Craving for sweets
Moodiness
Exhaustion
Insomnia
Depression
Anxiety
Irritability
Headaches
Forgetfulness
Nervousness
Constant worrying
Indecisiveness
Mental confusion
Crying spells
Phobias
Difficulty concentrating
Temper tantrums

Physical symptoms:

Tremor (internal trembling)
Heart palpitations
Muscle pain and backache
Numbness
Chronic indigestion
Cold hands and feet
Sighing, yawning
Ringing in ears
Dry mouth
Hot flashes
Noise and light sensitivity

While all digestible carbohydrates eventually break down to glucose, the "good" (natural) carbohydrates consist of complex chemical chains that are more difficult to break down, and thus release glucose slowly. Slow absorption leads to minimal disruptions in blood sugar levels. In addition to helping circumvent spikes and plunges in blood sugar, natural carbohydrates also contain important vitamins and minerals that aid in the proper absorption, distribution, and use of glucose.

Vegetables supply natural carbohydrates, essential and nonessential amino acids (the building blocks of proteins), fiber, vitamins (including C, A, and some B vitamins), and minerals such as calcium, magnesium, and iron. Leafy green vegetables (lettuce, spinach, cabbage, chard, collards, kale, watercress) are especially rich in nutrients. Broccoli, brussels sprouts, and cauliflower have anticancer effects. Fresh, raw vegetables are highest in vitamins and minerals, although raw vegetables may be difficult for some people to digest; lightly steaming vegetables retains most of their nutrients but makes them easier to digest. Frozen vegetables, especially those that are frozen fresh, are still high in nutrients. Avoid canned vegetables because many nutrients are lost in processing, and both sugar and salt are added for taste.

Fruits supply natural, slowly digested sugars, vitamins C and A, and minerals. Fruits are also high in fiber, have a high water content, and are low in fat, sodium, and calories. Eat fresh, organic fruits whenever possible. Always carefully wash fruit (even organic fruit) to remove any dirt or toxic residues. If you use canned fruits, always buy water-packed or natural-juice-packed products; avoid those packed in syrup. Drink unsweetened fruit juices, but limit them to two small glasses a day because fruit juice is concentrated and naturally sugar-laden. Limit intake of dried fruits such as raisins, prunes, apples, or pears because the fruit's natural sugar is heavily concentrated during the drying process.

Grains, nuts, and seeds supply bran and fiber, and are rich in B vitamins (particularly B_1, B_2, and B_3), vitamin E, amino acids, minerals, and essential fatty acids; they also supply significant amounts of fiber.

Eat two or three slices of whole-grain bread every day, three to four servings of whole-grain cereal per week, and add nuts and seeds to cereals and casseroles or eat them as snacks. Always use whole-grain pasta products and rice, which contain the germ of the grain and are rich in nutrients. Chew carefully in order to break down the whole grains.

Most processed cereals contain a lot of sugar, so choose carefully. Hot, whole-grain cereals such as oatmeal are low in sugar and fat, but watch out for the instant (heavily processed) varieties. *Consumer Reports* recently warned consumers to avoid cereals loaded with sugar (and low in fiber), a long list that includes *Apple Cinnamon Cheerios, Cinnamon Toast Crunch, Cocoa Puffs, Frosted Cheerios, Honey Nut Cheerios,* and *Trix* from General Mills; *Apple Jacks, Corn Pops, Froot Loops, Frosted Flakes, Smacks,* and *Smart Tart* from Kellogg; *Cocoa Pebbles, Golden Crisp, Honey Comb,* and *Waffle Crisp* from Post; and *Cap'n Crunch, Fruitangy Oh!s,* and *Honey Nut Oats* from Quaker.

In that same issue *Consumer Reports* recommends the following cereals for "best nutrition and taste": Post's *Original Shredded Wheat 'N Bran,* Post's *Original Shredded Wheat Spoon Size,* Kellogg's *Raisin Squares Mini-Wheats,* General Mills's *Multi-Bran Chex,* Kellogg's *Raisin Bran Crunch,* General Mills's *Wheat Chex,* and Kellogg's *Complete Wheat Bran Flakes.*

FATS

Fats provide the most concentrated source of energy of any food group, supplying twice the number of calories per gram as carbohydrates and proteins. Fat also contributes three essential nutrients provided by no other food: linoleic, linolenic, and arachidonic fatty acids. These are known as the essential fatty acids (EFAs), and as long as they are present, the body can make all the other fatty acids it needs. The essential fatty acids are integral to normal growth, especially of the blood vessels and nerves; they regulate blood clotting mechanisms and cholesterol levels; and they control inflammatory reactions.

Once again, there are "good" fats and "bad" fats. The bad fats are saturated fats and hydrogenated fats. Saturated fats include animal fats (lard, suet) and certain oils (coconut and palm). Unsaturated fats are either polyunsaturated (safflower, soybean, corn, soy, sesame, and cottonseed oils) or monounsaturated (olive, canola, peanut, and avocado oils).

Saturated fats will increase "bad" (low-density lipoprotein or LDL) cholesterol, which is especially damaging to the cardiovascular system and can lead to atherosclerosis (hardening of the arteries) and coronary artery disease. Foods high in saturated fat include beef, pork, lamb, chicken with the skin on, duck, whole milk (as well as cheese, ice cream, and yogurt made from it), butter, cream, and foods made with palm or coconut oil. If you think you never come in contact with tropical oils, check out the list of ingredients in packaged cookies.

Hydrogenated fats are found in numerous processed foods. Get in the habit of looking for the words *hydrogenated* or *partially hydrogenated* on food labels, because hydrogenated fats are unequivocally bad for you. These products have been subjected to the food-processing equivalent of a nuclear power reactor, getting their atoms bounced around and reconfigured by high heat and complicated chemistry. In this process, the atoms realign themselves, changing from a natural (cis) form to an unnatural (trans) form. Trans fatty acids (TFAs) are devastating to the immune system and can threaten the coronary artery system, increasing the risk of heart attacks and strokes.

Unsaturated fats come in two varieties: polyunsaturated and monounsaturated oils. Polyunsaturated oils include safflower, soybean, peanut, corn, and cottonseed oils. These oils are unstable at room temperature and when heated tend to form the toxic, potentially cancer-causing trans fatty acids.

Monounsaturated oils (olive, canola, peanut, avocado) are the safest of all the edible fats; without any question, the best choice of all is extra-virgin, cold-pressed olive oil.

Here are some general recommendations regarding fats:

1. Cut saturated fat by reducing meat and whole-milk products.

2. Avoid products containing hydrogenated or partially hydrogenated fats.

3. Use extra-virgin, cold-pressed olive oil in salads and for all cook-

ing needs. Brush or drizzle olive oil onto bread instead of using butter or margarine.

4.   Eat fish high in omega-3 fatty acids or take EFA (essential fatty acid) supplements, which work to halt inflammatory processes throughout the body, thus protecting against chronic immune disorders such as allergies, lupus, arthritis, eczema, and psoriasis. (See page 240 for more information on the health benefits of fatty acids.)

5.   Watch out for "low-fat" foods, which tend to be high in sugar—flavored low-fat or nonfat yogurt, for example, has fewer calories from fat but far more from sugar than plain whole-milk yogurt. Fats and sugars both taste good; when manufacturers remove the fat, they usually replace it with sugar.

FIBER

Vegetables, fruits, and whole grains contain significant amounts of dietary fiber, which is essential for a healthy digestive system. Fiber bulks the food particles, moving them quickly and efficiently through the stomach and intestines and contributing to the health of the digestive system. Most important for alcoholics, glucose molecules latch on to the fibrous materials, allowing a more gradual release of sugar into the bloodstream and reducing the risk of a sugar overload, which can trigger hypoglycemia and all its attendant symptoms.

Fiber also promotes regular bowel movements and helps propel the digestive contents through the small and large intestines, allowing the digestive organs to work more efficiently.

Dietary fiber can be a big help to a stressed digestive system. Soluble (mucilaginous) fiber, such as psyllium, pectin, and guar gum, works in two basic ways: First, it coats the bowel, which supports the healing process; and second, it bulks the stools, making them lighter and easier to eliminate. Psyllium is the main bulking agent in commercial laxatives such as Metamucil and Fiberall, but we recommend avoiding these products because they have artificial colors and flavors and, more important, are sweetened with sugar or artificial sweeteners. Most commercially grown psyllium is also heavily sprayed with pesticides.

For a completely organic source of psyllium, we recommend Yerba Prima Daily Fiber Formula. If you can't find Yerba Prima at your health food store, ask the store owner for another organic brand of psyllium.

Whenever you use fiber supplements, be sure to drink a full glass of water immediately afterward to expand and soften the fiber. If you don't have enough water in your system, the fiber can thicken, harden, and actually obstruct your colon. A good general rule is to drink eight to ten 8-ounce glasses of fresh, filtered water daily. (See pages 225–226 for an in-depth discussion on drinking water.)

SWEETENERS

Sugar is an antinutrient—it takes more from the body than it gives. Excess sugar depletes the vitamins and minerals needed to metabolize it and can overstimulate the pancreas and adrenal glands, causing problems with blood sugar control. Too much sugar can also weaken the immune system.

According to nutritional expert Elson Haas, M.D.:

> Sugar . . . is easily the most commonly addictive food/drug worldwide. . . . Many nutritional authorities feel that the high use of sugar in our diet is a major nutritional culprit in disease. This includes sugar in all forms—from pure white beet or cane sugar, soda pops, and candies to honey and fruit juices. Sugar often replaces other, more nutritious foods, and it weakens our tissue health and body resistance. Microorganisms and insects love sweet, simple sugar foods, and a sweet diet allows greater infestation with bacteria, fungi, and parasites, and then will support their growth, which may weaken our immunity. Reducing our entire dietary sugar load is important.

Everyone, alcoholic and nonalcoholic alike, can benefit by cutting back on their sugar intake—the average American consumes 156 pounds of sugar every year. Alcoholics have an added incentive, however, because they are often sugar sensitive and therefore vulnerable to blood sugar problems. Nutritionist Kathleen DesMaisons, Ph.D., explains the mechanics of sugar sensitivity in *Potatoes Not Prozac*:

> Sugar-sensitive people have a more volatile blood sugar reaction to eating sweet foods than do other people. If you are sugar sensitive, your blood sugar rises more quickly and goes higher than other people's, causing your body to release more insulin than is needed for the amount of food you have eaten. As a result of this spike in insulin, you experience a quicker and steeper drop in your blood sugar level. You are more vulnerable to low blood sugar level, also known as hypoglycemia.

Here are some suggestions for handling sweets during recovery:

• Cut back sugar and sugar-sweetened foods whenever possible (that includes candy, cakes, cookies, ice cream, sherbert, jams, jellies, pastries, and soda pop).

• If you eat sweets, always have them at the end of a nutritious meal; the fiber, protein, and complex carbohydrates will balance the effect of the concentrated sugar.

• Desserts containing fruit or natural grains such as fresh fruit, apple crisp, and granola bars are generally less disturbing to the body's biochemical balance.

• Honey is a natural sweetener that contains glucose, fructose, and small amounts of vitamins and minerals. Although slightly more wholesome than refined white sugar, honey can also throw off your blood sugar; always use it in moderation.

• Brown sugar is no healthier than white sugar.

What about artificial sweeteners? We recommend that you avoid them or cut way back on their use. DesMaisons explains some of the problems with aspartame, the main ingredient in NutraSweet:

> Aspartame is made from phenylalanine, which is an amino acid. High doses of any single amino acid can throw off the balance of aminos in your brain and body. Since phenylalanine is a precursor to dopamine and norepinephrine, which are both stimulating neuro-transmitters, high usage of NutraSweet can create an "upper"-like effect. You may find that you really like the effect you get from sugar-free products. I encourage my clients to stay away from products with aspartame both for their addictive potential and their reinforcement of the dependence upon sweet taste.

BEVERAGES

Coffee contains caffeine, a drug that, like alcohol, stimulates the release of the neurotransmitters dopamine and norepinephrine, brain chemicals that make you feel energized, mobilized, and happy. Add a few teaspoons of sugar to your coffee, and you give the brain an even stronger stimulating jolt. People who drink four, five, or more cups of coffee sometimes experience symptoms that mimic an anxiety attack—racing heart, shakiness, ringing in the ears, tingling in the fingers or toes.

As with all drugs, what comes up must come down. Caffeine withdrawal can induce headaches, nausea, fatigue, shakiness, and irritability. This withdrawal (like the drinking alcoholic's morning-after hangover) happens on a daily basis; within thirty to forty-five minutes after you drink a cup of coffee, you reach peak levels of caffeine in your brain. Approximately 15 percent is excreted each hour, which means that it takes about six hours for the body to metabolize and eliminate the drug.

Limit coffee (or other caffeinated beverages) to one or at the most two cups per day. If you drink more than three cups of coffee a day—and many recovering alcoholics drink five, ten, or more cups a day—you will need to cut back slowly in order to avoid the psychological and physical distress of full-blown withdrawal. Mix decaffeinated coffee with your caffeinated coffee; over a period of several weeks gradually increase the ratio of decaf to caffeine. If you drink several caffeinated sodas every day, cut out one can a day, replacing the caffeinated soda with a caffeine-free version.

Eliminating or severely restricting caffeine can do wonders for your mental state, clearing up anxiety, panic attacks, hyperactivity, mood swings, and depression. If these symptoms persist, or if you feel chronically depressed, panicky, or so tired you want to sleep all day, seek professional support from a specialist in addiction medicine. (See References section for help locating specialists.)

Carbonated sodas such as Coca-Cola, Pepsi, 7UP, and Dr Pepper have little or no nutritional value, are high in sugar (containing an average of three tablespoons per soda), often contain caffeine, and frequently contain phosphates, which can affect calcium levels, bone metabolism, and hormones. Caffeine levels are often high in sodas—one 12-ounce can of Mountain Dew contains 55 mg caffeine while a can of Diet Coke has 50 mg, Classic Coke has 45 mg, and Pepsi and Dr Pepper each have 37 mg. Avoid these products whenever possible, substituting unsweetened carbonated water mixed with a small amount of a low-sugar fruit juice such as grapefruit, orange, or apple.

Tea often contains caffeine, although generally not in the amounts found in brewed or instant coffee. (Twelve ounces of brewed tea, for example, contains 70 mg of caffeine compared to 206 mg caffeine in 12 ounces of brewed coffee.) Certain herbal teas do not contain caffeine; check the label to make sure.

Chocolate and cocoa products are prepared with large amounts of sugar and contain caffeine and theobromine, a stimulant that can stress the CNS and aggravate hypoglycemic symptoms. If you have a sweet tooth that you can't completely squelch, try carob products, available at most health food stores. Carob is a natural noncaffeinated food that tastes like chocolate and contains protein, calcium, phosphorus, and some B vitamins. Watch out for commercially prepared carob products, which generally contain lots of sugar.

Fruit juices are high in fructose, a natural sugar that provides calories and quick energy. Twelve ounces of grape juice contain more sugar (54 grams) than the same amount of Kool-Aid (38 grams); a 16-ounce McDonald's chocolate shake contains only 4 more grams of sugar than the 12-ounce glass of grape juice. Apple juice has 41 grams of sugar, orange juice has 38 grams, grapefruit juice has 28 grams, and tomato juice has 8 grams per 12 ounces. Orange juice, although it is fairly high in sugar, is a good choice if you drink it with the pulp, which is rich in fiber and will slow down the sugar jolt.

Vegetable juices offer a concentrated source of vitamins and minerals. Any vegetable can be made into a juice, but carrots, beets, celery, and spinach are the most common. The popular V8 juice is made from tomato juice concentrate, carrots, celery, beets, parsley, lettuce, watercress, and spinach; be aware, though, that an 11.5-ounce can of V8 also contains 880 milligrams of sodium, 37 percent of the recommended daily amount. Use the low-sodium version, especially if you have high blood pressure.

Whole milk, cream, and half-and-half are all high in saturated fat. Use 1-percent or nonfat (skim) milk products instead.

Water is essential to the integrity of every cell in your body. Water makes it easier for the liver to filter toxins and foreign substances from the blood and eases the kidneys' job of filtering and separating toxins by diluting the urine. Water also eases the digestive system's burden, softening and expanding the food particles, which makes them easier to eliminate.

According to Ralph Nader's Center for Study of Responsive Law, our drinking water is contaminated with twenty-one hundred toxic chemicals; our public water systems test for fewer than thirty of these. City water is treated with chlorine and other disinfecting agents. Well water, which comes from groundwater, may contain toxic heavy metals, pesticides, herbicides, nitrates, radon, asbestos, industrial wastes, or gasoline by-products (hydrocarbons). If you get your water from a well, have the water analyzed periodically for bacteria, mineral content, and organic chemical pollutants.

Whether you are on a municipal water system or have your own well, we recommend that you filter your water. Water filtration systems include:

- *Activated carbon filters,* which remove bacteria, parasites, chlorine, and other chemicals. These systems are relatively inexpensive and available at department stores, hardware stores, and health food stores.

- *Solid block and carbon block filters* are more expensive and harder to find, but they filter more contaminants from the water.

- *Reverse osmosis filters* include a sediment filter to remove larger particles, a reverse osmosis membrane, and an activated carbon filter. Many experts consider reverse osmosis units to be the best way to purify water.

What about bottled water? Recent reports show that many expensive bottled waters are contaminated with toxic substances. In 1999 the National Resources Defense Council (NRDC) tested 103 brands of bottled water and concluded that approximately one-third of the water tested was of "spotty quality." The NRDC recommends the following bottled waters, which "tested clean": Deer Park, Naya, Rocky Mountain Drinking, San Pellegrino, Vons Drinking Water, and Vons Natural Spring Water.

We recommend that you drink eight to ten 8-ounce glasses of fresh, filtered water daily. Many nutritionists believe that water taken with the meal dilutes the digestive enzymes and interferes with the digestive process. While it won't hurt you to sip a glass of water at mealtimes, try to drink the bulk of your water between meals.

Here's an idea to increase your water intake, reduce your caffeine consumption, and possibly benefit your vital organs: Substitute a cup of warm lemon water (simply add a slice of lemon to hot water) for coffee. Practitioners of traditional Chinese medicine believe that foods with a sour taste help stimulate and support the liver; in Western herbal traditions, lemon is frequently used to cleanse the liver and gallbladder, benefit the kidneys, lower high blood pressure, and reduce a fever.

SEASONINGS

The average American consumes two to four teaspoons of salt a day, approximately fifteen pounds every year; yet we need only one-tenth of a teaspoon daily. Salt contributes to abnormal fluid retention, loss of potassium, and, most significantly, high blood pressure. High blood pressure is the number one cardiovascular disease in this country and a contributing factor to heart attacks, congestive heart failure, and strokes.

Cut down on salt whenever and wherever possible. This isn't easy to do, because most foods we eat are loaded with salt. Keep the salt shaker off the table, use less salt in cooking, and avoid canned and processed foods that contain salt, as well as smoked, salted meats such as bacon, hot dogs, bologna, and sausage.

Other condiments such as catsup, mustard, mayonnaise, chili sauce, hot sauce, salsa, salad dressings, and soy sauce tend to be high in salt, and often in fat and sugar as well. Cut down on these foods or look for a "natural" (low-sugar, low-salt, low-fat) variety.

Be careful to avoid seasonings and condiments that contain alcohol. All natural flavor extracts—vanilla, almond, maple, orange, and so on— contain alcohol. If you use cooking extracts, always use imitation versions; read the label to make sure they are alcohol-free. Also, cooking wines contain 11 to 12 percent alcohol. Although the alcohol content is generally eliminated during cooking, we recommend avoiding recipes that call for wine, sherry, port, brandy, vodka, or various liqueurs.

In *Staying Healthy with Nutrition*, Dr. Elson Haas notes that he received less than ten hours of nutritional education in four years of study at a highly ranked medical school. Most physicians receive approximately the same number of hours of education about alcoholism. Even physicians and treatment professionals with training and experience in alcoholism often know very little about alcohol's effect on nutrition and the insidious impact of marginal nutritional deficiencies. Therefore, your physician may not be knowledgeable about your nutritional needs in recovery or even support your decision to change your diet. "Just eat three square meals a day" is the advice you are most likely to get.

You will need to educate yourself. This chapter represents only a beginning. For readers who want to know more about nutrition in general or the specific problems of hypoglycemia and sugar sensitivity, we recommend the following books:

Staying Healthy with Nutrition, by Elson M. Haas, M.D. (Celestial Arts Press, 1992)

Eating Right to Live Sober, by Katherine Ketcham and L. Ann Mueller (Signet, 1986)

How to Defeat Alcoholism: Nutritional Guidelines for Getting Sober, by Joseph D. Beasley, M.D. (Times Books, 1989)

Potatoes Not Prozac, by Kathleen DesMaisons, Ph.D. (Simon & Schuster, 1998)

Seven Weeks to Sobriety: The Proven Program to Fight Alcoholism Through Nutrition, by Joan Mathews Larson, Ph.D. (Fawcett Columbine, 1992)

Diet for a Small Planet: 20th Anniversary Edition, by Frances Moore Lappé (Ballantine, 1991)

Nutrition Against Disease, by Roger Williams (Pitman, 1971)

Prevention of Alcoholism Through Nutrition, by Roger Williams (Bantam, 1981)

We have one final caution to offer regarding diet and nutrition: Don't go overboard. Recovering alcoholics often feel that they've lost so much time being sick that they want to make up for it *right now*. In the early stages of recovery, broadly defined as the first year or two of sobriety, alcoholics should be counseled to take a realistic approach to diet and nutrition. We agree wholeheartedly with psychologist Jerome Levin's philosophy:

> Trying to be a health saint in one step is just setting yourself up for failure. So take care of the booze and consider doing something about the sugar, if that's a problem for you, later on. . . . I feel the same way about caffeine. Heavy coffee drinking is not good; it makes you jumpy and anxious. But, again, first things first and, if coffee is a good substitute for the hootch, use it. Later on, you can think about cutting down. . . . As long as you are giving up alcohol, you may very well also want to eat perfectly, drink nothing containing caffeine, not smoke, and be canonized this week. Forget it, just don't drink today and the rest of it will sort itself out down the pike.

15

Alternative Therapies: Exercise, Acupuncture, Vitamins, Herbs, and Amino Acids

My belief is that health and sickness are complementary opposites, that we cannot have one without the other, any more than good and evil can
stand alone. The challenge is to use sickness as
an opportunity for transformation.

—ANDREW WEIL

We know what works in alcoholism treatment and recovery. Lifelong abstinence from alcohol and other drugs is the first essential. Understanding the hereditary, neurophysiological nature of alcoholism is indispensable. Alcoholics Anonymous and/or other self-help groups offer continuing support and a sense of belonging to a caring community. Nutritional therapy repairs the cells and tissues damaged by alcohol. Psychological counseling and family support strengthen the alcoholic's sense of self and ability to develop and maintain intimate relationships. Paying attention to the needs of the spirit eases shame and guilt and offers a place of balance even in times of turmoil.

In recovery you will hear about many possibilities for healing and self-renewal, including various alternative approaches that can be used to restore physical and emotional well-being. Mainstream medicine is beginning to recognize the potential of alternative medicine to prevent disease, balance the emotions, and reinvigorate the human spirit, but health care practitioners are wise to advise their patients to be cautious and to stay well informed. Fads come and go, research is often contradictory, and a product or special treatment that looks promising can, in the long run, be dangerous. The uneducated consumer is easy prey for the sensationalistic claims and bogus cures of manufacturers hoping to make big bucks off overly trusting customers.

What works and what doesn't? Which remedies are safe and which should not be attempted? In this chapter we will offer a guide to various therapies that, for the most part, deliver on their promises—exercise, acupuncture, vitamin and mineral supplements, herbal remedies, and amino acid therapy. Our primary caution to anyone considering alternative therapies is this: Always maintain a skeptical, questioning attitude toward any provider or product claiming "instant" cures. If a particular treatment makes you feel better physically, mentally, or spiritually, and if your primary health care practitioner (who must be knowledgeable about the neurophysiological nature of alcoholism) assures you that it is safe, then by all means stick with it. Don't expect miracles, however, and don't jump from one method to the next, hoping to find a quick solution to your problems.

Stick with the basics, and if you feel the need for something more, cautiously explore the alternatives. "When you venture out of the world of standard medicine to look for alternative treatments," writes Andrew Weil, "it is even more important to be an informed consumer." Protect yourself by becoming an informed consumer and always seek professional guidance before trying something new. You don't want to risk your recovery—or your health.

EXERCISE

Exercise is a powerful antidote to the everyday stresses of modern life. From loud music to traffic jams, E-mail foul-ups, and long lines at the grocery store, not many of us get through the day without experiencing significant physical or emotional stress. Much of the time, oddly enough, we seem to enjoy the revved-up feeling of the stress-activated adrenaline response, easily adjusting our minds to the frenetic pace of our speeded-up heart rate, tense muscles, rapid pulse, and blood sugar rush.

Stress can actually feel good, and many people get hooked on that instantaneous adrenaline rush and the burst of energy it supplies. For every high, however, there must be a low, and eventually stress will take a toll on your body and mind. Tense muscles lead to headaches, muscle pulls, cramps, and strains. Blood sugar highs are inevitably followed by blood sugar lows, which contribute to depression, fatigue, and anxiety. A pounding heart and racing pulse are followed hours later by mental confusion, physical exhaustion, and a general sense of feeling wiped out.

Exercise reduces stress and tension and offers immediate benefits for the mind, body, and spirit. With regular exercise, muscle tension eases, heart rate stabilizes, mental confusion clears, and energy returns. Regular exercise also has long-term payoffs, including a stronger heart, increased muscle strength, greater bone density, an improved immune system, more efficient neurological functioning, and protection against weight gain.

Getting accustomed to a daily exercise routine will take both practice and persistence. Impulsive, perfectionistic behaviors will need to give way to patience and tolerance of gradual gains. It is always a good idea to work gradually into a fitness routine and set realistic goals for yourself. If you are overweight, weakened by illness, or unaccustomed to exercise, walking up and down one flight of stairs three times a day might be a good way to start. After several days you can try a five- or ten-minute walk, over a period of weeks working up to thirty minutes of brisk walking every other day.

Whether you walk, jog, run on a treadmill, practice yoga, swim, bike, lift weights, or climb rocks, it is critically important to warm up first, giving your muscles a chance to stretch and loosen; "cold" muscles, tendons, and ligaments are more likely to snap, tear, or rupture. Breathe regularly and deeply as you exercise. Most important of all, choose an activity you enjoy, or you'll soon lose the desire to exercise. Researchers report that 25 percent of individuals beginning an exercise program quit within a week, and another 25 percent quit before six months.

While the short- and long-term benefits of regular exercise are numerous and documented by research, most of us are confused about the type, frequency, and duration needed to maintain health and reduce the risk of disease. Here are some general recommendations.

FREQUENCY AND DURATION OF EXERCISE

Two long-term, well-respected studies offer solid information on the benefits of exercise for both men and women. The Harvard Alumni Study tracked approximately twenty-two thousand men for thirty-three years and found that maximum physical and emotional well-being was obtained by men who expended 1,500 calories a week in activities such as walking, jogging, cycling, and swimming.

The Boston Nurses' Health Study, which followed more than seventy-three thousand women, found that women who exercised for one hour four or five times a week had a 56 percent lower risk of stroke and a 44 percent lower risk of heart attack than those women who exercised for twenty minutes or less per week.

Despite the impressive benefits realized with regular exercise, researchers warn that overdoing it may cause more harm than good. Excessive exercise is *not* good for you. The International Society of

Exercise and Immunology reports that excessive exercise (more than ninety minutes at a time, for example) increases levels of cortisol; this immune-suppressing hormone releases free radicals, reactive molecules that can damage your cells, drain your immune system, and contribute to many chronic illnesses. For these reasons researchers at the highly regarded Cooper Aerobic Center in Texas recommend running no more than fifteen miles per week.

TYPE OF EXERCISE

Aerobic and anaerobic exercise are both needed to maintain health and reasonable weight. Aerobic exercise, which is dependent on oxygen for energy, consists of continuous low-intensity activity (running, swimming, fast walking) for a minimum of twenty minutes. Anaerobic exercise, which burns glycogen (stored sugar) for energy, consists of repeated short intervals of high-intensity exercise (weight lifting, strength training). Aerobic exercise conditions the cardiovascular system and builds stamina, while anaerobic exercises build strength, bone density, and muscle tone.

Try to include strength (weight) training, a form of anaerobic exercise, in your workout routine at least once or twice a week. Strength training involves using weights or resistance techniques (free weights or Nautilus) to build strength and muscle tone. If we do not use our muscles, we begin to lose muscle mass beginning in our thirties; as we lose muscle, our metabolism slows, which often results in weight gain. Many exercise physiologists believe the benefits of strength training are the most overlooked aspects of fitness and weight management.

Weight exercises run the greatest risk of injury, however, so you will need to use caution whenever beginning a new exercise program. Avoid dead lifts, overhead presses, seated leg extensions, squats, leg raises, and torso twisting with or without weights. Always avoid jerking weights to complete an exercise. Do not be preoccupied with lifting heavy weights when beginning a strength training program, for your muscles need time to adapt gradually to the strain of the workout. Weight exercises should always be performed slowly with controlled movements; any attempts to increase the weights too soon may result in injury.

To achieve the greatest aerobic gains and reduce body fat most efficiently, practice interval training. Interval training consists of alternating bursts of exercise intensity. Runners, for example, might race for short bursts and then return to a normal jog, while walkers can run for a minute and then return to normal-pace walking for two minutes.

Alternating between aerobic and anaerobic exercises has the added benefit of burning up to 40 percent more fat than exercising at a steady rate.

Cross-training, which involves alternating exercise routines so that you are doing more than one form of exercise on a regular basis, uses more muscle groups, burns more calories, and leads to better overall conditioning. Swimming, for example, develops the upper body, while bicycling conditions the lower body. If you combine running and bicycling, running will develop your hamstring muscles while bicycling works the quadriceps; the combination creates muscle balance and increases the number of muscle groups used.

Stretching is critical to flexibility and prevents muscle tightness and injury. If done improperly, however, stretching can actually cause injuries. Avoid bouncing, and do not try to compete with others; everyone is different in terms of flexibility, and if you push your stretches to the point of feeling pain, you risk injury. Yoga instructors are excellent teachers, as almost all stretches have their origin in this ancient art.

OTHER STRESS-REDUCING STRATEGIES

Laughter. Norman Cousins calls laughter "internal exercise . . . a form of jogging of the innards." Laugh often and much. Tell and listen to jokes. Watch funny movies. Learn how to laugh (gently) at yourself.

Relaxation techniques. Meditation, breathing exercises, visualization methods, massage, yoga, and other relaxation techniques can be potent stress relievers. Take a class (many hospitals now offer stress reduction clinics and other outpatient complementary medical services) or read well-researched books by recognized authorities on stress and fitness. We highly recommend Herbert Benson's classic *Relaxation Response* and Jon Kabat-Zinn's *Wherever You Go There You Are*.

Sleep. A good sleep does wonders to reduce stress and tension, while a restless night will affect your ability to concentrate, your mood, and your general outlook on life. Exercise, a healthy diet, nutritional supplements, and a network of strong, supportive relationships will help you get a good night's sleep. (Also see the section on herbs, pages 241–243, and amino acid therapy, pages 243–245.)

Relationships. You can exercise every day, eat well, and take every "miracle cure" available on the shelf, but if your relationships are unhealthy, your physical and emotional health will suffer. According to recent research, people who are isolated and lonely are two to five times more likely to get sick and die prematurely. Work hard to keep your relationships open, honest, and loving—your life literally depends on it.

ACUPUNCTURE

Acupuncture has been used for thousands of years to prevent and treat both chronic and acute illnesses, relieve pain, and induce relaxation. In the last thirty years clinicians have discovered its uses in the treatment and long-term recovery of drug addiction. Acupuncturists in Hong Kong in the early 1970s used auricular (outer ear) acupuncture with opiate addicts and noted surprising improvement in virtually every patient. Of forty patients treated, thirty-nine reported decreased pain and discomfort during withdrawal. A year after treatment began, 51 percent of the patients reported being free of drugs.

In the 1970s and 1980s, staff members at Lincoln Hospital, an inner-city addiction treatment program in the Bronx, New York, pioneered a needling method designed to reduce craving for alcohol and other drugs. This technique, which was later adopted and standardized by the National Acupuncture Detoxification Association (NADA), involves inserting very thin, very fine needles into the tough skin of the outer ear at five specific acupuncture points (acupoints). Two points ("Shen Men" and "Sympathetic") are believed to induce relaxation, while the others ("Kidney," "Liver," and "Lung") are thought to strengthen the function of these vital organs.

At Lincoln Hospital and many other treatment centers offering auricular acupuncture, patients can walk into the clinic off the street and be "needled" in a group setting, sitting in a chair and still in their street clothes. Acupuncture advocates claim that the group setting allows

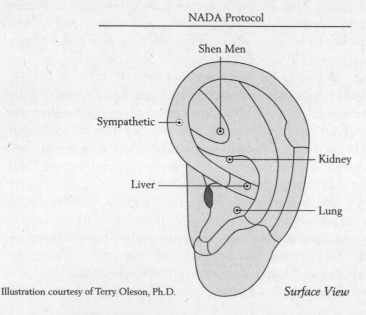

NADA Protocol

Shen Men

Sympathetic

Kidney

Liver

Lung

Illustration courtesy of Terry Oleson, Ph.D.

Surface View

patients to develop a rapport with staff members and other patients, enhancing the acupuncture experience. Alcoholics and other drug addicts who are very shy, withdrawn, fearful, or angry and who may find it difficult to express themselves verbally appear to thrive in this environment. Treatment staff report that when these patients receive the mild, calming acupuncture treatments, they are more likely to engage in positive relationships with the staff and other patients. As a result, they tend to stay in treatment longer and seem to be more willing to continue on with more structured counseling experiences.

The group setting also alleviates the fears and uncertainties that many people experience when thinking about getting "needled." When patients see that there is little if any pain, and that the other members of the group are experiencing relief from cravings, physical pain, nausea, anxiety, and fear, they are much more willing to go ahead with the procedure.

Auricular acupuncture is currently being used in approximately seven hundred chemical dependency programs in the United States and other countries to aid in acute detoxification and promote long-term recovery. In detoxification the goal is to reduce the primary symptoms of withdrawal and relieve associated aches and pains. In rehabilitation and recovery the goal shifts to promoting relaxation and relieving ongoing depression and/or anxiety. In the acute detox phase, patients may receive ear needling one or more times per day. As recovery advances, the frequency declines, although many recovering alcoholics report that periodic treatments—once a week or so—continue to be helpful even after a year or more of continuous abstinence. By reducing the symptoms associated with craving and encouraging relaxation, practitioners believe that acupuncture can be an important factor in preventing relapses.

Patients report that acupuncture treatments help them relax, reduce their cravings, and reestablish normal sleep patterns. The treatments also appear to have a definite effect on the individual's mood and receptivity to treatment, for patients report being more attentive to the overall treatment process and more hopeful about their long-term prospects. Detox nursing staff note fewer instances of elevated blood pressure and fewer patients needing antiwithdrawal medication. Treatment program managers claim that acupuncture reduces dropout rates and negative behaviors, including anger, aggression, and violence.

A growing body of research data on the use and effectiveness of acupuncture in the treatment of addiction tends to confirm these anecdotal reports. In a 1989 article that appeared in the British medical journal *Lancet*, a random sample of eighty male patients in a residential alcoholism treatment program in Minnesota were divided into two groups. The first group received the NADA-approved "real" acupuncture and the other received a "sham" version—the needles were placed in different spots on the outer ear than those specified by the NADA system. Over half (52.5 percent) of the men in the first group completed the eight-week treatment program, compared to only 2.5 percent of the second group. Six months later, the sham group had been readmitted to a detox center more than twice as often as those in the real acupuncture group.

At a New York City outpatient alcoholism treatment clinic, researchers randomly selected a group of thirty male patients. All thirty patients received the clinic's conventional counseling program, but sixteen also received the NADA acupuncture therapy. Fifteen of the sixteen in the acupuncture group completed the program or remained abstinent, while only six of the fourteen patients who did not get acupuncture completed the program or remained abstinent.

How, exactly, does acupuncture work? Researchers have discovered that acupuncture points have a higher electrical potential and are supplied by more peripheral nerves than other areas of the skin. When acupoints are stimulated with needles or firm pressure (acupressure), measurable biological changes occur. Acupuncture—like exercise— accelerates the release of natural opioids in the central nervous system; these substances inhibit pain and increase feelings of well-being. In studies with rats, acupuncture increases activity in areas of the brain responsible for relaying sensory and motor information and other regions of the brain that influence learning, memory, and emotions.

If you decide to give acupuncture a try, make sure that your practitioner is trained in the special protocols and techniques designed by the National Acupuncture Detoxification Association (NADA). Most people trained by NADA to perform this specialized form of acupuncture are not acupuncturists, which is a term ordinarily used for someone who has completed a three- or four-year course of graduate training in the general practice of Asian medicine. General acupuncturists (known in many states by the term "Licensed Acupuncturist," or L.Ac.) are not considered by NADA to be qualified to perform its system of treatment unless they have also received the NADA training.

VITAMIN AND MINERAL SUPPLEMENTS

When combined with a sensible, balanced diet, vitamin and mineral supplements will help repair damaged cells and tissues, mitigate the effects of stress and illness, reduce the risk of infection, balance blood sugar, increase energy, and protect the body's cells from pollutants in the air you breathe, the food you eat, and the water you drink.

We believe most people can benefit from taking daily vitamin and mineral supplements, but alcoholics have an added incentive due to alcohol's devastating effects on the body's ability to absorb and use nutrients, as we discussed in Chapter 14. To repair cellular damage and prevent illness, we recommend the following nutritional supplements for long-term recovery. Although these dosages are generally safe and nontoxic, it is always wise to seek the advice of a trained professional before taking these or other nutritional supplements.

MULTIVITAMIN

A standard multivitamin pill provides approximately 100 percent of the recommended daily allowance (RDA) or daily value (DV) for most vitamins, minerals, and trace elements. In addition to the multivitamin, take the additional nutritional supplements listed below.

VITAMIN A (BETA CAROTENE)

Vitamin A plays a vital role in maintaining the health of the body's mucous membranes and helping the cells and tissues establish a natural impermeability to external pathogens. This antioxidant action helps protect the cells from pollutants of all kinds and may be helpful in preventing problems such as ulcers, high blood pressure, and strokes. Vitamin A also:

- Supports the immune system by increasing antibody response, enhancing natural-killer-cell functions, supporting monocyte functions, and strengthening the activity of the thymus gland

- Helps repair tissues

- Protects tissues from infection

- Promotes healthy teeth

- Prevents night blindness and maintains the health of the cornea (the eye covering)

- Contributes to healthy skin by stimulating the growth of skin cells and contributing to their structural integrity

We recommend taking 10,000–25,000 IU of beta or mixed carotenes daily. Beta carotene is converted into vitamin A in the intestines, but unlike vitamin A is not toxic even in large doses. However, alcoholics with advanced liver disease (hepatitis or cirrhosis) should use vitamin A and beta carotene only under medical supervision.

B VITAMIN COMPLEX

Although the B vitamins differ chemically and perform varied functions in the body, they are grouped together because they have similar biochemical structures, are commonly found together in foods, and need each other to function optimally. The B vitamins:

- Provide the spark for numerous physiological and neurological processes, helping your body cope with everyday stress as well as the additional strain of chronic illness

- Stimulate the metabolism of carbohydrates, fats, and proteins

- Maintain the health of vital organs, including the brain, liver, and heart

- Improve nervous system functioning, relieving fatigue, stress, anxiety, depression, and irritability

Take a B-100 complex daily, rather than taking individual B vitamins. Many alcoholics have deficiencies in specific B vitamins (thiamine and niacin, for example); if you need to supplement individual B vitamins, be sure to follow your doctor's advice.

VITAMIN C

Vitamin C performs many essential functions in the body. This powerful, protective vitamin:

- Stimulates the immune system, which helps prevent infections and numerous chronic illnesses

- Acts as an antioxidant, protecting the body from free radicals (reactive molecules that can injure cells and contribute to many chronic diseases)

- Forms and repairs collagen, which is the basis of connective tissue

- Maintains healthy blood vessels

- Assists in the metabolism of the amino acid tryptophan, the precursor to serotonin

- Stimulates adrenal function

- Aids in cholesterol metabolism

- Assists in the detoxification of drugs such as cortisone, aspirin, and insulin

Take 1,000 to 3,000 milligrams daily. Because vitamin C works rapidly (it is used by the body in about two hours and is out of the bloodstream within three to four hours), divide the daily dose into two or three smaller doses. When increasing or decreasing your dose of vitamin C, do so gradually, over a period of several days or weeks, in order to allow your body to adjust. If you experience diarrhea or loose stools while taking vitamin C, cut back on the dosage until the symptoms disappear, and then maintain that new dosage.

VITAMIN E

Vitamin E, like vitamins A and C, is an antioxidant, protecting the body against oxidative damage which can lead to cellular irritation and damage and chronic inflammation throughout the body. Through its powerful antioxidant actions, vitamin E:

- Protects the body's cells and tissues most vulnerable to oxidation: skin, eyes, liver, breasts, and testes

- Defends the lungs from oxidative damage caused by environmental toxins

- Protects the membranes of red blood cells from oxidative damage

- Improves the functioning of heart and muscle cells, thus reducing cardiovascular risk

- May help prevent cancer, heart and vascular disease, and lung disease

Take 400 IU if you are under age forty and 800 IU if you are over forty; always take d-alpha tocopherol (natural vitamin E), which is the most active form of the vitamin.

ESSENTIAL FATTY ACIDS

The essential fatty acids (EFAs), which include linoleic, linolenic, and arachidonic acids, are critically important polyunsaturated fatty acids that need to be supplied through food sources or nutritional supplements because the body cannot make them on its own. Omega-3 fatty acids also have many beneficial effects on physical health and emotional well-being.

The essential fatty acids:

- Act as anti-inflammatory agents throughout the body, reducing inflammation and working to prevent and/or ease the symptoms of numerous autoimmune diseases such as asthma, allergies, arthritis, and lupus

- Function as skin lubricants, keeping the skin and other tissues soft and supple

- Reduce serum cholesterol levels

- Raise "good" (HDL) cholesterol

- Decrease risk of vascular thrombosis and cardiovascular disease

- Increase the production of serotonin, thereby reducing depression and suicidal behaviors

Evening primrose oil is an important source of gamma-linoleic acid (GLA), a substance that helps the brain convert essential fatty acids to the prostaglandin E1 (PGE1) series; these hormonelike substances work throughout the body to reduce inflammation, lower blood pressure, assist with insulin secretion, enhance nerve conduction, aid gastrointestinal function, and protect the liver. Take 1,500 milligrams daily. Black currant seed oil or borage seed oil are also good sources of GLA.

Omega-3 fatty acids are found in cold-water fish such as salmon, mackerel, herring, anchovies, sardines, and albacore tuna. Eat two or three servings of fish that are high in omega-3s weekly or take a 1,500-

milligram omega-3 fish oil supplement daily. If you can't tolerate fish oil because of allergies or the fishy aftertaste, flaxseed oil is a good substitute, providing a rich source of omega-3 fatty acids. Take one tablespoon daily. Because flaxseed oil can quickly go rancid, be sure to refrigerate it and store it in an amber, light-protective container. Flax meal (ground flaxseeds) is another alternative; you can sprinkle the crushed seeds over cereal and salads.

Omega-3 fish oils and GLAs are available in combined capsules. Whether you take the supplements separately or in a combined formula, make sure you get 1,500 milligrams *each* of omega-3s and GLA daily.

HERBAL REMEDIES

Alternative-medicine practitioners and increasing numbers of traditionally trained physicians are recommending various herbal remedies for recovering alcoholics. Herbs, like acupuncture, have been used for hundreds, even thousands of years, and are generally safe and nontoxic. Yet herbs are also powerful medicine and can be used inappropriately and even dangerously. It's a good idea to consult a professional herbalist, and also tell your doctor what herbal supplements you are taking.

With caution and careful supervision, the following herbal remedies may be useful for cellular repair, relaxation, insomnia, general immune support, and blood sugar problems. Remember, though, that herbs generally work slowly, with benefits occurring only after several weeks or months of use. Many recovering alcoholics find herbs too weak and either stop taking them or double or triple the recommended dosage in order to obtain a more potent effect.

For these reasons, always take herbs under the supervision of a trained professional and always take the herb(s) in the dosages specifically prescribed for you or follow the dosage instructions on the product label. Buy herbs that are labeled "standardized extracts," which guarantees you will get a sufficient amount of the active ingredient in the herb; extracts are available in both liquid or pill form. If you buy herbs in a liquid form, make sure the formula is alcohol-free—look for extracts in a glycerine base. Be sure to check the label for the expiration date.

FOR CELLULAR REPAIR

Milk thistle (Silybum marianum) is a gentle Mediterranean herb that has been used for more than two thousand years in treating liver disorders. The active ingredient silymarin, found in milk thistle seeds, protects the liver from damage and works to regenerate liver tissue. Researchers in Germany report that milk thistle is extremely effective in aiding recovery from alcohol-related liver disorders (fatty liver, alcoholic hepatitis, and cirrhosis).

Dandelion (Taraxacum officinale) is considered a blood purifier and has been used with great success for hundreds of years for conditions involving the liver and gallbladder, including food sensitivities, hepatitis, cirrhosis, gallstones, and gallbladder infections. A rich source of vitamins and minerals, dandelion supports the digestion and improves metabolism, reduces bloating and/or water retention, helps resolve many skin conditions, and helps regulate blood sugar levels.

For Symptom Relief

Valerian (Valeriana officinalis) is used worldwide as a calming, tranquilizing agent to ease anxiety, relieve tension, reduce anger and irritability, and induce sleep.

Passionflower (Passiflora incarnata) is also effective for insomnia and anxiety; herbalists sometimes combine passionflower and valerian to produce mild sedation and relaxation. Passionflower appears to act on the central nervous system as a mild tranquilizer, yet it also contains stimulants thought to aid in digestion, relief of menstrual pain, and dilation of coronary arteries.

Skullcap (Scutellaria laterifolia) is a member of the mint family and has been used traditionally for treating anxiety and insomnia; however, excessive use of this herb can cause stimulation rather than sedation. Herbalists sometimes combine skullcap, valerian, and passionflower to combat the craving for alcohol.

For Immune Support

Echinacea (Echinacea auqustifolia or echinacea purpura) is a traditional Native American remedy used to increase immunity and fight infection. Modern research confirms that echinacea boosts immunity by normalizing the white blood cells, which fight bacteria and viruses, and increasing levels of the antiviral substance interferon and the immune-related blood protein propardin.

Echinacea is best used preventively rather than curatively. When you start to feel the first symptoms of a cold or flu, take echinacea in the dosages recommended on the label; stop taking the herb when you begin to feel better.

FOR HYPOGLYCEMIA

Guar gum is a soluble fiber extracted from the guar plant, grown in the Middle East; it may help prevent and/or treat hypoglycemia. Glucose molecules latch on to the fibers, causing sugar to be released slowly into the bloodstream, which reduces stress on the pancreas. Whenever you take extra fiber, be sure to drink lots of fresh, filtered water to help the fiber bulk up and move food particles swiftly and efficiently through the digestive tract.

Gentian (Gentiana lutea) stimulates the digestion and encourages the production of saliva, stomach acid, and bile. This gentle, balancing herb relieves a variety of digestive disorders such as nausea, vomiting, heartburn, and flatulence. Gentian also has anti-inflammatory properties that may make it useful in arthritis treatment. Most herbalists advise pregnant women to avoid taking gentian.

Devil's club (Oplopanax horridum) helps to balance blood sugar levels. Considered part of the ginseng family, this herb grows abundantly in the Pacific Northwest. A soothing digestive tonic and metabolic stimulant, devil's club also seems to help people lose weight.

Dandelion root, a gentle but powerful liver tonic (see page 77), doubles as an excellent digestive remedy, assisting in the assimilation of nutrients, strengthening various digestive organs, and balancing blood sugar levels.

AMINO ACID THERAPY

Amino acids are the primary component of proteins; they are also the principal source of the "feel-good" neurotransmitters in your brain, including dopamine, serotonin, norepinephrine, and GABA. If you eat sufficient amounts of balanced, nutritious foods every day, you will be supplying your body with most, if not all, the essential amino acids you need to synthesize these neurotransmitters. However, because genetically transmitted neurotransmitter imbalances are implicated in the development of alcoholism, many researchers and clinicians believe that amino acid therapy may help restore normal brain function in alcoholics, reducing cravings, increasing energy, relieving depression, and easing anxiety and/or panic attacks. Many health care practitioners offer amino acid supplements as alternatives to the prescription antidepressants known as SSRIs (selective serotonin reuptake inhibitors), which include Prozac, Zoloft, and Paxil.

The following amino acids are the most frequently used in treatment and long-term recovery:

Glutamine is a precursor to GABA, an inhibitory neurotransmitter that induces calm, improves memory, and reduces craving for alcohol.

Leucine stimulates insulin release and inhibits protein breakdown, helping to stabilize or lower blood sugar levels.

Methionine stimulates memory, prevents fatigue, and helps to remove excess brain histamine, which can contribute to depression and obsessive-compulsive behaviors.

Phenylalanine is a precursor of the amino acid tyrosine, which is involved in the formation of two neurotransmitters: norepinephrine, which stimulates memory, alertness, and learning; and dopamine, which relieves anxiety and depression.

Tryptophan increases levels of the neurotransmitter serotonin, helping to relieve anxiety and depression and induce sleep.

Readers who want to know more about amino acid therapy should review Joan Mathews Larson's book *Seven Weeks to Sobriety*. Larson describes the innovative treatment program she directs at Health Recovery Center (HRC) in Minneapolis. With this program, which is based on abstinence, general nutritional repair, blood sugar stabilization, and amino acid therapy, Larson claims that more than 75 percent of patients treated at HRC "have broken their addiction to alcohol, maintained their sobriety, and regained their health." Larson's book details the physiological effects of various amino acids and offers numerous amino acid formulas designed to combat specific problems such as tremors, fatigue, aggression, memory loss, poor concentration, paranoia, insomnia, and so on.

For readers who want to understand the biochemical processes underlying neurotransmitter deficits and the reasons why amino acid therapy may help reduce cravings, withdrawal symptoms, depression, and anxiety in both treatment and long-term recovery, we highly recommend *Alcohol and the Addictive Brain* by pharmacologist Kenneth Blum. In Chapter 11 Blum details his efforts to synthesize an amino acid formula that can be used to reduce craving, and he describes the promising preliminary clinical trials with alcoholics using his formula (called SAAVE).

Blum also attests to the safety of amino acid therapy. "The amino acids have been studied extensively in both animals and humans since the 1930s, and the literature reports that they are safe and have few side effects in comparison to agents commonly used in therapy," Blum writes. "It has been shown, for example, that DL-phenylalanine is less toxic than vitamin C, vitamin B_1, or pantothenic acid."

Research on amino acids and their safety and effectiveness as adjunct therapies in the treatment of alcohol addiction is progressing rapidly with new studies published on a regular basis. Until all the facts are in and the long-term effects of amino acid therapy are rigorously assessed, we recommend a cautious, individualized approach to amino acids. If craving for alcohol is intense, persistent, and unrelieved by dietary changes and nutritional supplements, amino acid supplements may help. For recovering alcoholics who suffer from chronic depression, fatigue, irritability, or anxiety, amino acids may offer substantial relief.

Before taking amino acid supplements, always seek the advice of a knowledgeable professional who is educated and experienced in alcoholism treatment and long-term recovery.

PART III

The
Future

16

The Booze
Merchants

If the liquor industry does not start acting in a more
socially responsible way, it may soon find itself
held in the same kind of esteem in which the
tobacco companies are now held. The alcohol
industry can act now. Or it can deny reality and
pay later.

—FORMER U.S. DRUG CZAR WILLIAM BENNETT

Who's brave enough to stand up and shout that
the $100-billion-a-year alcohol industry is also . . .
the number 1 killer of young adults in our country?

—SUSAN POWTER

How is it that the vast damage that the drug alcohol does to millions of individuals and to our society as a whole has gone effectively unchallenged? Grapes have been fermented, beer has been brewed, and whiskey distilled for hundreds, even thousands, of years. Through the ages alcohol has been the drug of choice for humankind, and every passing year adds new pages to the catalog of horrors related to its use. Now, with the scientific advances of the last fifty years, we know why certain people become addicted to alcohol and what can be done to help them. Why does the misery continue unabated? Why, now that we understand the full extent of alcohol's dark side, has there been no concerted effort to stem the bloody tide?

Throughout history there have been many reasons for our silence. Certainly the stigma of alcoholism has been a factor, as people have been taught to blame the drinker and not the drug for alcohol-related problems. Ignorance about the physical nature of the disease has played a major role, too, as have denial and reluctance to pin the label "alcoholic" on fine, upstanding citizens. (Medical examiners, for example, routinely list other causes of death on official records, in an effort to spare the family shame and embarrassment.)

But the greatest single obstacle to spreading the truth about alcohol and alcoholism is the $100-billion-a-year alcoholic beverage industry—the booze merchants. The liquor industry spends millions to tell us they are reasonable folks with a social conscience. They disburse huge sums to promote programs encouraging us to "drink responsibly." They urge us to "know when to say when." And when we drink too much, they even remind us to find a designated driver, neglecting to mention that the one designated driver who stays clearheaded means that the other passengers in the car can drink to oblivion—designated drunks, if you will.

"We're the good guys," the liquor industry would like us to believe. "Our product is legal, we spend millions for our chosen alcohol education and prevention programs, and we do everything in our power to make sure our products don't get into the hands of underage drinkers."

Don't believe a word of it.

The drug alcohol kills 100,000 people every year. That's 274 deaths every day—11 every hour—from alcohol-related causes. The deaths are not limited to panhandling street drunks, winos, and bums; their number is tiny. Most of the dead are ordinary people with jobs, good reputations, and civic responsibilities. Sixteen thousand people are victims of alcohol-related car crashes. The dead are men, women, and children with families and friends who love them and grieve over their loss for a very long time. The funerals are private, and the fact that alcohol speeded up or caused their demise is noted briefly—in a whisper of shame—or not at all.

Once in a while, however, those who die of alcohol's effects have powerful relatives, such as U.S. Senator Strom Thurmond, whose twenty-two-year-old daughter was killed in 1993 by a drunk driver, or former presidential nominee George McGovern, whose forty-five-year-old daughter died of alcoholism. With their help and with the legions of ordinary folk whose lives have been forever altered by the drug alcohol, we believe that one day, not very far in the future, the anger, grief, and awareness about alcohol's deadly potential will be distilled into a finely focused outrage. Perhaps it will take the untimely death of a particularly famous and loved national leader, actor, or athlete to bring appropriate attention to the nation's alcohol problems. Perhaps it will happen after a catastrophic accident caused by a train driver tanked up on beer, or a whiskey-sotted school bus driver who loses control of his vehicle with dozens of children aboard, or an alcohol-addicted pilot who somehow falls through the cracks of the airline industry's monitoring system and kills hundreds aboard a 747 jumbo jet.

Whatever the precipitating event, the day will come when ordinary citizens are so sick and tired of the death and destruction caused by the drug alcohol that they will demand an accounting. Make no mistake: When that day comes, the booze merchants will rise up indignantly and in a concerted, well-orchestrated chorus insist that there is no risk in drinking alcohol except for the weak-willed among us who "abuse" it. As for beer, wine, or whiskey being addictive? No way, say the booze merchants; a few "irresponsible" drinkers are ruining alcohol's image, while the "neoprohibitionists" are threatening to take us back to the moral finger wagging of Prohibition.

In this chapter we will focus on the ways and means by which the liquor industry has achieved its goal of averting the nation's eyes from the human tragedies, economic costs, and public health consequences of problem drinking and alcoholism. We will show how Big Alcohol has succeeded by spending huge sums of money to keep lawmakers quiet, by cleverly advertising and promoting their products, by pitching their promotions to the impressionable underage drinker, by manipulating government at all levels (including those agencies charged with educating the public about the evils of drugs), and by a drumbeat of deceptive language intended to take the heat off alcohol and focus it on the person who drinks it.

With their ingeniously plotted, well-financed campaigns to glorify alcohol and cast aspersions on addicted drinkers, the booze merchants have insinuated themselves and their hugely profitable products with virtual impunity into all elements of American life.

THE MONEY MACHINE

For the booze merchants, money is the name of the game. The beer, wine, and whiskey pushers spend big to keep their products flowing out in a virtual flood, unimpeded. Thus they keep their profits streaming in. The liquor industry's annual gross of $100 billion is twice the size of the annual budget of California and nearly a third of what our country spends annually for its armed forces.

The alcohol money game is played with simple, circular rules. Billions earned. Hundreds of millions spent on advertising and promotion. Tens of millions lavished on politicians. "Abusers" blamed. Billions more earned. And the circle goes round.

The Beer Institute, a powerful lobby group, has a $2 million budget. The Wine Institute, with lobbyists in Washington, D.C., and forty states, spends $6.5 million a year to make friends in high places. The Distilled

Spirits Council has a $7.5 million budget and employs forty-five people. At the state level, those who protect Big Alcohol as well as Big Tobacco are among the highest-paid lobbyists.

The booze merchants pay their friends well. The liquor industry is legally entitled to give money, within certain prescribed federal and state limits, to any politician who wants to take it, and it gives lots of money to many politicians and even more to the political parties. Between 1993 and 1998 Big Alcohol handed $2.6 million to U.S. senators; in 1997 and 1998 the booze merchants gave U.S. representatives $1.5 million. State, county, and municipal politicians throughout the land also benefit from the booze industry's largesse, and the gifts always come hard and fast whenever there are proposals before state or local governments designed to restrict the flow of alcohol.

In its 1999 budget the Distilled Spirits Council (DISCUS) increased its budgeting for the free distribution of liquor. DISCUS gave Representative Carrie Meeks, a Democrat from Florida, two cases of booze for her birthday. Representative Mitch McConnell, a Republican from Kentucky, received a stash of Kentucky bourbon, and Representative Henry Bonilla, a Republican from Texas, got several cases of liquor for a party hosted at the Republican Capitol Hill Club.

DISCUS also gave four cases of liquor to the March of Dimes Birth Defects Foundation. Embarrassed by the disclosure that they were taking money from Big Alcohol at the same time they were raising millions to finance prevention efforts against fetal alcohol syndrome, a spokesperson explained that the liquor was used at a fund-raising event. March of Dimes employees are prohibited from drinking at such events, the spokesperson continued, and signs were posted near the bars urging pregnant women to abstain from drinking.

Post–World War II public disclosure laws give the citizens of this country the right and opportunity to know who accepts Big Alcohol's money and how these beneficiaries vote on alcohol education, prevention, treatment, research, taxation, licensing, and advertising. Here is a list of the top alcohol money recipients, compiled by the Center for Responsive Politics:

Top Ten House Recipients of Alcohol Political Action Committee and Individual Contributions, 1997–1998 Election Cycle

RANK	NAME	AMOUNT
1	Jim Bunning, R-KY	$56,273
2	Richard A. Gephardt, D-MO	$44,833
3	Anne Northup, R-KY	$35,414
4	Frank Riggs, R-CA	$31,480
5	John Ensign, R-NV	$29,197
6	Martin Frost, D-TX	$24,800
7	Newt Gingrich, R-GA	$22,000
8	Kenny Hulshof, R-MO	$19,472
9	Charles E. Schumer, D-NY	$18,300
10	Nancy Pelosi, D-CA	$17,500

Top Ten Senate Recipients of Alcohol Political Action Committee and Individual Contributions, 1993–1998

1	Dianne Feinstein, D-CA	$133,634
2	Tom Daschle, D-SD	$123,565
3	Alphonse M. D'Amato, R-NY	$119,099
4	Kay Bailey Hutchison, R-TX	$79,050
5	Bob Kerrey, D-NE	$72,200
6	Mitch McConnell, R-KY	$64,850
7	Gordon Smith, R-OR	$64,415
8	Bill Frist, R-TN	$56,395
9	Phil Gramm, R-TX	$54,500
10	John B. Breaux, D-LA	$51,475

The alcohol industry does not restrict its giving to individual politicians. It makes large "soft money" contributions—gifts that are dear to the heart of partisan leaders because contributions to political parties avoid the limitations of campaign contributions to individual candidates. During the 1992 presidential campaign, for example, Anheuser-Busch (brewers of Budweiser and Bud Light, among other brands) gave the Democratic National Committee $105,000. During the 1996 election cycle Anheuser-Busch donated more than $400,000 to the Democratic Party. In that same year Seagram's, the large whiskey distillers, gave the Democratic Party $1.2 million, with $595,000 of that coming directly from the checkbooks of Seagram's chairman, Edgar Bronfman, and his son, Edgar junior.

AVOIDING TAXES

The Reverend Dr. Alpha Estes Brown, an ordained minister with a law degree, master's degree in business administration, and doctorate, flew to Houston to attend the 1997 Anheuser-Busch shareholder meeting. He went to protest the company's marketing strategies specifically targeted at African-Americans. On the way to the meeting Dr. Brown stopped at a gas station, where he bought a 40-ounce bottle of King Cobra malt liquor and a 32-ounce bottle of Evian water. He took the bottles with him to the meeting to make a point about alcohol. The water, it turns out, cost $1.39, while the larger bottle of malt liquor was only 99 cents.

Brown's show-and-tell was mostly lost on the profit-oriented beer makers and their shareholders, but it has much to teach the rest of us. How can water cost more than booze? The answer is that alcohol is not taxed at the same rate as nonalcoholic beverages. The "real" price of alcohol—the price after accounting for inflation—has actually declined significantly over time, due in large part to stable federal, state, and local alcoholic beverage taxes. In 1950, alcohol taxes represented 6.2 percent of total federal revenues; by 1970 they had fallen to 2.5 percent, and by 1990 they were less than 0.5 percent of the total federal budget.

Inflation goes up every year, but booze is curiously immune to price increases. Between 1950 and 1989 legislators approved only one tax increase on alcohol, and that increase affected only distilled spirits. In late 1990, when Congress was trying to figure out how to tighten the reins on a federal budget that was awash in red ink, President George Bush took a hard look at the taxes on booze. Noting that the excise tax for beer—which accounts for more than one-half of the total annual U.S. consumption of alcohol—had not been raised in nearly forty years (since 1951), President Bush proposed a fivefold increase. Polls showed that 75 percent of the American people, despite being generally tax-averse, supported this proposed tax increase.

The beer companies were not happy. Higher taxes would mean higher beer prices, which would discourage some people—most notably low-income college and high-school students, who drink in excess of five billion cans of beer every year—from buying their brews. So Anheuser-Busch launched a multimillion-dollar "Can the Beer Tax" advertising campaign as part of its $300 million annual budget to promote beer drinking. Petitions, letter-writing materials, and prewritten messages were placed in bars and taverns throughout the country. Members of Congress were deluged with more than 2.4 million petition signatures and 1.6 million letters.

With that kind of money and influence being bullied around, the outcome was predictable. Congress voted down President Bush's five-fold tax increase on beer and instead approved a watered-down tax that doubled the 1951 tax from about 16 cents on a six-pack to 32 cents, an increase of less than 3 cents a bottle. The tax on wine was increased from 3 cents to 21 cents a bottle, a sevenfold increase that on the surface may seem like a lot. By any reckoning, however, a 21-cent tax on a 750-milliliter bottle with an average cost of several dollars is small.

Big Alcohol continued to wage war against higher taxes during President Bill Clinton's term. When Clinton announced his far-reaching, expensive plan for health care improvements in 1993, he was asked how he would pay for it. He answered that he would impose significantly higher taxes on tobacco and alcohol. Enter U.S. Representative Richard Gephardt, Democratic majority leader from Missouri, who got the president's ear when he accompanied him on a flight on Air Force One. It so happens that the brewing of Budweiser beer is the largest industry in Mr. Gephardt's district. When Mr. Clinton next spoke about taxes to pay for better health care, his speechwriters excised any mention of higher taxes on alcoholic beverages.

Big Alcohol's ability to sidestep taxes—and avoid accepting responsibility for the expensive toll exacted by its products—shifts the burden to the rest of us. Every taxpayer in this country ends up paying for the problems created by the people who produce, promote, and encourage the use of alcohol. We pay for the cops on the street who have to deal with rowdy and unruly drunks, the public defenders who are charged with defending the drinkers who commit crimes while high on alcohol, the judges who try their cases, the drunk tanks and detox centers that dry them out, and the jailers and prison officials who keep them locked up.

We pay for cleaning up the carnage on our highways created by drunk drivers. We help subsidize hospital services for the victims of alcohol-related accidents, domestic violence, and barroom brawls. We pay for veterans' hospitals, which spend hundreds of millions of dollars to treat and sustain alcoholics who served in the military. The list goes on and on and on.

Alcoholism and alcohol-related problems cost taxpayers in excess of $166 billion and claim more than a hundred thousand lives every year. It is therefore strange indeed that our elected officials don't assess the actual costs of alcohol and levy sufficiently heavy taxes on Big Alcohol to balance the scales.

TARGETING YOUTH

The liquor industry spends $1.8 billion a year telling us how beer, wine, and distilled spirits will enhance our sex lives, reduce our cares and woes, and make our boring lives more interesting. These messages are intended to reach anyone likely to pick up a bottle of beer, a glass of wine, or a drink made with hard liquor—and that includes millions of underage drinkers.

In fact, drinkers under twenty-one consume an estimated 10 percent of all the alcohol consumed in this country, which works out to billions of drinks a year sold illegally to young people. If the booze merchants are dedicated, as they assure us, to preventing underage drinkers from consuming their liquor, they are doing a lousy job of it. Retired four-star army general Barry McCaffrey, our nation's drug czar under President Clinton, put it this way: "There's no question that the worst drug among adolescents right now, from any standpoint, is alcohol."

To win over young drinkers before they become loyal to other brands, Budweiser, Miller, Coors (the three largest brewers), Colt 45, Absolut Vodka, Seagram's, Gallo, Cribari, and all the other alcohol peddlers spend fortunes on advertising and promotion; Budweiser alone spends $300 million on television advertising every year. Beer ads dominate not only professional games but also college sports, even though 70 percent of college students are below the legal drinking age.

Big Alcohol's advertising and promotion efforts influence the hearts and minds of kids who haven't even graduated from elementary school. During the 1998–99 football season, Anheuser-Busch reached an average of 1.3 million children under eleven years of age with their advertising during televised games. In the 1999 Super Bowl, seven of the ten top-rated ads were Budweiser plugs featuring creatures such as lizards, frogs, mice, and dogs, all hawking beer.

Kids love these ads. When Anheuser-Busch first introduced the

Budweiser frogs during the 1995 Super Bowl, the Center on Alcohol Advertising conducted a survey to see what kind of an impression the frogs made on youthful minds. Seventy-three percent of nine- to eleven-year-olds recognized the frogs croaking Bud's virtues, a recognition rate second only to the 80 percent who recognized Bugs Bunny. Lagging behind the bunny and the beer-hawking frogs were Smokey the Bear, Tony the Tiger, and the Mighty Morphin' Power Rangers.

Beer is unquestionably the drug of choice among adolescents. Despite the hype about "the beverage of moderation," beer has the same capability to create drunkenness and alcoholism as wine, whiskey, vodka, brandy, gin, rum, and other drinks. You just have to consume a little more liquid to get the same effect—and how many beer drinkers do you know who call it a night after drinking a 2-ounce shot of beer?

Beer, it turns out, accounts for more than half of the total annual U.S. alcohol consumption. More than 59 percent of males between twelve and twenty who drink alcohol say beer is their beverage of choice (compared to 9.1 percent citing hard liquor). And beer drinkers are notoriously immoderate in their drinking habits. Here are the statistics:

- Beer accounts for more than 80 percent of *excessive* alcohol consumption in the United States.

- Forty-nine percent of beer drinkers drink excessively (five or more drinks in one day).

- Only half of beer drinkers could accurately define how many drinks constitute "moderate" drinking, compared to 59 percent of distilled-spirits drinkers and 72 percent of wine drinkers.

- Sixty-three percent of beer drinkers under age twenty-four report binge drinking (five or more in a single day) compared to 53 percent of those twenty-five to forty-four years old and 30 percent of those forty-five or over.

Ignoring these carefully researched statistics, the beer pushers get really touchy when anyone suggests that their product may be dangerous. When the Cub Scouts published a pamphlet intended to educate parents about the dangers of drugs, the brewers of beer came out swinging. In a 1997 address to the annual meeting of the Beer Institute, the industry's watchdog and lobby group, institute president Ray McGrath blasted the Cub Scouts for handing out what he called biased information disparaging the liquor industry—and most especially beer—in its handbooks. Three million Cub Scout pamphlets titled "How to Protect

Your Children from Child Abuse and Drug Abuse: A Parent's Guide" contained what McGrath called "stunning examples of misinformation." He cited the following sections of the pamphlet as misleading:

- "Beer is a drug! Cocaine and crack are drugs! All drugs can be addictive. Once a person tries them, he or she builds up an appetite for them. They can be dangerous and deadly, and burn out the brain."

- "Number 2 Killer (second only to tobacco): Alcohol—one can of beer contains as much alcohol as one ounce of liquor. One can of beer can affect a person's reasoning, judgment, breathing and body coordination and can cause dizziness. After five beers a person is legally intoxicated and it takes as much as 3½ days to recover reflexes and normal brain function."

The Beer Institute couldn't dispute the facts used in the Cub Scout pamphlets, but that didn't dilute their outrage. They fell back on the message that beer is the "beverage of moderation." "With this volume of anti-alcohol advertising material and misinformation, we must work harder to get out our message of moderate and healthy consumption," McGrath declared. "We must challenge our adversaries, and we must not give them ammunition to bludgeon us with this kind of rhetoric."

Beer actually benefits society, says Peter Coors, the chief executive officer of Coors Brewing Company in Golden, Colorado. Mr. Coors recently suggested a creative solution to the nation's alcohol problem: Lower the drinking age. In a September 10, 1997, interview, Coors said: "If you chug a gallon of alcohol, you're going to die. We ought to be telling kids that in school. We shouldn't be preaching 'Don't drink.' We should be preaching responsible drinking. Maybe the answer is lowering the drinking age so that kids learn to be responsible about drinking at a younger age. I'm not an advocate of trying to get people to drink, but kids are drinking now anyway. All we've done is criminalize them.

"We have a legal, legitimate product that, when used properly, is a benefit to society . . . [and] makes life more enjoyable and more fun and more social."

PUSHING BOOZE IN THE AIR
AND OVERSEAS

Big Alcohol insinuates itself into virtually every aspect of our lives. Take the U.S. armed forces, for example. Until just a few years ago soldiers stationed in Korea could buy twenty-four cans (a full case) of beer every day. When the U.S. Army decided to cut the daily beer allocation to a mere six-pack, many GIs were not happy. The soldiers' grumblings were nowhere near as loud, however, as the howls of protest from Anheuser-Busch.

In a May 8, 1997, memorandum to Budweiser's top Washington lobbyist, the head of Anheuser-Busch's overseas military sales, Thomas A. Doherty, conjured up the specter of military interference with free enterprise: "This military ration-control directive subverts the [military] exchange business to the whims or moral dictates of a local military authority," Doherty wrote. Lawmakers, with their campaign coffers well lined with alcohol money (see pages 251–254), talked in somber terms about "troops not able to buy American beer for their morale."

The army defended itself by saying it was trying to cut back on black marketing. Some of the troops, it turns out, were buying beer for $12 a case in the military PXs and selling it for nearly four times that amount on the Korean black market.

That argument didn't cut it with the brewers of beer, and considering the money involved, it's no wonder. Military beer sales are a sweet deal for U.S. brewers, because the army foots the bill for the cost of shipping beer to its troops. In 1996 the 1.3 million cases of beer sent to Korea cost U.S. taxpayers $5.1 million.

Commercial airliners are another place where you can always find Big Alcohol. Lots of people get drunk in the air, and trouble sometimes ensues. Here are a few recent examples:

- An investment banker flying from Buenos Aires to New York in October 1996 was drunk. When the United Airlines flight attendant decided it was time to cut him off, he protested by lowering his pants, defecating on the beverage cart, and using napkins for toilet paper.

- When flight personnel on a November 1996 Northwest Airlines flight from London to Minneapolis stopped serving booze to a group of drunken British tourists, there was a near-riot.

- A drunken passenger assaulted the copilot of a USAirways Express plane in January 1997 and tried to grab the controls.

- Reverend Robert Schuller, a television evangelist who preaches to millions every week from his California-based Crystal Palace, was accused of assault by a United Airlines flight attendant for an incident that occurred in first class on a United Airlines flight from Los Angeles to New York in June 1998. The flight attendant said the seventy-year-old preacher, who had been drinking, "jumped" on him because he refused to serve him grapes without cheese on a dessert platter. Schuller entered into a plea-bargain to avoid a trial.

Why do the airlines put up with this nonsense? With passenger safety at risk, you would think the airlines would consider alcohol-free flights; after all, they banned smoking on airlines to protect the health of their passengers and air crews. The alcohol industry, however, has given the airlines a major incentive to keep the alcohol flowing. Distillers, hoping to win new customers, sell their little bottles to the airlines dirt cheap, charging part of the cost to their advertising budgets. In just one year the major airlines took in approximately $428 million from alcohol sales; $342 million was pure profit.

The liquor industry spends a lot of money hoping to convince the American public that it is interested in responsible, moderate drinking. These efforts are all smoke and mirrors, of course, for if it were not for the "irresponsible" and "immoderate" drinkers, the booze merchants would have much less money to throw around. Five percent of drinkers in this country are drinking half of the total booze consumed, according to Thomas Greenfield, a researcher for the Alcohol Research Group in Berkeley, California. The top 2.5 percent of drinkers average twelve drinks per day per person and consume one-third of all alcohol sold, Greenfield says, while the top 10 percent average three drinks per day each and account for 64 percent of all the alcohol sold. Light drinkers are a mere drop in the bucket.

INFLUENCING EDUCATION AND PREVENTION EFFORTS

Penny Norton, a Michigan alcohol prevention specialist, was attending an all-day training session sponsored by the local health department in Sanilac, Michigan. During the break, Ms. Norton picked up a box of educational materials featuring a photo of a group of teenagers and the words ALCOHOL—WE'RE NOT BUYING IT.

Norton then noticed a strip of heavy red plastic tape running across the forehead of one of the teenagers, which she thought was odd. When she removed the tape with the aid of a solvent, she discovered that it covered up five words. The original message, it turned out, was: ALCOHOL IS A DRUG, TOO, AND WE'RE NOT BUYING IT.

Who was responsible for putting that strip of red tape over the words *is a drug, too, and*? Why would anyone in the alcohol prevention field want to obscure the message that alcohol is a drug? Norton took her question to Bob Hammond, editor of *The Bottom Line*, a quarterly publication that tracks the activities of the booze merchants. Hammond called the Center for Substance Abuse Prevention (CSAP), the nation's leading public agency charged with alcohol prevention programs and the creator and distributor of the "Alcohol Is a Drug, Too, and We're Not Buying It" educational materials.

This is what CSAP's Heather Roberts told Hammond: "There were some . . . I'm not sure the word is compromise, but we had some pretty rough discussions with the alcohol industry, and it is my understanding that . . . uh . . . gosh, I'm not sure I should even be the one to answer this question. . . . It's kind of a sensitive issue, but I think the bottom line was that both the alcohol industry and ourselves have more to gain by working together than against one another. I think one of the concessions made was not to outright refer to alcohol as a drug."

The nation's alcohol prevention specialists apparently caved in to the liquor industry. Hoping to find out exactly what happened in discussions between government employees and alcohol industry representatives, Hammond hired an attorney, who filed a Freedom of Information Act request to obtain documents that might shed some light on the booze merchants' involvement. On February 28, 1998, ten months after the request was filed, someone from CSAP's office called Hammond with an apology for coming up empty-handed. "There are no records," he said. "They have been destroyed."

Here's another interesting story about Big Alcohol's influence on public and private agencies charged with educating citizens about the drug alcohol. In a report titled "Paying the Piper—The Effect of Industry Funding on Alcohol Prevention Priorities," the nonprofit Center for Science in the Public Interest (CSPI) compared the activities of forty-four local alcohol prevention groups on thirteen prevention measures, including increasing alcohol excise taxes, banning alcohol-promoting billboards, and lowering the legal blood alcohol limit.

Some of the prevention groups accepted liquor industry money. Others did not. The question CSPI hoped to answer was whether alcohol industry funding compromised prevention efforts. Here's what CSPI learned in answer to that question: Only 21 percent of the groups receiving liquor industry money backed an increase in federal alcohol taxes, compared to 65 percent of organizations with other sources of support. And 29 percent of the groups receiving liquor industry money supported a ban on alcohol-promoting billboards compared to 72 percent for groups that received no liquor industry funds.

"The alcohol industry is stepping up its efforts to buy friends among local prevention groups just as federal prevention funds are drying up in Washington," commented George Hacker, director of CSPI's Alcohol Policies Project. "Local groups are increasingly between a rock and a hard place when it comes to their own survival. This study reveals the compromises they may be asked to make—explicitly or implicitly—if they rely on the alcoholic-beverage industry for help."

TOUTING WINE'S HEALTH BENEFITS

The power and influence of the booze merchants to win friends and influence people in high places was proved once again in the recent decision to allow wine makers to tout the health benefits of their products. In February 1999 the Bureau of Alcohol, Tobacco, and Firearms—a federal agency whose name communicates that it is in the business of overseeing the most dangerous consumer products—approved two new labels allowing wine producers to promote the health benefits of their products on the label of any wine bottle sold in the United States.

The first approved label reads: "The proud people who made this wine encourage you to consult your family doctor about the health benefit of wine consumption." The second label reads: "To learn the health effects of wine consumption, send for the federal government's Dietary Guidelines for Americans." The message is followed by the address of the Center for Nutrition Policy and Promotion at the U.S. Department of Agriculture. The Dietary Guidelines note that moderate consumption of red wine may have certain health benefits. (These guidelines were released in 1995 and at this writing have not been updated; since that time, new research indicates that even one or two glasses of red wine a day may increase a woman's risk of breast cancer.)

Wine drinkers inclined to read the small print may be confused by the mixed messages, for right next to the health benefit labels are the federally required warning labels citing the risks of drinking alcohol. These warning labels appear on all cans and bottles containing alcoholic beverages and read as follows:

Government Warning: (1) According to the Surgeon General, women should not drink alcoholic beverages during pregnancy because of the risk of birth defects. (2) Consumption of alcoholic beverages impairs your ability to drive a car or operate machinery, and may cause health problems.

In its decision to allow the new health benefit labels, the Bureau of Alcohol, Tobacco, and Firearms overrode the loud protests of the most powerful and prestigious health care and disease prevention organizations in the country—the American Medical Association, the American Cancer Society, the American Heart Association, and the Center for Science in the Public Interest. The action also brought stern rebukes from two of the U.S. Senate's most powerful members—Strom Thurmond, a staunch conservative and dean of Senate Republicans, whose daughter was killed by a drunk driver; and Robert Byrd, a much-respected senior Democrat. The proposed labels, Thurmond and Byrd agreed, would encourage more people to drink and would push moderate drinkers to drink more heavily, with consequently steeper medical and social costs.

A year earlier, in April 1998, Senator Thurmond had filed a bill to strengthen the warning labels on all alcoholic beverages. The bill failed. Senator Thurmond's proposed additions are italicized:

Government Warning: (1) According to the Surgeon General, women should not drink alcoholic beverages during pregnancy because of the risk of birth defects. (2) Consumption of alcoholic beverages impairs your ability to drive a car or operate machinery, and *may lead to alcoholism.* (3) *Moderate consumption of alcoholic beverages* may cause health problems *such as hypertension and breast cancer.*

After the Wine Institute's success, Senator Thurmond introduced countering legislation that would bar "health messages" on wine bottles, transfer authority over labeling from the Bureau of Alcohol, Tobacco, and Firearms to the Department of Health and Human Services, and raise the taxes on wine. "Generally I do not favor increased taxes," Senator Thurmond explained, "but in this era of shrinking budgets, the only way in which we will be able to finance adequate, impartial and trustworthy research into alcohol-induced diseases such as hypertension, breast cancer and birth defects, is to generate a new revenue flow that will be used specifically for investigating such (alcohol-induced) killers."

USING BAD LANGUAGE

Big Alcohol talks dirty. Their favorite words, used often in smear campaigns intended to pin the blame for alcohol-related problems on alcoholics, are *abuse* and *irresponsible*. Thus, according to the booze merchants, "irresponsible" drinkers who "abuse" alcohol cause all the problems and give beer, wine, and hard liquor a bad name.

Through this language of abuse, the booze merchants have been remarkably effective at getting the rest of us to adopt both their vocabulary and their way of thinking. As alcoholism has been linked in the public mind with alcohol "abuse," efforts to teach "irresponsible" and "abusive" drinkers how to moderate their drinking have become increasingly popular. Critics of the disease concept (hardly a concept, given the volume of research supporting the fact that alcoholism is a disease) argue that controlled-drinking therapy—tellingly translated as "behavioral self-control"—should be considered a valid alternative to lifelong abstinence. Experimental bars instituted at publicly funded universities strive to teach students at high risk for alcoholism how to control their drinking.

The language we use when we talk about alcoholism has a profound influence on the way we treat its victims. The terms *abuse* and *abuser* are among the most pejorative terms in our vernacular, for as a society we hold in greatest contempt sexual abusers, child abusers, spouse abusers, and, not surprisingly, alcohol "abusers." It is long past time that we got rid of the phrases *alcohol abuse* and *alcohol abuser*, which focus the blame on the drinker, and put the emphasis back where it belongs—on the drug, the addiction, the disease. The idea of "abuse," encouraged by the alcohol industry and abetted, unfortunately, by federal and state government, leads directly to the problem of stigma about the disease. And the stigma serves to keep alcohol's victims and their families from seeking help for their problem.

With their bad language, the booze merchants are trying to manipulate the public into thinking that the problem is not with their booze but with us. The advice "Drink responsibly" is no more sensible for those genetically inclined to alcohol addiction than "Shoot up responsibly" is for heroin addicts. Cocaine junkies don't "abuse" their chemical—they are addicted to it.

In an industry with billions of dollars to buy the most talented advertising and marketing copywriters available, is it any wonder the booze merchants continue to play word tricks, hoping to deceive us and thus enhance their profits? One of the most effective—even brilliant—word games played by the booze barons is the use of the label *neoprohibitionist*. With that word we are taken back more than eighty years to the failed social movement of Prohibition, with its religious and moral zealots, Al Capones, Billy Sundays, bootleggers, and corrupt cops bribed to look the other way when booze was manufactured and sold. By implication, neoprohibitionists are backward-looking, pulpit-pounding fanatics intent on demonizing alcohol. (It is worth noting that the reduced consumption of alcohol during Prohibition also brought a substantial reduction in domestic violence, accidents of all kinds, and the incidence of alcoholism and related diseases such as cirrhosis of the liver. Productivity, on the other hand, increased during Prohibition.)

People who want to see better education about the drug alcohol, extensive prevention programs, affordable treatment, reductions of advertising to underage drinkers, and higher taxes to reduce consumption, particularly among underage drinkers, are not "neoprohibitionists." They are men and women who know from studying the facts, and often from firsthand experience with the disease, that alcohol is a drug more pernicious and deadly than all the illegal drugs combined. They are Republicans and Democrats, conservatives and liberals, rich and poor, Catholic, Protestant, and atheist, black, white, yellow, and brown. They care about the health and welfare of other human beings and our society as a whole. These are the people who are raising their voices and using their clout to put an end to the power and influence of the booze merchants.

Whenever you hear the word *neoprohibitionist*, you can be sure that someone who is employed by the liquor industry or its large network of affiliates is using it. Don't be fooled by the abusive language.

DAY OF RECKONING

On April 20, 1999, millions of Americans wept openly. We grieved on a national scale for the twelve high-school students and one teacher who were massacred in an afternoon of madness at Columbine High School in Littleton, Colorado. That same day—and the next day and the next, for every day of every year—eight young people died in equally gruesome, equally bloody alcohol-related car accidents. Their deaths, for the most part, went unnoticed and unremarked by the larger society.

Putting guns in the hands of frustrated, alienated, impulsive teenagers is a frightening scenario, but no less horrific is the everyday reality of boozed-up teenagers climbing into their cars. Put a bottle of beer in an adolescent's hand, and you have a weapon as powerful as any handgun. Put a drunk behind the wheel of an automobile, and you have a remarkably efficient killing machine.

Of course, we do it every day. That's part of the problem—we've come to accept the body count. We don't think about the dead and the maimed. We blame the deaths on the "abusers" who are "irresponsible." We pay the bills without protest. We shut our eyes and close our hearts. We have allowed ourselves to be duped into silence by the booze merchants.

It is long past time that Big Alcohol's free ride, with all its bloody sideshows, ended. When will the frogs and lizards go the way of Joe Camel and the Marlboro Man? What will it take to stand up and say no to the liquor industry? Who will step forward to make the booze merchants pay for the damage and destruction caused by the drug alcohol in the same way the assembled attorneys general made Big Tobacco pay for the damage caused by the drug nicotine? When is the day of reckoning for Big Alcohol?

These questions demand answers.

17

A River Runs
Through Us

You do not win a war by treating its victims.

—JAMES ROYCE

Our country's problems—and, indeed, the world's problems—with alcohol often seem beyond solution. After all, alcoholism and problem drinking have been with humankind since grains and grapes were first fermented, at a time lost in the ages. Through history alcohol has insinuated itself into the world's cultures and institutions. It has become ubiquitous.

The power of alcohol to disturb the mind and body was known early. "How exceeding strong is wine! It causeth all men to err who drink it" is included in the early Greek version of the Old Testament, dating from nearly two millennia ago. The industrial revolution of the nineteenth century created the capability to produce whiskey in million-barrel amounts, wine by the hundreds of thousands of cases, and beer by the billions of bottles. Fast assembly-line production of booze—and its concomitant mass marketing—greatly reduced the cost of alcoholic beverages.

Suddenly, a century ago, alcohol was affordable and available in the most remote African village and affordable and available as well to teenagers and even children throughout the industrialized world. Even the poorest characters in the Victorian era about which Charles Dickens wrote could afford gin. Gin-induced alcoholism was rampant and devastating to British society during Dickens's time and long after.

Before the industrial revolution, the drug alcohol was integrated into religions. Drinking wine in its various forms became traditional in many of the ancient religions of Asia, in the rituals of Judaism in the Middle East, and later around the world after the Jews were forced to leave their homeland and took their wine drinking services with them. The equation of red wine and the blood of Christ in the communion service remains part of the liturgy of the large, mainstream Christian faiths; hundreds of years ago the Catholics took this ritual with them as part of their global missionary outreach, introducing alcoholic beverages for the first time to many susceptible native peoples in the New World of North and South America.

It is a fact that gin, whiskey, beer, and wine have been and can be enjoyed with impunity by most drinkers. It is understandable why many such drinkers ask of alcoholics and problem drinkers, "Why do you drink to excess?" and clearly they deserve an answer. That is why in Part 1 we cited new knowledge about alcoholism, derived from solid scholarly research. But having established that for neurochemical reasons alcoholism afflicts a minority of alcohol's users doesn't dispel the dilemma posed by the disease. The hard fact is that though alcoholics and problem drinkers are in the minority, the drug alcohol has a devastating effect on drinkers and nondrinkers alike.

History has shown us that prohibition of alcohol use, though well motivated and indicative of the profoundly damaging effects of the drug, is not a practical solution to an obvious and serious problem. Though Prohibition in the United States reduced the consumption of alcohol and consequently lessened its negative consequences, it failed because it forbade what was an enjoyable beverage for most drinkers. Even Alcoholics Anonymous, which was established in 1935, just two years after Congress ended national Prohibition, took pains in its written principles not to indict the drug alcohol nor its users, at least not users who were not predisposed to addiction. In an early chapter of AA's "Big Book," the founders wrote, "We are careful never to show intolerance or hatred of drinking as an institution." In the tenth of AA's Twelve Traditions, the founders also said that "no AA group or member should ever, in a way as to implicate AA, express an opinion . . . on alcohol reform."

In this chapter we consider what we can do as individuals and as a society to reduce the incalculable costs of the problem incurred by a legal drug. A river runs through us, and that river is called alcohol. Since the beginning of time, people have been falling into the river, and far too many have been lost in the currents. For every alcoholic who is rescued, five, ten, or twenty more drown. That is the way it has been in the past, and some say that is the way it will always be. For this river will never dry up—alcohol is legal, and it is here to stay.

If we can't stop the river from flowing, however, we can at least attempt to slow its course. Fully aware of the life-threatening dangers the river poses to our communities, we can restrict access, practice

flood control, and post warning signs along the water's edge. We can educate people about the unpredictable nature of the river, detailing where
the rapids are and pointing out ways to avoid the most dangerous
stretches. Walking upstream, we can talk to people before they jump in,
informing them of the dangers that lie ahead. If they decide to take the
plunge, they will at least know the risks—hazards that exist even for
those who stay in the shallows, even for those who appear to be the
strongest swimmers.

In this chapter we look to the future and recommend specific action
in three broad categories—education, prevention, and treatment. In
considering the approaches outlined in these pages we suggest a realistic approach, recognizing the fact that we will never completely eliminate the death and destruction caused by the drug alcohol. There can be
no question, however, that these strategies will have a beneficial effect
on our society as a whole and directly impact the lives of tens of millions of people.

This statistic bears repeating: Forty-three percent of U.S. adults—
seventy-six million Americans—have been exposed to alcoholism in
their families, either growing up with an alcoholic, marrying an alcoholic, or having a blood relative who is an alcoholic. The river runs deep,
and it runs wide.

EDUCATION: TEACHING OUR CHILDREN
ABOUT THE DRUG ALCOHOL

Jeremy Jones is eleven years old and in the fifth grade. After eight
weeks in the Drug Abuse Resistance Education (DARE) program, he
believed he knew enough about alcohol to make a strong case for prohibition. Late one afternoon Jeremy removed all the booze from the
refrigerator at home (two beers and two-thirds of a bottle of white
wine), emptied it into the sink, and then proceeded to lecture his parents about their bad habits. "You're drug users," Jeremy said, "and I don't
want to live in a house where drugs are abused."

In his education about drugs, Jeremy learned that alcohol is a
drug—a true and important fact. Nobody told him, however, about the
peculiar nature of this drug (its stimulant, sedative, intoxicating, and
addicting qualities) or the fact that it affects different people in different ways. Nobody told him that his parents—who drink, on the average, one or two beers a week and have no family history of alcoholism—
are not at high risk for alcoholism. Nobody told him that alcoholism is
inherited and passed down from one generation to the next. Nobody

explained what a brain addiction is and how it affects the drinker's thoughts, emotions, and behaviors.

Are eleven-year-old children capable of understanding the basic nature of alcoholism and neurological addiction? We believe they are. The facts about the drug and the disease are not all that complicated when they're broken down, and even young children can be captured by the subject if the information is presented clearly and forcefully, with real-life stories used to dramatize the major points.

Here are the essential facts that must be communicated to our children in their education about alcohol and the problems it causes:

- *Alcohol is a drug.* Alcohol is both a stimulant and a sedative—it can get you high, and it can also make you sleepy, depending on how much you drink. Alcohol can make you throw up because in large doses it's a poison and the body tries hard to get rid of it. Alcohol slows down your brain, which makes it harder for you to walk, talk, think, and react—that's why it is dangerous to ride a bike or walk along the street after you have been drinking. You can overdose on alcohol the same way you can overdose on illegal drugs such as heroin and cocaine. Sometimes people—even kids—die when they drink too much alcohol.

  Whenever you hear someone use the phrase "alcohol and drugs," correct them. Tell them that alcohol is a drug, too, and that the right phrase is "alcohol and other drugs." Tell them, too, that alcohol causes more death and destruction than all the other illegal drugs combined.

- *Alcohol causes addiction in some drinkers.* If you smoke cigarettes, snort cocaine, or shoot heroin, you will probably get hooked, yet most people can drink alcohol regularly without ever becoming addicted. Alcohol is a unique drug because it is addictive only for a minority of its users—approximately one out of ten. Most people can take it or leave it.

- *People don't become addicted because they are weak-willed.* People become addicted because their brains adapt to the drug alcohol and need it to function. Alcoholics are not bad people—the drug alcohol disturbs their brains, making them say and do bad things.

- *Your genes control your reaction to the drug alcohol, just as they control your height, your eye color, and the size of your feet.* If someone in your family is an alcoholic—a parent, grandparent, uncle, aunt, brother, or sister—you have a much greater risk of getting the disease if you drink. That's because alcoholism is inherited—it's passed down from one generation to the next. People with a family history of alcoholism should either abstain from drinking alcohol or closely regulate and monitor their alcohol intake, always remaining attentive to the early-stage symptoms of the disease (see pages 54–60)

• *If you start drinking alcohol at a young age, your chances of becoming an alcoholic are greatly increased.* A young person's brain is extrasensitive to the drug alcohol, and drinking alcohol may cause permanent damage to your brain. People who begin drinking before age 15 are four times more likely to develop alcoholism than those who start drinking at age twenty-one.

Some people should not drink alcohol. These include:

• People under the age of twenty-one, because alcohol is illegal for minors

• Pregnant or nursing women, and women who are trying to get pregnant

• Anyone operating any kind of vehicle, including a bicycle, all-terrain vehicle, motorcycle, boat, snowmobile, or car

• Athletes and others who participate in strenuous physical activities or who want to do their best when they perform

• People who are responsible for the safety of others, such as school bus drivers or airplane pilots

• People who take prescription or over-the-counter drugs that can interact with alcohol

• Alcoholics and recovering alcoholics

In middle school, high school, and college, alcohol education programs should become increasingly detailed and explicit, focusing on the immediate harmful effects of alcohol, with particular emphasis on the early and middle stages of the disease. Teens and young adults can be taught how to identify alcoholism in its early stages, avoid dangerous situations that involve alcohol or people who have been drinking alcohol, and help those who are experiencing problems with alcohol. Some particularly important areas to emphasize:

• *Early-stage symptoms.* People who love to drink and can drink a lot without getting drunk are at high risk for alcoholism. The early stages of alcoholism are marked by benefits, not penalties, because the addicted brain is able to tolerate much more alcohol than the nonaddicted brain. If you have a friend who loves to drink and is known as the life of the party, who keeps drinking long after others have called it quits and yet is still able to drive everyone else home, he or she may be an early-stage alcoholic. If your friend has a family history of alcoholism, the risk rises dramatically. Experts estimate that people who have a family history of alcoholism are four or five times more likely to become alcoholics themselves.

• *The negative side of alcohol.* Drinking does not make you sexy, popular, cool, or funny, no matter what those Budweiser and Miller ads might say. After one or two beers you may feel relaxed and confident, but if you continue to drink (and as one fifteen-year-old put it, "Why drink if you're not going to get drunk?"), you'll start slurring your words, lurching and stumbling around when you try to walk, saying things that the next day you could kick yourself for, and doing things you may regret for the rest of your life.

• *People who drink too much are a nuisance to others.* Three out of four college students complain about the problems they experience as a result of other students' drinking behavior, including being insulted or humiliated, getting into a serious argument, being pushed or hit, interruption of sleeping or studying, damage to personal property, and sexual assault.

A survey conducted by *Sports Illustrated* found that 100 percent of the spectators at sporting events had witnessed at least one of the following behaviors as a result of drinking alcohol: yelling of obscenities, racial slurs, abusive sexual remarks to women, fistfights between strangers, fights between friends, having beer accidentally or purposely spilled on them, vomiting in a nearby seat or urinating in the aisles, indecent exposure, and being spit on by someone who was intoxicated.

• *Beer is a drug, too.* A 12-ounce can of beer contains approximately the same amount of alcohol as 1.5 ounces of 80-proof distilled spirits or 5 ounces of wine. Middle-school and high-school kids consume 1.1 billion cans of beer every year. College undergraduates drink 4 billion cans a year (averaging fifty-five six-packs apiece). Nearly two-thirds of males between twelve and twenty name beer as their beverage of choice. More than half of the total U.S. alcohol consumption is of beer, and beer accounts for 80 percent of all *excessive* alcohol consumption.

- *Alcohol can kill you.* Young people can and do die when they drink too much. Alcohol is the number one killer of young people.

What can you do when friends or acquaintances have too much to drink? First, don't let them drive. Take away their keys, find someone sober to drive them home, or call their parents. Don't worry about betraying a friend; you may be saving a life. Second, don't try to sober them up with coffee, a cold shower, or a quart of fruit juice—it won't work because the liver eliminates alcohol at a steady pace. Third, stay with them to make sure they don't pass out and stop breathing or choke on their own vomit. If someone has passed out, place the person on his or her side with the head elevated, and call for help. If you notice any changes in breathing, call 911 or immediately take the intoxicated person to the nearest emergency room. Never leave someone alone who has passed out after drinking too much.

This isn't the kind of information that most kids learn in alcohol education classes, but it needs to be taught. A little knowledge can save a lot of lives.

- *Liquor industry shenanigans.* If the people who sell, advertise, and promote alcohol truly wanted people to drink "moderately," they would agree to define what they mean by "moderate." Instead they leave it up to the individual drinker to decide "when to say when," a strategy that more often than not leads to an immoderate consumption of alcohol. The booze merchants refuse to define what they mean by "moderate" because they know that if all drinkers limited their intake to the federal guidelines of one drink a day for women and two drinks a day for men, their profits would vanish.

Teens and preteens need to understand that the liquor industry is not particularly interested in their health and well-being; it's primarily interested in selling lots of booze in order to make lots of money. It's worth repeating here what August Busch III, chief executive officer of Anheuser-Busch, said at the 1997 shareholders meeting. "We are not a social services agency that happens to make beer," said Busch. "We are a beer company whose primary goal is to maximize profit for our shareholders, and that means selling as much beer as we can."

Kids can be taught how to recognize the alcohol industry's deceptions. In Washington, D.C., for example, Dr. Alpha Estes Brown, a United Methodist minister with a law degree and a doctorate, is teaching elementary- and secondary-school kids about misleading advertising and the harm caused by the drug alcohol. Dr. Brown's work is motivated by his concern about the size and scope of the alcohol problem in the nation's capital. Based on a drinking population age fourteen and older, annual per capita consumption in our capital city is nearly four gallons of pure alcohol—almost double the national average.

Dr. Brown is especially concerned about the liquor industry's heavy marketing to young inner-city minorities. Alcohol and cigarettes are the biggest profit-makers for mom-and-pop grocery stores in the city's African-American and Latino neighborhoods.

People who teach children and young adults about alcohol and alcoholism should avoid horror stories about what will happen to them forty years down the pike. Teens and preteens are much less interested in the far-distant ("It will never happen to me") incidence of cirrhosis of the liver, alcoholic heart disease, suicide, and divorce than the immediate, short-term risks associated with drinking.

What if teenagers could actually see into the future, imagining themselves in a car wreck and witnessing the effect of the crash on their families? This is one of the real-life scenarios portrayed in the documentary *The Truth About Drinking*. In one heartbreaking segment, the teenagers attend their own mock burial services at a local cemetery and listen to their parents' grief-stricken statements. One mother was so overwhelmed with emotion just imagining that her son lay in the coffin that she couldn't read the farewell letter she had written to him. Later, when she had calmed down enough to read, her son started sobbing and begged her to stop.

Being injured or killed in a drunk driving accident is not the only immediate danger associated with drinking. Teenagers also need to know that if they drink excessively, they will almost certainly make poor decisions. One of these decisions could change the course of their lives. Maybe they'll get in a car with someone who has been drinking, have sex with someone they don't really like, get pregnant, get caught at a party and kicked off the football or softball team, be fined $1,000, have their driver's license revoked, have their insurance premiums increased, or see their insurance policy canceled.

Educators should always emphasize that alcohol problems are not just in the future—they're right here, right now, and they can ruin your life and the lives of those you love.

Keep in mind that the purpose of education is not to "promote responsible drinking," as one college alcohol policy puts it, but to enlighten students about the nature of the drug alcohol and the problems it creates for drinkers and those who interact with them. Promoting "responsible drinking" is a clever alcohol industry ploy—don't buy it.

Repetition is the key. Offering a ten-week Drug Abuse Resistance Education course in fifth grade won't do it. Every year, from elementary school through high school and then continuing into college, students need to be educated and enlightened about alcohol and the problems associated with its use.

Tell stories, since while kids (and adults) are quickly bored by statistics, a true, well-told story will always hold their attention. In health, science, and specifically designed drug education classes, teachers trained in the facts about alcohol and alcoholism can tell stories about their own experiences and bring in speakers whose lives have been altered by the drug and/or the disease.

Stories are wonderfully powerful. From a story, this book and its predecessor, *Under the Influence*, were born. Twenty-five years ago Kathy Ketcham and Bill Asbury worked together at the *Seattle Post-Intelligencer*, the largest morning daily in the state of Washington. Bill was editor in chief of that paper, and Kathy was his part-time assistant. On slow news days Bill would pull up a chair next to Kathy's desk and talk. The conversations often drifted to the past: his drinking days.

Listening to those stories of alcoholic shame and misery, told by a sober, intelligent, honest, hardworking man who used to be a drunk, Kathy grasped the basic truths about alcoholism. She learned that this is a disease not of morals but of biology. Under the influence of alcohol, good, intelligent, sane people do bad, stupid, and insane things. When they recover from their addiction, they are returned to themselves.

With those basic insights, gifts generously bestowed by Bill's stories, Kathy began to research *Under the Influence*, a classic work on alcoholism that debunks many of the prevailing stereotypes and misconceptions about the disease. As the years passed, more facts and stories piled up, leading eventually to this book.

In a culture saturated with alcohol, the stories aren't hard to find. They are everywhere. Tell them. Listen to them. Learn from them. Spread them far and wide.

PREVENTION

Alcohol is an intoxicating drug with addictive potential, and it's legal. Taken together, those facts explain why we will always have an "alcohol problem." We will never be able to eliminate these problems, but we can do everything within our power to make sure that the smallest number of people are affected and that those who become addicted to the drug receive appropriate help for their problem.

Education is the first line of defense in any program designed to prevent alcohol problems. Teaching kids about the many and diverse problems associated with drinking alcohol allows them to make intelligent choices if and when they decide to drink. When we educate our children about the perils of alcohol use, we meet them at the river's headwaters. Given accurate, fact-based information, many will be dissuaded from taking the plunge. Those who do decide to brave the waters will know the risks and the consequences. Everyone who lives near the river—and that includes most of us—will understand what to do in case of an emergency.

In this section we look at prevention efforts in several critically important areas: programs that seek to reduce deaths and injuries on our highways, and innovative interventions in our hospitals' emergency rooms designed to identify alcoholics and refer them for treatment.

DRINKING AND DRIVING*

Alcohol and the automobile have been a lethal combination since Henry Ford's turn-of-the-century invention. Early in 1998 the United States took sad note of its three millionth highway fatality. By conservative estimates, half of those deaths were caused by drinking and driving, a number that approximates very closely the total deaths in all of our country's wars.

Three in every five Americans (60 percent) will be involved in an alcohol-related automobile accident at some point in their lives. With those odds, you can count yourself lucky if you or someone you love isn't seriously or fatally injured in a drinking-connected road accident. Every year more than a million people are injured in alcohol-related car crashes—about one every thirty seconds. Every thirty-two minutes someone dies in a drinking-and-driving accident. Drinking and driving is the number one killer of teens and young adults.

Enforcing the laws against drinking and driving has significantly reduced the death toll. From 1987 to 1997 alcohol-related deaths decreased by almost one-third, dropping from 23,641 deaths in 1987 to 16,189 in 1997. That's more than 7,000 lives saved every year. Experts credit the decline in highway deaths to the minimum drinking age of twenty-one, reduced highway speed limits, safer cars, and tougher drinking-and-driving laws.

---

* The term drinking and driving *is used instead of "drunk driving," since you don't have to be drunk to get in an accident.*

We can continue to reduce the deaths and injuries on our highways by implementing the following strategies, some tried and true, some innovative and still in the trial stages.

Penalties

In March 1998, while the Washington State legislature was in session, Representative Kelli Linville was arrested at 1:41 A.M., just three blocks from the state capitol. Her car had narrowly missed colliding with a security guard's vehicle. Her blood alcohol level was .11. Under a law passed the year before—a law Linville supported—the legal limit for drinking and driving in Washington State had been reduced from .10 to .08; under either law, she was legally drunk.

Linville agreed to an alcohol assessment, which showed she was in the early stages of alcoholism. Under a deferred-prosecution agreement, Linville was referred for alcoholism treatment, followed by monitoring, for a total of two years. She was put on probation for five years and ordered to install an ignition lock on her car that disabled the starting mechanism unless her breath was alcohol-free when she blew into the breath analyzer connected to the ignition.

The ignition lock was mandated for six months. During her five-year probationary period, the judge ordered her to abstain from drinking and stay away from bars and taverns. She did not lose her driver's license, but she had to pay nearly $1,500 in fees and court costs.

This true story illustrates what can be done legally to keep drivers who drink (and get caught) off the road and to guide them into treatment for their drug problem. The penalties that can be imposed by lawmakers are many and varied. Stiff fines for drinking and driving are a definite deterrent as long as they are consistently and uniformly imposed. For a first offense, $1,000 is a reasonable fine; the penalty for repeat offenses should be doubled or even tripled. Hefty insurance increases offer another strong deterrent.

In addition to financial penalties, people convicted of drinking and driving should receive an automatic license revocation until they have undergone assessment and treatment and proven to the court that they will not drink and drive again.

Vehicle impoundment, vehicle immobilization, and vehicle forfeiture make it physically more difficult for the convicted driver to operate a vehicle. In late 1998 in New York City, Mayor Rudolph Giuliani ordered that drunk drivers' cars be seized to make the city safer. If the vehicle was owned by the drunk driver, forfeiture proceedings began immediately. Thus, drunk drivers faced criminal proceedings for driving drunk and civil proceedings if they wanted their cars returned. Civil liberties groups vowed to fight the tough procedures, which the city called its "Zero Tolerance Drinking and Driving Initiative."

Breath interlock devices prevent repeat offenders from operating their cars if their blood alcohol level is above a predetermined level. These devices, however, cannot prevent the drinker from enlisting the help of a sober person to disable the ignition lock. That's what happened in Howardsville, Virginia, when a thirty-four-year-old man with several previous drunk driving convictions asked an eleven-year-old girl to circumvent the interlock system on his car's ignition. The man was too drunk to drive, so the child got behind the wheel and promptly crashed the van on a bridge crossing the James River. She cut her head in the accident. He was charged with child neglect.

In some states, black-and-white striped stickers, called "zebra stickers," have been placed on the license plates of drinking-and-driving offenders who are stopped for driving on a suspended license. These stickers, which remain on the license plate until the person's license has been reinstated, are being used in pilot programs in Oregon and Ohio. They work. After the "zebra law" was enacted in Oregon, drivers whose licenses were suspended and who were at risk of getting a zebra sticker if caught had a 33 percent reduction in moving violations and a 23 percent reduction in crashes.

A Boston judge recently had a novel idea: Instead of special license plates or stickers, the judge ordered that signs be placed in the rear windows of those convicted of repeatedly driving drunk. The signs say: "Convicted Repeat Drunk Driver. Report Erratic Driving to Police."

If you think these penalties for drinking and driving are overly harsh, consider what other countries do to their drunk drivers. In Australia, drivers are subjected to random breath testing; if they are guilty, they receive stiff fines and possible license revocation for a year. Random testing also takes place in Scandinavian countries, where the legal blood alcohol level is 0.05 percent. In Czechoslovakia, Hungary, Japan, and Russia, the BAC standard is 0.00 percent, which means that drunk driving penalties are imposed if you even have a trace of alcohol on your breath. In Japan, the penalties include immediate imprisonment, stiff fines, permanent loss of driver's license, and, for those who work in the public sector, possible loss of their job. Repeat offenders in Russia may be sentenced for up to two years of "correctional labor."

Alcoholism Assessment and Treatment

All drivers arrested for driving under the influence should undergo an assessment for alcoholism or problem drinking. Local authorities should be given the power to mandate appropriate treatment, but judges and law enforcement personnel should defer to qualified professionals for this assessment process. ("Qualified" means that the individual is educated and experienced in the diagnosis and treatment of alcoholism as a neurologically based addiction.) Repeat offenders should not be allowed to drive until they have completed alcoholism treatment and can prove their commitment to sobriety. The more severe the drinking problem, the more intensive the treatment. Follow-up after treatment is crucial.

Tougher Laws

By the end of 1999, seventeen states and the District of Columbia had lowered the legal limit for driving under the influence to a blood alcohol concentration of 0.08 percent. Experts estimate the lower limits will save hundreds of lives every year. Lowering the limit to 0.05 percent would save even more lives.

Zero-tolerance laws for minors—no alcohol at all in the bloodstream—must stay in place. (Only South Carolina does not have such a law.) These laws are effective—studies in Maine, New Mexico, North Carolina, and Wisconsin show that zero-tolerance laws reduce drinking and driving among minors when combined with alcohol awareness programs and aggressive law enforcement.

Forty-four percent of fatally injured drivers between the ages of fifteen and twenty have positive blood alcohol levels at the time of the accident. Young drivers account for 17 percent of fatal alcohol-related accidents, even though they comprise only 9 percent of the population. Alcohol is illegal for people under age twenty-one, and our drinking-and-driving regulations must strictly enforce the law.

Making Drinking-and-Driving Deaths Personal

"A few weeks ago, I wrote and told you about the tragic drunk driving crash that took the life of 9-year-old Lorien Denham and injured her father David so badly he still has memory loss and difficulty walking seven years later." So begins a recent fund-raising letter from the national president of Mothers Against Drug Driving (MADD). Personal stories are the trademark of MADD, a volunteer agency founded in 1980 in California by Candy Lightner after her thirteen-year-old daughter was struck down and killed by a drunk hit-and-run driver with three previous arrests and two convictions for drunk driving.

Through the grassroots activities of MADD and its offshoot Students Against Drunk Driving (SADD), Lightner and thousands of other MADD volunteers have succeeded in their efforts to create tougher laws against drinking and driving and harsher penalties leveled at drunk drivers. By personalizing the damage caused by drinking and driving, MADD has become a powerful lobbying organization nationally.

Any attempt to educate people about the dangers of drinking and driving should focus on the fact that real people die in these accidents. A photograph of a mother holding a two-year-old child who was later killed by a drunk driver does a lot more to get the point across than a two-inch obituary in the local newspaper. A personal story sinks in where statistics often glance off.

In eastern Washington State, residents have discovered a way to make drinking-and-driving deaths personal. Every ten miles or so by the side of Highway 12, drivers and their passengers see plain white signs indicating where someone died in an alcohol-related crash. The words PLEASE DON'T DRINK AND DRIVE are followed with IN MEMORY OF . . . and the name of the person who died there.

PREVENTION IN THE EMERGENCY ROOM

On the adrenaline-pumping weekly TV series *Trauma*, featuring real-life scenes in hospital emergency rooms, a physician puts his head in his hands and sighs. It has been a rough shift—it was prom night at the local high school—and the ER doctors and nurses have been working nonstop to piece together the bloodied bodies of young men and women who are brought in all dressed up in their party clothes. Pulled from the wreckage of their automobiles, they either had too much to drink or had the bad luck of running into someone else who had been drinking.

Looking at the camera, the ER doctor attempts a bit of black humor. "My one fear is that people will stop drinking and driving," he says with a weak smile. "Because that would put us out of business."

Half the patients admitted to emergency rooms have alcohol in their bloodstream. In a groundbreaking study conducted at Seattle's Harborview Medical Center, which houses the only regional class I trauma center in the Northwest, researchers studied the connection between alcohol and trauma in more than thirty-five hundred patients

age eighteen and older between March 1989 and February 1991. The
results:

- Fully one-half of the patients had a positive blood alcohol content. Approximately one-third were intoxicated on admission to the
emergency department. Of those with alcohol in their blood, the
median blood alcohol level was 0.179, more than double the .08
legal limit established in 1999 by the state of Washington.

- Intoxication was most common among men, patients between
twenty-five and thirty-four years of age, Native Americans,
Hispanics, and African-Americans.

- The highest proportion of intoxicated patients were victims of
stab wounds. More than one-half of all assault victims were intoxicated at the time of admission, as were more than one-third of
patients with self-inflicted wounds.

- Chronic alcoholics were twice as likely to develop complications, particularly pneumonia.

- The risks of respiratory failure and the need for a subsequent
operation were higher among patients with strong evidence of
chronic alcohol abuse.

- Three-fourths of acutely intoxicated patients had evidence of
chronic alcoholism.

The Harborview medical researchers concluded that in addition to
treating the patient's immediate injuries, trauma centers need to properly diagnose alcoholics and refer them for appropriate treatment. "Most
trauma centers fail to appreciate the chronic nature of alcohol abuse in
most intoxicated patients," said Dr. Fred Rivara, coauthor of the research
and director of the Harborview Injury Prevention and Research Center.
"A simple 'don't drink and drive' message is not appropriate counseling,
and in most instances, trauma victims aren't even hearing that. I think
trauma centers need to take a more aggressive role in getting these
patients into alcohol treatment programs. We don't even come close to
scratching the surface on what can and should be done."

Statistics tell only part of the story. Behind each statistic is a human
being whose life—and, in too many cases, death—affects dozens of others. In an effort to piece together the human side of the story,
Harborview researchers spent hours talking to trauma victims. From stories like these, which take place every moment of every day in the

bloodied hallways of our nation's emergency rooms, we can begin to glimpse the depth and breadth of the suffering caused by the drug alcohol and the potential for life-saving strategies implemented in our hospital's emergency rooms.

Mary

Mary, thirty-six, asked the interviewer to move closer so she could whisper; she was embarrassed to have the other patient in the room hear her story. For fourteen years, Mary confided, she had struggled with her addiction to alcohol. Seven years earlier she signed herself into a four-week treatment program; she had been in and out of various kinds of treatment ever since. For the last year she had been able to stay sober, but then she relapsed. Overcome with guilt and shame, she tried to kill herself by crashing her car into the back of a tractor-trailer.

When Mary was brought into Harborview's ER, her blood alcohol level was 0.46, nearly five times the .10 legal driving limit. (The legal limit in Washington State has since been changed to .08.) Doctors and nurses worked hard to save her life; she was nearly decapitated in the high-speed collision. After she was stabilized, surgeons tried to repair Mary's multiple facial and skull fractures, peeling her facial tissues back over her forehead and resculpting her face using bone taken from her hip.

Three days after the surgery Mary was able to speak. She was suffering deeply, lying in bed with her face so swollen that her eyes were shut and her mouth could barely form words. She was also in withdrawal, fading in and out of consciousness from the drugs, the pain, and the exhaustion. In her lucid moments, she talked about how she had alienated her parents, her ex-husband, and her eight-year-old son.

Mary had lost custody of her son because of her previous battles with alcoholism. She rarely saw him, and she was afraid that her ex-husband might try to prevent him from visiting her in the hospital. Even if he was allowed to visit, she feared that he would be too frightened by her appearance to stay very long.

Mary was concerned, too, about disappointing her alcoholism counselor. Before her recent relapse, she had actively been involved in outpatient treatment.

Mary spoke openly about her struggle to "want to want" recovery and her fears that she would not be able to put together another full year of sobriety. The circumstances of her life, she said, were simply too miserable to endure without taking a drink.

In the last few days of her hospital stay, Mary seemed to feel more hopeful. "Maybe I survived the crash for a reason," she said just before she was released. "Maybe, when I am ready, the reason will be revealed to me."

Ben

Ben, forty-seven, was admitted to Harborview with a blood alcohol level of .11. He was the driver in a one-car crash that killed his fourteen-year-old passenger, Darren. Darren was the only child of his best friend.

The crash occurred on a Saturday afternoon. A self-employed electrician, Ben had spent his day off helping his best friend wire a new basement room; when it was finished, it would be Darren's bedroom. They had been drinking beer, but Ben didn't recall feeling drunk or even high, and it never occurred to him that he shouldn't drive. When he left for a quick trip to the hardware store, Darren asked if he could ride along.

The sun was shining, and the roads were clear and dry, but the car suddenly swerved off the road, slid down an embankment, and flipped over. Ben and Darren were rushed to Harborview, where Darren died a few hours later of massive head injuries.

Ben's spine was badly fractured, and he sustained a minor brain injury. He lay in the hospital bed, his body tightly strapped into a rigid blue plastic shell that made it hard for him to breathe and impossible to bend his spine; he would wear the brace day and night for six weeks. He said he had no feeling in his feet, but he could wiggle his toes and bend his knees. The orthopedic surgeons expected him to walk again, but with permanent difficulty.

Darren's mother, Susan, visited Ben in the hospital. She sat by his bed, made small talk, and asked what she could do to make him more comfortable. Neither of them mentioned Darren.

Ben and his wife had no health or disability insurance, and Ben's injuries prevented him from returning to work. His wife worked two jobs to pay the hospital bills. A year after he was released from Harborview, Ben was still unable to climb stairs, and they were forced to sell their house and rent a smaller, one-level home. The marriage began to disintegrate. A gentle, easygoing man before the accident, Ben experienced sudden, uncontrollable rages caused by his brain injury. His wife eventually filed for divorce.

After the accident, Ben never took another drink.

TREATMENT

Treatment for alcoholism should be readily available to anyone who needs it. This isn't just humanitarianism or utopianism—it's a matter of economics. Treatment is cost-effective.

A 1998 government study reports that alcoholism and alcohol-related problems cost our society $166 billion. Two-thirds of that cost— almost $100 billion—is shouldered by business in the form of lost productivity due to alcohol-related illness or premature death. An estimated 8 percent of Americans working in full-time jobs are heavy drinkers who consume five or more drinks per drinking occasion. These drinkers contribute to 41 percent of business losses due to absenteeism, errors on the job, accidents, heavier turnover, excessive sick benefits, and higher insurance costs.

Alcohol is involved in 47 percent of industrial accidents and 40 percent of work site fatalities, but it is not just on-the-job drinking that costs money. A 1997 study sponsored by the National Institute on Alcoholism and Alcohol Abuse (NIAAA) and the Robert Wood Johnson Foundation, a health-care philanthropy, showed that workers who drank heavily away from the workplace "accounted for a large proportion of unproductive work days."

Alcoholism treatment can save businesses bundles of money. "Treatment is expensive but it's usually a one-time charge," concludes an analysis in *Business Week* magazine. "Many companies have learned that skirting the problem or skimping on treatment means paying full price, in salary and benefits, for a less than fully functional employee— sometimes for years."

Put in simple terms, if a company has a $45,000-a-year employee working at two-thirds efficiency because of alcohol, that worker costs the company $15,000 in lost productivity every year. The cost of a twenty-eight-day treatment program at the Betty Ford Center—one of the most effective treatment clinics in the world—is around $13,000; twenty-one days at Sundown M Ranch, the treatment program featured in Chapter 10, costs less than $3,000. The company saves money the very first year after treatment, and in ten years, assuming the treatment of just one alcoholic is successful, the company's bottom line will be improved by more than $150,000.

THE MANAGED-CARE BUGABOO

Managed care is like alcohol: the long-term penalties eventually far outweigh the short-term benefits. Years ago, when we were offered the idea of a $5 copayment versus $25 for an office visit, we figured it was a no-brainer—who wouldn't choose the cost-cutting alternative? Years later, however, when a request for alcoholism treatment, knee surgery, or even a yearly physical is denied, we realize the consequences of allowing for-profit organizations uninvolved in patient care to call the shots.

Business organizations, if they have the will and the common sense, can include ample provisions for treating alcoholics in their health plans. Unfortunately, as corporations have sought to control rapidly rising health insurance costs, alcohol treatment and other so-called mental health treatments have felt the pinch. While few companies have completely eliminated benefits, many have asked their insurers to "manage" (that is, limit) the usage by employees.

Treatment for alcoholism and other drug addictions is subject to a higher level of "management" than other health care services. As a result, most of us no longer have access to private inpatient treatment programs. Benefits are often denied because alcoholism is classified as a mental disorder and is not covered under many insurance policies. According to a report by the benefits consulting firm A. Foster Higgins and Company, 87 percent of the two thousand employers surveyed now limit "substance abuse" and mental health benefits for their employees.

Cutting benefits for alcohol treatment doesn't make sense any way you look at it. Research conducted over the last five decades confirms that alcoholism is a chronic, progressive, physiological disease that disrupts the activities of every vital organ, most notably the brain. When treatment focuses on abstinence, education, AA attendance, psychological counseling, and spiritual issues, it works. The sick person is restored, almost miraculously, to full health. With how many diseases can we claim that kind of success?

As a society with seventy-six million adults directly affected by the disease of alcoholism, we have the obligation to find ways to pay for treatment. The most obvious solution, in the absence of a complete overhaul in our current health care system, is to increase taxes on the drug itself, earmarking such revenues to pay for treatment, education, and prevention programs. Higher taxes on distilled spirits, beer, and wine can be collected by the federal and state governments and then distributed to local governments.

Here are a few real-life examples showing how it can be done:

- In 1989, 63 percent of Kansas City, Missouri, voters approved a quarter-cent sales tax increase to finance drug treatment, prevention, and law enforcement programs; the antidrug tax has been credited with reducing violent crime by 30 percent and helping as many as seven hundred people a month enter treatment.

- In 1995, citizens in Little Rock, Arkansas, passed a half-cent sales tax increase to pay for outpatient treatment services for any of the twenty-seven thousand students who needed it in the Little Rock School District.

- The state of New Mexico imposed a statewide liquor tax of just a penny a drink in 1993. Though the state's population is small, $11 million was raised in the first year on the sale of 1.1 billion drinks. Unfortunately, the extra money went into the state's general fund instead of being targeted specifically for alcoholism treatment, education, and prevention.

Those in corporations or managed-care organizations responsible for identifying good treatment centers should look for certain essentials:

- Educated, qualified staff members—preferably recovered persons—who understand that alcoholism is a disease and not bad behavior

- Insistence on lifelong abstinence from alcohol and other drugs

- Education about the biochemical, neurophysiological nature of the disease and the need for lifelong abstinence

- Attention to the alcoholic's physical, psychological, spiritual, and social needs

- Education and psychological counseling services for family members

- Careful monitoring and follow-up care to reduce relapses and provide help if relapses occur

- Introduction to the program of Alcoholics Anonymous and required AA attendance during treatment

- An environment in which alcoholics are treated with dignity and respect

These are the general principles guiding the most successful and well-respected treatment programs in this country, including the Betty

Ford Center in Rancho Mirage, California. To the astonishment of many, the former First Lady was diagnosed as an alcoholic and prescription drug addict in 1978, two years after leaving Washington, D.C. Her own experiences with the shame and misery of drug addiction motivated her to use her influence and prestige to create a treatment program dedicated to helping alcoholics and other drug addicts recover from their disease.

The Betty Ford Center, founded in 1982, stands as a monument to an alcoholic who wanted to help other alcoholics and their families. Because many famous personalities, including baseball great Mickey Mantle and actress Elizabeth Taylor, have been treated there, an assumption persists that the center is restricted to the rich and famous. In truth only one tenth of one percent of the patients at Betty Ford are celebrities, although Mrs. Ford is careful to point out that her mission "is to provide 'star treatment' to all who enter." Mrs. Ford's willingness to speak openly about her addiction emboldened other women to accept the need for help. By 1996, there were more than 450,000 women in this country in various treatment centers for their addictions. That figure represents almost 30 percent of the 1.5 million persons being treated for alcoholism and other drug problems during that year.

TREATMENT IN THE WORKPLACE

In the 1940s, when American business was growing explosively because of World War II, business managers began to be aware that alcohol was cutting deeply into their profits. They decided to search for solutions. Executives, human resource managers, supervisory personnel, and labor leaders collaborated to develop what were then known as OAPs—occupational alcoholism programs.

One of the earliest OAPs was created by the mammoth DuPont Corporation during World War II. The war effort created a high demand for engineers, and DuPont was placed in the unenviable position of having to compete with the government for that scarce human resource. Rather than abruptly terminating their alcoholic employees—the typical solution before the war—DuPont executives tried to salvage them, turning to Alcoholics Anonymous for help. Under the tutelage of one of AA's founders, DuPont used recovering alcoholics to teach supervisors how to recognize alcoholism and offer assistance through AA.

Hundreds of DuPont employees who might otherwise have been fired got sober and returned to full productivity. They were grateful for the company's interventions. In a survey conducted by the National

Council on Alcoholism, the largest volunteer organization on alcoholism at the time, recovering workers praised DuPont's efforts and even offered a helpful suggestion. The disease could be identified even earlier, they advised, if supervisors would document unacceptable work performance rather than waiting for physical and psychological symptoms to appear.

The development of OAPs had a twofold positive effect. First, with the threat of job loss and the promise of referrals to competent professionals, alcoholics could be identified and treated with a relatively high degree of success. Second, with supervisors paying closer attention to their employees' work performance, chronic problems other than alcoholism—divorce, death or illness in the family, problems with supervisors, financial difficulties—could also be identified. Gradually the OAPs expanded their function to assist employees with various personal problems, leading to a change of terminology in the 1970s from OAP to EAP—employee assistance program. Ironically, while that evolution allowed many more troubled workers to seek help for their problems, it eventually opened the door to a decreased emphasis on alcoholism in the workplace.

Measured in terms of dollars and cents (not to mention the impact on human suffering), the new EAPs were a huge success from the outset:

- United Airlines, the nation's largest air carrier, established EAPs in all its divisions. For every $1 invested in helping identify and treat problem drinkers, the airline was rewarded with almost $17 in improved productivity and other cost savings. Despite these impressive savings, United canceled most of its EAP programs in 1995, when the airline began to experience financial problems. Two developments helped to cushion the blow. First, when United workers demanded that EAP services be restored, the company offered to contract for some services at many of their larger operational centers. Second, many United employees, such as pilots and flight attendants, have an excellent peer-referral program that has successfully helped thousands of addicted and otherwise troubled personnel into treatment and successful recovery programs.

- The Northrup Corporation saw a 43 percent increase in the productivity of each of its first hundred employees to enter an alcohol treatment program. After three years of sobriety, the average savings per worker was nearly $20,000, for a total of $2 million saved.

• The Philadelphia Police Department discovered that personnel who underwent alcohol treatment reduced the number of their sick days by an average of 38 percent and their injured days by 62 percent.

• Oldsmobile's Lansing, Michigan, plant saw the following results in the year after its alcoholic employees went through treatment programs: lost man-hours declined by 49 percent, health care benefits paid dropped by 29 percent, sick leaves were down by 56 percent, grievances were off by 78 percent, disciplinary problems fell by 63 percent, and accidents were reduced by 82 percent.

• A four-year study commissioned by the giant McDonnell-Douglas aerospace company (now part of Boeing) to assess its investment in its EAP concluded that employees treated for "chemical dependency" missed 44 percent fewer workdays, had an 81 percent lower attrition rate, and filed $7,300 less in health-care claims than those who did not use the EAP. (The McDonnell-Douglas study made the front page of the *Wall Street Journal*.)

The big growth in EAPs occurred in the 1970s, when more than 80 percent of Fortune 500 companies instituted such programs. In those days, EAP consultants and specialists were mostly recovered alcoholics who had learned firsthand about alcoholism, the alcoholic's denial system, and the subtle symptoms of this complicated disease. But in the late 1970s and continuing into the 1980s and '90s, the EAP movement steadily deteriorated as psychologists and social workers with little or no experience in the field of alcoholism replaced recovered alcoholics as EAP consultants. Poorly managed programs became increasingly dependent on "self-referrals," in which employees with alcohol problems were asked to decide for themselves if they needed treatment or counseling. Alcoholic denial being what it is, few workers came forward.

When managed care took over our nation's corporate health care system in the 1980s and '90s, most health care plans reduced coverage for alcoholism, offering only minimal treatment paid for by the company (a day or two in detox is the current norm) or denying benefits altogether. Henry Govert, a former EAP specialist for several large East Coast corporations, put it this way: "EAPs surrendered to managed care about ten years ago."

Here, then, is one of the greatest challenges facing those who are concerned about the millions of working men and women with alcohol problems. We need to convince both large and small companies to return to an EAP system that is staffed by people who understand how to diagnose and treat alcoholism, and then encourage these companies in their own self-interest to provide health care plans that cover the cost of effective treatment.

TREATMENT IN OUR PRISONS

On October 25, 1993, football superstar O. J. Simpson blackened the eye and bruised the face of his wife, Nicole, during a domestic quarrel. A police photograph taken after that incident shows Nicole Simpson's badly battered face. (This is the photograph that was broadcast around the world after Simpson was accused of murdering his wife eight months later.)

After the battering incident, Simpson explained to a television sports commentator that he and Nicole had been drinking and got into an argument. Nicole Simpson never pressed charges. No big deal, right? A little booze. A minor argument. A battered wife. Happens every day.

Indeed it does. According to a 1998 report by the federal Department of Justice, "three out of four incidents (of violence against spouses) . . . involved alcohol use by the offender." The report goes on: "Two-thirds of the violent crime victims who were attacked by an intimate—a current or former spouse or a boyfriend or girlfriend—reported that alcohol had been a factor."

Domestic abuse is only one variant of alcohol-related crime. "Alcohol and crime are joined at the hip," state the authors of a 1998 study published by the National Center on Addiction and Substance Abuse (CASA) at Columbia University. The report, titled "Behind Bars: Substance Abuse and America's Prison Population," reveals the following facts about the relationship between alcohol and violent crime:

• Eighty percent of the men and women in state and federal prisons and local jails—1.4 million individuals out of a total prison population of 1.7 million—are seriously involved with alcohol and/or other drugs.

• These 1.4 million individuals either violated drug or alcohol laws, were high at the time they committed their crimes, stole property to buy drugs, and/or have a history of drug and alcohol abuse and addiction.

• Alcohol is more closely associated with crimes of violence, including murders, rapes, assaults, and child and spouse abuse, than any other drug. Alcohol is implicated in most homicides arising from disputes or arguments.

• Twenty-one percent of inmates in prison for violent crimes were under the influence of alcohol—and no other substance—when they committed their crime. Only 3 percent of violent offenders were under the influence of cocaine or crack alone, and only 1 percent were under the influence of heroin alone.

• Among these 1.4 million inmates are the parents of 2.4 million children, many of them minors.

The United States has the lamentable distinction of having more of its people behind bars than any nation on this planet. According to a Department of Justice report released in April 1998, the number of prison inmates in the United States has more than doubled since 1980. The great majority of those prisoners—80 percent, according to the CASA study—have "serious" alcohol and/or other drug problems.

We can make an immediate difference in our criminal justice system by implementing and supporting treatment services for alcoholics and other drug addicts. Since prisons and jails are places where treatment can be coerced, it makes great sense to treat chemically dependent convicts for their addictions while they are locked up. Unfortunately, that's not happening. In fact, rather than increase the availability of treatment for alcoholism and drug addiction, our federal and state legislators have dramatically reduced it.

The 1998 Justice Department report reveals that only 9.7 percent of inmates in state prisons received treatment for their addictions, compared to 24.5 percent in 1991; federal prisons reported a similar decrease. Asked why treatment had been cut back, prison officials said that the huge increase in populations of prisoners caused them to reduce counseling and education in order to free up space and funds for more beds.

Treatment specialists know that jailed criminals can be successfully treated. While the drug problems of many prison inmates are complicated by poverty, lack of education, polyaddictions, and many years of drug use, treatment efforts are often successful. In fact, after learning the facts about the physiology of the disease and the connection between alcohol and violent crime, prisoners are sometimes even more responsive to the well-established treatment techniques used outside prison walls.

Considering what we are now paying to incarcerate criminals, treatment pays for itself many times over. The per-inmate cost of treatment is approximately $7,000. The Columbia University researchers estimate that for each inmate who successfully completes treatment and becomes a taxpaying, law-abiding citizen, the annual economic benefit to society, when measured in terms of avoided incarceration, health care costs, salary earned, taxes paid, and general contribution to the economy, is $68,800—a tenfold return on investment in the first year.

If we successfully treat only 10 percent of our prisoners, the increased economic benefits after their release from prison would amount to a savings of more than $11.5 billion.

18

Walking the Walk

We are here to do,
And through doing to learn;
and through learning to know;
and through knowing to experience wonder;
and through wonder to attain wisdom;
and through wisdom to find simplicity;
and through simplicity to give attention;
and through attention
to see what needs to be done.

—RABBI BEN HEI HEI

When Bill Asbury first considered whether to include his personal history of alcoholism in this book, he was reluctant. He feared hurting his family. As a prominent figure in Washington journalism and state politics and chairman of the state's legislative ethics committee, Bill was concerned that his wife and children might suffer personal attacks leveled by those who consider alcoholism a behavioral disorder characterized by weak character, failed moral resolve, or lack of willpower.

Myths and misconceptions, Bill knows full well, shape the thoughts and actions of many people. So his ultimate decision to share his experience points to the larger need for open discussion about this disease called alcoholism. The shame and stigma associated with alcoholism will not be completely eliminated until the people who are directly affected by the disease tell their stories, holding nothing back. Every time a sober, healthy alcoholic stands up and says, "I'm an alcoholic," the old myth of the alcoholic as a late-stage, morally destitute drunk takes a direct hit. Every time someone who loves an alcoholic stands up and says, "This is the way it used to be when my loved one was drinking, but then she got sober, and now things are different," people in similar situations find new reason for hope. Every time someone who hears these stories stands up and says, "I didn't understand before, but now I do," the death grip of this disease loosens its hold.

Facts about the drug and the disease cannot by themselves change the course of the river that runs through us. After all, we have been gathering statistics for decades, and the river of alcohol runs just as wide and just as deep. As we amass the facts, we must also collect the stories, telling them to anyone and everyone who will listen: stories of men, women, and children who died too soon; stories of those who survived and whose lives were transformed when they stopped drinking; stories of people who are suffering right now, and of those who are struggling to save their lives.

If we tell the stories, the stigma will fade. Not immediately, but slowly, over time, we will begin to think about alcoholics and their disease in different ways. We will become increasingly impatient with ignorance and misconception and much less willing to tolerate the senseless loss of life.

The stories will guide us along the way. When we listen to another person's story, that story becomes part of our own story. "Once upon a time," we remember, "I did not understand this disease and its victims. But then I heard these stories, and something changed. Now I understand. Now I see what I could not see before. Now I know what must be done."

In the end it is the stories that will make the difference. The stories will set us free.

We end our book, as we began it, with a story about Terry McGovern, who died on a frigid December night at the age of forty-five. After his daughter's death, former senator George McGovern wrote a book about her struggle with alcoholism, hoping to make some sense of her short life and unexpected death. In one of the book's most moving passages, he reflects on what he would have done if he had had a second chance to save her.

> *I wish I could tell her: "Dear Terry, I hope you know how much I love you. And I wish I had told you that more when you were alive and struggling with the demon that controlled your brain." I try not to berate myself for the things that I cannot now correct, but if I had those months to live over again . . .*
>
> *Well, I will tell you what I would do with a second chance. I would never forget that alcoholism is a disease, that I should hate the dis-*

ease but care for its victim—just as I would react if a loved one were
suffering from cancer or diabetes. . . .

There is no such thing as too much compassion, understanding,
support, and love for the sick and dying. Alcoholics are sick unto
death. They won't make it through the night without our love and
protection—and sometimes our repeated direct intervention. It is not
easy to live with alcoholics, but it is far harder to live without them
when death steals them away. I do not regret one single act of kind-
ness, patience, or support that I gave to Terry. What I regret is her
slowly developing death and the feeling that I could have done more
to prevent it.

Who can read this passage written by a grieving father and not be
moved to tears? Who can listen to Terry's story and not wish that we
could turn back the clock and have just one more chance to save her
life? For years Terry fought for her life, and her family and friends bat-
tled just as hard and for just as long to save her. Even at the very end,
after nearly three decades of trying and failing to help her, the people
closest to Terry knew that she had been taken over by a "demon," as her
father describes the disease, something so fiercely powerful that it
seemed that all the love in the world could not break its grip.

Terry also knew that she was possessed by a craving for alcohol so
desperate and unrelenting that it overpowered every other need. She
understood that the disease had captured her body, mind, and spirit, and
yet she blamed herself, as all alcoholics do. Nevertheless, despite all the
sad, sordid situations she thought she had brought on herself, Terry never
stopped believing that she was a good, decent human being: "I am the
problem," she wrote in her journal, "and I am the solution."

During one of Terry's many attempts to get sober at various inpatient treatment programs and detox centers, a counselor asked her to list
ten good things about herself. Terry listed twelve:

1. I have a very caring heart.

2. When not drinking, I am a creative and loving mother.

3. I have a good sense of humor.

4. No matter how many times I have fallen into relapse, I keep
striving to get sober.

5. I'm willing to help people in pain.

6. I love a lot of different people.

7. I go out of my way to not step on ants.

8. I believe that the political and social causes I've worked for have been very humane.

9. I'm devoted to my family.

10. All the volunteer work and professional work I've done has been in service to others: elderly, mentally ill, children, handicapped children, hospice work.

11. I long for spiritual growth and have been consciously drawn to it for many years.

12. I am intuitive and perceptive.

Terry knew, in her heart, that she was a kind, compassionate human being. She knew that it was the drug that compromised her values and sapped her spirit. She never stopped fighting to free herself from the addiction that threatened her sanity and her life.

When Terry McGovern was forty-five years old, she lost her battle with alcohol. We lost something, too. We lost the promise and the potential of a kind, intelligent human being. We lost the loving mother of two young children. We lost someone who cared about people in pain and who was committed to helping them. We lost the opportunity to save a life.

Sometimes, when we hear a story like Terry's, our hearts break. Doubts creep in. We wonder if anything will ever change, for the problem seems too vast, the victims too many, the pain too overwhelming. Filled with grief, overcome by despair, we question whether we should even try.

An old story is told about a woman who experienced a similar sense of futility. "Why?" she pleaded with God. "Why don't you do something about the pain and the misery?" Her questions are our questions. Her answer is our answer.

As she walked through the streets of the city, searching for answers to the questions that gave her no rest, the seeker was surrounded by the destitute, the downtrodden, the drunk, and the crippled. Filled with a great, crushing sadness, she fell to her knees and cried out, "Oh my God, where are you? Surely you must see the pain and misery suffered by so many in this world you have created. Why do you do nothing to help them?"

A great silence descended, and the seeker was filled with fear and wonder as she waited for a response. When the answer came, she was prepared.

"I did do something. I made you."

We have an obligation, as human beings, to do what we can to ease the suffering of others. This is not superficial charity or the work of do-gooders—this is our responsibility as individuals who are part of a larger community. When a fellow human being is in pain, we are called upon to do what we can to alleviate the suffering. When people are powerless to help themselves, we are asked to do what we can to assist. When we are presented with an opportunity to change what does not work and in the process save even one life, it is our duty to seize the moment with all the passion that we can muster.

At some point in the not-too-distant future, we will stop thinking about alcoholics as "weak-willed" or "immoral." We will understand the hidden prejudice in the phrases "alcohol abuse" and "responsible drinking," and we will work hard to banish them from our collective vocabulary. We will never again use the expression "lost cause" about an alcoholic.

Looking with compassion at the panhandlers on our streets, the drunks passed out in our city parks, and the broken, bloodied bodies in our emergency rooms, we will renew our commitment to helping those who cannot help themselves. We will ask what we can do to make the world a less hospitable environment for the drug alcohol and a more humane place for people who are addicted to alcohol. We will begin to walk the walk and not just talk the talk.

Now is the time.

Now is our chance.

REFERENCES

Note: In various chapters and sections of this book we deal with statistics and politics. While we have made every effort to obtain both accurate and up-to-date information, political and statistical data are always and inevitably fluid. We are nevertheless confident that the information provided identifies prevailing trends.

INTRODUCTION

Page x footnote: We use the six years of sobriety figure to distinguish between *recovering* and *recovered*, drawing on research conducted by Harvard psychiatrist George Vaillant. He defines stable abstinence as "how long abstinence must persist before an individual's recovery can be considered truly secure. With each passing year . . . the likelihood of long-term abstinence became greater. After six years of abstinence, subsequent relapse to abuse of alcohol seemed quite unlikely."

Even after six years of continuous sobriety, however, alcoholics can and do relapse—just as people who have been in remission from cancer for five or ten years can suffer a relapse. Of thirty-seven men in Vaillant's study who were abstinent for more than six years, three eventually relapsed after abstinences of 8, 10, and 13 years. It is for this reason that some alcoholics continue to describe themselves as *recovering*, even after decades of sobriety, as a reminder of the power of the physiological addiction to alcohol.

See George E. Vaillant, *The Natural History of Alcoholism Revisited* (Cambridge, Mass.: Harvard University Press, 1995), pages 234–35.

PART I   THE PROBLEM

CHAPTER 1   STILL UNDER THE INFLUENCE

Page 3: "Don't remember where . . .": *Terry: My Daughter's Life-and-Death Struggle with Alcoholism* (New York: Villard, 1996), page 142.

Page 4: The Supreme Court ruling on "willful misconduct" was released on April 20, 1988. The case before the Court involved two veterans, Eugene Traynor and James P. McKelvey, who were denied benefits by the Veterans' Administration on the grounds that alcoholism is not a disease but the result of "willful misconduct." On a 4–3 vote, the Court upheld the rights of the VA to define primary alcoholism (as distinguished from secondary alcoholism, which is considered by the VA to be the result of a psychiatric disorder and therefore a disease) as "the result of willful misconduct." Supreme Court Justice Byron R. White, writing for the majority, noted that "a substantial body of medical literature . . . contests the proposition that alcoholism is a disease, much less that it is a disease for which the victim bears no responsibility."

Justice White, citing a 1970 article by philosopher Herbert Fingarette, stated that ". . . even among many who considered alcoholism a 'disease' to which its victims are genetically predisposed, the consumption of alcohol is not regarded as wholly voluntary."

H. Fingarette (1970), "The perils of *Powell:* In search of a factual foundation for the 'disease concept of alcoholism'," *Harvard Law Review* 83 (793): 802–8.

For in-depth examinations of the Supreme Court ruling, see J. Larry Goff, "Alcoholism: Disease or willful misconduct? A look at the Veterans' Administrator position in Traynor v. Turnage," *The Journal of Psychiatry & Law* (Spring-Summer 1990): 59–107.

Gerard J. Connors and Robert G. Rychtarik, "The Supreme Court VA/Disease model case: Background and implications," *Psychology of Addictive Behavior* 2, 3 (1988), 101–7.

Pages 5–6: These myths and realities represent an abridged and revised version of the list that appears in James R. Milam and Katherine Ketcham, *Under the Influence: A Guide to the Myths and Realities of Alcoholism* (New York: Bantam, 1983), pages 11–15.

Page 6: Milam and Ketcham, *Under the Influence: A Guide to the Myths and Realities of Alcoholism* (New York: Bantam, 1983).

Page 6: "maladaptive lifestyle habits . . .": G. A. Marlatt, "The Controlled Drinking Controversy: A Commentary," *American Psychologist*, Oct. 1983, pages 1097–1110.

In this paper Marlatt, a behavioral psychologist at the University of Washington, suggests that we redefine alcohol problems as problems in living or maladaptive lifestyle habits used to cope with stress:

Excessive drinking can be redefined as behavior that people do, not a symptom of what people are (i.e., you are an alcoholic). Problem drinking is a health-risk behavior, a maladaptive habit pattern that can be modified through the application of basic learning principles, cognitive reframing, stress management, and life-style change. Moderation will become the key for many individuals who seek a reduction in their drinking to a level that does not pose a serious risk to their health or well-being.

Page 7: "No leading research authorities accept the classic disease concept...": Herbert Fingarette, *Heavy Drinking: The Myth of Alcoholism as a Disease* (Berkeley: University of California Press, 1988), page 3.

Page 7: Stanton Peele, *The Diseasing of America: Addiction Treatment Out of Control* (Lexington, Mass.: Lexington Books, 1989), page 27.

Page 7: "The act of lifting a drink...": Audrey Kishline, *Moderate Drinking* (New York: Crown, 1995), page 19.

Page 7: "The Drinking Dilemma," *U.S. News and World Report* cover story, Sept. 8, 1997, pages 55–65.

Pages 8–10: The references on these pages are drawn from varied sources:
* An estimated 14 million alcoholics: Statistics on the prevalence of alcoholism vary enormously. According to research published in *Alcohol Health & Research World* (vol. 18, no. 3, 1994: 243–45), 13.8 million Americans have drinking "problems," while of those, 8.1 million are alcoholics. In *The Natural History of Alcoholism* George Vaillant writes: "Depending on how one defines alcoholism, it will afflict, at some time in their lives, between 3 and 10 percent of all Americans" (p. 1). In James Royce and David Scratchley, *Alcohol and Other Drug Problems* (New York: Free Press, 1996) the authors use the conservative "rule of thumb that alcoholics constitute 4 percent of the general population" (p. 13). If we use the 4 percent figure and calculate according to figures released in 1999 by the U.S. Census Bureau, which put the U.S. population at 270,298,000 in July 1998, there were 10.8 million alcoholics in the U.S. at that time, with the numbers rising as the population increases. If early-stage and middle-stage alcoholics are included in these figures, the number may be as high as 20 to 25 million.
* Economic costs: According to a January 14, 1998, news release from NIAAA, from 1985 to 1992 the economic costs of alcoholism and alcohol-related problems rose 42 percent to $148 billion. Lost productivity, either due to alcohol-related illness (45.7 percent) or premature death (21.2 percent) accounted for two-thirds of the costs; the remaining costs were in the form of health care expenditures to treat alcohol use disorders and the medical consequences of alcohol consumption (12.7 percent), property and administrative costs of alcohol-related motor vehicle crashes (9.2 percent), and various additional costs of alcohol-related crime (8.6 percent). Based on inflation and population growth, the estimated costs for 1995 totaled $166.5 billion.

* More than 100,000 Americans die every year: in J. McGinnis and W. Foege, "Actual causes of death in the United States," *Journal of the American Medical Association* 270, 18 (11/10/93): 2208.

* In 1998, 15,935 people ... 1998 statistics released by the National Highway and Traffic Safety Administration (NHTSA).

* Alcoholics are five times ... NIAAA, Eighth Special Report to U.S. Congress on Alcohol and Health, September 1993, p. 233.

* 280 babies will die: NHTSA, 1996.

* Drownings and accidents: Department of Transportation, United States Coast Guard, Boating Statistics 1994, September 1995.

* Industrial fatalities: M. Bernstein and J. J. Mahoney, "Management perspective on alcoholism: The employer's stake in alcoholism treatment, *Occupational Medicine* 4, 2 (1989): 223–32.

* Pedestrian accidents: NHTSA, 1995. In 1993, 39.3 percent of all fatal pedestrian accidents involved alcohol.

* Rapes and assaults: "Alcohol and crime: An analysis of national data on the prevalence of alcohol involvement in crime," U.S. Department of Justice, April 1998. Based on victim reports, each year 183,000 (37 percent) of rapes and sexual assaults involve alcohol use by the offender, as do just over 197,000 (15 percent) of robberies, about 661,000 (27 percent) of aggravated assaults, and nearly 1.7 million (25 percent) of simple assaults.

* Domestic violence: J. Collins and P. Messerschmidt, "Epidemiology of Alcohol-Related Violence," *Alcohol Health and Research World* 17, 2 (1993): 96.

* 1.7 million Americans behind bars: S. Belenko, "Substance abuse and America's prison population," the National Center on Addiction and Substance Abuse (CASA) at Columbia University, January 1998.

* 6.6 million children: NIAAA, Alcohol Alert 9 (July 1990): 1.

* Middle and high school drinkers: U.S. Surgeon General, 1991.

* Forty-three percent of college students: Henry Wechsler, "Getting serious about eradicating binge drinking," *The Chronicle of Higher Education*, November 20, 1998. See also an earlier report by H. Wechsler and N. Isaac, " 'Binge' drinkers at Massachusetts colleges: Prevalence, drinking style, time trends and associated problems," *Journal of the American Medical Association* 267, 21 (1992): 2929–31. Reprinted in "Rethinking Rites of Passage: Substance Abuse on America's Campuses," CASA at Columbia University, June 1994.

* Campus crimes: C. R. Bausell et al., "The links among drugs, alcohol and campus crime," Towson State University Center for Study and Prevention of Campus Violence, Maryland, 1990.

* 47 percent of ER admissions: F. P. Rivara et al., "The magnitude of acute and chronic alcohol abuse in trauma patients," *Arch Surg* 128 (August 1993): 907–13; and G. J. Jurkovich et al., "The effect of acute alcohol intoxication and chronic alcohol abuse on outcome from trauma," *Journal of the American Medical Association* 170, 1 (July 7, 1993): 51–56. (See also the editorial in the same issue, pp. 93–94.)

* Alcoholism among minorities: Eduardo Hernandez, "The effects of alcohol on Latinos in California," *The Bottom Line* 19, 3 (Fall 1998): 15–25. For an in-depth look at the alcohol industry's global marketing strategies see D. Jernigan, *Thirsting for Markets: The Global Impact of Corporate Alcohol* (San Rafael, CA: The Marin Institute, 1997). For copies contact: The Marin Institute for the Prevention of Alcohol and Other Drug Problems, 24 Belvedere St., San Rafael, CA 94901.

Page 10: "How could this have happened? . . .": McGovern, *Terry*, pages x–xi.

CHAPTER 2   ALCOHOL: A "SIMPLE" CHEMICAL

Basic texts used as references for this chapter include H. Wallgren and H. Barry, *Actions of Alcohol* (Amsterdam: Elsevier Publishing Co., 1970) and Kathryn E. Crow and Richard D. Batt, eds., *Human Metabolism of Alcohol*, 3 vols. (Boca Raton, FL: CRC Press, 1989).

We are indebted to James Russo, Ph.D., professor of biology at Whitman College, for his careful review of chapters 2 and 3.

Page 12: Jack London tells his story of youthful drinking in his autobiographical book *John Barleycorn or, Alcoholic Memoirs* (New York: Signet, 1990), pages 22–34.

Page 12: Jack London died: In Clarice Stasz's introduction to Jack London's *John Barleycorn* (Signet 1990) she notes: "Jack London died of uremic poisoning on November 22, 1916, following months of physical suffering and fearless self-exploration." Uremic poisoning is considered an old, imprecise term for what is now commonly called "renal failure." We interviewed Dr. Richard Tremblay, a urologist and board member of the American Society of Addiction Medicine (ASAM), who notes that renal failure refers to the buildup of damaging metabolic products in the kidneys and throughout the body as a consequence of ingesting large amounts of alcohol. In most cases alcohol-damaged livers drag down the renal functions; only if alcoholics have a malfunctioning kidney or kidneys before they start drinking heavily is renal failure likely to be a serious consequence of heavy drinking.

In Jack London's case, as Stasz notes in her introduction (p. 11), kidney failure may have been caused by "the arsenic- and mercury-based medicines he took for various ailments, the side effect of a tropical disease like malaria, or perhaps even lupus."

Page 13: "I had got into the cogs . . .": London, *John Barleycorn*, page 49.

Page 16: BAC and hormone levels in women: NIAAA Alcohol Alert, no. 35, PH371, January 1997.

Page 17: "In one study . . ." A. W. Jones and K. A. Jönsson, "Food-induced lowering of blood-ethanol profiles and increased rate of elimination immediately after a meal," *Journal of Forensic Sciences* 39, 4 (1994): 1084–93.

Page 19: According to the NIAAA Alcohol Alert no. 35 (January 1997), a standard drink is defined as 12 ounces of beer, 5 ounces of table wine, or 1.5 ounces of 80-proof distilled spirits, all of which contain the same amount of alcohol.

Page 22: The Dietary Guidelines, published in 1995, also warn that some people should not drink alcoholic beverages at all, including women who are trying to conceive or who are pregnant; individuals who plan to drive or take part in activities that require attention or skill; individuals using prescription and over-the-counter medications; individuals of any age who cannot restrict their drinking to moderate levels; and children and adolescents. For more information, check the website of NCADD at www.ncadd.org.

Pages 22–23: Variations in ADH and ALDH enzymes: Table 2-2, "Occurrence of ADH alleles in different populations," from J. B. Hittle and D. W. Crabb, "The molecular biology of alcohol dehydrogenase: Implications for the control of alcohol metabolism," *Journal of Laboratory and Clinical Medicine* 112 (July–December 1988): 7–15.

For a description of ALDH*2 deficiencies in Asians, see T. L. Wall et al., "Alcohol metabolism in Asian-American men with genetic polymorphisms of aldehyde dehydrogenase," *Annals of Internal Medicine* 127, 5 (Sept. 1, 1997): 376–79.

Pages 24–26: Section on the microsomal enzyme oxidizing system (MEOS): Charles S. Lieber, chief of the research program on liver disease and nutrition at the Bronx Veterans Administration Hospital in New York, has been researching the metabolism of alcohol for several decades. See his book *Medical and Nutritional Complications of Alcoholism: Mechanisms and Management* (New York: Plenum, 1992). Lieber discusses the role of P-4502E1 in "Cytochrome P-4502E1: Its physiological and pathological role," *Physiological Reviews* 77, 2 (April 1997): 517–44.

Page 25: Alcohol's interactions with other drugs: The NIAAA Alcohol Alert no. 27, January 1995, details alcohol's interactions with other drugs. The complexity of these interactions is evident:

> The extent to which an administered dose of a drug reaches its site of action may be termed its availability. Alcohol can influence the effectiveness of a drug by altering its availability. Typical alcohol-drug interactions include the following: First, an acute dose of alcohol (a single drink or several drinks over several hours) may inhibit a drug's metabolism by competing with the drug for the same set of metabolizing enzymes. This interaction prolongs and enhances the drug's availability, potentially increasing the patient's risk of experiencing harmful side effects from the drug. Second, in contrast, chronic (long-term) alcohol ingestion may activate

drug-metabolizing enzymes, thus decreasing the drug's availability and diminishing its effects. After these enzymes have been activated, they remain so even in the absence of alcohol, affecting the metabolism of certain drugs for several weeks after cessation of drinking. Thus, a recently abstinent chronic drinker may need higher doses of medications than those required by nondrinkers to achieve therapeutic levels of certain drugs. Third, enzymes activated by chronic alcohol consumption transform some drugs into toxic chemicals that can damage the liver or other organs. Fourth, alcohol can magnify the inhibitory effects of sedative and narcotic drugs at their sites of action in the brain.

A few examples: Chronic alcoholics may require higher doses of certain anesthetics such as propofol (Diprivan) prior to surgery. Chronic alcohol consumption reduces the availability of the antiseizure medication phenytoin (Dilantin), meaning that the alcoholic patient's protection against epileptic seizures, even during a period of abstinence, is significantly reduced. Chronic drinking decreases the availability of propranolol (Inderal) used to treat high blood pressure, the anticoagulant warfarin (Coumadin), and tolbutamide (Orinase) used to lower blood sugar levels in diabetics, potentially reducing the therapeutic effects of these drugs. The combination of chronic alcohol ingestion and antipsychotic drugs such as chlorpromazine (Thorazine) may result in liver damage. Acute or chronic alcohol consumption enhances the sedative effects of barbiturates and can lead to coma or fatal respiratory depression. The combination of the opiates (morphine, codeine, Darvon, Demerol) enhances the sedative effect of both substances, increasing the risk of death from overdose.

For more information on drug interactions, see NIAAA's Alcohol Alert 27, available at the web address: www.health.org. In the search box type "alcohol and medication" and then click on Alcohol Alert No. 27.

Page 26. Alcohol and acetaminophen: See L. B. Seeff et al., "Acetaminophen hepatotoxicity in alcoholics: A therapeutic misadventure," *Annals of Internal Medicine* 104, 3 (1986): 399–404; C. Girre et al., "Increased metabolism of acetaminophen in chronically alcoholic patients," *Alcoholism: Clinical and Experimental Research* 17, 1 (1993): 170–73; and M. Black, "Acetaminophen hepatotoxicity," *Annual Review of Medicine* 35 (1984): 577–93.

CHAPTER 3   THE DRUG CALLED ALCOHOL

Pages 27–28: "It's Only Beer" billboard and story appeared in *The Bottom Line* (published by the Alcohol Research Information Service in Lansing, Mich.), Spring 1997, pages 29–33. We tried to find out what billboard replaced the offending hypodermic better bottle, but our sleuthing came to no avail. Five different sources told us they didn't know what happened to the replacement billboard. It is possible that the billboard was simply dismantled and never replaced.

However, if you would like to order a bookmark featuring the hypodermic beer bottle, call FACE (Facing Alcohol Concerns Through Prevention),

(888) 822-3223. The cost for 200 bookmarks is approximately $50. Along with the hypodermic illustration, the bookmarks feature this message: "Beer contains alcohol. Alcohol is a drug. Alcohol is the number one drug problem in this country. Not marijuana. Not cocaine. Alcohol. Get the point?"

Page 28: 120 million Americans drink: In a Gallup poll taken from June 27 to 30, 1996, 42 percent of American adults said they were total abstainers and did not use beer, wine, or distilled spirits on any occasion. Of those who did drink, three percent said their last drink was more than a year ago; another nine percent said their last drink was "over three months to within the last year." Robert L. Hammond, editor of *The Bottom Line*, comments in the Winter 1996 issue that this "translates into 54 percent of our adult population using alcohol very seldom or not at all, which represents the highest rate of abstinence in the world, where data are available on such subjects" (p. 19).

Hammond then turned to the Eighth Special Report to the U.S. Congress on Alcohol and Health (September 1993), prepared by the National Institute on Alcohol Abuse and Alcoholism (NIAAA) to get the number of persons represented by the percentages.

Page 29: "Imagine a cocktail party . . .": This story is adapted from lectures given by James R. Milam at Alcenas Hospital, the treatment center he founded in Kirkland, Washington.

Page 30: "Most studies of nerve conduction . . .": Wallgren and Barry, *Actions of Alcohol*, 2:797.

Page 30: Actor John Larroquette appeared on CNN's *Larry King Live* on January 7, 1998.

Page 31: Sir William Osler is quoted in James E. Royce and David Scratchley, *Alcoholism and Other Drug Problems* (New York: Free Press, 1996), page 53.

Page 31: "It is said that alcohol attacks judgment . . .": Royce and Scratchley, *Alcoholism and Other Drug Problems*, pages 54–55.

Page 33: "If alcoholism were just a symptom . . .": George Vaillant, *The Natural History of Alcoholism Revisited* (Cambridge, Mass.: Harvard University Press, 1995), pages 77–78.

Page 33: Anxiety levels in hospitalized alcoholics: S. A. Brown et al., "Changes in anxiety among abstinent male alcoholics," *Journal of Studies on Alcohol* 52 (1988): 55–61.

Page 34: "I thought I had all these problems . . .": Actor/novelist Thomas Tryon, quoted in Dennis Wholey, *The Courage to Change* (New York: Houghton-Mifflin, 1984), pages 115–16.

Page 34: Alcohol as anesthetic: Kenneth Blum, Ph.D., writes in *Alcohol and the Addictive Brain:* "Once considered a simple anesthetic that caused general depression of brain neurons, alcohol is now seen as a substance that can cause specific changes in the biochemistry and electrophysiology of brain function" (p. 243).

Page 35: "In higher doses . . .": J. N. Santamaria, "The effects of ethanol and its metabolism on the brain," in Crow and Batt, eds., *Human Metabolism of Alcohol,* vol. 3, *Metabolic and Physiological Effects of Alcohol.*

Page 35: Beneficial effects of alcohol are reported in M. J. Thun et al., "Alcohol consumption and mortality among middle-aged and elderly U.S. adults," *New England Journal of Medicine* 337, 24 (1997): 1705–14; R. Doll, "One for the heart," *British Medical Journal* 315 (December 20–27, 1997): 1664–8.

Page 36: For articles that raise questions about the benefits of moderate drinking, see M. Criqui, "The reduction of coronary heart disease with light to moderate consumption: Effect or artifact?" *British Journal of Addiction* 85 (1990): 854–57; P. Boffetta and L. Garfinkel, "Alcohol drinking and mortality among men enrolled in an American Cancer Society prospective study," *Epidemiology* 1 (1990): 342–48.

Page 36: "It must be borne in mind . . .": Vaillant, *Natural History,* page 141.

Page 37: Forcing rodents to drink: For several decades researchers have been force-feeding alcohol and other drugs to rats and mice to try to create addiction. Robert D. Myers at Purdue University in Indiana implanted plastic tubes into the cerebral spinal fluid of rats that had never drunk alcohol, pumping regulated quantities of different alcohol solutions directly into the animals' brains. Each rat received 1,000 brain injections during the experiment. Myers found that the more alcohol he injected into the animals' brains, the greater the tendency to drink large amounts of alcohol. Kenneth Blum comments on this research in *Alcohol and the Addictive Brain* (p. 97): "We were now seeing the first evidence linking an increase in alcohol-craving behavior to permanent biochemical changes induced by long-term ingestion of alcohol." See R. D. Myers, "Alcohol consumption in rats: Effect of intracranial injections of ethanol," *Science* 142 (1963): 240–41.

Researcher John R. Nichols injected morphine into rats that normally did not drink morphine solutions, until the animals became addicted and suffered withdrawal symptoms when the morphine was withheld. See J. R. Nichols and S. Hsiao, "Addiction liability of albino rats: Breeding for quantitative differences in morphine drinking," *Science* 157 (1967): 561–63.

One of the most ingenious methods for inducing rapid alcohol dependence in rodents was the vapor chamber developed by Stanford University researcher Dora Goldstein. Within three days of breathing the vapor, the animals were dependent on alcohol. See D. B. Goldstein, "Alcohol withdrawal reactions in mice: Effects of drugs that modify neurotransmission," *Journal of Pharmacology and Experimental Therapeutics* 186 (1973): 1–9.

Page 38: "The physical loathing for alcohol . . .": London, *John Barleycorn*, page 35.

CHAPTER 4   THE ADDICTED BRAIN

Page 39: "Every human soul . . .": J. E. Todd, "Drunkenness a vice not a disease." This paper was read at the General Association at Middletown, Conn., June 21, 1882, and by vote of that body printed and distributed to the churches. Quoted in E. M. Jellinek, *The Disease Concept of Alcoholism* (New Haven, CT: Hillhouse Press, 1960), page 139.

Page 39: "1979 survey . . .": "The General Mills American Family Report: Family health in an era of stress," survey conducted by Yankelovich, Skelly and White, Inc.

Page 39: The Recovery Institute's study, titled "The road to recovery: A landmark national study on public perceptions of alcoholism and barriers to treatment," conducted by Peter D. Hart Research Associates, Inc. (October 1997 to February 1998) is available from the Recovery Institute, 332 Pine Street, Suite 707, San Francisco, CA 94104, tel. (415) 249-3956, fax (415) 249-3960, E-mail recovinst@aol.com. The section quoted here appears on pp. 19–20 of that report.

As a result of this national survey, the Recovery Institute has created a course for the clergy (52 percent of whom believe that alcoholism is a moral weakness) at the Graduate Theological Union, Pacific School of Religion in Berkeley, California. R. Stockton Rush, chairman and president of the Recovery Institute, told us the course was created in an effort to "put into practice the destigmitization of alcoholism."

A historical aside: Stockton Rush is the great-great-great grandson of Dr. Benjamin Rush, signer of the Declaration of Independence as a Pennsylvania delegate, Physician-General of the Continental Army, and often called the "Father of Psychiatry." The first American to designate alcoholism as a disease, Benjamin Rush identified the addictive nature of alcohol in *An Inquiry into the Effects of Ardent Spirits on the Human Mind and Body*, written in 1784.

Page 41: For adoption studies and familial incidence of alcoholism, see D. W. Goodwin et al., "Alcohol problems in adoptees raised apart from alcoholic biological parents," *Archives of General Psychiatry* 28 (1972): 1132–36; D. W. Goodwin, *Is Alcoholism Hereditary?* (New York: Oxford University Press, 1976); D. W. Goodwin, "Alcoholism and heredity," *Archives of General Psychiatry* 36 (1979): 57–61; D. W. Goodwin, *Alcoholism: The Facts* (New York: Oxford University Press, 1994); N. S. Cotton, "The familial incidence of alcoholism," *Journal of Studies on Alcohol* 40 (1979): 89–116.

Page 41: Henri Begleiter's work on P3 brain waves is reported in H. Begleiter et al., "Event-related brain potentials in boys at risk for alcoholism," *Science* 225 (1984): 1493–95. See also H. Begleiter and B. Porjesz, "Potential biologic markers in individuals at high risk for developing alcoholism," *Alcoholism: Clinical Experimental Research* 12 (1988): 488–93; R. Elmasian et al., "Event-related brain potentials are different in individuals at high and low risk for developing alcoholism," *Proceedings of the National Academy of Sciences of the USA* 79 (1982): 7900–3; S. M. Berman et al., "P3 in young boys as a predictor of adolescent substance use," *Alcohol* 10 (1993): 69–76.

Page 42: The Blum/Noble collaboration is described in Kenneth Blum (in collaboration with James E. Payne), *Alcohol and the Addictive Brain* (New York: Free Press, 1991), pages 226–36. We confirmed the details in numerous personal interviews with Dr. Blum and in correspondence with Dr. Ernest Noble at UCLA.

See also: E. P. Noble, "The gene that rewards alcoholism," *Scientific American Science & Medicine*, March/April 1996, pages 52–61; E. P. Noble, "The D2 dopamine receptor gene: A review of association studies in alcoholism and phenotypes," *Alcohol* 16, 1 (1998): 33–45; E. P. Noble, K. Blum et al., "Allelic association of the D2 dopamine receptor gene with receptor-binding characteristics in alcoholism," *Arch Gen Psychiatry* 48 (1991): 648–54; E. P. Noble, Kenneth Blum et al., "Allelic association of the D2 dopamine receptor gene with cocaine dependence," *Drug and Alcohol Dependence* 33 (1993): 271–85; and "Case-control study of the D2 dopamine receptor gene and smoking status in lung cancer patients," M. Spitz et al., *Journal of the National Cancer Institute* 90, 5 (March 4, 1998): 358–63.

Page 42: Civelli's studies are reported in D. K. Grandy et al., "The human dopamine D2 receptor gene is located on chromosome 11 at q22–q33 and identified as Taq1RFLP," *American Journal of Human Genetics* 45 (1989): 778.

Page 43: "For a person to be considered alcoholic . . .": Wallgren and Barry, *Actions of Alcohol*, chapter 11.

Page 44: Diagnostic criteria from *Diagnostic and Statistic Manual*, 4th ed. (Washington, D.C.: American Psychiatric Association, 1994), pages 108–9.

Page 45: NCADD and ASAM definition: This definition was prepared by the 23-member Joint Committee to Study the Definition and Criteria for the Diagnosis of Alcoholism of the National Council on Alcoholism and Drug Dependence and the American Society of Addiction Medicine. It was approved on February 3, 1990, by NCADD and by ASAM on February 25, 1990.

Page 48: Figure 4–1: Adapted from Blum, *Alcohol and the Addictive Brain*, page 103.

Page 48: R. D. Myers and C. L. Melchior, "Alcohol drinking: Abnormal intake caused by tetrahydropapaveroline in brain," *Science* 196 (1977): 554–56.

Page 49: Fewer dopamine receptors in alcohol-loving rats and mice: J. A. Severson et al., "Genotypic influences on striatal dopamine regulation in mice," *Brain Research* 210 (1981): 201–15; E. R. Korpi, J. D. Sinclair, and O. Malminen, "Dopamine D2 receptor binding in striatal membranes of rat lines selected for differences in alcohol-related behaviors," *Pharmacology and Toxicology* 61 (1987): 94–97.
Blum quotation from *Alcohol and the Addictive Brain*, page 188.

Page 50: Blum details his "reward deficiency syndrome" in *Alcohol and the Addictive Brain*, Chapter 12 ("The Reward Cascade") and in K. Blum et al., "Reward deficiency syndrome," *American Scientist* (March–April 1996): 132–45.
See also K. Blum et al., "Allelic association of human dopamine D2 receptor gene in alcoholism," *Journal of the American Medical Association* 263, 15 (April 18, 1990): 2055–60; K. Blum et al., "The D2 dopamine receptor gene as a determinant of reward deficiency syndrome," *Journal of the Royal Society of Medicine* 89 (July 1996): 396–400.

Page 52: Research on Fyn tyrosine kinase is reported in "Enzyme linked to alcohol sensitivity in mice," *Science* 278 (October 24, 1997): 573.

Page 52: "Initial insensitivity seems to be a predictor . . .": Pharmacologist Adron Harris is quoted in "Enzyme linked to alcohol sensitivity in mice," *Science* 278 (October 24, 1997): 573.

Page 52: The Human Genome Project is an international effort, which formally began in October 1990, to discover all the sixty thousand to eighty thousand human genes (the human genome) and determine the complete sequence of the three billion DNA subunits.

CHAPTER 5   ALCOHOLISM: THE EARLY AND
                   MIDDLE STAGES

Page 53: Dylan Thomas story told in Clifton Fadiman, ed., *The Little Brown Book of Anecdotes* (Boston: Little, Brown, 1985), page 541.

Page 54: Mary Kerr, *The Liar's Club* (New York: Penguin, 1995), page 237.

Page 55: "A great feeling of peace . . .": Malachy McCourt, *A Monk Swimming* (New York: Hyperion, 1998), page 116.

Page 55: "Before drinking I felt unloved . . .": Jean Kirkpatrick, *Goodbye Hangovers, Hello Life: Self-Help for Women* (New York: Ballantine, 1986), p. 54.

Pages 55–57: On lower-intensity reaction, see M. A. Schuckit, "Low level of response to alcohol as a predictor of future alcoholism," *American Journal of Psychiatry* 151 (1994): 184–89; M. A. Schuckit, "A clinical model of genetic influences on alcohol dependence," *Journal of Studies on Alcohol* 55 (1994): 5–

17; M. A. Schuckit, "A long-term study of sons of alcoholics," *Alcohol Health and Research World* 19, 3 (Nov. 3, 1995): 172–75.

Schuckit's study on acetaldehyde levels in sons of alcoholics: M. A. Schuckit and V. Rayses, "Ethanol ingestion: Differenes in blood acetaldehyde concentrations in relatives of alcoholics and controls," *Science* 203 (1979): 54–55. See also C. J. P. Eriksson and J. E. Peachey, "Lack of difference in blood acetaldehyde of alcoholics and controls after ethanol ingestion," *Pharmacology, Biochemistry and Behavior* 13, suppl. 1 (1980): 101–5.

Page 57: Ken Blum discusses Schuckit's study on page 141 of *Alcohol and the Addictive Brain*.

Page 57: "I could drink everybody under the table . . .": Marty Mann, is quoted in Nan Robertson *Getting Better: Inside Alcoholics Anonymous* (New York: Fawcett Crest, 1988), page 120.

Pages 57–58: "I had a splendid constitution . . .": London, *John Barleycorn*, pages 46–47.

Page 59: "I loved those moments . . .": Caroline Knapp, *Drinking: A Love Story* (New York: Dial Press, 1996), pages 63–64.

Page 61: "It is as if a coiled spring . . .": Jerome David Levin, *Introduction to Alcoholism Counseling: A Bio-Psycho-Social Approach* (Washington, D.C.: Taylor and Francis, 1995), page 41.

Page 62: Henri Paul's drinking: see Thomas Sancton and Tamal M. Edwards, "Drunk and drugged," *Time*, September 22, 1997, pages 27–30. On page 28 the article cites a French journalist's claim that two employees at Harry's New York Bar positively identified photos of Paul and confirmed he drank "two or three whiskeys" from about 7:30 P.M. to 9:45 P.M. in the bar the night of the accident. A Ritz employee is quoted as saying Paul drank pastis in the hotel bar after he was called back to work.

Page 65: "In spite of a great diversity . . .": Jellinek, *The Disease Concept of Alcoholism*, page 153.

Page 65: The most famous of all prospective studies is George Vaillant's research, reported in *The Natural History of Alcoholism Revisited*. Other perspective studies discussed by Vaillant on pages 48–52 of his book include W. McCord and J. McCord, *Origins of Alcoholism* (Stanford: Stanford University Press, 1960); L. N. Robins, W. N. Bates, and P. O'Neal, "Adult drinking patterns of former problem children," in D. J. Pittman and C. R. Synder, eds., *Society, Culture and Drinking Patterns* (New York: Wiley, 1962); M. C. Jones, "Personality correlates and antecedents of drinking patterns in adult males," *Journal of Consulting and Clinical Psychology* 32 (1968): 2–12; M. C. Jones, "Personality antecedents and correlates of drinking patterns in women," *Journal of*

Consulting and Clinical Psychology 36 (1971): 61–69; R. G. Loper, M. L. Kammeier, and H. Hoffmann, "M.M.P.I. characteristics of college freshman males who later became alcoholics," *Journal of Abnormal Psychology* 82 (1973): 159–62.

Page 65: "Alcoholics are selectively . . .": Vaillant, *Natural History*, page 381.

Page 66: "Just as light . . .": Vaillant, *Natural History*, page 48.

Page 66: Terry McGovern's story is told in McGovern, *Terry*, pages 87–89.

Page 67: PBS debate: "Is abstinence the answer to alcoholism," *Debates* #219, taped November 19, 1997, aired the week of December 10, 1997. HBO Studio Production, 120A East 23rd Street, New York, NY 10010.

Page 67: Family denial: McGovern, *Terry*, page 101.

Page 69: "I need to write this . . .": McGovern, *Terry*, page 149. This journal entry was written on November 13, 1993, thirteen months before Terry died on December 13, 1994.

CHAPTER 6   LATE-STAGE ALCOHOLISM

Page 70: "At no point in my life . . .": Joseph D. Beasley, *How to Defeat Alcoholism: Nutritional Guidelines for Getting Sober* (New York: Times Books, 1989), page 8.

Pages 70–71: Jeff Jay's story appeared in *The Bottom Line* 17, 4 (Winter 1996) and was confirmed through several email conversations. Jay has produced a video and series of audiotapes focusing on intervention techniques. For more information, write or call *Take Charge! with Jeff Jay*, Brighton Hospital, 12851 East Grand River, Brighton, MI 48116; tel. (800) 523-8198.

Page 71: "By this time . . .": Doc Severinsen is quoted in Wholey, *The Courage to Change*, page 28.

Page 72: "The drinker's position . . .": Levin, *Introduction to Alcoholism Counseling*, page 41.

Pages 73–74: "I don't know how long . . .": Mark Twain, *The Adventures of Huckleberry Finn* (New York: Random House, 1997), page 38.

Page 74: William Madsen, *The American Alcoholic: The Nature-Nurture Controversy in Alcoholic Research and Therapy* (Springfield, IL: Charles C. Thomas, 1974), page 71.

Page 74: "When strongly urged . . .": This quotation is attributed to Benjamin Rush, M.D. We found the quote in H. G. Levine, "The discovery of addiction," *Journal of Studies on Alcoholism* 39, 1 (1978): 143–74; Levine cites B. Rush, *Medical Inquiries and Observations Upon the Diseases of the Mind* (New

York: Hafner, 1810). In Donald Goodwin, *Alcoholism: The Facts*, this same quote is attributed to 19th century psychologist and philosopher William James, but with no specific citation.

Pages 75–76: The Reward Cascade Theory: See Blum, *Alcohol and the Addictive Brain*, pages 200–15. As Blum is careful to point out, the problem with craving behavior involves many chemical messengers. The brain is dependent on dopamine—its content, its receptors, its storage in the neuron, its release—but the reward cascade involves a number of neurotransmitters (serotonin, GABA, norepinephrine, the enkephalins, and so on) all working in concert.

Page 76: "Forty years of research . . ." in Blum, *Alcohol and the Addictive Brain*, page 237.

Pages 76–80: The section on the medical complications of alcoholism draws on numerous references, specifically: James E. Royce and David Scratchley, *Alcoholism and Other Drug Problems*, pages 62–73; Frederick A. Montgomery, *Alcoholism and Chemical Dependency: A Current Medical View* (Selah, WA: Sundown M. Foundation), chapter 3; Donald Goodwin, *Alcohol: The Facts*, chapter 6; and *Topics in Addiction Medicine* (Chevy Chase, MD: American Society of Addiction Medicine, Inc., April 1995), section V: Medical Disorders of the Addicted Patient.

Page 79: Young people's brains more vulnerable to alcohol: See B. Grant and D. Dawson, "Age at onset of alcohol use and its association with DSM-IV alcohol-abuse and dependence: Results from the National Longitudinal Alcohol Epidemiologic Survey," *Journal of Substance Abuse* 9 (1997): 103–10; B. Grant and D. Dawson, "Age at onset of drug use and its association with DSM-IV drug abuse and dependence: Results from the National Longitudinal Alcohol Epidemiologic Survey," *Journal of Substance Abuse* 10 (1998): 163–73.

Page 80: The Maryland study on Alzheimer's is cited in James West, *The Betty Ford Center Book of Answers* (New York: Pocket Books, 1997), page 78.

Page 81: "In two studies . . .": S. Brown and M. A. Schuckit, "Changes in depression among abstinent alcoholics," *Journal of Studies on Alcohol* 49 (1988): 412–17; M. A. Schuckit and V. Hesselbrock, "Alcohol dependence and anxiety disorders: What is the relationship?" *American Journal of Psychiatry* 15 (1994): 1723–34.

Page 81: "The conclusion from all . . .": M. A. Schuckit, *Educating Yourself About Alcohol and Drugs: A People's Primer* (New York: Plenum, 1995), page 116. See also S. Brown, M. Irwin, and M. A. Schuckit, "Changes in anxiety among abstinent male alcoholics," *Journal of Studies on Alcohol* 52 (1991): 55–61.

Pages 83–84: Rob Larson's story is told in Joan Mathews Larson, *Seven Weeks to Sobriety: The Proven Program to Fight Alcoholism Through Nutrition* (New York: Fawcett Columbine, 1992), pages 6–8. For additional resources on alcoholism and suicide, see H. Van Praag, "Depression, suicide and the metabolism of serotonin the brain," *Journal of Affective Disorders* 4 (1982): 275–90; Schuckit, *Educating Yourself About Alcohol and Drugs,* page 296.

Page 84: "Of over 100 alcoholics . . .": William Madsen, *The American Alcoholic,* page 69.

Page 86: "Here are some of the methods . . .": Bill Wilson in *Alcoholics Anonymous,* 3rd ed. (New York: Alcoholics Anonymous World Service, Inc., 1976), page 31.

Page 86: Linda C. and Mark B. Sobell, *Individualized Behavior Therapy for Alcoholics: Rationale, Procedures, Preliminary Results, and Appendix,* California Mental Health Research Monograph no. 13 (California Dept. of Mental Hygiene, 1972); M. B. and L. C. Sobell, "Individualized behavior therapy for alcoholics," *Behavior Therapy* 4 (1973): 49–72; M. B. and L. C. Sobell, *Behavioral Treatment of Alcohol Problems: Individualized Therapy and Controlled Drinking* (New York: Plenum, 1978); M. B. and L. C. Sobell, "The aftermath of heresy: A response to Pendery et al.'s (1982) Critique of 'individualized behavior therapy for alcoholics,' " *Behavioral Research Therapy* 22 (1984): 413–40; M. B. and L. C. Sobell, "Conceptual issues regarding goals in the treatment of alcohol problems," in M. B. Sobell and L. C. Sobell, eds., *Moderation as a Goal or Outcome of Treatment for Alcohol Problems: A Dialogue* (New York: Haworth, 1987); M. B. and L. C. Sobell, "Stalking white elephants," *British Journal of Addiction* 82 (1987): 245–47.

Pages 86 – 87: M. L. Pendery, I. M. Maltzman, and L. J. West, "Controlled drinking by alcoholics? New findings and a reevaluation of a major affirmative study," *Science* 217 (1982): 169–75; I. M. Maltzman, "Why alcoholism is a disease," *Journal of Psychoactive Drugs* 26, 1 (Jan.–Mar. 1994): 13–31; I. M. Maltzman, "Controlled drinking and the treatment of alcoholism," *Journal of the American Medical Association* 257 (1987): 927–28.

Page 87: "In no known respect . . .": Fingarette, *Heavy Drinking,* page 59.

Page 87: Fingarette's case of the alcoholic convicted of drunk driving appears on page 38 of *Heavy Drinking.* For a fascinating analysis of Fingarette's position on the disease concept, see William Madsen, *Defending the Disease: From Facts to Fingarette* (Akron, OH: Wilson, Brown & Co., 1988). See also J. E. Helzer et al., "The extent of long-term moderate drinking among alcoholics discharged from medical and psychiatric treatment facilities," *New England Journal of Medicine* 312, 26 (June 27, 1985): 1678–82. Helzer and colleagues studied the five- to seven-year outcomes for 1,289 diagnosed alcoholics and found that only 1.6 percent met their definition of stable moderate drinking at follow-up. "The evolution to stable moderate drinking appears to be a rare outcome among alcoholics," the authors conclude.

Page 87: "If those who advocate . . ." in Madsen, *The American Alcoholic*, pages 72–73.

CHAPTER 7   THE SOCIAL DRINKER, THE PROBLEM
                         DRINKER, AND THE DRUNK

Pages 90–92: The Henri Paul story is based on facts presented in numerous print and broadcast reports following Princess Diana's death.

"If Mr. Paul had ever betrayed . . ." in "Diana and the paparazzi: A morality tale," *The New York Times*, September 6, 1997.

"Innocent bystanders" (Prozac and tiapride) remark was made by Richard A. Friedman, M.D., director of the psychopharmacology clinic of New York Hospital–Cornell Medical Center and appeared in "Diana to rescuers: Leave me alone," *The Oregonian*, September 11, 1997, page A3.

Remarks about Henri Paul's drinking behavior are found in numerous articles. As *The New York Times* reports in "Diana and the Paparazzi," Henri Paul was "viewed by some in the hotel as a pillar of reliability and by others as a swaggering tough guy with a weakness for alcohol and a Rambo-like machismo." In "Drunk and drugged," *Time*, September 22, 1997, Thomas Sancton and Tamala Edwards cite an article that appeared in the French daily *Libération* saying that Paul drank in the Ritz bar in the hours before the accident, and when he got up to go, he staggered and "knocked into a customer" (p. 28). *Time* correspondent Thomas Sancton was also interviewed on CNN and *Time* magazine's *Impact* program during the week of September 22, 1997. According to Sancton, *Time* tracked Henri Paul to Harry's New York Bar, where at least two sources said he was there from around 7:30 P.M. to around 9:45 P.M.; during that period, according to one of the bartenders, Paul had two or three whiskeys.

In Thomas Sancton and Scott MacLeod, *Death of a Princess: The Investigation* (New York: St. Martin's Press, 1998), the facts about Paul's "fondness for the bottle" (p. 172) and his drinking in the bar the night of the fatal accident (p. 183) are reported, along with many other facts about Paul's drinking behavior. (See Chapter 10, pages 165–86.)

The facts about the champagne bottle in Paul's refrigerator, the quote "His life was a series of water-tight compartments," and other facts about Paul's drinking problems appear in "The demons that drove Diana's chauffeur," *The Sunday Times* (London), September 14, 1997, page 1.

Comment about Paul in Willi's bar appears in "New questions about Diana's driver," *The Oregonian*, September 4, 1997.

Pages 92 – 93: Statistics about drinking behavior: NIAAA, *Alcohol Health & Research World* 18, 3 (1994): 243–45; and NIAAA, "Sixth Special Report to

U.S. Congress on Alcohol and Health," U.S. Department of Health and Human Services, January 1987, page 3. See also Donald Goodwin, *Alcohol: The Facts*, pages 24–25.

Alcohol problems in the elderly: NIAAA News Alert no. 40, April 1998; see also *The Bottom Line* 20, 2 (Summer 1999): 76–81, which cites a 1997 Gallup poll finding that 39 percent of drinkers age 50 and older reported having a drink within 24 hours of the Gallup interview, compared with 28 percent of drinkers age 18 to 29 who did.

Page 93: "No longer at risk . . .": Vaillant, *Natural History*, page 162.

Page 93: "If you need a drink . . .": The first public awareness campaigns by NIAAA in 1973–74 included a poster with the message "If you need a drink to be social, it's not social drinking." This slogan was devised by Gray-North advertising agency under contract with NIAAA. We thank Jay Lewis, former editor of *The Alcoholism Report*, for bringing these facts to our attention.

Page 95: "Alcoholics and social drinkers are two different kinds of people . . .": Dan E. Beauchamp, *Beyond Alcoholism: Alcohol and Public Health Policy* (Philadelphia: Temple University Press, 1980), page 32.

Page 96: *Diagnostic and Statistical Manual*, 4th ed., page 112.

Pages 97–98: D. Cahalan, *Problem Drinkers: A National Survey* (San Francisco: Jossey-Bass, 1970).

Pages 98–99: Vaillant's problem-drinking scale is published in his "Natural history of male psychological health, II: Antecedents of alcoholism and 'orality,' " *American Journal of Psychiatry* 137 (1980): 181–86.

Page 100: "Conservatively, the average . . .": Vaillant, *Natural History*, page 43.

Page 101: "The modal problem drinker . . .": Vaillant, *Natural History*, page 166.

Page 101: "A 1995 study . . .": "Binge drinking on American college campuses," by the Harvard University School of Public Health, Henry Wechsler, Ph.D., principal investigator, made possible by a grant from the Robert Wood Johnson Foundation, published in *Journal of the American Medical Association*, December 7, 1994. This study was updated four years later; see H. Wechsler, "Getting serious about eradicating binge drinking," *The Chronicle of Higher Education* 45, 13 (November 20, 1998): B4–B5.

Pages 102–3: "A 1998 report . . .": C. A. Presley, P. W. Meilman, and J. R. Cashin, *Alcohol and Drugs on American College Campuses: Use, Consequences, and Perceptions of the Campus Environment*, vol. 4 (Carbondale: Southern Illinois University, 1996). Information on this survey and previous SIU surveys is available on the Internet at www.siu.edu/departments/coreinst/public html/index.html#pubs.

Page 104: "Heavy college drinking turned out . . .": Vaillant, *Natural History*, page 167.

Page 106: "The fact is . . .": Knapp, *Drinking: A Love Story*, pages 12–13.

Page 107: "She was a very reassuring presence . . .": Knapp, *Drinking: A Love Story*, page 26.

Pages 107–8: Malachy McCourt's story of his alcoholic father: *A Monk Swimming*, pages 282–85.

PART II

CHAPTER 8   AM I AN ALCOHOLIC?

Page 112: "Studies show that paper-and-pencil tests . . .": Harvard psychiatrist George Vaillant states in *The Natural History of Alcoholism Revisited*, page 386:

> [B]iochemical tests have consistently provided too little sensitivity and specificity. However, by using the MAST, a problem-based measure, the simple CAGE, and even by simply asking individuals "Have you ever had a drinking problem?" and "When was your last drink?" clinicians have achieved much greater sensitivity and specificity of diagnosis.

Vaillant cites M. G. Cyr and S. A. Wortman, "The effectiveness of routine screening questions in the detection of alcoholism," *Journal of the American Medical Association* 259 (1988): 51–54.

Pages 112–13: The National Council on Alcoholism questionnaire is published by the National Council on Alcoholism and Drug Dependence, Inc., New York City, 1987 (revised March 1990).

Pages 113–14: The Johns Hopkins University Drinking Scale is printed in our book as it appears in Jerome David Levin's book *Introduction to Alcoholism Counseling: A Bio-Psycho-Social Approach* (Washington, D.C., Taylor & Francis, 1995), pages 106 – 7.

Pages 115–19: The Michigan Alcohol Screening Test (MAST): M. L. Selzer, "The Michigan Alcoholism Screening Test: The quest for a new diagnostic instrument," *American Journal of Psychiatry* 127 (1971): 1653–8; M. L. Selzer et al., "A self-administered Short Michigan Alcoholism Screening Test (SMAST)," *Journal of Studies on Alcohol* 36, 1 (1975); A. D. Pokorny, B. A. Mill, and H. B. Kaplan, "The brief MAST: A shortened version of the Michigan Alcoholism Screen Test," *American Journal of Psychiatry* 129 (1972): 342. F. C.

Blow et al., "The Michigan Alcoholism Screening Test—Geriatric Version (MAST-G): A new elderly-specific screening instrument," *Alcoholism: Clinical and Experimental Research* 16 (1992): 372. Our thanks to G. Douglas Talbott, M.D., for bringing this test to our attention.

In an April 1998 news release (News Alert no. 40), NIAAA addressed the problem of alcohol and the elderly: "People age 65 and older constitute the fastest growing segment of the American population. Although the extent of alcoholism among the elderly is debated, the diagnosis and treatment of alcohol problems are likely to become increasingly important as the elderly population grows."

Pages 120–21: The CAGE questionnaire: J. A. Ewing, "Detecting alcoholism: The CAGE questionnaire," *Journal of the American Medical Association* 252 (1984): 1905–7.

Page 120: The CAGE has a sensitivity of 85 percent: B. Bush et al., "Screening for alcohol abuse using the CAGE questionnaire," *American Journal of Medicine* 82 (1987): 231–35.

Page 120: Harborview Medical Center study: F. P. Rivara et al., "The magnitude of acute and chronic alcohol abuse in trauma patients," *Arch Surg* 128 (August 1993): 907–13. See also G. J. Jurkovich et al., "The effect of acute alcohol intoxication and chronic alcohol abuse on outcome from trauma," *Journal of the American Medical Association* 270, 1 (July 7, 1993): 51–56.

Page 121: "He told me how de-humanized he felt . . .": Levin, *Introduction to Alcoholism Counseling*, page 43.

Page 122: Drinking underestimated by 50 percent: See P. F. Smith et al., "A comparison of alcohol sales data with survey data on self-reported alcohol use in 21 states," *American Journal of Public Health* 80 (1990): 309–12.

Page 122: "10 percent of physicians . . .": This often quoted statistic was confirmed in conversations with Dr. Richard Tremblay, an addiction medicine specialist.

Page 123: "To overcome their own myopia . . .": Vaillant, *Natural History*, pages 362–63.

Pages 124 – 25: "Warning Symptoms of Alcoholism" and "Physical Signs of Alcoholism" (tables) from L. Ann Mueller, M.D., and Katherine Ketcham, *Recovering: How to Get and Stay Sober* (New York: Bantam, 1987), pages 50– 57. These tables were created by Dr. Mueller, an addiction medicine specialist who has worked as medical director in alcohol/drug rehabilitation centers for thirty years. Dr. Mueller is currently involved in prison medicine at Clarinda Correctional Facility in Clarinda, Iowa, where she notes that 85 percent of the inmates are affected by alcohol and/or other drugs.

Page 131: "Alcoholism Lab Profile" from Mueller and Ketcham, *Recovering*, pages 258–60; revised with Dr. Mueller's help, November 1999.

CHAPTER 9   INTERVENTION

Page 133: "Our family doctor was on vacation . . .": Robertson, *Getting Better*, page 208.

Page 134: "The truth dawned . . .": Robertson, *Getting Better*, pages 213–14.

Page 134: Physician interventions: See M. F. Fleming et al., "Brief physician advice for problem alcohol drinkers," *Journal of the American Medical Association* 277, 13 (April 21, 1997): 1039–45.

Page 135: "Chemical dependency forces . . ." in Daniel Angres, G. Douglas Talbott, and Kathy Bettinardi-Angres, *Healing the Healer: The Addicted Physician* (Madison, Conn.: Psychosocial Press, 1998), page 201.

Page 136: Help for the family: Alcoholism affects the entire family. Education, support, and treatment programs specifically designed for family members provide critical life skills for the alcoholic's spouse and children and also enhance the treatment effectiveness for the alcoholic/addict. For information on family issues, contact the National Association for Children of Alcoholics (NACoA), 11426 Rockville Pike, Suite 100, Rockville, Maryland 20852. Telephone: (888) 554-COAS or (301) 468-0895. Fax: (301) 468-0987. E-mail: nacoa@erols.com. Website: www.health.org/nacoa.

Many families find the following books and references helpful: *It Will Never Happen to Me* by Claudia Black, Ph.D. (Ballantine, 1991); *"It's Never Too Late to Have a Happy Childhood": Inspirations for Adult Children* by Claudia Black (Ballantine, 1989); *Codependent No More: How to Stop Controlling Others and Start Caring for Yourself* by Melody Beattie (Hazelden, 1996); *Another Chance: Hope and Health for the Alcoholic Family* by Sharon Wegscheider-Cruse (Science and Behavior Books, 1989); *Struggle for Intimacy* by Janet Woititz (Health Communications, 1986); and *Adult Children of Alcoholics* by Janet Woititz (Health Communications, 1990).

For health care providers we strongly recommend this special supplement to the journal *Pediatrics*: Hoover Adger, Donald Macdonald, and Sis Wenger, "Core competencies for involvement of health care providers in the care of children and adolescents in families affected by substance abuse: Report from a conference held at the White House, September 15, 1997, Washington, D.C." *Pediatrics* (May 1999), volume 103, number 5, pages 1083–1144.

Page 137: "The world looked unrelievedly grim . . . felt numb, anesthetized . . .": Robertson, *Getting Better*, page 211. "My gloom and despair lightened . . ." page 213.

Page 138: The intervention process is carefully and thoroughly outlined in Vernon Johnson, *I'll Quit Tomorrow* (New York: Harper & Row, 1973). We highly recommend this book for friends and family members who are considering an intervention. You might also look in your library for Katherine

Ketcham and Ginny Lyford Gustafson, *Living on the Edge: A Guide to Intervention for Families with Drug and Alcohol Problems* (New York: Bantam, 1989, out of print).

Page 139: "For some reason . . .": Betty Ford, *The Times of My Life* (New York: Harper and Row, 1978), pages 281–82.

Page 139: W. R. Miller and E. Kurtz, "Models of alcoholism used in treatment: Contrasting AA and other perspectives with which it is often confused," *Journal of Studies on Alcohol*, March 1994, pages 159–66.

Page 140: Quotes from *Alcoholics Anonymous* (New York: Alcoholics Anonymous World Services, Inc., 1976): "call on him" (p. 91); "continue to speak" (p. 92); "when dealing with" (p. 93); "outline the program" (p. 94); "if your talk" (p. 94); "never talk down" (p. 95); "burn the idea" (p. 98).

CHAPTER 10   TREATMENT

Pages 142–44: The Susan West story was compiled from numerous documents including police reports, newspaper articles, and verbatim transcripts.

Page 143: "It's too late for that . . ." (judge's remark): *The Seattle Post-Intelligencer*, August 6, 1997, page B2.

Pages 144–62: "They simply find drunkenness . . ." in William Madsen, *The American Alcoholic*, pages 19–20.

Page 149: We would like to thank researcher William White, author of *Slaying the Dragon*, for his careful reading of this section and his helpful suggestions for improvements.

Pages 149–51: The Minnesota Model: These basic tenets are outlined in William White, *Slaying the Dragon*, page 209, and reprinted with his permission. As White notes:

> An implicit element of the Minnesota Model is a treatment milieu within which the primary characteristic of the service relationship is one of respect. Jerry Spicer, who traced the emergence of these ideas in his book *The Minnesota Model*, rightly notes the importance of seeing this element within the historical context of the 1940s and 1950s. The Minnesota Model represented a radical shift from the prevailing view that alcoholism was both a hopeless condition and a reflection of moral inferiority. The Minnesota Model provided a marked contrast to the "degradation rituals" that alcoholics were subjected to within the psychiatric asylums of the mid–20th century and the mutual contempt that had long marked the relationship between alcoholics and professional helpers.

For anyone interested in the history of alcoholism treatment and recovery in the U.S., we strongly recommend White's thoroughly researched, beautifully written book *Slaying the Dragon*, the winner of the 1998 Terry McGovern Foundation Award for best nonfiction book.

Pages 151–62: The description of Sundown M's treatment program is compiled from facts gathered during an on-site visit in January 1999, and from personal interviews with executive director Scott Munson, director of treatment Chuck Buttrey, and youth director James Barth.

Coauthors William Asbury and Mel Schulstad visited the Betty Ford Center on February 1, 1999. Mark Greenberg, vice president for business development, took them on a three-hour tour of the facilities and introduced them to counselors, intervention specialists, medical director Gail Schultz, M.D., and John T. Schwarzlose, the treatment center's president and chief executive officer.

Page 153: Increase in methamphetamine-related emergency-room admissions: Cynthia Kuhn, Scott Swartzwelder, and Wilkie Wilson, *Buzzed: The Straight Facts about the Most Used and Abused Drugs from Alcohol to Ecstacy* (New York: W. W. Norton, 1998), page 199.

Page 158: Study of 65,000 patients and AA attendance: This study was published in 1994 by CATOR Independent Treatment Outcome Evaluation Service, St. Paul, MN., 1994.

Page 160: The American Society of Addiction Medicine (ASAM) publishes detailed *Patient Placement Criteria* to assist treatment providers in selecting the appropriate level of care for each individual. According to these criteria, intensive outpatient/partial hospitalization services involve "a structured day or evening program" that provides "comprehensive biopsychosocial assessments and individualized treatment plans [including] problem formulation, treatment goals and measurable treatment objectives." Intensive outpatient treatment programs "generally provide nine or more hours of structure programming per week, consisting of counseling and education," while partial hospitalization programs provide "20 hours or more of clinically intensive programming per week based on individual treatment plans" with "ready access to psychiatric, medical and laboratory services."

The *Patient Placement Criteria* (2nd edition) can be purchased through ASAM's website: www.asam.org.

CHAPTER 11   RELAPSE PREVENTION

Page 163: "Stopping isn't hard . . .": The interview with Robert Downey appears in *Playboy*, December 1997.

Page 163: "I have come to realize . . .": *Alcoholics Anonymous*, page 559.

Page 163: Quotations are from interviews we conducted with recovering alcoholics.

Page 164: "Researchers estimate that 75 to 95 percent . . ." in Terence T.

Gorski and Merlene Miller, *Staying Sober: A Guide for Relapse Prevention* (Independence, Mo.: Herald House, 1986), page 57.

Page 167: Cortical improvements: Physicians who work with alcoholics sometimes refer to this gradual improvement as a "restorative process" that takes place in the central nervous system with prolonged abstinence. Recent research indicates that nerve cells can regenerate; see, for example, R. Rosenblatt, "New hope, new dreams," *Time* 148, 10 (August 26, 1996).

Page 169: "There are three times . . .": Bob Welch is quoted in Wholey, *The Courage to Change*, page 91.

Page 170: "We must learn how . . .": Kirkpatrick, *Goodbye Hangovers, Hello Life*, page 172.

Page 171: "Life isn't fair . . .": William Goldman, *The Princess Bride* (New York: Harcourt Brace Jovanovich, 1973), page 308.

Pages 173–74: The studies on naltrexone include J. R. Volpicelli et al., "Naltrexone in the treatment of alcohol dependence," *Archives of General Psychiatry* 49 (1992): 876–80; S. O'Malley et al., "Naltrexone and coping skills therapy for alcohol dependence: A controlled study," *Archives of General Psychiatry* 49 (1992): 881–87; J. R. Volpicelli et al., "Naltrexone and alcohol dependence: Role of subject compliance," *Archives of General Psychiatry* 54 (1997): 737–42.

Page 173: Joseph Volpicelli is quoted in *The Bottom Line*, Winter 1998, pages 72–73.

Page 174: Avram Goldstein, *Addiction: From Biology to Drug Policy* (New York: W. H. Freeman and Co., 1994), page 142.

Pages 174–75: The studies on acamprosate include R. S. Croop et al., "The safety profile of naltrexone in the treatment of alcoholism: Results from a multicenter usage study," *Archives of General Psychiatry* 54 (1997): 1130–5; A. Whitworth et al., "Comparison of acamprosate and placebo in long-term treatment of alcohol dependence," *Lancet* 347 (1996): 1438–42; J. Besson et al., "Combined efficacy of acamprosate and disulfiram in the treatment of alcoholism: A controlled study," *Alcoholism: Clinical and Experimental Research* 22 (1998): 573–79.

Pages 176–77: The studies on SSRIs include M. O. Lawrin et al., "Identification and testing of new drugs for modulating alcohol consumption," *Psychopharmacology Bulletin* 22 (1986): 1020–5; C. A. Naranjo et al., "Modulation of ethanol intake by serotonin uptake inhibitors," *Journal of Clinical Psychiatry* 47 suppl. (1986): 16–22; C. A. Naranjo and E. M. Sellers, eds., *Research Advances in New Psychopharmacological Treatments for Alcoholism* (Amsterdam: Elsevier Science Publishers, 1985); Z. Amit et al., "Zimelidine: A review of its effects on ethanol consumption," *Neuroscience Biobehavioral Review* 8 (1984): 33–54; Schuckit, *Educating Yourself,* pages 390–93.

Page 176: "The antidepressant drugs . . .": Schuckit, *Educating Yourself,* page 392.

Page 177: Enoch Gordis, "An update on neuroscience research at the National Institute on Alcohol Abuse and Alcoholism," *Neuroscience Newsletter,* July/August 1997.

CHAPTER 12   PSYCHOLOGICAL COUNSELING

This chapter features several case histories drawn from Arthur P. Ciaramicoli's clinical psychology practice. All identifying details have been changed to protect patients' privacy.

For a detailed review of individual and group therapy approaches, see Arthur P. Ciaramicoli, *Treatment of Abuse and Addiction: A Holistic Approach* (Northvale, N.J.: Jason Aronson, 1997).

Pages 178–80: Grant and Xanax: Xanax is a central nervous system depressant similar to Valium; both Valium and Xanax are benzodiazepine drugs. In addition to the benzodiazepines, central nervous system depressants include alcohol, the barbiturates, the barbiturate-like hypnotics (Quaalude), and meprobomate (Miltown or Equanil). All of these drugs can produce physical dependence, cross-tolerance, severe depression, and anxiety during withdrawal; they can also be lethal in overdose or when used in combination.

Page 181: Daniel Goleman, *Emotional Intelligence: Why It Can Matter More than IQ* (New York: Bantam, 1995).

Page 181: "There is no evidence . . .": Schuckit, *Educating Yourself,* page 116.

Page 182: Michael's story is told in *Portraits of Recovery: Sixty Stories of Hope and Faith* (New York: Penguin Books, 1997), page 65.

Page 186: For additional studies on the efficacy of group psychotherapy, see J. S. Maxmen, "Group therapy as viewed by hospitalized patients," *Archives of General Psychiatry* 28 (1973): 404–8; J. S. Maxmen, "Helping patients survive theories: The practice of an educative model," *International Journal of Group Psychotherapy* 34 (1984): 355–68.

Pages 185–86: Groups in early recovery: See H. Getter et al., "Measuring treatment process in coping skills and interactional group therapies for alcoholism," *International Journal of Group Psychotherapy* 42, 3 (1992): 419–30.

Page 188: "Different alcoholics have different needs . . ." in Levin, *Introduction to Alcoholism Counseling,* page 241.

Page 190: "I was neurotic for years . . .": Anthony de Mello, *The Song of the Bird* (New York: Doubleday Image, 1982), pages 67–68.

CHAPTER 13   THE SPIRITUAL CONNECTION

The authors owe a great debt of gratitude to historian and author Ernest Kurtz for his ideas and inspiration. For readers interested in Alcoholics Anonymous, twelve-step programs, and the evolution of spirituality in this country, we highly recommend *The Collected Ernie Kurtz* (Wheeling, WV: The Bishop of Books, 1999), available from The Bishop of Books, Charlie Bishop Jr., 46 Eureka Ave., Wheeling, WV; tel. (304) 242-2937.

Page 191: "Sometimes people get . . .": Brussat and Brussat, *Spiritual Literacy*, page 29, who cite David Steindl-Rast and Sharon Lebell, *The Music of Silence* (New York: HarperCollins, 1995).

Page 191: "We must find some spiritual basis . . .": Bill Wilson, personal correspondence, 1961. For a related quote, see *Alcoholics Anonymous*, page 44.

Page 192: "[Rowland's] craving for alcohol . . ." The correspondence dated January 30, 1961, between Carl Jung and Bill Wilson has been reprinted several times in the *A. A. Grapevine*; see January 1963 and January 1968. As Kurtz and Ketcham explain in *The Spirituality of Imperfection*, page 113:

> In his letter Jung explained that he had not been able to reveal to Rowland H. the full extent of his belief that spirituality is essential to recovery, for he feared that any talk of spirituality would be misinterpreted. How could one formulate such an insight in a language that is not misunderstood in our days? Jung asked. But he took the risk in his letter to Wilson, explaining his intuition of the connection between spirituality and recovery.

Page 192: "Alcoholics begin to peel off layers . . .": G. Douglas Talbott, M.D., quoted in Wholey, *The Courage to Change*, page 21. Dr. Talbott is also featured in the recent nonfiction book *The Tennis Partner*, by Abraham Verghese (New York: HarperCollins, 1998).

Page 193: "Time before time . . .": This beloved story is told in many different versions. See Wilkie Au, *By Way of the Heart* (New York: Paulist Press, 1989), page 46, who cites Belden C. Lane, "Rabbinical stories: A primer on theological method," *Christian Century* 98, 41 (Dec. 16, 1981): 1307–8. Versions of the story also appear in William Bausch, *Storytelling: Imagination and Faith* (Mystic, CT.: Twenty-Third Publications, 1984), pages 68–69, and Anthony de Mello, *Taking Flight* (New York: Doubleday Image, 1990), page 60.

Page 194: "Staying is nowhere . . .": Rainer Maria Rilke's quote is translated by Margaret Miles, *Practicing Christianity* (New York: Crossroad, 1988), page 75; Miles cites the source as Rilke's *Denn Bleiben ist nirgends*.

Page 194: "The spiritual person . . .": Francis Baur, *Life in Abundance: A Contemporary Spirituality* (Mahwah, NJ: Paulist Press, 1983), page 112.

Page 195: William James on "the essential achievement of the will . . .": *Principles of Psychology* (Mineola, New York: Dover, 1950), vol. II, page 561. Italics and caps are in the original.

Page 195: "Every exit . . .": Tom Stoppard, quoted in *Little Zen Companion* (New York: Workman, 1994), page 75.

Page 197: The "drop the damn anvil" story has been told and retold in many different versions. See, for example, Goodwin, *Alcoholism: The Facts*, pages 153–54.

Page 197: The Serenity Prayer: According to Robert O'Brien and Morris Chafetz, M.D., in *The Encyclopedia of Alcoholism*, 2nd ed. (New York: Facts on File, Inc., 1999): "The prayer is based on one delivered by the Protestant theologian Reinhold Niebuhr at a church near Heath, Massachusetts, in the summer of 1934. Since then it has been widely quoted. It reads, 'O, God, give us the serenity to accept what cannot be changed, courage to change what should be changed, and the wisdom to distinguish one from the other.' "
The Serenity Prayer was adapted by AA in the early 1940s. According to *Pass It On: The Story of Bill Wilson and How the AA Message Reached the World*, (New York: AA World Services, 1984), the Serenity Prayer may date back to Boethius, a philosopher who lived about 500 A.D. and was martyred by the Christians, although it is usually credited to Niebuhr, who in turn credits Friedrich Oetinger, an 18th-century theologian.

Page 198: Father Joseph Martin is an internationally renowned speaker, author, and creator of educational films. His film *Chalk Talk on Alcoholism* (released September 1999) has become the principal educational vehicle on alcoholism for most branches of the federal government as well as schools, treatment centers, and state alcohol programs. Father Martin has produced twenty-five other films on various aspects of alcoholism and other drug addictions. His book *No Laughing Matter* (New York: Harper & Row, 1982) continues to be a bestseller. He is the president and cofounder of Ashley, Inc., a treatment center located in Havre de Grace, Maryland.

Page 198: The Mat-su story appears in many different versions; see, for example, Frederick Franck, "The mirrors of Mahayana," *Parabola* 11, 2 (May 1986): 66, and Anthony de Mello, *One Minute Wisdom* (New York: Doubleday, 1985), page 7.

Page 198: "With all the earnestness . . .": *Alcoholics Anonymous*, page 58.

Page 199: "Spirituality is one of those realities . . .": Ernest Kurtz and Katherine Ketcham, *The Spirituality of Imperfection* (New York: Bantam, 1992), page 143.

Page 199: "First of all . . .": Bill Wilson in *Alcoholics Anonymous*, page 62.

Page 199: "A long, long time ago . . .": This story is adapted from one told in Abbot Zenkei Shibayama, *A Flower Does Not Talk* (Rutland, Vt.: Charles E. Tuttle, 1993), pages 189–90.

Page 200: "Pulled around by Zen . . .": The Homeless Kodo was Roshi Uchiyama's teacher. See Kosho Ujiyama Roshi, *Approach to Zen* (Japan Publications, Inc., 1973).

Page 200: Derrick's story is told in Adam Gaynor, *Portraits of Recovery: Sixty Stories of Hope and Faith* (New York: Penguin Books, 1997), page 7.

Page 201: "The scary thing . . .": Laura Baugh, interviewed in *People*, November 16, 1998, pages 215–18.

Page 201: "The way our 'worthy' alcoholics . . .": *The Language of the Heart: Bill W's Grapevine Writings* (New York: The A.A. Grapevine, 1988), page 37.

Page 202: "Resentment is the 'number one' offender . . .": *Alcoholics Anonymous*, page 64.

Pages 202–3: Susan Powter's AA story is told in *Staying Sober* (New York: Simon & Schuster, 1997), pages 91–94.

Page 203: "I pushed a drink . . .": *Alcoholics Anonymous*, page 9.

Page 204: "I didn't like the idea . . .": *Alcoholics Anonymous*, page 12.

Page 205: "The spiritual life is not a theory . . .": *Alcoholics Anonymous*, page 83.

Page 205: "It's seeing a mystical power for good . . .": *Came to Believe: The Spiritual Adventures of A.A. as Experienced by Individual Members* (New York: Alcoholics Anonymous World Services, Inc., 1973), pages 5–6. The quotation is adapted from the original version, which reads: "The single thing that is spirituality cannot be given to a fellowman by word of mouth. If every man is to have it, then every man must earn it, in his own way, by his own hand, stamped by the seal of himself, in his own individual right."

CHAPTER 14 · A DIET FOR SOBRIETY

Page 207: Candace Pert quotation is taken from her foreword to Kathleen DesMaisons, *Potatoes Not Prozac* (New York: Simon & Schuster, 1998), page 12.

Pages 207–8: "Frank had been sober . . ." This story is adapted from a story told in Katherine Ketcham and L. Ann Mueller, M.D., *Eating Right to Live Sober* (New York: Signet, 1983), pages 61–63. "Frank" was Dr. Mueller's patient, and this story is adapted with her permission.

Page 209: "How Alcohol Works Against Nutrition" (figure): This figure first appeared in Ketcham and Mueller, *Eating Right to Live Sober*, pages 68–69.

Page 212: "Body Systems Affected by Alcohol-Induced Nutritional Disorders": This table first appeared in Ketcham and Mueller, *Eating Right to Live Sober*, page 77.

Page 213: "All alcoholics are malnourished . . .": Beasley, *How to Defeat Alcoholism*, page 197.

Page 214: Healthy diet guidelines: *The University of California at Berkeley Wellness Encyclopedia* (New York: Houghton Mifflin), 1995.

Page 217: "The Good and Bad Carbohydrates" (box): This table first appeared in Ketcham and Mueller, *Eating Right to Live Sober*, page 165.

Page 218: Hypoglycemic symptoms: This list is adapted from symptom lists in Paavo Airola, Ph.D., *Hypoglycemia: A Better Approach* (Phoenix, Ariz.: Health Plus Publishers, 1977). See also Ketcham and Mueller, *Eating Right to Live Sober*, chapter 4.

Page 219: Cereals containing fiber, fat, and sugar: "Separating the wheat from the chaff," *Consumer Reports* 64, 10 (October 1999): 30–33.

Page 222: "Sugar is easily . . .": Elson Haas, M.D., *Staying Healthy with Nutrition: The Complete Guide to Diet and Nutritional Medicine* (Berkeley, Calif.: Celestial Arts, 1992), page 932. We heartily recommend this book for anyone interested in learning more about nutrition.

Page 222: 156 pounds of sugar every year: This statistic is cited in Jane E. Brody, "Increasingly, America's sweet tooth is tied to sour health," *New York Times*, September 21, 1999, Personal Health section. "That we load up with more sugar than ever is unquestionable—156 pounds of added sugars per person last year, up from 144 pounds in 1994, which in turn was up from 127 pounds in 1986," Brody writes. "The average American now consumes more than 20 teaspoons of added sugars a day, twice the amount recommended by health experts worldwide."
In her foreword to DesMaisons, *Potatoes Not Prozac*, page 11, researcher Candace B. Pert, Ph.D., comments: "If sugar were to be put on the market for the first time today, it would probably be difficult to get it past the FDA."

Page 223: "Aspartame is made from . . .": DesMaisons, *Potatoes Not Prozac*, page 123.

Page 224: Caffeine levels in coffee, tea, soda pop: See DesMaisons, *Potatoes Not Prozac*, page 170.

Page 225: Contaminated drinking water: Ralph Nader statistic is cited in Debra Lynn Dadd, *Nontoxic, Natural and Earthwise* (New York: Tarcher/

Putnam, 1990), page 41. Also see Haas, *Staying Healthy with Nutrition*, pages 15–29, 422–30.

Page 226: Clean and "spotty" drinking water: See "Bottled-Water Controversy Bubbles Up," *USA Today*, March 31, 1999, page 1D.

Page 227: Elson Haas's education in nutrition: Haas, *Staying Healthy with Nutrition*, page 4.

Page 228: "Trying to be a health saint . . .": Levin, *Recovery from Alcoholism*, page 171.

CHAPTER 15   ALTERNATIVE THERAPIES: EXERCISE, ACUPUNCTURE, VITAMINS, HERBS, AND AMINO ACIDS

Page 229: "My belief . . .": Andrew Weil, *Spontaneous Healing* (New York: Knopf, 1995), page 109.

Page 230: "When you venture out . . .": Weil, *Spontaneous Healing*, page 238.

Page 231: Quitting exercise: B. Huebner, "Burning cash not calories," *Boston Globe*, May 27, pages 31–32.

Page 231: The Harvard Alumni Study: I-Min Lee et al., "Body weight and mortality," *Journal of the American Medical Association* 270, 23 (Dec. 15, 1993): 2823–8; on the Boston Nurses' Study, see J. Manson et al., "Body weight and mortality among women," *New England Journal of Medicine* 333, 11 (Sept. 14, 1995): 677–85.

Page 232: Running no more than fifteen miles a week: Kenneth Cooper, *Antioxidant Revolution* (Nashville: Thomas Nelson, 1994).

Page 233: Laughter as "internal exercise": Norman Cousins, *Anatomy of an Illness* (New York: Bantam, 1981), pages 145–48.

Page 233: Relaxation techniques: Herbert Benson, *Relaxation Response* (New York: Morrow, 1975); Jon Kabat-Zinn, *Wherever You Go There You Are: Mindfulness Meditation in Everyday Life* (New York: Hyperion, 1994).

Page 233: Research on loneliness: The abundant research on the connection between loneliness and disease is covered in detail in Dean Ornish, *Love and Survival: The Scientific Basis for the Healing Power of Intimacy* (New York: HarperCollins, 1998). See especially pages 23–72.

Pages 234–36: The section on acupuncture was written with the help of Jay Renaud. Resources include M. Bullock et al., "Controlled trial of acupuncture for severe recidivist alcoholism," *Lancet*, June 24, 1989, pages 1435–9; H. Lao, "A retrospective study on the use of acupuncture for the prevention of alcoholic recidivism," *American Journal of Acupuncture* 23, 1 (1995): 29–33; A. Margolin et al., "Investigating alternative medicine therapies in randomized controlled trials," *Journal of the American Medical Association* 280, 18 (1998): 1628–30; A. T. McLellan et al., "Acupuncture treatment for drug abuse: A technical review," *Journal of Substance Abuse Treatment* 10 (1993): 569–76; A. M. Washburn et al., "Acupuncture heroin detoxification: A single-blind clinical trial," *Journal of Substance Abuse Treatment* 10 (1993): 345–51; D. R. Wesson, "Detoxification from alcohol and other drugs," Treatment Improvement Protocol, Series 19, U.S. Dept. of Health and Human Services #SMA 95-3046, 1995; National Institutes of Health, "Acupuncture," *NIH Consensus Statement* 15, 5 (1997); M. Smith, "Acupuncture in addiction treatment," *Encyclopedia Britannica 1998, Medical and Health Annual,* pages 350–55. For more information on acupuncture and addiction, contact the National Acupuncture Detoxification Association Literature Clearinghouse, PO Box 1927, Vancouver, WA 98668-1927; tel. (360) 254-0186.

Page 234: We are grateful to Terry Oleson, author and illustrator of *Auriculotherapy Manual: Chinese and Western Systems of Ear Acupuncture,* for his permission to use his illustration of the five ear points commonly used in auricular therapy. Oleson's book is available from Health Care Alternatives in Los Angeles, (323) 656-2084. Web site address: www.auriculotherapy.com.

Pages 237–40: Vitamin and mineral supplements: This section was compiled from several sources, specifically Ketcham and Mueller, *Eating Right to Live Sober;* Haas, *Staying Healthy with Nutrition;* Ciaramicoli, *Treatment of Abuse and Addiction;* Andrew Weil, M.D., *Spontaneous Healing: How to Discover and Enhance Your Body's Natural Ability to Maintain and Heal Itself* (New York: Ballantine, 1996); and Larson, *Seven Weeks to Sobriety.*

Pages 241–43: Herbal Remedies: This section was compiled with the help of Jason Elias, M.A., L.Ac. Jason is a licensed acupuncturist, trained practitioner of Western and Chinese herbal medicine, and author of several books, including *The A to Z Guide to Healing Herbal Remedies* (New York: Dell, 1995). He is a founder of Integral Health Associates in New Paltz, New York.

PART III   THE FUTURE

The research and statistics in Chapters 16 and 17 have been culled from several sources. We relied specifically on three major information sources:

The Bottom Line on Alcohol in Society, a quarterly publication of the Alcohol Research Information Service (ARIS), 1106 East Oakland Avenue, Lansing, MI 48906. ARIS's stated purpose is "to collect, correlate and disseminate information regarding alcohol and alcoholic products, their manufacture, sale and use for beverage, industrial, or other purposes." Robert L. Hammond is the editor of

The Bottom Line and other ARIS publications, including *The Monday Morning Report*, which is published 24 times a year. Tel. (517) 485-9900, fax (517) 485-1928.

The Center for Science in the Public Interest (CSPI), 1875 Connecticut Avenue, NW, Washington, D.C. 20009. CSPI's mission is to identify health problems in the U.S. and to alert the public to such problems. For the purposes of this book we consulted George Hacker, who heads CSPI's Alcohol Policies Project. That project played a leading role in the enactment of the federal law which requires warning labels on all alcoholic beverage containers. E-mail: cspi@essential.org; Web site: www.cspinet.org.

The Marin Institute for the Prevention of Alcohol and Other Drug Problems, 24 Belvedere Street, San Rafael, CA 94901. We depended on the considerable research and information services of the Marin Institute, which tracks the political, marketing, and promotional activities of the liquor industry. We are particularly indebted to Hilary Abramson, the institute's media specialist, and Eris Weaver, head librarian, for their assistance. Tel. (415) 456-5692, fax (415) 456-0491; library E-mail: erisw@marininstitute.org; website: www.marininstitute.org.

ARIS, CSPI, and the Marin Institute are all privately supported, non-governmental organizations.

CHAPTER 16   THE BOOZE MERCHANTS

Page 249: "If the liquor industry..." William Bennett quoted in Michael Massing, "Strong stuff," *The New York Times Magazine*, March 22, 1998, page 34ff.

Page 249: "Who's brave enough..." Susan Powter, *Sober ... and Staying That Way* (New York: Simon & Schuster, 1997), page 87.

Page 250: "Alcohol kills 100,000 people every year...": *U.S. Department of Health and Human Resources* report, January 1995. Statistics cited on the NCADD Web site: www.ncadd.org/problems.html.

Pages 251–52: "The Beer Institute..." These statistics about budgets and lobbying efforts are reported in Massing, "Strong stuff," *The New York Times Magazine*, March 22, 1998, pages 36–46.

Page 252: "The booze merchants pay their friends well..." in "Liquor flows again on Capitol Hill," *The Bottom Line* 20, 1 (Spring 1999): 11–12.

Page 253: PAC contributions to senators and representatives are posted and periodically updated on the Center for Responsive Politics (CRP) Web site: www.opensecrets.org.

Page 254: Reverend Brown story is reported in *The Bottom Line* 19, 2 (Summer 1998): 1.

Pages 254–55: Taxes on alcohol: Statistics on these pages are cited in Frank J. Chaloupka, "The effects of price on alcohol consumption," a report given at the Alcohol Policy XI Conference held at the American Medical Association in Chicago, May 10–13, 1998. This report is reprinted in *The Bottom Line* 19, 2 (Summer 1998): 111–36. See also Peter Hernon and Terry Ganey, *Under the Influence: The Unauthorized Story of the Anheuser-Busch Dynasty* (New York: Avon, 1991), pages 396–98.

Page 255: "Can the Beer Tax" advertising blitz is covered in Hernon and Ganey, *Under the Influence*, pages 396–97.

Page 255: Taxes during the Clinton years: See Associated Press story, "Book reveals lawmakers' 'career patrons,' " *The Daily Olympian*, September 10, 1993, page A3. The book referred to in the article is Charles Lewis, *The Buying of the Congress* (Washington, D.C.: Center for Public Integrity, 1998). See also William F. Asbury, "The Government's Wrong War," *Professional Counselor*, December 1994, pages 28–32.

Pages 256–58: Targeting Youth section: Statistics are reported in *The Bottom Line* 17, 2 (Summer 1996). Center on Alcohol Advertising study was presented by researcher Laurie Lieber at a press conference prior to the April 24, 1996, Anheuser-Busch annual stockholder meeting (see *The Bottom Line*, pages 7–8).

Beer statistics on page 257 appear in *The Bottom Line* 19, 1 (Spring 1998): 20–22; *The Bottom Line* 18, 1 (Spring 1997): 7–8; and *The Bottom Line* 20, 1 (Spring 1999): 19, 34.

Page 257: Drinkers under 21: According to the 1998 National Household Survey on Drug Abuse (NHSDA) published by the National Institute on Drug Abuse, there were 10.5 million drinkers between the ages of 12 and 20 in 1998 (up from 9.5 million in the 1996 survey). Of these, 5.1 million are listed as binge drinkers (up from 4.4 million in 1996), while 2.3 million (up from 1.9 million in 1996) are also considered heavy drinkers.
Binge drinkers, according to the survey, consume five or more drinks in a row on a single occasion, while heavy drinkers consume five or more drinks on the same occasion on at least five different days.
See also an excerpt of L. D. Eigen and J. Noble, "The extent of underage drinking in the United States," *The Bottom Line* 19, 1 (Spring 1998): 42–45. The full paper was originally published in *Prevention File*, available from Lewis Eigen, 11426 Rockville Pike, Suite 100, Rockville, MD 20852.

Pages 257–58: Cub Scouts pamphlet: "Brewers frustrated over 'misinformation' in Cub Scout handbooks," *The Bottom Line* 18, 1 (Spring 1997): 34–35.

Page 258: Peter Coors was quoted in *Beverage World*, October 1997, page 14, and in *USA Today*, September 10, 1997, page 4B.

Pages 258–59: U.S. armed forces and beer: Eric Schmitt, "Army cuts its beer ration and brewers are furious," *The New York Times*, July 5, 1997, page 1.

Pages 259–60: "Flying high" stories are reported in *The Bottom Line* 18, 3 (Fall 1997): 73–77. The Reverend Schuller story is reported in *The Bottom Line* 20, 1 (Spring 1999): 39.

Page 260: Thomas Greenfield statistics are reported in *The Bottom Line* 20, 1 (Spring 1999): 79–81.

Pages 260–61: Penny Norton and CSAP story reported in *The Bottom Line* 18, 1 (Spring 1997): 13–28 and *The Bottom Line* 19, 1 (Spring 1998): 7–16.

Pages 261–62: CSPI report: See *The Bottom Line* 18, 1 (Spring 1997): 37–39.

Pages 262–63: Wine Labels: George Hacker, director of the Alcohol Policies Project at the Center for Science in the Public Interest, gave a presentation on the new wine labels at the Alcohol Policy XI conference in May 1999; his talk is discussed in *The Bottom Line* 19, 2 (Summer 1998): 180–83.

This section also draws from research presented in *ASAM News* 14, 2 (March–April 1999) and *ASAM News* 14, 3 (May–June 1999) (available on ASAM's website: www.asam.org). See also *Booze News*, a publication of the Center for Science in the Public Interest, 10, 1 (August 1998): 2; and *Monday Morning Report*, published by the Alcohol Research Information Service, November 9, 1998.

Page 263: Alcohol and breast cancer: see references for page 36.

Page 263: "Generally I do not favor . . ." Strom Thurmond is quoted in D. Stout, "Bill would bar health referral on wine label," *The New York Times*, February 22, 1999.

CHAPTER 17   A RIVER RUNS THROUGH US

Page 268: "We are careful never to show intolerance . . .": *Alcoholics Anonymous* (New York: AA World Services, Inc., 1976), page 103. AA's Twelve Traditions appear on page 564.

Page 269: Jeremy Jones: This is a true story taken from the authors' experience. Names and identifying details have been changed.

Page 269: The DARE Program: A recent study of the long-term usefulness of DARE (Drug Abuse Resistance Education) raises questions about its effectiveness and popularity. "Our results are consistent in documenting the absence of beneficial effects associated with the DARE program," concluded the study, which was funded by the National Institutes of Health and conducted by a team of researchers at the University of Kentucky. See D. R. Lynam et al., *Journal of Consulting and Clinical Psychology* (September 1999).

Page 271: People who begin drinking before age fifteen: B. Grant and D. Dawson, "Age at onset of alcohol use and its association with DSM-IV alcohol-abuse and dependence: Results from the National Longitudinal Alcohol Epidemiologic Survey," *Journal of Substance Abuse* 9 (1997): 103–10.

See also: B. Grant and D. Dawson, "Age at onset of drug use and its association with DSM-IV drug abuse and dependence: Results from the National Longitudinal Alcohol Epidemiologic Survey," *Journal of Substance Abuse* 10 (1998): 163–73.

Page 272: Three out of four college students complain: 1995 study "Binge drinking on American college campuses," by the Harvard University School of Public Health, Henry Wechsler, Ph.D, principal investigator, made possible by a grant from the Robert Wood Johnson Foundation, published in *Journal of the American Medical Association*, December 7, 1994. This study was updated four years later; see H. Wechsler, "Getting serious about eradicating binge drinking," *The Chronicle of Higher Education* 45, 13 (November 20, 1998): B4–B5.

Page 272: *Sports Illustrated* survey was reported in *The Bottom Line*.

Page 272: Beer is a drug, too. Statistics from *The Bottom Line* 19, 1 (Spring 1998): 7–8; and *The Bottom Line* 19, 2 (Summer 1998): 95.

Page 273: "We are not a social services agency. . ." August Busch III is quoted in *The Bottom Line* 19, 1 (Spring 1998): 22. This statement was made at the 1997 Anheuser-Busch shareholder meeting.

Page 273: Kids need to be taught: According to the Center for Substance Abuse Protection (CSAP) 1996 news release, 2.6 million teenagers don't know that a person can die from an alcohol overdose.

Page 273: Dr. Alpha Estes Brown described his work in Washington, D.C., at the Alcohol Policy XI Conference in Chicago, Illinois, in May 1998. His talk is partially reprinted in *The Bottom Line* 19, 2 (Summer 1998): 205–7.

Page 274: *The Truth About Drinking* video is available from Aims Multimedia, (800) 367-2467.

Page 276: Drinking and driving statistics: These statistics are from the MADD Web site: www.madd.org. MADD publishes up-to-date statistics from the National Highway Traffic Safety Administration (NHTSA) and other agencies.

Page 277: Representative Kelli Linville: This story was reported in Bob

Parlow, "Lawmaker arrested on DWI charge," *The Daily Olympian*, March 20, 1999, page 1; and "Lawmaker in court on DWI charges," *The Daily Olympian*, March 23, 1999, page C-1. A sidebar on page 1 of the March 20, 1999, edition of *The Daily Olympian* reports that the Eagle Forum, a conservative political organization in Linville's hometown of Bellingham, Washington, called for her resignation.

Page 277: "In late 1998 . . . Mayor Rudolph Giuliani . . ." "Police to seize cars of people accused of drunken driving," *The New York Times*, February 23, 1999, page 1.

Page 278: Howardsville, Virginia, story reported in *The Bottom Line* 20, 1 (Spring 1999): 38.

Page 278: Boston judge: Associated Press report on District Judge Daniel Winslow appeared in *The Daily Olympian*, June 12, 1998, page A-10.

Page 278: Statistics about drinking and driving penalties in other countries are often exaggerated in reports widely circulated among teachers, legislators, and law enforcement officials. In a 1999 handout offered to students at Walla Walla High School in Walla Walla, Washington, for example, the penalty in Libya is listed as public flogging and/or loss of limb; in Bulgaria a second conviction is said to result in execution and in El Salvador the first offense is death by firing squad. As Bob Hammond reports in *The Bottom Line* 12, 2 (Summer 1991): 62–67, these reports have been exaggerated to the point that they have become myths. A spokesperson for the Salvadorian Embassy in Washington, D.C., told Hammond that the most severe penalty for drinking and driving in that country is loss of driving privileges for a year.

Page 279: States with 0.08 BAC: confirmed in October 1999 in interview with the Insurance Institute for Highway Safety.

Page 279: Statistics on drinking and driving are from MADD Web site. According to the NHTSA Traffic Safety Facts 1996, drivers ages 21–24 had the highest intoxication rates (27 percent) for fatal crashes in 1996, the most recent year for which statistics are available.

Pages 280–82: Harborview Medical Center study: This groundbreaking research appears in several journal articles. See L. M. Gentiello et al., "Alcohol interventions in trauma centers: Current practice and future directions," *Journal of the American Medical Association* 274 (1995): 1043–8; J. G. Gurney et al., "The effects of alcohol intoxication on the initial treatment and hospital course of patients with acute brain injury," *Journal of Trauma* 33, 5 (1992): 709–13; G. J. Jurkovich et al., "The effect of acute alcohol intoxication and chronic alcohol abuse on outcome from trauma," *Journal of the American Medical Association* 270, 1 (1993): 51–56; A. L. Kellerman et al., "Utilization and yield of drug screening in the emergency department," *American Journal of Emergency*

Medicine 6 (1988): 14–20; O. Nilssen et al., "The 'WAM' score: Sensitivity and specificity of a user-friendly biological screening test for alcohol problems in trauma patients," *Addiction* 91, 2 (February 1996): 255–62; F. P. Rivara et al., "A descriptive study of trauma, alcohol and alcoholism in young adults," *Journal of Adolescent Health* 13 (1992): 663–67.

See also a related article about alcohol and trauma by Harborview's F. P. Rivara, "Alcohol and illicit drug abuse and the risk of violent death in the home," *Journal of the American Medical Association* 278 (1997): 569–75; and F. P. Rivara et al., "The magnitude of acute and chronic alcohol abuse in trauma patients," *Archives of Surgery* 128 (August 1993): 907–13.

Pages 282–83: These stories were generously offered to us by Harborview Medical Center researcher and practitioner Chris Dunn, Ph.D.

Page 284: 1998 government study: H. Harwood et al., "The economic costs of alcohol and drug abuse in the U.S., 1992," Bethesda, Md.: DHHS, NIH, NIH Publication No. 98-4327 (September 1998).

Page 284: "An estimated 8 percent . . .": National Institute on Drug Abuse, "National household survey on drug abuse: Main findings, 1994," September 1996, page 100.

Page 284: "47 percent of industrial accidents and 40 percent of work site fatalities . . .": M. Bernstein and J. J. Mahoney, "Management perspectives on alcoholism: The employer's stake in alcoholism treatment," *Occupational Medicine* 4, 2 (1989): 223–32; for more information, see NCADD's "Alcohol and other drugs in the workplace" facts, available on the NCADD Web site: www.ncadd.org.

Page 284: The 1997 study sponsored by the NIAAA and Robert Wood Johnson Foundation is described in *The Bottom Line* 20, 1 (Spring 1998): 55–59.

Page 284: "Treatment is expensive . . .": William C. Symonds, "Is business bungling its battle with booze?" *Business Week*, March 25, 1991, page 76.

Page 285: A. Foster Higgins report: This statistic was supplied by Henry Govert, who has twenty-five years' experience developing and administering EAPs. Govert currently manages the Washington State Drug-Free Workplace Discount Program, which provides financial incentives to employers who implement comprehensive treatment plans and offer employee rehabilitation through an approved EAP. In several interviews, Govert offered helpful comments and insights on the Treatment in the Workplace section of this chapter. We are also indebted to Jay Lewis for his insights and suggestions regarding EAPs. The editor and publisher of the highly respected *The Alcoholism Report* for twenty years, Jay served as director of public policy for the NCADD in 1983, and he was a member of President Reagan's National Commission on

Alcoholism and the board of directors of Rutgers University's *Journal of Alcohol Studies*.

Page 286: Cities and states that imposed taxes to pay for treatment: reported in "Lessons Learned" seminar report 1998, pages 6–7. The Lessons Learned series is published by the nonprofit organization Join Together: A National Resource for Communities Fighting Substance Abuse and Gun Violence, 441 Stuart Street, 7th Floor, Boston, MA 02116, (617) 437-1500; Email: info@jointogether.org; website: www.jointogether.org.

Page 287: Betty Ford tells her story in *The Times of My Life*, (New York: Harper & Row, 1978).

Pages 287–90: Treatment in the workplace: Once again we gratefully acknowledge the assistance of EAP specialist Henry Govert and alcoholism expert Jay Lewis in researching and writing this section.
See also Royce and Scratchley, *Alcoholism and Other Drug Problems*, chapter 13, pages 209–21.

Page 288: Jay Lewis offers this analysis of the change in terminology from OAP to EAP in a September 1999 letter to the authors:

> The EAP terminology was first used in the 1970s and was an outgrowth of an effort by NIAAA to foster what was originally called troubled employee programs. Willard Foster, Special Assistant to NIAAA Director Morris Chafetz, was the foremost advocate of this approach, called the "broad brush." The EAP terminology was vigorously opposed by the National Council on Alcoholism and the AFL-CIO in the 1970s when the term Occupational Alcoholism Program still prevailed.

Pages 288–89: These EAP examples were supplied by Henry Govert and from statistics cited in Royce and Scratchley, *Alcoholism and Other Problems*, pages 209–21.

Page 289: Jay Lewis offers this perspective on EAPs in the 1970s:

> The big growth in programs occurred in the 1970s, under impetus of NIAAA funding. The Conference Board, the prestigious business research organization, in a study on Occupational Alcoholism released in 1978, reported a "phenomenal" increase in OAPs in major U.S. corporations in the 1970s. Based on a survey of 3,600 large domestic corporations, 340 said they had OAPs. In 1970, when its last report on the subject was made, the Conference Board said only 15 percent of these OAPs were in existence. The Conference Board study was released at the Association of Labor-Management Administrators and Consultants on Alcoholism (ALMACA) annual meeting in San Francisco, Oct. 3–6, 1978. ALMACA did not change its name to Employee Assistance Program Association until the 1980s.

Page 290: "According to a 1998 report . . .": Lawrence A. Greenfield, "Alcohol and crime: An analysis of national data on the prevalence of alcohol involvement in crime," U.S. Department of Justice, Bureau of Justice Statistics, 1998, page v.

Page 290: "Alcohol and crime are joined at the hip...": S. Belenko, "Substance Abuse and America's prison population," January 1998. Available for $25 from the National Center on Addiction and Substance Abuse (CASA) at Columbia University, 152 West 57th Street, 12th floor, New York, NY 10019-3310, tel. (212) 841-5200; or visit the CASA website at www.casacolumbia.org.

Page 291: More Americans in prison: This statistic is cited in various reports. *On the Inside*, an hour-long feature on prisons, which aired on October 3, 1999, on The Discovery Channel, reported: "There are two million Americans behind bars, more than in any other nation. California has more inmates behind bars than all the nations of Europe combined."

CHAPTER 18   WALKING THE WALK

Page 293: "We are here to do . . ." Rabbi Ben Hei Hei is quoted in Frederic and Mary Ann Brussat, *Spiritual Literacy*, page 353. The Brussats list the source as Rabbi Rami M. Shapiro, *Wisdom of the Jewish Sages* (New York: Bell Tower, 1995). No page number is cited.

Page 294: "I wish I could tell her . . .": McGovern, *Terry*, pages 18–19.

Page 295: "I have a very caring heart . . .": McGovern, *Terry*, pages 171–72.

Page 296: "As she walked through the streets . . .": This favorite story is often told; see, for example, Frederic and Mary Ann Brussat, *Spiritual Literacy: Reading the Sacred in Everyday Life* (New York: Scribner, 1996), page 327.

RESOURCES

WEBSITES

National Institute on Alcohol Abuse and Alcoholism (NIAAA)
www.niaaa.nih.gov

NIAAA supports and conducts biomedical and behavioral research on the causes, consequences, treatment, and prevention of alcoholism and alcohol-related problems. It is one of eighteen federal institutes that comprise the National Institutes of Health under the Department of Health and Human Services in Washington, D.C.

The National Council on Alcohol and Drug Dependence (NCADD)
www.ncadd.org

Founded in 1944, NCADD is a voluntary, nonprofit health organization with a network of affiliates that provide education, information, and assistance in the fight against alcoholism and other addictions.

The National Center on Addiction and Substance Abuse at Columbia University (CASA)
www.casacolumbia.org

A think tank and action organization headed by former Health, Education, and Welfare Secretary Joseph AÏ. Califano Jr., CASA is affiliated with Columbia University and located on its campus. The center's mission statement explains that CASA engages all academic disciplines to study and prepare reports on every form of substance abuse in American society.

The National Clearinghouse for Alcohol and Drug Information
www.health.org

The Clearinghouse is the information service for the Center for Substance Abuse Prevention in the Department of Health and Human Services. The world's largest resource for current information and materials concerning substance abuse, the Clearinghouse distributes free or at low cost fact sheets, brochures, pamphlets, posters, and videotapes.

The American Society of Addiction Medicine (ASAM)
www.asam.org

The American Society of Addiction Medicine, the addiction specialty arm of the American Medical Association, offers a "doctor finder" on its Web page. On the left side of the screen click on "AMA Physician Select." When the next screen appears, click on "search by name or medical specialty." You will then be asked to accept the conditions; click "accept." On the next screen click on "medical specialty" and then "search for an expanded list of medical specialties." Fill in your state, city, and zip code, and then click on the circle next to "addiction medicine."

The search results will give you a list of physicians in your city who practice addiction medicine. Click on the specific doctor's name and you will be given details about the doctor including gender, medical school and year of graduation, residency training, board certification, primary practice specialty, office location, and phone number.

The Center for Science in the Public Interest (CSPI)
www.cspinet.org

CSPI is a nonprofit educational and advocacy organization headquartered in Washington, D.C. Its stated purpose is "to reduce the carnage caused by alcoholic beverages." It is also active in promoting the safety and nutritional quality of American food supplies.

Mothers Against Drunk Driving (MADD)
www.madd.org

MADD is a volunteer advocacy and education organization headquartered in Irving, Texas. It was established to stop drunk driving, support the victims of drunk drivers, and prevent underage drinking.

Students Against Destructive Decisions (SADD)
www.saddonline.com

Headquartered in Marlborough, Massachusetts, SADD, which originally stood for Students Against Drunk Driving, limits its activities and membership to students. It seeks to teach students about the hazards of drunk driving through its local chapters.

Join Together Online (JTO)
www.jointogether.org

Join Together is a project of the Boston University School of Public Health, a national resource for communities working to reduce substance abuse and gun violence. Join Together has volunteer, community-based organizations throughout the United States.

The Marin Institute
www.marininstitute.org

The Marin Institute in San Rafael, California, was established to prevent alcohol and other drug problems. It serves as a watchdog of the alcoholic beverage industry, particularly of the industry's sales and marketing practices, and of government action or inaction as it relates to the alcoholic beverage makers and distributors. The institute has a large library with a research database on alcohol policy.

The Alcohol and Drug Abuse Institute at the University of Washington (ADAI)
www.depts.washington.edu/adai

Established in 1973, ADAI is an interdisciplinary research organization in Seattle, Washington. ADAI distributes research on alcohol and drug abuse; much of this research is done by University of Washington faculty and UW Medical School professors. ADAI has a large library open to the public.

Alcohol Research Group (ARG)
www.arg.org

ARG collects and disseminates information on national alcohol problems. The group's focus is solely on alcohol and not other drugs. It has available a large collection of studies and reports.

Alcohol Research Center (Medical University of South Carolina)
www.musc.edu/arc

The Alcohol Research Center, which was founded in the early 1970s, is part of the medical school of the University of South Carolina. Its primary mission is to conduct research on pharmacotherapy and dual diagnosis (alcoholism and comorbid psychiatric disorders). Funds to support the center come from the National Institute on Alcohol Abuse and Alcoholism (NIAAA), the National Institute on Drug Abuse (NIDA), and the University of South Carolina.

The Betty Ford Center
www.bettyfordcenter.org

The Betty Ford Center, in Rancho Mirage, California, is one of the best known treatment centers for alcoholism and other drug addictions. Its Web site includes information about admission for treatment at the center and extensive data on alcoholism and treatment techniques.

Alcoholics Anonymous (AA)
www.alcoholics-anonymous.org

The AA Web site from AA World Services, New York, has a broad offering of information about the pioneer 12-step self-help program for alcoholics. It describes AA and offers information about available reading materials.

Hazelden Foundation
www.hazelden.org

The Hazelden organization is one of the oldest treatment and alcohol information centers in the United States. It was founded fifty years ago in Center City, Minnesota. The website describes Hazelden's treatment program and offers information about materials on alcoholism and other drug addictions that are available from Hazelden's extensive catalogue of books, pamphlets, and audio- and videotapes.

National Association for Children of Alcoholics (NACoA)
www.health.org/nacoa

NACoA is a national nonprofit voluntary membership and affiliate organization headquartered in Rockville, Maryland, and dedicated to helping the more than 28 million people in this country whose lives have been affected by family alcohol addiction, eleven million of whom are under the age of eighteen. "If we are ever to break the intergenerational transmission of alcoholism, we must come to terms with the impact on the children who live in the addicted home environment during their critical developmental years," writes NACoA executive director Sis Wenger.

In November, 1999, a group of consulting researchers and program experts drafted a list of program criteria for services to children of addicted parents. Titled "Meeting Children's Needs," these services include the following:

Services to Adult Clients in Treatment: Teach clients about family addiction and recovery; emphasize the fact that children of alcoholics are at greater risk for addiction, mental health, and behavioral problems; discuss how to find and connect with specific age-appropriate services for children; improve parenting skills.

Services to the Children of Clients in Treatment: Provide information about addiction, treatment programs, community-based supports, and other resources; reassure children that they are not alone, the disease is not their fault, they deserve help, and with appropriate help they will feel better; teach children problem-solving skills, safety plans, communication skills, relationship, and intrapersonal skills.

Program Design Criteria: Develop a family plan with various options for family members; develop and communicate clear objectives for children's program; provide support for kinship and foster care; provide special group services for sexually abused children; address personnel issues including staff training and interpersonal skills; provide community collaboration, referrals, and outreach services.

Note: Whether services for children of alcoholics are part of a treatment program or school-based student assistance program, developmentally appropriate educational support groups are the preferred method of delivering information, messages, and skills because:

- Children learn that they are not alone.

- Group work provides opportunities for group validation.

- Group work allows children to try out new approaches to old problems.

- Group work increases the likelihood of breaking denial.

- Children can experience healthy social interactions.

- Group work builds trust in social situations.

- Groups build protective factors.

- Group work provides safety and protection.

PERMISSIONS

Grateful acknowledgment is made for permission to reprint the following:

The Terry McGovern material: Reprinted with the permission of George McGovern, author of TERRY: MY DAUGHTER'S LIFE-AND-DEATH STRUGGLE WITH ALCOHOLISM. Copyright © 1996 by George McGovern. Published by Villard, a division of Random House, Inc.

The THP/Morphine diagram: Reprinted with permission of The Free Press, a Division of Simon & Schuster, from ALCOHOL AND THE ADDICTIVE BRAIN: New Hope for Alcoholics from Biogenetic Research by Kenneth Blum, Ph.D. with James Payne. Copyright © 1991 by The Free Press.

The Caroline Knapp material: From DRINKING: A LOVE STORY by Caroline Knapp. Copyright © 1995 by Caroline Knapp. Used by permission of The Dial Press/Dell Publishing, a division of Random House, Inc.

The Vaillant Problem Drinking Scale: Reprinted by permission of the publisher from THE NATURAL HISTORY OF ALCOHOLISM REVISITED by George E. Vaillant, Cambridge, MA: Harvard University Press. Copyright © 1983, 1995 by the President and Fellows of Harvard College.

The MAST: M. L. Selzer, "The Michigan alcoholism screening test: The quest for a new diagnostic instrument" *American Journal of Psychiatry* 127 [1971]: 1653 – 58.

The CAGE: D. Mayfield, M.D., G. McLeod, MSW, and P. Hall, MSW, "The CAGE questionnaire: Validation of a new alcoholism screening instrument," *American Journal of Psychiatry* 131 [1974]: 1121 – 23.

The Nan Robertson material: From GETTING BETTER: INSIDE ALCOHOLICS ANONYMOUS by Nan Robertson. Copyright © 1988 by Nan Robertson. Used by permission of Nan Robertson.

The ear illustration: Courtesy of Terry Oleson, Ph.D. Reprinted with permission from AURICULOTHERAPY MANUAL: CHINESE AND WESTERN SYSTEMS OF EAR ACUPUNCTURE, (Health Care Alternatives, 1996) by Terry Oleson.

ACKNOWLEDGMENTS

This book builds on the hard work and dedicated efforts of many men and women. With the understanding that a mere listing could never adequately convey the depth of our respect or our gratitude, we would like to acknowledge the contributions of:

• James R. Milam, Ph.D., co-author with Katherine Ketcham of *Under the Influence: A Guide to the Myths and Realities of Alcoholism*, who paved the way for so many of us;

• Kenneth Blum, Ph.D., researcher, professor, and author of *Alcohol and the Addictive Brain*, for guiding us through the neurophysiology and biochemistry of addiction;

• Ernest Kurtz, Ph.D., historian and co-author with Katherine Ketcham of *The Spirituality of Imperfection*, whose brilliant insights into the spiritual role of recovery form the foundation of Chapter 13;

• George McGovern, U.S. ambassador to the U.N. Food and Agricultural Organization in Rome, former Democratic nominee for President of the United States, and former U.S. Senator, for his support, his encouragement, and especially his compassionate concern for alcoholics and their families;

• Dr. Richard Tremblay, M.D., member of the Board of Directors, American Society of Addiction Medicine, for his insights, knowledge, and specific comments on various drafts of the manuscript;

• G. Douglas Talbott, M.D., past president of the American Society of Addiction Medicine, founder and director of the Talbott Recovery Campus in Georgia, and co-author of *Healing the Healer: The Addicted Physician*, for his suggestions on improving the manuscript;

• Ernest Noble, M.D., Ph.D., national authority on alcoholism and other drug addictions, researcher, professor of alcohol studies and director of the Alcohol Research Center, University of California, Los Angeles, and former director of the National Institute on Alcohol Abuse and Alcoholism for reading and reviewing the manuscript;

• William White, Senior Research Consultant at Chestnut Systems in Bloomington, Illinois and author of *Slaying the Dragon: The History of Addiction Treatment and Recovery in America*, for his many helpful suggestions throughout the manuscript;

• Jeff Jay, president of the Terry McGovern Foundation in Washington, D.C., and director of program development at Brighton Hospital in Brighton, Michigan, for offering his insights on intervention and treatment and for introducing us to George McGovern;

• Jay Renaud, MPA, MAC, publisher of *Guidepoints: Acupuncture in Recovery*, for reviewing the manuscript and offering specific help with the acupuncture and detoxification sections in Part II;

• James Russo, associate professor of chemistry, Whitman College in Walla Walla, Washington, for his detailed critique of Chapters 2 and 3;

• L. Ann Mueller, M.D., addiction medicine specialist and co-author with Katherine Ketcham of *Eating Right to Live Sober* and *Recovering: How to Get and Stay Sober*, for her help with the chapters on diagnosis, treatment, and nutrition;

• Jay Lewis, national authority on alcoholism and former editor and publisher of *The Alcoholism Report*, for reviewing the manuscript and offering detailed suggestions;

• Robert Hammond, executive director of the Alcohol Research and Information Service in Lansing, Michigan, and editor/publisher of *The Bottom Line*, for his many fascinating stories about the liquor industry;

• George Hacker, Director, Alcohol Policies Project, Center for Science in the Public Interest in Washington, D.C., for helping us understand the politics of alcohol and showing us how to follow the money from the liquor industry to Congress and the White House;

• Neil Scott, secretary of the Alliance for Recovery based in Washington State and former editor of *The Alcoholism and Addiction Magazine* and *The Alcoholism Report*, for his friendship and his willingness to act as a general advisor throughout the organization and writing of this book;

• Irving Maltzman, Ph.D., researcher and professor at University of California, Los Angeles, for insights into the controlled drinking controversy;

• Dr. Christopher Dunn, Ph.D., Injury Prevention and Research Center, Harborview Medical Center, University of Washington, Seattle, for supplying the trauma stories in Chapter 17;

- Dr. James LoGerfo, Medical Director, Harborview Medical Center, Seattle, Washington, and Harborview's alcohol-trauma research team including Fred Rivara, M.D., Richard Ries, M.D., and Michael Copass, M.D., for their groundbreaking research on the relationship between alcohol and trauma;
- Scott Munson, Charles Buttrey, and James Barth, executives of the Sundown M Ranch treatment center for alcohol and other drug addictions in Selah, Washington, for allowing us to spend the day at Sundown and offering invaluable insights into the treatment and recovery process;
- John T. Schwarzlose, president/CEO, and Mark Greenberg, vice president for development, Betty Ford Center, Rancho Mirage, California, for giving us a comprehensive tour of the Betty Ford Center and offering detailed explanations about current treatment methods and followup therapies;
- Tim O'Farrell, Ph.D., chief of Harvard Families and Addiction Program, Department of Psychiatry, Harvard Medical School, for his dedication to helping alcoholics and their families;
- The alcohol specialists at MetroWest Medical Center in Natick, Massachusetts, especially Patrick Rice, LMHC, and the treatment team at MetroWest's Partial Hospital Program including Kathy Natale, O.T., Patricia Morse, M.A., LMHC, and Benjamin D'Aprile, M.S., LMHC, for their commitment to quality care in the treatment of alcoholics;
- Bob Cherney, Ph.D., the Reverend Richard Fleck, and Dennis Sweeney, M.A., LMHC, for their friendship, support, and many years of dedication to treating alcoholics;
- Ken Stark, director, Division of Alcohol and Substance Abuse, Washington State, for encouraging his competent staff to answer our many questions and direct us to appropriate resources;
- Henry Govert, Program Manager, Washington State Drug-Free Workplace Program in Olympia, Washington, for offering a comprehensive history of Employee Assistance Programs in corporate America and giving us his expert advice about present-day needs;
- Dr. Tony Krupske, Ph.D., Research Director, Division of Alcohol and Substance Abuse, Washington State, for directing us to the latest data on the incidence of alcoholism in the United States;
- Denise L. Fitch, Supervisor, Safe and Drug-Free Schools, Office of the Superintendent of Public Instruction, Washington State, for information on public education and intervention services;
- R. Stockton Rush, chairman and president of the Recovery

Institute in San Francisco, California, and Zara Lenora Mirmalek, project manager, for their ongoing efforts to educate the public about the enduring stigma of alcoholism;

• Hilary Abramson, Director of Public Affairs, and Eris Weaver, librarian, at the Marin Institute for the Prevention of Alcohol and Other Drug Problems in San Rafael, California, for keeping us informed about the liquor industry's lobbying efforts;

• Nancy Sutherland, associate director, and Pamela Miles, librarian, the library of the Alcohol and Drug Abuse Institute (ADAI) at the University of Washington in Seattle, Washington, for research assistance;

• Nancy Zussy, chief librarian, and Judy DeBuse, librarian, Washington State Library in Olympia, Washington, for source and reference information;

• Linda Grace-Kobas, director of the Cornell University Information Service, for her help with tracking the incidence of binge drinking and alcohol-related problems on our nation's college campuses;

• Diane Hall, president of the Chemical Dependency Professionals of Washington State and the president and CEO of Safe Harbor, an addiction clinic and counseling service in Kirkland, Washington, for information about the newest treatment techniques;

• David Beebe, Addiction Program Manager, Veterans Administration Medical Center, Walla Walla, Washington, for his insights into current treatment issues;

• Patria Robinson-Martin, Special Assistant to the Secretary of Corrections, Washington State for her help with the Susan West story;

• Earlyse Swift, director of Together! in Olympia Washington, for the latest information on drug problems among underage drinkers;

• Jonna Van Dyk and Richard Doane of the Washington State Traffic Safety Commission and Neill Raymond and Mike Baldwin of the National Highway Traffic Safety Administration, Region X, Seattle, Washington, for supplying us with the necessary facts and statistics on drunk driving laws;

• Ann Bradley, press liaison officer for the National Institute of Alcohol Abuse and Alcoholism, for her seemingly endless knowledge of facts, statistics, and resources on alcoholism and alcohol-related problems;

• Claudia Black, Ph.D., M.S.W., author, lecturer, and a founder of the Adult Children of Alcoholics (ACOA) movement, for reviewing the manuscript and offering many helpful comments on codependency, family issues, and current treatment concerns;

• Sis Wenger, executive director of the National Association for

Children of Alcoholics (NACoA), for answering our questions and for her ongoing efforts to raise public awareness about the effects of alcoholism on children and families;

• Julianna Hughes, longtime alcoholism activist and widow of Senator Harold Hughes, for her support and encouragement;

• Terry Oleson, author and illustrator of *Auricular Manual: Chinese and Western Systems of Ear Acupuncture*, for his generous permission to use the illustration in Chapter 15;

• Jason Elias, M.A., L.Ac., Integral Health Associates in New Paltz, New York, for advice on herbs and acupuncture;

• Patrick Spencer (Kathy Ketcham's husband) for research assistance, countless errands, and unfailing support;

• Janet, April, and Alex Asbury (William Asbury's wife and daughters) for research assistance, transcriptions, and computer know-how;

• David Asbury for skillful research, referencing, and Internet assistance;

• Marcel Ferland, Claire Gagnon, DMR Corp., Quebec City, Quebec, Canada, for computer and Internet services;

• Sue Seese for her friendship;

• Beth E. Elness-Hanson for taking the author photograph;

• Jane Dystel, Miriam Goderich, and Jo Fagan of Jane Dystel Literary Management for their competent assistance;

• Literary agent Kathleen Anderson of Anderson Grinberg Literary Management, Inc., in New York City for her support of this book;

• The Bantam staff including Robin Michaelson, editor; Toni Burbank, executive editor; Laura Hoguet, editorial assistant; Sue Warga, copy editor; and Kelly Chian, title administrator;

• And, finally, with the deepest gratitude to our families: Patrick, Robyn, Alison, and Benjamin Spencer (Kathy Ketcham's family); Janet, Jeff, Sarah, April, David, and Alex Asbury (William Asbury's family); and Karen, Erica, and Alaina Ciaramicoli (Arthur Ciaramicoli's family). For everything.

INDEX

ABOUT THE AUTHORS

Katherine Ketcham has been writing nonfiction books for two decades. *Beyond the Influence* is her eleventh book. Her other books include *Under the Influence: A Guide to the Myths and Realities of Alcoholism* (Bantam, 1983) co-authored with James Milam, Ph.D.; *The Spirituality of Imperfection: Storytelling and the Journey to Wholeness* (Bantam, 1992), co-authored with Ernest Kurtz, Ph.D.; *Witness for the Defense: The Accused, the Eyewitness, and the Expert Who Puts Memory on Trial* (St. Martin's, 1991) and *The Myth of Repressed Memory: False Memories and Allegations of Sexual Abuse* (St. Martin's, 1994), both co-authored with Elizabeth Loftus, Ph.D.; *The Five Elements of Self-Healing: Using Chinese Medicine for Maximum Immunity, Wellness, and Health* (Harmony Books, 1998) with Jason Elias; and *The Power of Empathy: A Practical Guide to Creating Intimacy, Self-Understanding, and Lasting Love in Your Life* (Dutton, 2000), co-authored with Arthur Ciaramicoli, Ed.D., Ph.D.

Kathy lives in Walla Walla, Washington, with her husband, Patrick Spencer, a college professor, and her three children, Robyn, 17, Alison, 15, and Benjamin, 13.

William F. Asbury is a journalist and former editor in chief of *The Seattle Post-Intelligencer.* After retiring from the newspaper business, Bill served as director of the Washington State Office of International Relations and chief of protocol for Washington Governors John Spellman and Booth Gardner. He was appointed by Governor Mike Lowry to help write new ethics and campaign finance laws for the state. He was then appointed to the state's Legislative Ethics Board and elected chairman of the board. Bill has lectured and written frequently about the need for changes in alcohol policies at all levels of government.

In addition to writing and lecturing about alcohol problems, Bill is at work on a book about his solo voyage at age 70 up Alaska's famed Inside Passage in a 25-foot sloop. Three years later he spent his 73rd birthday working as a deck hand on a fishing vessel headed for the fishing grounds of the Aleutian Islands and the Bering Sea. In Fall 1999, at 75, he climbed California's Mt. Whitney, the highest peak in the lower forty-eight states, as prelude to a series of articles on adventuring for older Americans.

Bill lives in Tumwater, Washington, with his wife Janet.

Mel Schulstad is the cofounder and former president of the National Association of Alcoholism and Drug Abuse Counselors. In 1978, the editor/publisher of *The Alcoholism Report* established the "Mel Schulstad Award" to recognize outstanding contributors to the then-new profession of addiction counseling. This annual award is given to the nation's most outstanding alcoholism counselor. In 1994, Mel received the National Association of State Alcoholism and Drug Addiction Directors Lifetime Achievement Award for outstanding work in the field of alcoholism and drug addiction. Mel served on the Washington State Citizens Advisory Council on Alcoholism and Substance Abuse for nine years and as its chairman for four years.

In 1979, Mel took a position as the director of Plans and Programs with the prestigious Johnson Institute in Minneapolis. Following in the footsteps of its founder, the Reverend Vernon Johnson (author of *I'll Quit Tomorrow*), Mel continued to devise and implement cutting-edge training programs for alcoholism professionals.

A retired colonel in the U.S. Air Force, Mel was twice awarded the Distinguished Flying Cross for valor in air combat operations over Europe during World War II.

Mel lives in Redmond, Washington.

Arthur P. Ciaramicoli, Ed.D., Ph.D. is a licensed clinical psychologist and director and chief psychologist at the Alternative Therapy Center, MetroWest Wellness Center in Natick, Massachusetts. Dr. Ciaramicoli is also an instructor of psychology in the Department of Psychiatry at Harvard Medical School, where he supervises the Harvard Couples Project for alcoholics and their spouses. He has worked with alcoholics in inpatient, outpatient, and day treatment alcohol programs for more than twenty-five years; in the last decade he has developed an expertise in advising alcoholics in alternative medicine modalities. Twice a week he co-hosts Boston's WRPT 650 AM morning radio show, "Health and Fitness Today."

Dr. Ciaramicoli is the author of *Treatment of Abuse and Addiction: A Holistic Approach* (Northvale, New Jersey: Jason Aronson, 1997) and co-author with Katherine Ketcham of *The Power of Empathy* (Dutton, 2000). He maintains a private practice in Hopkinton, Massachusetts, where he lives with his wife and two daughters.

William F. Asbury, Arthur Ciaramicoli, Katherine Ketcham, and Mel Schulstad